Oekologie & Gesellschaft
Herausgegeben von Peter Knoepfel und Helmut Weidner

Band 10

Oekologie & Gesellschaft
Herausgegeben von Peter Knoepfel und Helmut Weidner

Band 10

Lösung von Umweltkonflikten durch Verhandlung

Beispiele aus dem In- und Ausland

Solution de conflits environnementaux par la négociation

Exemples suisses et étrangers

Peter Knoepfel (Hrsg./im Auftrag der SAGUF)

Helbing & Lichtenhahn
Basel und Frankfurt am Main
1995

Publikation des IDHEAP und der SAGUF

Alle Rechte vorbehalten. Das Werk und seine Teile sind urherberrechtlich geschützt. Jede Verwertung in anderen als den gesetzlich zugelassenen Fällen bedarf deshalb der vorherigen schriftlichen Einwilligung des Verlags.

Die Deutsche Bibliothek – CIP-Einheitsaufnahme:
Lösung von Umweltkonflikten durch Verhandlung : Beispiele aus dem In- und Ausland = Solution de conflits environnementaux par la négociation / Peter Knoepfel et al. – Basel ; Frankfurt am Main : Helbing und Lichtenhahn, 1995
  (Oekologie & Gesellschaft ; Bd. 10)
   ISBN 3-7190-1441-X
NE: Knoepfel, Peter; Solution de conflits environnementaux par la négociation; GT

ISBN 3-7190-1441-X
Bestellnummer 21 01441
© 1995 by Helbing & Lichtenhahn Verlag AG, Basel

VORWORT

Die Hälfte der in diesem Band enthaltenen Beiträge gehen auf Referate zurück, die am Symposium der SAGUF (Schweizerische Akademische Gesellschaft für Umweltforschung und Ökologie) im November 1991 in Chur gehalten wurden. Die Beiträge wurden auf den neuesten Stand gebracht und ergänzt durch sechs weitere Aufsätze, die dem Herausgeber zur Abrundung der Thematik und im Hinblick auf die Aktualität der vorliegenden Publikation als notwendig erschienen. Ich bin der Meinung, dass die elf Beiträge aus den USA, aus Deutschland, Frankreich, den Niederlanden und aus der Schweiz ein repräsentatives Bild über die Ursprünge und die mitteleuropäische Praxis von Verhandlungslösungen über Umweltkonflikte in der ersten Hälfte der neunziger Jahre abgeben. Den 15 Autoren bin ich insbesondere deshalb zu Dank verpflichtet, weil sie im Hinblick auf die Aktualisierung ihrer Beiträge erhebliche Aufwendungen geleistet haben. Dank gebührt dem Organisator der damaligen Tagung (Christian Hedinger) und der Schweizerischen Akademie der Naturwissenschaften, die das Symposium und diese Publikation finanziell unterstützt hat. Ohne die tatkräftige Unterstützung seitens von Erika Blanc und des Institut de hautes études en administration publique (IDHEAP) wäre dieses Buch kaum zustande gekommen; auch ihnen möchte ich an dieser Stelle meinen Dank aussprechen.

Die Anregung zur Beschäftigung mit dem Thema "Mediation" erhielt ich seinerzeit von der Mediationsforschungsgruppe[1] am Wissenschaftszentrum der Sozialforschung in Berlin. Im Sommersemester 1993 hatte ich Gelegenheit, die Arbeiten dieser Gruppe (Helmut Weidner, Hans Joachim Fietkau, Karin Pfingsten und Katharina Holzinger) aus nächster Nähe zu studieren. Aus jenem Aufenthalt stammten schliesslich die Grundüberlegungen zu meinem Schlussartikel, den ich anlässlich einer Tagung der Evangelischen Akademie Loccum im November 1993 erstmals einem breiteren Publikum vortragen konnte. Auch aus jener überaus interessanten Veranstaltung[2] habe ich zahlreiche neue Anregungen für die Ausgestaltung dieses Buches erhalten. Ich möchte an dieser Stelle auch den Organisatoren jener Tagung herzlich danken.

Peter Knoepfel
Chavannes-près-Renens, den 3. März 1995
Institut de hautes études en administration publique (IDHEAP)

---

[1] Der Schlussbericht zum Neusser Verfahren wird demnächst erscheinen.
[2] A. Dally, Helmut Weidner, Hans Joachim Fietkau (Hrsg.): *Mediation als politischer und sozialer Prozess, Loccumer Protokolle 73/93*, Evangelische Akademie Loccum, 1994.

INHALTSVERZEICHNIS

VORWORT   V

INHALTSVERZEICHNIS   VII

Peter Knoepfel:
EINLEITUNG   1
1. Blockierung und Deblockierung: Der Zwang zur Verhandlungslösung?   1
2. Zum Inhalt dieses Buches   4
Literaturverzeichnis   15

Arturo Gàndara:
FROM CONFLICT TOWARDS COLLABORATIVE PROCESSES: CONCEPTS AND EXPERIENCES FROM THE UNITED STATES   17
1. Introduction   17
2. Administrative Agencies and Constitutional Scheme   18
3. Modes of Administration Agency Decision Making   19
4. The Federal Negociated Rulemaking Act as a Collaborative Model   21
5. Comparison With Two State Collaborative Processes   23
6. Conclusion   24
References /Court Decisions   26

Daniel A. Mazmanian, Michael Stanley-Jones:
RECONCEIVING LULUS: CHANGING THE NATURE AND SCOPE OF LOCALLY UNWANTED LAND USES   27
1. Conventional Explanations for LULUs   29
2. Initial Responses of the 1980s   32
3. Confronting the Need for Fundamental Change   35
4. Conditions of Cooperative Decision Making   46
5. LULUs and Policy Democracy   49
References   51

Robert Nakamura, Thomas Church, Philip Cooper:
ENVIRONMENTAL DISPUTE RESOLUTION AND HAZARDOUS WASTE CLEANUPS: A CAUTIONARY TALE OF POLICY IMPLEMENTATION 55
1. Introduction 55
2. Hazardous Waste Cleanup: The Policy Environment 56
3. ADR: A Solution Seeking A Problem 58
4. Policy Design: ADR and the Phohl Brothers Landfill 60
5. Policy Implementation 63
6. Analysis of Implementation Outcomes: How Does the Implementation Literature Inform the Analysis of ADR? 66
7. Conclusions 76
References 78

Wolfgang Hoffmann-Riem, Irene Lamb
VERHANDLUNGSLÖSUNGEN/MEDIATION: ERFAHRUNGEN AUS DEN USA UND ÜBERTRAGBARKEIT AUF DEUTSCHE VERHÄLTNISSE 83
1. Grenzen einseitigen Verwaltungshandelns 83
2. Zu Begriffen und Modellen von Verhandlungslösungen und Konfliktmittlung 84
3. Verhandlungslösungen/Mediation in den USA und grundsätzliche Fragen ihrer Übertragbarkeit 85
4. Erfahrungen mit mittlergestützten Verhandlungsverfahren in der Bundesrepublik Deutschland 87
5. Einpassung in die bundesdeutsche Rechtsordnung 89
6. Die Beteiligung an Verhandlungsverfahren 92
7. Inhaltliche Erfolgsvoraussetzungen für Verhandlungsverfahren 96
8. Die Letztverantwortung der Verwaltung und die Umsetzung des Konsenses 99
9. Schlussbemerkung 100
Literaturverzeichnis 102

Helmut Weidner:
INNOVATIVE KONFLIKTREGELUNG IN DER UMWELTPOLITIK DURCH MEDIATION: ANREGUNGEN AUS DEM AUSLAND FÜR DIE BUNDESREPUBLIK DEUTSCHLAND 105
1. Mediationsverfahren im Ausland, insbesondere in den USA 105
2. Mediationsverfahren in der Bundesrepublik Deutschland 111
3. Fazit 122
Literaturverzeichnis 124

Patrice Duran:
LES DIFFICULTES DE LA NEGOCIATION INSTITUTIONNALISEE, LE PARC NATIONAL DES PYRENEES OCCIDENTALES OU LA COOPERATION CONTRARIEE 127
1. Introduction 127
2. Une institution en miettes 134
3. Logique de bouc émissaire et fonction tribunicienne 141
4. Reconstruire la négociation 151
5. Passer d'une vision éclatéé des missions à une vision homogène 153
6. Au delà de l'illusion pédagogique... 164
References 169

Ida J. Koppen:
REGULATORY NEGOTIATION IN THE NETHERLANDS: THE CASE OF PACKAGING WASTE 171
1. Negotiating waste reduction 171
2. Consultation, negotiation and consensus-building 173
3. The origin of regulatory negotiation 176
4. The legalist critique 179
5. Strategic discussions and covenants as the answer? 180
6. The Packaging Covenant: a concrete example 182
7. Consultation, negotiation and consensus-building: evaluating Dutch policy practice 185
References 188

Ortwin Renn, Thomas Webler:
DER KOOPERATIVE DISKURS: THEORIE UND PRAKTISCHE ERFAHRUNGEN MIT EINEM DEPONIEPROJEKT IM KANTON AARGAU 191
1. Einleitung 191
2. Notwendigkeit zum offenen zweiseitigen Risikodialog 196
3. Theoretische und methodische Vorgehensweise 199
4. Fallbeispiel: Kooperativer Diskurs für eine Standortfestlegung "Deponie Aargau Ost" 204
5. Der Verfahrensablauf 208
6. Ergebnisse der Bürgerbeteiligung 213
7. Besonderheiten der Schweizer Politischen Kultur 217
8. Lernerlebnis: Beteiligung 221
9. Gruppendynamische Beobachtungen 222
10. Subjektive Zufriedenheit der Teilnehmer 225
11. Schlussbemerkung 231
Literaturverzeichnis 235

Michel Rey:
LA GESTION DU PROCESSUS DE CONSULTATION ET DE DECISION: UN NOUVEL ENJEU EN AMENAGEMENT DU TERRITOIRE 245
1. Le rôle de l'ISDS dans la politique suisse des déchets spéciaux 245
2. Une législation lacunaire en matière de procédure d'étude 246
3. De l'intérêt d'une étude préliminaire 247
4. Une démarche ouverte mise en oeuvre pendant cinq ans 248
5. Les effets concrets de la consultation sur la prise de décision 256
6. Les conditions du succès d'une consultation 257
7. Epilogue 259

Rolf Maegli
LÖSUNG VON UMWELTPROBLEMEN DURCH VERHANDLUNG WAS IST VON VERHANDLUNGS- LÖSUNGEN ZU ERWARTEN? STELLUNGNAHME AUS DER SICHT DER PRAXIS DES KANTONS SOLOTHURN 261
1. Einleitung 261
2. Verhandlungslösungen im Kanton Solothurn - bisherige Erfahrungen 263
3. Schlussfolgerungen und Ausblick 273
Literaturverzeichnis 282

Peter Knoepfel
VON DER KONSTITUTIONELLEN KONKORDANZ ÜBER ADMINISTRATIVE KONSENSLÖSUNGEN ZUM DEMOKRATISCHEN DEZISIONISMUS - ZUR VIELFALT VON VERHANDLUNGSARRANGEMENTS IN KONFLIKTLÖSUNGSVERFAHREN DER SCHWEIZ 283
1. Einleitung 283
2. (Impressionistische) geschichtliche Reminiszenzen: Die Schweiz und ihre Mediation 285
3. Typische helvetische Konfliktkonstellationen der Gegenwart 290
4. Acht Mediations- oder mediationsähnliche Verfahren aus der jüngsten Vergangenheit und der Gegenwart 293
5. Andere (weniger auf Verhandlung basierende) Konfliktlösungsmechanismen 314
6. Schlussfolgerungen: Die Schweiz hat und braucht keine Mediatoren 318
Literaturverzeichnis 320

AUTORENVERZEICHNIS 323

EINLEITUNG

Peter Knoepfel

1. BLOCKIERUNG UND DEBLOCKIERUNG: DER ZWANG ZUR VERHANDLUNGSLÖSUNG?

Der Empfang von mindestens 20 Fernsehprogrammen in jedem Schweizer Haushalt gilt heute als Selbstverständlichkeit. Darüber, dass man auch in der abgelegensten Wohnung einfach den Kalt- oder Warmwasserhahn drehen muss, um sich das nötige Trink- oder Badewasser zu beschaffen, wird heute schon gar nicht mehr diskutiert. Bebaut und bewohnt wird nur erschlossenes Land; standartkonforme Verkehrserschliessung, Wasserzufuhr und Abwasseranschluss sowie Elektrizitätszufuhr sind von der Gemeinde zur Verfügung zu stellen. Selbstverständlich müssen auch die Abfälle entsorgt werden. Und wehe der Gemeinde, die nicht an die öffentlichen Verkehrsmittel bzw. an ein leistungsfähiges Strassennetz angeschlossen ist. Spitäler, Schulen, öffentliche Sportanlagen, etc., aber auch Telefon-, Telefax-, etc. -verkabelung oder Postbüros gehören zur Grundausstattung einer öffentlichen Infrastruktur. Flughafennähe und nahegelegene ruhige Erholungsgebiete gelten als (mietpreissteigernde) Faktoren für ein angenehmes Wohnklima.

Es leuchtet dem Normalverbraucher durchaus ein, dass diese Leistungen nur über Grosssysteme kostengünstig erbracht werden können. Denn das Gesetz der abnehmenden Grenzkosten gebietet eine minimale Grösse für das Einzugsgebiet öffentlicher Leistungserbringung; meist lassen sich die investierten Mittel nur auf diese Weise optimal amortisieren. So wird der Strom aus einem grossen Stausee billiger sein als Strom, den 10 Kleinkraftwerke produzieren. Kleine, für jede Gemeinde errichtete Abfallverbrennungsanlagen führen in der Regel zu höheren Entsorgungspreisen als regionale Grossanlagen, und eine gemeinschaftliche Empfangsanlage für das Fernsehen arbeitet vermutlich preisgünstiger als eine Vielzahl kleiner Geräte. Der Wunsch der Benützer öffentlicher Infrastrukturwerke nach einem kostengünstigeren Angebot ist neben angeblichen technischen Optimierungsimperativen denn auch der Hauptgrund für die gegenwärtig beobachtbare Tendenz zur Schaffung immer neuer öffentlicher Grosssysteme im Infrastrukturbereich. Vermutlich wird ein solches Grenznutzungskalkül auch dann zugunsten relativ grosser Systeme sprechen, wenn neben den betriebswirtschaftlichen in Zukunft auch die ökologischen Kosten im engeren Sinne konsequent miteinbezogen werden. Denn das Gesetz der abnehmenden Grenzkosten gilt in der Regel auch für Investitionen, die zugunsten des Umweltschutzes getätigt werden.

Wenn diesen hochkomplexen und kolossalen Riesen des postindustriellen Zeitalters auch nicht aus unmittelbar umweltökonomischen Gründen Gefahr droht, so deutet doch vieles daraufhin, dass ihnen dereinst eine bereits heute wachsende sozio-ökologische Bewegung den Garaus machen könnte: Denn solche Grossysteme verfügen regelmässig über ein Aktivitätszentrum, das der örtlichen Bevölkerung im Interesse "des Ganzen" Umweltbelastungen beschert. Diese übermässig betroffene Bevölkerung ist zahlenmässig meist erheblich kleiner als die grosse Mehrheit jener, die sich vom Grossystem ausschliesslich Vorteile versprechen können. Nach den Regeln der demokratischen Mehrheitsentscheidung ist es daher gewöhnlich ein leichtes, die Vertreter der betroffenen Minderheiten zu überstimmen. Rein formal lassen sich daher die Umweltbelastungen von Grossystemen auf dem Weg über demokratische Mehrheitsentscheide beliebig in Raum und Zeit verteilen.

Aber diese Feststellung wird selbst den "rein formal" argumentierenden Juristen nicht befriedigen. Denn nach wie vor gültig ist der Rechtssatz, wonach der Staat seine Bürgerinnen und Bürger gleich zu behandeln hat. Ausserdem sind staatliche Eingriffe in zentrale Grundrechte auch bei Vorliegen demokratisch korrekt zustandegekommener Gesetze nicht zulässig. So ginge es nicht an, eine bezeichenbare Personengruppe übermässigen radioaktiven oder elektromagnetischen Strahlungen, gesundheitsgefährdenden Lärmpegeln und Vibrationen oder Luftbelastungen auszusetzen, um der grossen Mehrheit der Bevölkerung billige Elektrizität, Fernsehprogramme, Schienen- und Strassenverbindungen oder Abfallbeseitigungsanlagen zu sichern. Zu Recht werden ähnliche Grundrechtspositionen zunehmend auch zugunsten der Natur gefordert, die nicht mehr unwidersprochen als Grossbaustelle für aberwitzige Grossysteme des Homo sapiens angesehen werden darf. In beiden Fällen gilt übrigens auch der unbestrittene Rechtsgrundsatz, dass niemand rechtsgültig auf seine Grundrechte verzichten kann, indem er etwa in derartige Belastungen einwilligt. Bereits vor diesem juristischen Hintergrund wird deutlich, dass jedem Grossystem der grundrechtliche Schutz der betroffenen Bevölkerung Grenzen setzt. Praktisch äussert sich dieser Sachverhalt denn auch darin, dass sich heute Grossysteme kaum mehr ohne langwierige Rechtsmittelverfahren projektieren und realisieren lassen.

Aber all den auf Bundesebene oft widerspruchslos beschlossenen Infrastrukturpolitiken, deren Umsetzung auf die Errichtung solcher Grossysteme angewiesen ist, erwächst in den betroffenen Gebieten zunehmend politischer Widerstand. Dieser wird nicht nur auf juristischem Wege, sondern auch auf dem Parkett von Politik und Verwaltung ausgetragen: Ganz im Sinne des amerikanischen Schlachtrufes "not in my backyard" ("Nimby-Syndrom"), wehren sich etwa Bewohner begüterter Stadtquartiere gegen den Bau einer Kehrichtverbrennungsanlage in ihrer Nähe; die Stadt soll diese verkehrsintensive Anlage doch bitte in einer Gemeinde des städtischen Umlandes bauen. Umgekehrt errichten ländliche Gemeinden Sperren gegen den Bau von Sondermülldeponien, protestieren laut gegen die ihre Landschaft "zu Tode liebenden" städtischen Zeitgenossen und deren Tourismusgebahren oder errichten Strassenblockaden gegen den Transitverkehr. Welche konkreten Formen diese Konflikte auch immer annehmen, ihr Grundauslöser ist immer derselbe: Die sich als besonders betroffen betrachtende Personengruppe wirft der von der geplanten Grossanlage profitierenden Bevölkerungsmehrheit mangelnde Solidarität, Übervorteilung, ja sogar Überrumpelung vor. Denn der Normalverbraucher vermag zwar in der Regel noch einzusehen, dass für das Erbringen der von ihm geforderten Leistung Grossysteme notwendig sind. Aber es ist ihm nur in den seltensten Fällen bewusst, dass solche Grossysteme eben nicht irgendwo im Äther, sondern auf konkretem Grund und Boden errichtet werden müssen. Welcher Stadtbewohner denkt schon daran, dass er mit dem Öffnen des Wasserhahns eventuell mit für eine Grundwasserabsenkung und entsprechende Feuchtgebietverluste im ländlichen Raum verantwortlich ist? Wer wird schon beim Einschalten der Tagesschau an den landschaftsverunstaltenden Sendeturm und wer beim Klosettspülen an die üblen Gerüche der Klärschlämme unten in der Talgemeinde denken?

Grossysteme führen zu gefährlichen Polarisierungen. Diese müssen recht eigentlich als ihre sozialen und politischen Kosten betrachten werden. Die Polarisierung zwischen Land und Stadt, zwischen reichen und armen Stadtquartieren, zwischen heutigen und zukünftigen Generationen, etc. führen trotz demokratischer Mehrheitsentscheiden in ein Zeitalter eines neuen ökologischen Faustrechts. Die politisch und gesellschaftlich bereits heute privilegierten Gruppen werden sich dank ihrer Macht vor zusätzlichen Umweltbelastungen schützen können. Sie können gleichzeitig die mit ihrem Lebensstil zwangsläufig verbundenen Umweltbelastungen auf diejenigen Gruppen abwälzen, die mangels derartiger Machtpositionen nicht in der Lage sind, sich dagegen erfolgreich zur Wehr zu setzen. Darin liegt vermutlich eine der wesentlichsten sozialen Fragen ökologischer Politik. Diese lautet nicht nur: "Wie lässt sich vermeiden, dass bestimmte heutige oder künftige Bevölkerungsgruppen bzw. Ökosysteme unzumutbaren Umweltbelastungen ausgesetzt werden?", sondern zusätzlich auch: "Wie lässt sich vermeiden, dass bestimmte Bevölkerungsgruppen bzw. Ökosysteme heute oder in Zukunft an sich zumutbaren Umweltbelastungen ungleich stärker ausgesetzt werden als andere?". Das zentrale politische Instrument zur Lösung dieser neuen sozialen Frage ist im Prinzip dasselbe wie jenes, das sich bereits bei der alten bewährt hat: Es ist dies der Solidaritätsvertrag zwischen Bevorzugten und Benachteiligten, zwischen Mensch und Natur bzw. zwischen den Generationen.

2. ZUM INHALT DIESES BUCHES

Solche Verträge müssen ausgehandelt werden, aber zwischen wem? Bei allen Verhandlungslösungen ist zunächst die Frage zu beantworten, wer als Verhandlungsbeteiligter und damit als potentieller Vertragspartner zu bezeichnen ist. Wie lässt sich die besonders betroffene minoritäre Personengruppe im Zentrum, wie die grosse Gruppe der Nutzniesser im gesamten Einzugsgebiet von Grossystemen definieren, und nach welchen Verfahren sollen ihre Vertreter bestimmt werden? Solidaritätsverträge setzen zudem voraus, dass es gelingt, die einmal bestimmten Partner am runden Tisch zu versammeln und für Verhandlungen im Hinblick auf einen bindenden Vertrag zu gewinnen. Dies kann wohl kaum ohne Engagement seitens der Behörden bzw. Festsetzung verbindlicher staatlicher Rahmenbedingungen geschehen. Erforderlich ist allerdings auch, dass bei der Gruppe derjenigen Personen, von denen solidarisches Handeln verlangt wird, Einsicht in die Notwendigkeit eines Solidaritätsbeitrags zugunsten der besonders betroffenen Gruppe besteht. Diese ist aufgrund der sachlichen Wirkweise der entsprechenden Grossysteme aufzuzeigen. Wie entsteht eine solche Solidargemeinschaft und welche Strategien haben namentlich Behörden im In- und Ausland zu deren Aufbau angewandt?

Das Zustandekommen von Solidarverträgen setzt vermutlich aber auch voraus, dass sämtlichen beteiligten Kontrahenten daraus irgendwelche Vorteile erwachsen. Inwieweit dies der Fall ist, hängt wiederum von der Art der wechselseitig ausgetauschten Leistungen ab. Während hier auf der Seite der Betroffenen sicherlich letztlich der Verzicht auf Widerstand gegen an sich hinnehmbare Umweltbelastungen steht, werden sich auf der Seite der Nutzniesser eine Vielzahl möglicher Abgeltungsleistungen finden. Ihre Ausgestaltung dürfte mitunter auch durch den Mittler zwischen den beteiligten Gruppen figurierenden Staat mitbestimmt sein (z.B. Planungsleistungen, Nachteilungsausgleich durch Verzicht auf die Errichtung anderer Infrastrukturwerke, etc.). Man wird bezüglich dieser Abgeltungsleistungen wegkommen müssen von der bisher allzu raschen Bewertung als "Stimmenkauf" bzw. "Übertölpelung" der Behörden der betroffenen Gebiete durch Steuergeschenke, etc.. Anzustreben ist gerade nicht ein rechtswidriger Übertölpelungsvertrag, sondern ein fairer Interessenausgleich. Welche Leistungen wurden in derartigen Verhandlungen bisher im In- und Ausland von den Verfahrensbeteiligten angeboten, und welche Kriterien könnten herangezogen werden, um einen solchen fairen Interessenausgleich tatsächlich sicherzustellen?

Diese und andere Fragen wurden am SAGUF-Symposium 1991 von berufenen Fachleuten aus den USA, der Bundesrepublik Deutschland, Frankreich und aus der Schweiz beantwortet. Die vorgetragene Publikation, die u. a. die Beiträge zu jenem Symposium enthält, richtet sich nicht nur an Umweltjuristen und Vertreter von Umweltverwaltungen, sondern auch und gerade an Vertreter der erwähnten betroffenen Minderheiten und an Gemeindebehörden. Angesprochen sind auch Infrastrukturplaner, die mit solchen Verhandlungsstrategien heute noch kaum Erfahrungen sammeln konnten. Das Buch bezweckt, einer breiteren Öffentlichkeit Inhalt und Tragweite möglicher Strategien zur Konfliktbewältigung durch Verhandlungen vorzuführen, die gegenwärtig unter den Stichworten "Mediation", "Collaborative Processes" oder "Approche par la négociation" zunehmend auch in Europa und in unserem Lande diskutiert werden.

Der vorliegende Band umfasst elf Beiträge, die Verhandlungslösungen von Umweltkonflikten aus fünf Ländern (USA, Deutschland, Frankreich, Niederlande und Schweiz) behandeln. Die Hälfte davon geht auf Referate am *Symposium der Schweizerischen Akademischen Gesellschaft für Umweltforschung (SAGUF) vom November 1991* in Chur zurück. Die sechs anderen Arbeiten wurden vom Herausgeber im Hinblick auf eine sinnvolle Abrundung der vorliegenden Publikation zusätzlich angefordert. Damit enthält der Band eine solide Übersicht über die Debatte zur Lösung von Umweltkonflikten durch Verhandlung in den USA, in einigen europäischen Ländern und insbesondere in der Schweiz.

Unzweifelhaft ist die USA (neben Japan) jenes Land, in dem die Lösung von Umweltkonflikten durch Verhandlung am intensivsten studiert und seit fast zwei Jahrzehnten auch praktiziert wird. Die ersten drei Beiträge stammen deshalb aus der Feder *amerikanischer Autoren*. *Arturo Gàndara*, der an der Universität Berkeley Rechtswissenschaft lehrt, umschreibt die wesentlichen Inhalte des US-amerikanischen Verhandlungslösungsmodells ("alternative dispute resolution - ADR") auf der Ebene des Bundes und des Staates Kalifornien anhand der entsprechenden Regulierungen für den Umweltbereich. Er zeigt, wie in der amerikanischen Umweltpolitik sowohl auf der Ebene der Gesetzgebung ("rulemaking") als auch auf der Ebene der Umsetzung Verhandlungslösungen zunehmend institutionalisiert wurden. Dadurch kann allerdings die korrekte Durchsetzung öffentlicher Interessen in Frage gestellt werden. Die beiden Politikwissenschafter der Claremont Graduate School, *Daniel E. Mazmanian* und *Michael Stanley-Jones* behandeln anhand zweier Beispiele aus den Staaten Colorado und Kalifornien mögliche Strategien zur Überwindung lokaler Konflikte rund um regional- bzw. national bedeutsame Grossanlagen (sog. "locally unwanted landuses - LULUs"). Auch in den USA sind derartige Anlagen (Gefängnisse, Flughäfen, Stauwehre oder Abfallanlagen) infolge ausgesprochen negativer Risikoperzeptionen umstritten. Eine erste Reaktion auf diese Opposition bestand in einer Zentralisierung der Zuständigkeiten. Aber der Widerstand hielt an, weshalb Mediations- und Verhandlungslösungen notwendig wurden. Die Umkehr vom NIMBY ("Not-In-My-Backyard") zum YIMBY ("Yes-In-Many-Backyards"), mit der eine gerechte soziale und räumliche Verteilung neuer Umweltbelastungen angestrebt wurde, ist nach Auffassung der Autoren nur über einen grundlegenden Wertwandel erreichbar. Dies demonstrieren sie anhand des Konflikts über die Errichtung eines Stauwehrs in der Region Denver und einer Sondermüllanlage in Kalifornien. Dabei werden Möglichkeiten und Grenzen von Lösungen diskutiert, die über eine Ausweitung der Systemgrenzen, Kompensationsmechanismen oder mittels technischer Risikominimierungen arbeiten. Im Zentrum steht die Frage nach der "Fair-share" von Risiken in demokratischen Gesellschaften.

Robert Nakamura, Politikwissenschafter an der State University of New York diskutiert mit seinen beiden Kollegen *Thomas W. Church* und *Phillip J. Cooper* die Strategie des Staates New York zur Sanierung von Altlastgebieten mittels alternativen Konfliktlösungsverfahren (ADR). Die Autoren stellen das Mediationsverfahren im Lichte dreier Generationen von Implementationsforschungen dar. Ihre kritische Würdigung des ADR-Verfahrens, das im New Yorker Fall zur Anwendung gelangte und scheiterte, zeigt gleichzeitig den Nutzen und die Grenzen der bisherigen Implementationsforschung für konkrete Mediationsprozesse auf. Der Beitrag kommt zum Schluss, dass ADR-Verfahren nur dann erfolgreich sein können, wenn die beteiligten Akteure darin mehr Vorteile erwarten können als in einem klassischen konfliktorientierten Verwaltungsverfahren. Wenn einer der beteiligten Akteure (im vorliegenden Falle die staatliche Verwaltung) seine Machtposition im Mediationsverfahren darauf aufbaut, dass er sich die Möglichkeit ihrer Nutzung während des ganzen Verfahrens offenhält, besteht nach der vorliegenden Studie kein genügender Anreiz für die übrigen Akteure, am Spiel mitzumachen. ADR-Verfahren lassen sich nur dann erfolgreich einsetzen, wenn die Rahmenbedingungen jedenfalls während einer gewissen Zeit konstant gehalten werden und die Chance besteht, dass das Ergebnis nicht nachträglich durch einen Rückzug der staatlichen Behörden auf ihre Verwaltungsbefugnisse in Frage gestellt wird.

Auch die Beiträge aus der *Bundesrepublik Deutschland* analysieren Möglichkeiten und Grenzen der Lösung von Umweltkonflikten durch Verhandlungen aus juristischer und politikwissenschaftlicher Sicht. *Wolfgang Hoffmann-Riem* von der Universität Hamburg und die Verwaltungsrichterin *Irene Lamb* gehen in ihrem Beitrag von den Grenzen des traditionellen einseitigen Verwaltungshandelns aus, das den Belangen der Betroffenen oft zu wenig Rechnung tragen kann. "Mittlerunterstützte Aushandlungsprozesse", in denen ein neutraler Dritter eingeschaltet wird, um das Aushandeln unter Beteiligung der Verwaltung und der Betroffenen moderierend zu erleichtern, sind in diesem Zusammenhang besonders erfolgversprechend. Erfahrungen aus den USA lassen sich auch in der Bundesrepublik Deutschland anwenden. Die Autoren stellen ausführlich das Verfahren zur Konfliktmittlung im Streit um die Sondermülldeponie Münchenhagen dar. Dieses Beispiel zeigt die Grenzen von Mediationsverfahren, die (gleichermassen wie im präsentierten New Yorker Altlastsanierungsverfahren) in der Doppelfunktion der Behörde als Partei und neutralem Verhandlungsleiter liegen kann. Sie unterstreichen, dass Mediationsverfahren Verwaltungsentscheidungen nicht ersetzen können. Analysiert wird schliesslich das Problem der Auswahl der Beteiligten, und es wird als Grundsatzbedingung für den Erfolg solcher Verfahren das Vorliegen sog. "Win-Win"-Situationen postuliert. Diese Bedingung lässt sich nicht selten durch Kompensationsleistungen zugunsten der Betroffenen schaffen. Schliesslich sind auf Konsens angelegte Konfliktlösungsverfahren generell nur in jenen Gesellschaften ein erstrebenswertes Ziel, die zugleich auch den Konflikt akzeptieren.

Thematisch deckt *Helmut Weidner* vom Wissenschaftszentrum Berlin für Sozialforschung (WZB) mit wenigen Ausnahmen genau dasselbe Feld ab wie sein seine juristischen Kollegen. Allerdings kommt in diesem Beitrag die politikwissenschaftliche Betrachtungsweise zum Tragen. Auch Weidner geht von den Mediationserfahrungen in den USA aus, vor deren Hintergrund sich sieben unterschiedliche Formen alternativer Streitbeilegungsverfahren herleiten lassen. Diese Verfahren führten gerade im Umweltbereich zu faireren, effektiveren, effizienteren, flexibleren, schnelleren und für alle Konfliktparteien zufriedenstellenderen Ergebnissen. Diese Auffassung werde von US-Beobachtern mehrheitlich geteilt. (Eine etwas kritischere Beurteilung findet sich bei Robert Nakamura und seinen Mitautoren in diesem Buch.) Bei der Darlegung der Notwendigkeit von Mediationsverfahren für die Bundesrepublik geht der Autor mit der bundesdeutschen Umweltpolitik recht hart ins Gericht. Immer häufiger beklagten sich Vollzugsbehörden darüber, dass die bundesdeutsche Umweltpolitik von einem bürokratisch-hierarchischen Staatsverständnis und einem staatlichen "Regelungswahn" geprägt würden. Dem Bürger würden Anforderungen vorgespielt, die in der Praxis nicht umsetzbar seien. Deshalb seien konsensorientierte Verfahren, in denen auf "juristische und politische Konfliktrituale, auf Diskriminierung und Manipulationstechniken" verzichtet würde, immer noch recht selten. Unter diesen Ausnahmen finden sich gegenwärtig in der Bundesrepublik auch zwei "richtige" Mediationsverfahren. Es sind dies die Verfahren zur Sondermülldeponie in Münchenhagen und das Mediationsverfahren im Kreis Neuss (Nordrhein/Westfalen) zum Abfallwirtschaftskonzept. Dieses letztere war Gegenstand einer sozialwissenschaftlichen Begleituntersuchung, an der der Autor massgeblich beteiligt war. Der Aufsatz enthält denn auch eine ausführliche Darstellung dieses Verfahrens. Auch Weidner ist in seinen Schlussfolgerungen zurückhaltend: Es wäre ein überzogener Anspruch, von Mediationsverfahren zu erwarten, dass sie einen "Königsweg in der Umweltpolitik ebnen könnten". Insbesondere jene, die an der Zunahme solcher Verfahren ein geschäftliches Interesse hätten, schilderten die Mediation oft in viel zu rosigen Farben. Noch keineswegs abgeklärt sei die Frage, ob Mediationsverfahren unter den rechtlichen Rahmenbedingungen und in der politischen Kultur der Bundesrepublik Deutschland erfolgreich durchgeführt werden könnten.

Sowohl thematisch als auch in Bezug auf den stärker der politischen Soziologie verpflichteten Ansatz unterscheidet sich die Analyse des *Franzosen Patrice Duran* von der Universität Bordeaux zum vielschichtigen und erst ansatzweise durch Verhandlungen angegangenen Konflikt rund um den französischen Nationalpark in den Pyrenäen. Der auf eigene Konfliktlösungsbemühungen des Autors zurückgehende Aufsatz schildert die seit der Parkgründung durch Dekret der Zentralregierung (1967) latent schwelenden Konflikte zwischen den Parkorganen, den Parkgemeinden und vor allem den Gemeinden in der unmittelbaren Parkumgebung. Der gewählte Ansatz anaylisiert die Steuerung gesellschaftlicher Probleme durch die Schaffung partnerschaftlicher Kooperationsformen zwischen Hierarchie und Markt. Institutionell wird der Park in Anlehnung an March & Ohlsen als organisierte Anarchie beschrieben, die nur über vage abstrakte Ziele verfügt, unklare und widersprüchliche Handlungskompetenzen besitzt sowie mit wechselnden und wechselhaften Partnern umzugehen hat. So soll der Park gleichzeitig einen Beitrag zum Naturschutz, aber auch zur wirtschaftlichen Entwicklung der Park- und Umliegergemeinden beitragen. Eine angemessene Organisationsform, in denen Park- und Umliegergemeinden im Interesse einer sowohl tourismuswirtschaftlich als auch umweltpolitisch befriedigenden Entwicklung mit den vom Zentralstaat eingesetzten Parkbehörden kooperierten, ist bis heute nicht zustande gekommen. Das konflikthafte Nachbarschaftsverhältnis zwischen den zwei (verschiedenen Departementen angehörigen) Parkgemeinden liess sich ebenso wenig überwinden wie die Strukturschwäche der von Abwanderung und zahlreichen Umweltauflagen bedrohten lokalen Wirtschaft der Umliegergemeinden. Die Schwächen des Arrangements vor der Einleitung eines bewussten Verhandlungsprozesses bestanden im Mangel starker Koalitionen unter den auf eigene Interessen bedachten Akteuren, im Fehlen eines gemeinsamen Nenners und in mangelhaften Ressourcen. Die Mediationslösung sollte das immobilisierte Netzwerk gewissermassen am eigenen Schopf aus dem Sumpf ziehen. Der Autor beschreibt auch diese Verhandlungsoperationen minutiös. Im Zentrum sollte das gemeinsame Bemühen um Erhalt und Förderung der natürlichen und kulturellen Ressourcen der betroffenen Gemeinden stehen ("patrimoine"). Dabei sollte der Park nicht als Problem, sondern als Ressource für die Realisierung unterschiedlicher Zielsetzung der beteiligten Akteure angesehen werden. Und der Interessenkonflikt sollte nach Auffassung der Mediatoren Anlass zur Schaffung institutioneller Kommunikationsformen unter den verfeindenden Akteuren dienen. Anhand zweier Konfliktgegenstände (Schutz des - symbolträchtigen - Bären und Bau einer Autostrasse mit Tunnel im Herzen des Westteils des Parks) zeigt der Autor die Anwendung dieser zwei Prinzipien.

Der *niederländische* Beitrag aus der Feder von *Ida J. Koppen* (Europäisches Institut für Politikwissenschaft in Florenz) zeigt die Mechanik von Verhandlungslösungen in der Abfallwirtschaft Hollands. Anfänglich nur in Einzelfällen eingesetzt, wurde die Verhandlungsstrategie 1988 in einem regierungsamtlichen "Memorandum" zum generellen Bestandteil der holländischen Abfallpolitik erklärt. Der Beitrag analysiert den Verhandlungsprozess, der 1991 zu einem Vertrag zwischen der Verpackungsindustrie und der Regierung geführt hat. In theoretischen Vorüberlegungen legt auch dieser Beitrag dar, dass Verhandlungen nur dann zum Erfolg führen können, wenn sich beide Seiten daraus realistische Vorteile versprechen können. Während sich bei den Branchen diese Vorteile in ihrer relativen Freiheit über die Wahl der Mittel zur Zielerreichung niederschlagen, liegen sie bei der Regierung darin, dass die Zielgruppen auf Obstruktion bzw. Opposition verzichten und sich vertraglich zur Einhaltung der gesetzten Ziele verpflichten. Als Gegenleistung verzichtet die Verwaltung auf den Einsatz einseitig festgelegter hoheitlicher Regulierung über die Art und Weise der Zielerreichung. Die Autorin legt dar, dass die im Beitrag beschriebenen Verhandlungen und der abschliessende Vertrag nicht als voller Erfolg angesehen werden kann. Der Widerstand der Industrie gegen die Forderungen der Umweltschutzorganisationen und der Regierung hielt länger an als anfänglich erwartet. Die unter Handlungsdruck stehende Regierung sah sich in der Endphase gar zum Übergang zu bilateralen Verhandlungen und damit zum Ausschluss der Umweltschutzorganisationen veranlasst. Trotz Abschluss des Vertrags bliebt der Konflikt zwischen Verpackungsindustrie und Umweltschutzorganisationen weiterhin bestehen. In der Schlussfolgerung warnt die Autorin denn auch vor unechten Verhandlungslösungen, die nichts anderes seien als eine Fortführung der alten bilateralen Gesetzesaushandlungsprozesse zwischen Staat und Industrie unter neuem Namen.

Die vier *Schweizer Beiträge* geben aus der Sicht des Herausgebers einen recht vollständigen Überblick über Vorhandensein und Stellenwert von Verhandlungslösungen in der helvetischen politisch-administrativen Praxis. Analysiert werden zunächst zwei, inzwischen wohl als schweizerische ADR-Klassiker zu bezeichnende Standortsuchverfahren aus der deutschen und aus der französischen Schweiz und die ausserordentlich Facettenreiche Praxis zur Kooperation zwischen Behörden und Zielgruppen der Umweltpolitik in einem schweizerischen Kanton (Solothurn). Im letzten Kapitel werden diese und andere Verfahren nochmal im Lichte einiger Grundprinzipien des schweizerischen politisch-administrativen Systems diskutiert.

Ortwin Renn, Leiter der Akademie für Technikfolgenabschätzung für Baden-Württemberg und sein ehemaliger Mitarbeiter *Thomas Webler* vom Polyprojekt "Risiko und Sicherheit technischer Systeme" der ETH Zürich situieren ihre detaillierte Analyse des Standortsuchprozesses für eine Deponie im Ostteil des Kantons Aargau in einem breit ausgelegten theoretischen Kontext zum kooperativen Diskurs. Entsorgungsanlagen sind nach Auffassung der Autoren besonders geeignet, bei Betroffenen und Benützung eine Sankt-Floriansmentalität zu führen, weil Risiken und Nutzen nicht gleich verteilt sind, weshalb trotz eines generellen Konsenses über ihre Notwendigkeit sich immer Kontroversen über die Standorte einstellten. Solche Anlagen sind daher auch besonders geeignete Einsatzgebiete für den kooperativen Diskurs. Entscheiden sollen weder Experten noch der Markt. Kompetente Problemlösung soll mit fairer Beschlussfassung verbunden werden. Kompetenz müsse an der Leistung des Verfahrens gemessen werden, "die im Dialog gemachten Aussagen nach dem Stand des jeweiligen Wissens intersubjektiv nachvollziehbar beurteilen" zu selektieren. Aufbauend auf Überlegungen von Jürgen Habermas und Peter Dienel entwickeln die Autoren ihr Modell des kooperativen Diskurses, das sich u.a. durch einen Konsens über das einzuschlagende Verfahren, über die Gleichberechtigung unterschiedlicher Interpretationsmuster und Rationalitäten und über die Abstinenz strategischen Handelns charakterisiert. Der kooperative Diskurs für die Standortfestlegung für eine Restabfalldeponie für den östlichen Teil des Kantons Aargaus verlief in drei Phasen und führte von 32 möglichen Deponiestandorten schliesslich zu deren 13. Die Entscheidfindung oblag vier parallel aber unabhängig voneinander tagenden Bürgerkommissionen, in denen die Kriterien für eine Nutzwertanalyse aller möglicher Standorte entwickelt wurden. Alle vier Kommissionen gelangten zu einstimmig gefassten Standortempfehlungen. Auf dem ersten Platz landete bei allen Gruppen der schliesslich ausgewählte Standort Eriwis. Im internationalen Vergleich zeichneten sich die schweizerischen Bürgerkommissionen durch hohes Durchhaltevermögen, ein grösseres Vertrauen in die Experten und ein teilweise beachtliches Misstrauen gegenüber den Behörden aus. Interessante gruppendynamische Beobachtungen und Ergebnisse einer Umfrage über die subjektive Zufriedenheit der Teilnehmer zu Beginn und am Schluss des Verfahrens runden den Beitrag ab.

Erstaunlich ähnlich verlief das in der Suisse romande durchgeführte Verfahren zur Suche eines Standorts für eine Sondermülldeponie, die *Michel Rey* von der an diesem Verfahren beteiligten Communauté d'études pour l'aménagement du territoire (C.E.A.T.) beschreibt. Auch hier bestand ein hoher Problemdruck und ein durch die Bundesgesetzgebung Anfang der neunziger Jahre deutlich akzentuierter Handlungsbedarf. Ähnlich wie im Falle des Kantons Aargau hatten die Westschweizer Behörden aufgrund eines gescheiterten Standortausweisungsverfahrens, das nach dem normalen Planungsverfahren verlief, gelernt, dass nur ein "alternatives" Prozedere zum Erfolg führen könnte. Die Notwendigkeit eines solchen Verfahrens resultierte aus einer 1987 in Auftrag gegebenen Vorstudie. Im Frühjahr 1988 begann der Stapellauf von ursprünglich 32 über 14, 5 zu den drei im März 1993 definitiv und oppositionslos ausgewiesenen Standorten. Dem Aargauer Verfahren ebenfalls auffallend ähnlich ist das Modell der Bürgerbeteiligung: Auch hier erarbeiteten vier regionale Gruppen die (gewichteten) Kriterien für die Standortauswahl, die dann allerdings nochmal durch wiederum unterschiedlich zusammengesetzten Bürgergruppen auf die 14 Standorte angewandt wurden. Die Kriterien der verschiedenen Gruppen fielen sehr ähnlich aus. Als Erfolgsbedingungen nennt der Autor zunächst den Umstand, dass die Akteure des Verhandlungsprozesses während der ganzen Verfahrensdauer über eine breite Unterstützung seitens der politisch Verantwortlichen verfügten. Wichtig war auch, dass die Anlage als solche nicht umstritten war, und dass sämtlich relevanten Akteure zur Mitwirkung bewegt werden konnten. Weiter angeführt werden die Verfügbarkeit von Zeit, die Möglichkeit der Entschädigung der Bürger für ihre Mitwirkungsarbeit und der

Umstand, dass die Verhandlungsleiter über eine gute Schulung in Verhandlungstechnik verfügen.

Wie reichhaltig die Praxis zum Kooperationsprinzip auf der Ebene eines schweizerischen Kantons sein kann, zeigt der Beitrag von *Rolf Maegli*, der die dargestellten Aktivitäten des Kantons Solothurn als Spitzenbeamter selbst aus nächster Nähe kennt. Verhandlungslösungen seien auf der kantonalen Ebene um so notwendiger, als hier Konflikte bereits auf Gesetzgebungsebene vorprogrammiert seien. Kooperative Elemente sind im Kanton Solothurn bereits in der beachtlichen Mitwirkung des Kantonsrates an der Gesetzgebung vorgesehen (insbesondere: Veto-Möglichkeit des Kantonsrats gegen Verordnungen). Anwendungen des Kooperationsprinzips finden sich denn auch im Kanton bereits auf der Gesetzgebungsebene. In der Verwaltungspraxis findet das Kooperationsprinzip nachhaltig Anwendung in der Lufteinhaltung (Sanierungsverfügungen), im Natur- und Landschaftsschutz (Schutzverträge mit Landwirten) und in der Durchführung der Umweltverträglichkeitsprüfung. In der Schlussfolgerung weist der Autor darauf hin, dass im Kanton Solothurn Vermittlungslösungen seit längerer Zeit mit Erfolg praktiziert würden. Diese Lösungen hätten sich meistens pragmatisch "und ohne dogmatischen Hintergrund" ergeben. "So gesehen ist die Auseinandersetzung um Sinn und Vorteile von Mittlermodellen nicht neu." In erster Linie sei es Aufgabe der Verwaltung, als Vermittlerin aufzutreten. Nur in Ausnahmefällen, in denen die Kantonsverwaltung selbst Partei sei, wäre der Beizug von aussenstehenden Mittlern zu prüfen. Gleichwohl müsse auch bei solchen Verfahren die Exekutive und die Verwaltung schlussendlich die Verantwortung für Entscheidungen übernehmen. Mittlermodelle müssten kreativ und innovativ eingesetzt werden; sie dürften nicht von Anbeginn an in die Verfahrensgesetzgebung und in ritualisierte Abläufe gepresst werden. Schliesslich stellt der Verfasser die Frage, ob Konfliktmittlung nicht als Aufgabe der Konfliktverursacher anzusehen sei. Verwaltungsseits biete sich für die Durchführung konflikthafter Verfahren auch ein Ausklinken aus der ordentlichen Verwaltungsstruktur in Ad-hoc-Strukturen eines Projektmanagements an.

Es möge dem Leser selbst überlassen bleiben, ob er den vom *Herausgeber* am Schluss vorgetragenen Versuch der Einordnung von Mediationsverfahren in das politisch-administrative System Helvetiens als realistische Analyse oder als gewagte Vision betrachtet. Nach dem Studium vieler ausländischer Mediationsverfahren und dem Versuch, unsere politisch-administrative Alltagspraxis im Lichte der ausländischen Überlegungen neu zu interpretieren, gelange ich jedenfalls zum Schluss, dass wir in unserem Lande trotz (oder wegen?) vielfältiger, historisch und kulturell bedingter Konfliktlinien bereits heute über derart vielfältige verhandlungsgestützte Konfliktlösungsmechanismen verfügen, dass wir Mediatoren im engeren Sinne in der Regel nicht haben und auch nicht brauchen. Die Beweisführung dieser These führt über eine (impressionistische) historische Reminiszenz vom "Stanser Verkommnis" bis zur "helvetischen Mediationsakte", von der "Kappeler Milchsuppe" über den "Sonderbundskrieg" bis zur Niederschlagung des "Generalstreiks" und schliesslich zur "Zauberformel". Herausgearbeitet werden vier typische Konfliktkonstellationen, die den helvetischen Alltag seit der Gründung des Bundesstaates prägen. Vor diesem Hintergrund werden schliesslich aufgrund von Fallstudien acht Mediations- oder mediationsähnliche Verfahren aus der jüngsten Vergangenheit und Gegenwart der schweizerischen Umweltpolitik dargestellt. Immerhin kennt auch die Schweiz mit ihrer ausgeprägten Verhandlungskultur Streitbeilegungsverfahren, die auf dem Prinzip des "kurzen" bzw. des "kürzeren" Prozesses beruhen. Aber selbst diese Verfahren, aus denen schliesslich Sieger und Besiegte resultieren, sind durch Verhandlungselemente durchsetzt, in denen Gegensätze zumindest teilweise abgebaut werden können. Vor diesem Hintergrund ist eine der vorgetragenen Schlussfolgerungen wenig erstaunlich, wonach unsere gesamte politisch-administrative Kultur und ihre Institutionen mit einer Vielzahl von Verhandlungselementen durchsetzt sei, weshalb heute und morgen "der Stellenwert von Mediationsverfahren äusserst gering bleiben wird".

Literaturverzeichnis

W. Hoffmann-Riem, E. Schmidt-Assmann (Hrsg.): *Konfliktbewältigung durch Verhandlungen,* I, Baden-Baden (Nomos-Verlag), 1990, und: dies. (Hrsg.): *Konfliktbewältigung durch Verhandlungen, Konfliktmittlung in Verwaltungsverfahren*, Band II, Baden-Baden (Nomos-Verlag), 1990.

Ministère de l'Equipement, du Logement, des Transports et de la Mer, Ministère de la Recherche et de la Technologie (ed.): *"Evaluation et décision"*, Séminaire de méthode, CEOPS, Ecole Nationale des Travaux Publics de l'Etat, Vaulx en Velin, septembre 1990.

L. Susskind, J. Cruikshank: *Breaking the Impass - Consensual Approaches to Revolving Public Disputes*, New York, 1987.

FROM CONFLICT TOWARDS COLLABORATIVE PROCESSES:
CONCEPTS AND EXPERIENCES FROM THE UNITED STATES

Arturo Gàndara

1. INTRODUCTION

The resolution of complex environmental disputes in the United States is rarely a matter involving only private parties. Usually at issue as well is a federal or state interest which of necessity usually involves an administrative agency - and occasionally the legislature. Consequently, alternatives to resolution before the courts in these situations are faced with additional challenges not normally faced by alternative forms of dispute resolution involving private parties. Nevertheless, much of the effort at involving government in alternative dispute resolution has as a basic analog the alternative dispute resolution (ADR) methodology developed for and used by private parties[1]. We must, however, keep in mind the limitations and opportunities posed by such special application of alternative dispute resolution techniques.

There has always been a spectrum of alternatives to the traditional mode of conflict resolution, litigation, which includes arbitration, mediation, facilitation, negotiation, cooperative problem solving, workshops, and roundtables. The traditional alternative, arbitration, stayed close to the traditional adjudication model. As experience and comfort was gained with that alternative and as some of the limitations became evident in its application to disputes in new and complex areas such as those of the environment, interest in the other forms of ADR developed.

These other forms are decidedly less judicial and although distinctive from each other in concept and practice they can generally be characterized by the avoidance of the adversarial model of fact determination and by the avoidance of appealing to a third party, judge or arbitrator, for a decision of the dispute. More affirmatively, these forms of ADR are

---

[1] M. Millhauser and C. Pou Jr., *Sourcebook: Federal Agency Use of Alternative Means of Dispute Resolution*, Administrative Conference of the United States, June 1987.

characterized by voluntariness, face-to-face discussions, and consensus building[2].

Clearly, some of these efforts may involve a mediator or facilitator and discussions may, in fact, be negotiations. Nevertheless, the most apt characteristic of the process is its collaborative nature. When utilized in the resolution of complex disputes by policymakers we can characterize, the process as a "collaborative policy forum"[3]. This characterization captures best the combination of result, policy, and process, non-adversarial discussion, which we seek in resolving environmental disputes.

This paper reviews a recent federal statutory initiative which encourages federal agencies to engage in "collaborative policy forums" when undertaking the resolution of complex environmental policy disputes. The paper will also review two non-federal instances of environmental collaborative policy forum undertakings in California which met with opposite results. The paper concludes with some thoughts and observations on the realistic expectations and appropriateness of collaborative policy forums in the resolution of environmental disputes.

2. ADMINISTRATIVE AGENCIES AND THE CONSTITUTIONAL SCHEME

To appreciate the significance of the federal government's recent approbation and encouragement of collaborative policy forums for the resolution of environmental disputes, one must have an understanding of the relationship of agencies to the three branches of government. To understand that relationship one must understand the federal constitutional scheme which allocates all governmental power. Although the following discussion refers solely to the federal scheme, for the most part it is also applicable to the governing arrangements of the individual states whose constitutions contain very similar provisions.

Article I of the constitution allocates "all legislative powers" to the Congress of the United States[4]. Article II allocates all executive power to

---

[2] G. Bingham, *Resolving Environmental Disputes*, The Conservation Foundation, 1986.
[3] T. Trzyna and I. Gotelli, Editors, *The Power of Convening: Collaborative Policy Forums for Sustainable Development*, California Institute of Public Affairs, 1990.
[4] U.S. Const. art I, Sec. 1.

the President of the United States[5]. Article III allocates the judicial power in one Supreme Court and in such inferior courts as the Congress may establish[6]. The Tenth Amendment reserves all powers not allocated to the United States by the constitution to the states or the people[7].

The basic constitutional scheme is distrustful of the accumulation of powers in any one branch of government. This constitutional scheme has separated the powers of the sovereign and instituted checks and balances on the exercise of the power allocated to any one branch of government. The allocation of governmental power is complete and none is allocated to administrative agencies. Indeed, administrative agencies are not created by the constitution although reference is made to several agency functions.

The administrative agencies of government, whether executive or "independent," are created by the congress and ironically, have been allocated a combination of the powers so carefully separated by the constitution. Although this appears to be violative of the constitutional scheme, judicial review of challenges to agency exercise of the combination of functions[8], to delegation of legislative power[9] and to delegation of adjudicatory power[10] has resulted in approval of the recombination of these powers - within certain guidelines. These limits to agency exercise of delegated legislative and judicial powers have important consequences for the design of collaborative procedures and the extent to which governmental agencies can engage in collaborative policy forums for resolution of environmental disputes.

3. MODES OF ADMINISTRATIVE AGENCY DECISION MAKING

Agency decision making authority and procedures derive from two sources, legislation and court interpretation. Each in turn has a couple of components.

---

[5] U.S. Const. art. II, Sec.1.
[6] U.S. Const. art. III, Sec. 1.
[7] U.S. Const. amend. X.
[8] *Withrow v. Larkin*, 421 U.S. 35 (1975).
[9] *Panama Refining Co. v. Ryan*, 293 U.S. 388 (1935); *A.L.A. Schecter Poultry Corp. v. United States*, 295 U.S. 495 (1935); *Carter v. Carter Coal Co.*, 298 U.S. 238 (1936).
[10] *Commodity Futures Trading Commission v. Schor*, 478 U.S. 833 (1986).

When congress creates an agency the enabling legislation defines the powers delegated to that agency. While it may also set forth some procedures to be used by that agency, agency procedures are generally governed by a more generic legislative source, the Administrative Procedure Act (APA). The APA sets forth two basic modes of agency decision making, adjudication[11] and rulemaking[12].

With respect to authority arising from court interpretation of the powers and procedures of administrative agencies, there are two important court derived concepts, the non-delegation doctrine[13] and the obligation of agencies to adhere to procedural due process[14], that accompany the modes of decision making. The former basically permits the delegation of legislative authority to administrative agencies as long as the delegation is accompanied by some guidance for the exercise of agency discretion when it acts in a legislative mode (rulemaking). The latter requires that agency adjudication adhere to some due process protections such as notice, opportunity to comment, possibly a hearing, and a decision by an independent decisionmaker based on the administrative record when the agency acts in a judicial mode (adjudication).

Therefore, the extent to which an administrative agency can use collaborative processes is constrained. For example, with respect to rulemaking the non-delegation doctrine would prohibit the delegation of that power to a collaborative policy group since it has been held that legislative authority cannot be delegated to private persons[15]. With respect to adjudication, the constitutional due process requirements may require trial-type elements thereby effectively precluding a collaborative process. Arbitration which is non-collaborative, may be the most likely alternative dispute resolution mechanism to administrative adjudication.

---

[11] 5 U.S.C. Secs. 551(7), 554. An agency adjudication is a determination of particular applicability that resolves, through an order, the rights or duties of a specified person or entity based upon circumstances unique to that person or entity.

[12] 5 U.S.C. Secs. 551(4), 553. A rule is typically an agency statement which regulates the future conduct of groups or persons and primarily concerned with policy considerations.

[13] *Yakus v. United States*, 321 U.S. 414 (1944).

[14] *Mathews v. Eldridge*, 424 U.S. 319 (1976).

[15] *Carter v. Carter Coal Co.*, 298 U.S. 238 (1936).

4. THE FEDERAL NEGOTIATED RULEMAKING ACT AS A COLLABORATIVE MODEL

Dissatisfaction with the increasing formality of the traditional modes of agency decision making, process inefficiencies and the near certainty of parties in disagreement with agency determinations pursuing judicial review coincided with the increasing visibility of alternative dispute resolution successes in private disputes. Consequently, the feasibility of alternative dispute resolution techniques to agency determinations began to be explored in the late 1970s and early 1980s. By 1982, the Administrative Conference of the United States (ACUS)[16] made formal its recommendation that administrative agencies employ a form of ADR, regulatory negotiation, in their rulemaking efforts[17].

The recommendation fit the definition of a collaborative policy process in that it called for the use of a "convener" who would organize "negotiations" whose goal would be a consensus on a proposed rule. To avoid the constitutional prohibition against delegating legislative authority to a private group, the consensus proposed rule would then be issued by the administrative agency as a proposed rule whose procedure towards adoption would be in accordance with the APA.

Less than one year later the Environmental Protection Agency (EPA) announced a "Regulatory Negotiation" demonstration project to test the utility and value of developing regulations by "negotiation"[18]. A year later the ACUS issued a recommendation to EPA for the use of negotiations in the cleanup of hazardous waste sites under the Comprehensive Environmental Response Compensation and Liability Act (CERCLA)[19].

By 1985, there had been four occasions in which agencies had used the regulatory negotiation procedures recommended by the ACUS in 1982 and the experience had been considered positive by the ACUS. Three of those instances involved the promulgation of environmental regulations. Encouraged by this the ACUS issued Recommendation No. 85-5, Proce-

---

[16] The Administrative Conference of the United States is itself an independent agency created by Congress in 1964. Its purpose is to promote improvements in the efficiency, adequacy and fairness of procedures by which the federal agencies conduct regulatory programs, administer benefits, and perform related government functions.
[17] 1 C.F.R. Sec. 305.82-4 (1982).
[18] 48 Fed. Reg. 7494 (1983)
[19] 1 C.F.R. Sec. 305.84-4 (1984).

dures for Negotiating Proposed Regulations[20]. This recommendation reaffirmed Recommendation 82-5 and asked agencies to be cognizant of some of the potential problems that could develop with negotiated rulemaking such as unrealistic expectations, uneven participatory skills among the "negotiators", constituency disagreements, confidentiality, and costs of participation.

The following years saw an increasing experimentation of negotiated rulemaking by executive branch agencies, particularly EPA. There appears to have been little interest by the "independent" regulatory agencies[21] and one, the Securities and Exchange Commission (SEC) specifically rejected the idea stating that it was "neither necessary nor appropriate"[22]. In 1988, however, the Congress required negotiated rulemaking from an "independent" regulatory agency, the Nuclear Regulatory Commission in order to determine whether to enter into indemnity agreements with persons licensed by the Commission or by the Agreement State for the manufacture, production, possession, or use of radioisotopes or radiopharmaceuticals for medical purposes[23].

This activity and interest in using a collaborative process in developing regulations finally culminated in the passage of the Negotiated Rulemaking Act of 1990[24]. Most aspects of the act followed ACUS's Recommendation No. 82-4 with a few differences. Rather than accepting ACUS's invitation to modify the Federal Advisory Committee Act (FACA) to facilitate negotiated rulemaking Congress required compliance with FACA which reflected what the agencies had been doing anyway. The ACUS was given a facilitator role and funds to assist these efforts. A sunset provision of six years was included. Most importantly, judicial review was precluded of any agency action relating to establishing, assisting, or terminating a negotiated rulemaking committee. The Act did not require negotiated rulemaking but maintained its voluntary aspect which also

---

[20] 1 C.F.R. Sec. 305.85-5 (1985).

[21] The "executive branch" agencies refers to the various Departments whose heads form the President's Cabinet. The "independent" agencies are generally the regulatory agencies characterized by a Commission form of organization. Some would add a third category of "quasi-independent" agencies wherein they would place the Environmental Protection Agency.

[22] 53 Fed. Reg. 2336 (1988).

[23] Price Anderson Amendments Act, Pub. L. No. 100-408 (1988).

[24] Pub. L. No. 101-648, 104 Stat. 4969.

maintained, for our purposes, the character of a collaborative policy process.

While the experience with negotiated rulemaking had not been extensive in the eight years since Recommendation No. 82-4 was issued, nevertheless, negotiated rulemaking proceeded without an act of Congress and could conceivably continue after the sunset of the Negotiated Rulemaking Act. Yet the passage of the Act must be perceived as a congressional endorsement of negotiated rulemaking and the resolution of complex environmental disputes through a collaborative policy process.

5. COMPARISON WITH TWO STATE COLLABORATIVE PROCESSES

In January of 1990 the four major investor-owned public utilities in the State of California announced that they had reached agreement with consumer groups, environmental organizations and government agencies on "An Energy Efficient Blueprint for California." In early 1991 several major environmental organizations and Sierra Pacific Industries, California's largest holder of private timberlands announced agreement on a "Sierra Accord" which resolved many timber controversies that had existed for decades. Both agreements were the result of collaborative policy processes, however, they met very different fates.

The Energy Efficient Blueprint was translated into specific conservation programs by the utilities and approved by the Public Utilities Commission of the State of California within the year. The Sierra Accord was translated to a legislative bill which was amended numerous times and eventually passed by the legislature over the opposition of the Governor. The Sierra Accord, as amended, is on the Governor's desk and it is expected that he will veto the bill.

Although there is the very major difference that one process led to a rule-type of agreement and the other led to a legislative proposal, nonetheless, it would appear that the collaborative policy process used by the developers of the energy efficiency blueprint comes close to the collaborative model represented by the negotiated rulemaking guidelines. That is, the regulatory agency directed the parties to engage in a dialogue, was involved as a participant, included all the major players (all the potential intervenors), and consensus by a time definite was the goal[25]. By contrast, the Sierra Accord process, although involving major stakeholders, did not include other timber companies and grassroots environmental organizations that had engaged in major court battles to control logging on lands inhabited by endangered wildlife. The legislature was not a participant and the process was open-ended[26]. Correlating the contrasting collaborative processes with their very different outcomes suggests that the guidelines and principles of the Negotiated Rulemaking Act, as a collaborative process model, might have some merit.

6. CONCLUSION

It would appear that years of refinement in alternative dispute resolution and its subsequent application to administrative decision making have resulted in a model process, a collaborative policy process, which has potential merit. The basic elements of that process are now most clearly set forth in the Negotiated Rulemaking Act of 1990. Although the Negotiated Rulemaking Act is only applicable to the federal government, the elements of the process are useful as a model, as is suggested by the California experiences reviewed. This model might very well be more widely applicable outside the confines of the United States. This would not be too surprising since these collaborative model elements are derived from alternative dispute resolution techniques honed in many governmental and non-governmental settings.

There is some irony, however, in the fact that the administrative rulemaking and adjudication which collaborative policy processes displace are also alternative dispute resolution methodologies - originally efficient alternates to their progenitors, legislation and court adjudication. What surely needs to be addressed sometime, then, is not only what has been

---

[25] Of the 18 speakers who appeared at the July 1989 hearing, many suggested that the issue...might be better resolved in a collaborative process in which parties with a stake in energy efficiency could meet and develop a consensus approach to propose to regulators. The idea of creating a collaborative process was promptly endorsed by the CPUC Commissioners, who further challenged the group to `begin and begin quickly,' and requested a blueprint within six months..." Report of the Statewide Collaborative Process: An Energy Efficiency Blueprint for California, January 1990.

[26] "Coalition Seeks a Peaceful End to Forest Fray", Los Angeles Times, page 3, September 2, 1991.

gained by moving from more adversarial processes to collaborative policy processes but also what has been lost. In asking our administrative agencies to seek consensus, especially with respect to complex environmental disputes, one must not overlook the fact that we are being less demanding of the application of technical expertise in the promulgation of policy and more accepting of our administrative agencies assuming a legislative or political role. In an era of judicial deference to administrative agencies we might pause to be concerned about whether anyone is looking out for the normative values that should comprise the public interest.

REFERENCES

G. Bingham, *Resolving Environmental Disputes*, The Conservation Forum, 1986.

Coalition Seeks a Peaceful End to Forest Fray, Los Angeles Times, p. 3, September 2, 1991.

M. Millhauser and C. Pou Jr., *Sourcebook: Federal Agency Use of Alternative Means of Dispute Resolution*, Administrative Conference of the United States, June 1987.

T. Trzyna and I. Gotelli (eds.), *The Power of Convening: Collaborative Policy Forums for Sustainable Development*, California Institute of Public Affairs, 1990.

COURT DECISIONS

A.L.A. Schecter Poultry Corp. v. United States, 293 U.S. 495 (1935).

Carter v. Carter Coal Co., 298 U.S. 238 (1936).

Commodity Futures Trading Commission v. Schor, 478 U.S. 833 (1986).

Mathews v. Eldridge, 424 U.S. 319 (1976).

Panama Refining Co. v. Ryan, 293 U.S. 388 (1935).

Withrow v. Larkin, 421 U.S. 35 (1975).

Yakus v. United States, 321 U.S. 414 (1944).

RECONCEIVING LULUS:
CHANGING THE NATURE AND SCOPE OF
LOCALLY UNWANTED LAND USES

Daniel A. Mazmanian[1]
Michael Stanley-Jones

One of the more intriguing developments in the social sciences that is changing our way of looking at natural and human behavior is the introduction of catastrophe theory. In contrast to the conventional linear or smooth and continuous models, catastrophe models apply to the less common but often extremely important cases of processes that experience abrupt "discontinuities" or step jumps[2]. The implications for students of politics and society are significant. If it is true that for certain kinds of policy problems taking one small and logical step after another - incrementally moving along the smooth and continuous curve - will only lead to an unbridgeable gap, then it becomes imperative to begin approaching these problems in qualitatively different ways.

How to make such a jump in the policy process is not so obvious. We know that bold new ideas are important in triggering fundamental policy reformulation and ways of thinking about problems[3], but we know embarrassingly little about where these ideas come from or how they are translated into practice. The conventional human pattern is to think and move inch-by-inch along a line. To expect to do otherwise is all the more frustrating in a political system designed to pit groups against one another in the legislative, executive, and judicial arenas, rather than to join groups together for dialogue, long-range thinking, and change. Equally troublesome is knowing just when it is necessary to break with convention. Differences of opinion will always exist on this score and the "facts" of the matter are rarely a sufficient guide.

---

[1] This contribution was published in: Joseph Di Mento, Le Roy Graymer (eds.), *Confronting Regional Challenges: Approaches to LULUs, Growth, and Other Vexing Governance Problems*, Cambridge, MA, Lincoln Institute of Land Policy, 1991. We thank the editor for the copyright.
[2] Zeeman 1976.
[3] Reich 1988.

The case of today's highly charged issue of siting hazardous-waste and toxic facilities illustrates the point. How is one to interpret the fact that in California, a state with over 27 million people, hundreds of large and thousands of small firms combine to generate somewhere between 3 and 10 million tons of hazardous waste per year? Or, while some readings of the figures on hazardous-waste disposal show a decline in the past several years others show little or no change[4]? This is no trivial matter given the push in the state to site an "adequate" number of hazardous-waste treatment and storage facilities in the face of substantial public opposition. Should hazardous-waste disposal problems be viewed conventionally as the unavoidable by-product of ever-expanding industrial production, then the invariable answer is a call for more and more waste-disposal sites. Or simply to send the wastes elsewhere. Alternatively, should it be framed in terms of the physical limits of the earth's surface to absorb and assimilate hazardous materials or the threat to human health, the past approach of adding landfills and waste facilities will only lead to an eventual policy disaster.

While we are just beginning to understand the politics and psychology of Locally Unwanted Land Use (LULUs), one of their defining features appears to be that they involve dramatic differences in the framing of the issue by contending parties. Some see progress while others see impending doom. Viable, long-term solutions, moreover, usually require redefining the nature of the problem at its core; they fit the catastrophe model[5]. This in turn requires radically new ways of thinking about the issue along with the development of new political institutions that facilitate redefinition and convergence on mutually acceptable solutions.

With this in mind, we begin by outlining the commonly identified causes of LULUs followed by a review of conventional responses. We then turn to more promising and comprehensive approaches evolving today, which provide a forum for reframing issues and developing policy processes through which lasting accords can be reached. Two illustrations are presented from the environmental-business-government confrontations over water development in Colorado and toxic-waste management in California. While only a limited range of examples are presented, they illustrate the underlying dynamics involved. The lessons drawn are summa-

---

[4] Mazmanian 1988.
[5] Rowland, Lee, and Goetz 1988.

rized in a matrix of conditions contributing to the resolution of LULUs and the implications drawn for democratic policy making.

1. CONVENTIONAL EXPLANATIONS FOR LULUS

Explanations of the failure to site a growing number of major industrial and public facilities, from prisons, airports, dams and water transport systems, solid- and hazardous-waste landfills, to high-tech toxic-waste management facilities usually fall into one of several categories.

1.1. Differences in Risk Perception

People simply do not see the risks of LULUs in the same way. Local citizens, environmentalists, and health advocates "frame" the issue as one of neighborhood and community health and safety or some generalized protection of the environment. Proponents of a LULU focus on the specific and more measurable economic benefits of a proposal and its "technical" feasibility and safety. Thus projects are adamantly opposed despite expert, dispassionate, and neutral determination that the benefit-cost ratio for a project is acceptable (at least by conventional criteria), or that the potential risks involved are less even than continuing with existing practices.

Researchers have suggested that this is affected by one or more dimensions of the way people respond to risk. For example, people resist involuntary risk exposure more keenly than voluntary risk exposure. They fear and have damaging psychological repercussions far less from naturally occurring risks, like earthquakes and floods, than man-made risks such as exposure to industrial toxins or harmful drugs[6]. Risks readily perceived through eyes, ears, nose, and touch turn out to be less frightening. Those that cannot be detected, such as chemicals in drinking water or radiation, are more mysterious, emotionally charged, and to be avoided. Politically this leads to calls for zero exposure.

Willingness to tolerate risk is also related to the perceived balance between beneficiaries and cost bearers. This is possibly more a matter of

---

[6] Baum 1988.

perceptions of "justice" than risk; the greater the symmetry between the costs and benefits, the more willing are people to tolerate risks for themselves and others. Finally, people are more prone to accept the risks associated with new technologies when they are clearly linked to new jobs, economic growth, and an increased standard of living[7].

1.2. The Not-In-My-Backyard (NIMBY) Syndrome

At the beginning of the 1980s many policy makers and project advocates saw opposition to LULUs largely in terms of irrational and selfish behavior. Public behavior was characterized in this fashion whenever the public resisted in the face expert opinion that a project was essential for society and the risk involved small and acceptable[8]. Yet, from the point of view of democratic process, JUST SAYING NO was actually quite rational - it was often the only recourse available to the public[9].

The NIMBY response takes on greater credence in view of recent documentation that LULUs can have a clearly adverse effect on adjacent residential property values[10]. Moreover, it is not the existence of risk from facilities per se so much as the negative publicity about the risks and the public's perceptions of risk that have the greatest downward effect on value. The implication is a perverse one: If you live near a troublesome LULU, don't blow the whistle or your property value will suffer. The corollary is: When in doubt, err on the side of keeping a potentially harmful LULU out of the neighborhood.

1.3. Uncertainty about the Need for and Technical Capability of a Facility

There are significant unknowns in almost every proposed LULU, especially any that involve new technologies. This always opens the door to competing claims about efficacy and safety. When combined with any of

---

[7] Otway and Von Winterfeldt 1982.
[8] Morell and Magorian 1982.
[9] Kraft and Clary, 1991.
[10] Payne, Olshansky, and Segel 1987.

the other factors noted, this can bring a project under enormous pressure, and often lead to its demise.

1.4 The Double-Edged Sword of Government Regulation

All LULUs are hit with the "too-many-checkpoints" problems of multiple jurisdictions, delays, permits, and ever-changing governmental regulations. For almost any project proponent, the frustrations of gaining numerous clearances, responding to different rules and expectations, and wading through numerous bureaucracies can be maddening. Combined with vocal public opposition, these can effectively kill a project.

1.5 Public Distrust in Business and Government

A more general problem is the pervasive public distrust of the ability of business and government to guide American society[11], which undermines any claim either makes on behalf of a LULU. Distrust has been rising for more than two decades and stems from many and complex causes: the Vietnam War and the Watergate scandal of the 1970s; a president who, throughout the 1980s, constantly reminded the public of the failures of the public sector; and a seemingly endless string of technological and environmental calamities, which government and business have been ill-prepared to handle.

Credibility on the question of toxic-waste management is particularly telling. The apparent failure of business and government to anticipate and then, when discovered, act decisively to remedy has made them suspect. The public's attitude today toward the waste-management practices promoted by political and economic leaders has been summarized in two words: danger and distrust[12].

---

[11] Lipset and Schneider 1987; Kraft and Clary, 1991.
[12] O'Connor and Shaw 1988.

2. INITIAL RESPONSES OF THE 1980S

2.1. Preemption

Suggestions for breaking out of the policy gridlock of LULUs are numerous and drawn from various understandings of the root cause of the problem. An initial tendency by business is often to try to out-muscle project opposition locally. This typically meets with failure and only leads to more public anger and grassroots organization and opposition. Efforts are then made to shift land use decisions over LULUs from local jurisdictions to the states. In certain instances, like freeways and utility lines, without the coordination provided by regional or state level control, the system would quickly degenerate into a hodgepodge of mismatched segments and excessive costs. Most of today's LULUs, however, have not historically been managed centrally nor been so politically visible as to capture the level of public attention and rancor experienced in recent years. They have the character neither of natural monopolies nor of inherently integrated systems that can justify removing local siting authority. And, as in the case of hazardous-waste facilities, shifting formal authority to the states has not lessened the ability of local citizens and opponents to prevent their siting[13].

2.2. Education and Incentives

Recent experiences in states such as Florida, Wisconsin, New Jersey, Massachusetts, and California nonetheless suggest that state government can play a useful role in the siting process through their ability to facilitate dialogue, provide technical assistance, create incentives for breaking deadlocks, and require comprehensive and binding local and regional planning as a condition for the many other services that states provide. Moreover, as local officials begin to appreciate the "paradox of home rule", which is that in a crowded metropolitan area officials have neither the resources nor the authority to resolve most major problems, a move

---

[13] Morell and Magorian 1982; Legislative Commission on Toxic Substances and Hazardous Wastes 1987.

toward collaborative regional or state planning is probably the only viable option[14].

2.3. Mediation and Negotiation

With the evident failure of conventional legislative, regulatory, and judicial approaches to solving LULU controversies, there has been a concerted effort to find alternative and less adversarial, procedural, and time-consuming mechanisms of dispute resolution[15]. Requirements for mediation and negotiation are common now in nearly one-half of the states as the preferred way of resolving LULU disputes. Likewise, the Omnibus Water Resources Development Act of 1986 makes "alternative dispute resolution" processes the preferred method of resolving all disputes that affect federal water projects. Even without formal requirements, mediation is being used to address a myriad of disputes, which just a few years ago would have been addressed through regulatory processes or the courts.

The literature in this field is rich and growing, from case studies to theoretical treatises to "how-to" guidebooks[16]. One of the most intriguing of the newest experiments is the Policy Jury Program initiated at the Center for New Democratic Processes, in Minnesota. The policy jury is modeled on the jury system, and is intended to recreate, in modern setting, some of the virtues of the New England town meeting[17].

Not all issues lend themselves to alternative dispute resolution, however, especially those that raise fundamental policy questions or involve more than a one-time siting issue.

2.4. Offsetting Compensation

A typical response to LULUs by many economists and traditional politicians is to think of the problem as one of compensating affected communities for the burden of taking a new facility. The implicit assumption is

---

[14] O'Neill 1988.
[15] Ury, Brett, and Goldberg 1988; Bacow and Wheeler 1984; Raiffa 1982.
[16] Fisher and Ury 1981.
[17] Crosby 1987.

that citizens and communities are rational economic actors and will readily respond to an attractive package of goods, e.g., more school aid in exchange for accepting a LULU[18]. A variation of this is conventional logrolling among legislators, exemplified by the recent decision in the Arizona legislature to break two long-standing stalemates by locating a toxic-waste facility in one part of the state and a prison in the other.

2.5. YIMBY as a Response to NIMBY

The concept of YIMBY, or "Yes-In-Many-Backyards," was introduced in the mid-1980s in Southern California as a guiding principle for the distribution of unwanted hazardous-waste facilities among all the counties participating in the Southern California Hazardous Waste Management Authority. The YIMBY philosophy requires that everyone takes responsibility for their fair share of the waste problem. For example, a heavily populated industrialized community with large volumes of hazardous wastes can accept a treatment facility designed to accommodate not just its own waste, but also that from surrounding rural areas. In turn, the rural area can accept a residuals repository for the permanent storage of treated waste. Alternatively, each community might agree to accept facilities adequate to handle their own waste stream or possibly share modular, transportable treatment systems. Whichever the case, the waste-management problem is addressed at a comprehensive regional level. The cost of creating the treatment network is borne by all according to a mutually acceptable formula[19].

The YIMBY approach that is evolving in toxic-waste management suggests an alternative to the NIMBYism that plagues most LULU proposals. Prison populations could be housed in small-scale facilities in or near their communities. Transportation could be scaled down to service neighborhoods through multiplication of light-rail or "light" bus services, rather than through the introduction of super-scale, super-costly mass transit systems. Decentralization and diversity are goals compatible with the YIMBY philosophy of supplying needed but hard-to-site public infrastructure.

---

[18] O'Hare, Bacow, and Sanderson 1983.
[19] Morell 1984.

To summarize, LULUs have emerged as one of the central dilemmas facing society in the 1980s[20]. Examples abound of how projects have been delayed and terminated to the point where vital services and economic progress are being threatened. The policy gridlock that results prevents even "good" projects from going forward. We have learned a great deal from these examples about the causes of opposition and seen several experiments in ways of containing the accompanying political firestorm through efforts at preemption, compensation, and successful mediation efforts[21].

Nevertheless, there remains a widely held view among government officials and business and community leaders that despite all the effort, very little real progress is being made toward development of either specific facilities or comprehensive and enduring solutions to the LULU phenomenon.

3. CONFRONTING THE NEED FOR FUNDAMENTAL CHANGE

The problem, it would appear, is a mega-problem that goes deeper than the need to educate the public better, or to negotiate, or to buy off opposition through a compensation package. America appears to be facing a profound crisis of political legitimacy that reaches from the local up through the national level of government. Opposition to LULUs stems often from narrow self-interest or differing perspectives and viewpoints; but possibly most profoundly it stems from a public that does not trust its leaders to make wise decisions. Without confidence in its public and business leaders, the public has used legal and formal mechanisms of democratic government to stop the wheels of society from turning.

Symptomatic of the leadership vacuum, the push for everything from massive freeways and economic expansion to environmental protection goes on with little consideration of overall impacts of incompatible objectives. This is obvious to those who have an opportunity to step back from their particular interests to a broader vantage point, but most everyone is too busy engaging issues of the moment. As a consequence, within communities and across the nation there is little in the way of a shared vision

---

[20] Popper 1985.
[21] Bingham and Mealey, 1991.

of the future, and there are few legitimate political mechanisms to ensure that society's long-term resource and infrastructure needs are met. There is also no justifiable rationale for asking any one group in society to make sacrifices for the good of the whole.

We believe that the problems of political legitimacy and the lack of a shared vision of the future are inextricably linked. What is most lacking is a political process in which the public can invest its trust. Only through a political process that the public sees as legitimate will it be possible to reconcile differences and come to a mutual understanding about common needs and shared fates.

How this may come about is suggested in several experiments in policy making that have taken as their primary mission the reframing of an issue in a way that all major participants can agree, and only then focus on the shaping of general policy goals and the guidelines for specific projects. Each has been a response to a colossal failure of the conventional policy process, which had produced stalemate at the very time dramatic action was critical. Each was motivated far more by pragmatic considerations than by lofty principles or noble goals. Each, however, ultimately meets the tests of legitimacy and vision and better fits the catastrophe model than conventional policy frameworks.

3.1. *Case 1*: **The Denver Metropolitan Water Roundtable**[22]

The Denver Metropolitan Water Roundtable was organized in October 1981 to design an equitable water system for the region's burgeoning population. The Denver (east slope) water-supply problem flows from two factors: the uneven distributions of population and water within the state; and the phenomenal growth experienced in the greater Denver region since the 1970s. While eighty percent of Colorado's population resides east of the Continental Divide, seventy percent of the state's native water supply lies west of the Divide. The state must therefore depend on transmountain water diversion projects to meet the eastern slope's rising water demand.

---

[22] The material in this section is drawn from Carpenter and Kennedy 1988 and Bingham 1986: 36-41. Both Carpenter and Kennedy are from ACCORD Associates.

Historically these projects had been a continual source of conflict and litigation between citizens living on opposite sides of the Divide, different classes of water consumers, developers, and environmentalists. Poor relations and coordination between the Denver Water Board, suburban water suppliers, and west-slope interests have made gaining acceptance for new water diversion projects a difficult and costly process.

In 1974 a proposal for the Foothills water treatment complex, which included a diversion dam, reservoir, tunnel, and treatment plan on Colorado's South Platte River, led to a five-year dispute between the Denver Water Department and the west-slope interests. The stalemate was finally broken when Colorado Congressman Tim Wirth stepped in and mediated a compromise. At the conclusion of the project's development cycle, the proposal was substantially amended - but not before much "bloodletting" had occurred between Colorado interests. Colorado's leaders began to wonder if it was time to rethink the entire process of developing the state's valuable water resources.

A new proposal for construction of the Two Forks Dam and Reservoir near the Foothills complex brought things to a head. The proposal was made by the Denver Water Department within a year of resolution of the Foothills controversy. In a sense, the proposal suggested that water matters were returning to business-as-usual for east-slope water developers, who were simply reaching for more and more supply. It carried the potential of renewing the cycle of conflict. The Water Department may have felt that it was forced by delays in gaining approval for the previous project "to play catch-up" by quickly proposing a new project, or it may have concluded that greater lead time for new projects was necessitated by the increasing opposition (and consequent delays) to expanding water services. The previous year's hard-won compromise appeared an ephemeral victory.

But the lessons of the previous decade were not lost on the state's political leadership. The governor's office asked ACCORD Associates, a Denver-based foundation, to study mediation options to avert another crippling policy stalemate. Here at least was recognition that the adversarial policy-making process had broken down. ACCORD members, assisted by Charles Jordan, the governor's assistant on water issues, set about laying the groundwork for negotiations between all interested parties. These negotiations concluded successfully in April 1983, when all parties accepted a process for creating a comprehensive water plan for the region. Of importance is how this was accomplished.

As a first step in preparation for negotiations, ACCORD sought to identify through an extensive interview process all major interests affected by metropolitan Denver's water-resource policy. A preliminary list of organizations and names was compiled; these were then contacted concerning possible participation in the Metropolitan Water Roundtable negotiations. As a principle in selecting participants, ACCORD held that representatives of the various interests should be policy-level people, e.g., mayors and county commissioners, able to implement any agreements reached. ACCORD recognized that mediation could succeed only if the participants understood that the broader issue of how best to provide water to the Denver area, rather than the narrower question of the specific Two Forks proposal, must be addressed. ACCORD promoted the view that resolving the conflict would entail both a new, more encompassing vision of the long-term needs of the region and a new political structure through which those needs could be effectively represented. Key to the strategy of broadening the policy vision was the careful balancing of interests within the Metropolitan Water Roundtable. Roundtable membership included two representatives each from the Denver Water Board (governing body of the Denver Water Department) and their opponents in the environmental community, one for each major affected suburban government and water group, and one each for metropolitan area businesses, front-range agriculture, and western-slope government and water interests. ACCORD acted as process mediators; Governor Lamm lent his prestige to the process by serving as the Roundtable moderator.

ACCORD next turned its attention to designing the process of negotiation. Ground rules and a procedural framework to ensure that the sessions would be productive were suggested. As a complement to the non-adversarial approach of mediation, ACCORD insisted that a consensus decision rule was essential to encourage participation and eventual implementation of any agreed-upon plan.

Procedural agreements were also reached on the behavior of participants (no personal attacks, no delaying tactics); on operating procedures for meetings and activities outside of general meetings; on participation by non-members (limited under specified circumstances); and on interactions with the media. To prevent grandstanding, the meetings were closed to the public. A twenty-five member limit was set for the Roundtable with no substitute members allowed. After each meeting a statement was issued and a press conference held by the governor's office. Discussion of other participants' negotiating positions was prohibited outside of the Roundtable. No specific time limit was set for discussion and negotiation.

Critical to the outcome of the negotiation was the setting of the geographic scope of the Roundtable's area of concern. This was defined broadly to include all areas affected by the Denver Water Board, i.e., nearly all the communities within the primary service area of the Denver Regional Council of Governments. Similarly, the time horizon of the plan to be considered was extended to 2010. By that year, according to the Regional Council's estimate, the population of the service area would reach 2.76 million. Expanding the discussion to include a larger geographic region and longer time horizon forced the participants to reframe their ideas and positions on the future development of the state's water resources.

Four small working groups were formed to address typical interests (west-slope management; environment; agriculture; inter-urban supply and coordination) and to promote individual interaction.

To prevent insularity and build public support for the mediation effort, a list of some 400 individuals and organizations was assembled to receive regular updates on the progress of the Roundtable. Roundtable representatives continually updated their constituencies, and general public meetings (forums), attended by Roundtable members, were held around the region.

A Systemwide Environmental Impact Statement (SEIS) was conducted through the United States Army Corps of Engineers with financial participation by the Denver Water Board and forty-six suburban water suppliers. A committee was created to develop information and projections regarding the geographic service area, expected population growth to 2010, system water supply, and water savings expected from conservation.

The basic ground rules included developing a series of cumulative plans and strategies that could be amended over time. Both short- and long-term water needs would be considered. There would not be an effort to use the water issue as a way to place growth limits on Denver. Final plans would include provisions for improving management and expansion of existing facilities where feasible, environmental impact mitigation, maximization of exchange and reuse of west-slope water, efficiency measures, and interregional compensation.

Roundtable members opposed to the Denver Water Board proposals were challenged to develop alternatives and given access to resources for such development. Significant funding ($ 65,000) from Metropolitan Water Providers and the Denver Water Board was given to Environmental Caucus, a local environmental coalition, for ongoing technical review of SEIS. This unprecedented approach to cooperative planning became the model for other west-slope developers around the state. Denver water providers formed a new entity, Metropolitan Water Conservation, Inc., while the governor created the West Slope Water Advisory Council to concertate that area's diverse interests. The Colorado Water Resources and Power Development Authority funded a $ 2 million study of joint east slope-west slope projects.

Agreement was reached in 1983 on the need for additional east-slope water storage, the institution of a significant water conservation program, and the development of a joint use facility on the west slope. In a unique procedural breakthrough, a subcommittee of the Roundtable, working closely with the Army Corps, developed the concept of combining systemwide environmental impact statements with site-specific analysis, thus streamlining the project-planning phase and significantly reducing costs. The final task of determining the best package of specific methods to meet the region's water needs was assigned to a special negotiating team, consisting of representatives of the Denver Water Board, other regional water providers, the Northern Colorado Water Conservancy District, west-slope communities, environmentalists, and developers.

The conditions contributing to the Roundtable's success are several: policy gridlock with a crisis looming; high-level political leadership, and a governor who saw his role as convenor and facilitator; avoidance of partisanship and narrow advocacy; a support network of interest representation and concertation; a well-structured decision-making forum operating under a consensus decision rule, a "no substitutes" rule, and closed meetings; development of trust between adversaries; extension of resources to environmental representatives; and an iterative step-by-step agreement process.

3.2. *Case 2*: Hazardous-Waste Management in California[23]

3.2.1. The Tanner Council

In California, in the early 1980s, policy makers found themselves locked over the first big toxic-waste issue they encountered - the siting of new hazardous-waste landfills and treatment facilities. A crisis atmosphere was created when implementation of the Federal Resources Conservation and Recovery Act of 1976, combined with mounting public pressure, resulted in the closure of four of the five landfills in metropolitan Southern California alone. This left political leaders keenly aware that the region was totally dependent on the single BKK disposal site in West Covina. Meanwhile, the Stringfellow Acid Pits made the nightly news and the Superfund clean-up list, only to be followed by many lesser hazardous-waste stories and Superfund controversies.

California business leaders found themselves with literally no place to take their mounting volumes of hazardous waste. Other factors contributed to the crisis atmosphere, from Governor Jerry Brown's 1981 executive order, which banned six categories of toxins from disposal on the land and called for new hazardous-waste treatment technology, to the growing public concern (and in some cases hysteria) over the toxic poisoning of workplaces and the environment, to the escalating number of state and federal laws affecting hazardous waste and materials management. Key business leaders realized that if they did not get out in front on the problem, environmentalists surely would. They saw their future, and the future of the state's economy, on the line.

What to do? The prospects for local approval of new hazardous-waste landfills looked dim. None had been sited in the state throughout the entire decade of the 1970s, even before the issue had become politically volatile. Business turned to Sacramento and pleaded its case before the legislature, asking for state-level preemption over local land use siting decisions for hazardous-waste LULUs. After two years and several attempts at passing legislation favoring preemption, it was evident that the opposition from local and county governments, together with the environmentalists, was too strong. At this point, attempts to site new landfills

---

[23] The material in this section is drawn from Mazmanian, Stanley-Jones, and Green 1988 and Mazmanian and Morell 1988

ground to a halt at all levels of government in the state with little expectation that the situation would change at any time soon.

Assemblywoman Sally Tanner (D-El Monte), chair of the legislature's new Toxics Committee and in whose district contaminated underground wells were being discovered, then stepped in to move the process off of dead center. She had concluded that a genuine solution might be found only if the issue could be addressed outside the adversarial arena of the legislature and if all the relevant parties in the controversy would join together. In brief, both a new political process and a new shared view of the problem and its solution were imperative.

In contrast to the Denver experience, no facilitators or third-party mediators were called in. Rather, Tanner and her staff went to work drawing in key leaders of the warring factions and other interests for a legislatively sponsored Hazardous Waste Management Council, securing from all only their pledge to give the process a try. In truth, many were skeptical but dared not offend Assemblywoman Tanner; too much was at stake. The Council had sixteen members representing key participants from state and local government, the legislature, industry, health care, environmentalists, and university experts. It was given twenty-four months (1982-84) to report back to the legislature on how to resolve the state's hazardous-waste siting problem.

It was a rather amazing two years. The first several months and meetings were devoted simply to getting to know competing positions. What the participants learned, in part, is that they had been talking past each other. Once they overcame their posturing, movement toward a shared understanding of the issue and new solutions became possible. Also, the group implicitly developed the same kind of operating rules about not posturing outside the group, as well as other good-faith measures, that were spelled out more formally by the mediators in the Denver experience. A genuine dialogue began in early 1983 at a Council retreat where the major actors - industry, local government, and environmentalists - recognized the importance of each others' positions and began to rethink the entire issue.

The turning point for the Council came a month later on a group tour of Danish and German hazardous-waste management facilities. The Council's representatives were impressed by the European approach to toxins management, which incorporates integrated collection networks, tight public monitoring, recycling, incineration, and well-protected permanent residuals storage facilities. Combined with an emerging commitment to source reduction, these options began to form the central pieces of an overall state strategy aimed at the safest possible management, dramatic reduction in the waste stream, public-private cooperation, and the elimination of most land disposal of hazardous materials. Siting per se was no longer the priority, but only one (albeit important) option for the long-term management of hazardous waste in the state.

The new thinking both about waste management and cooperative planning needed to be introduced statewide, of course. The Council used itself as a guide and incorporated, in large measure, its own cooperative decision-making process into its recommendation to the legislature for establishing hazardous waste and materials planning across the state. The legislature adopted both the goals and planning strategy suggested by the Tanner Council in their entirety. However, this came just at the moment when the governorship had passed from Jerry Brown, who supported the effort, to George Deukmejian who, at least initially, did not. For reasons never made clear to any of the Tanner Council or legislative participants, for two years the governor vetoed Tanner planning bills. He gave statewide local hazardous waste and materials planning his support only after his own blue ribbon commission recommended it on the eve of his 1986 gubernatorial reelection contest.

Planning is now underway in all of California's fifty-eight counties and at the state level, aided by $ 10 million in state monies. These efforts replicate the state-level Tanner Council by including representatives of business, government, the environmental and health communities, and local citizenry. The law calls for the plans to be guided by the principles of "fair share," with each county addressing its needs for at least a decade. In practice, however, the state has placed pressure on the counties to identify any and all feasible toxic-facility sites rather than just those needed under a fair-share program, and it is unclear what this will produce. Experience to date has also shown that it can be as difficult to reconcile the interests of cities within the counties, as it is to reconcile the interests of the counties within the state.

Industry is looking to the process to ensure the availability of adequate hazardous-waste facilities. Environmentalists see it as a way of introducing businesses and local governments to safe hazardous-waste management practices, in a manner that underscores how a greater commitment to recycling and a reduction in the production of toxic wastes lessens the burden of siting and monitoring hazardous-waste management facilities. The process is clearly designed to strike a balance between local control and state preemption. Planning and implementation are left to the cities and counties working with local business and community interests, yet their plans must be reviewed and approved by the California Department of Health Services. Additionally, the Tanner Act provides for an appeals process to a multimember statewide board should a local community reject siting a facility that falls within its adopted plan.

3.2.2. The Southern California Hazardous Waste Management Project/Authority

As the legislature was mulling over how to respond to the outcry from the public and industry to the hazardous-waste crisis of the early 1980s, Southern California most keenly felt the pinch from the closure of its hazardous-waste landfills. Few of the region's public leaders were pleased at the inability of Sacramento to take decisive action; yet they shuddered at the prospect of state preemption that threatened to strip them of their traditional land use authority.

Peggy Sartor, Councilwoman from the high desert community of Victorville - just outside the Los Angeles basin - is credited with initiating a region-wide assault on the problem by prodding the Southern California Association of Governments to take up the issue. Her community was alarmed by the increasing incidence of illegal dumping of hazardous waste, suspected of being trucked in from the Los Angeles basin. Los Angeles Mayor Tom Bradley stepped in to provide important political leadership by convening, late in 1980, a group of regional officials to form the basis of a region-wide task group. Meanwhile, the Los Angeles County Sanitation District, under pressure to find new hazardous-waste landfills, joined the group, as did the State Water Resources Control Board, which faced the growing problem of drinking water contamination from leaking toxic-disposal sites. Within a short time all the counties and major cities from Santa Barbara south to the Mexican border united under Bradley's auspices to form a region-wide Southern California Hazardous Waste Management Project (later reformulated and renamed an Authority).

The Authority initially focused on the siting of new landfill and hazardous-waste treatment facilities. But attention soon moved to collecting and sharing waste stream and siting information on a region-wide basis; developing equitable formula for allocating treatment facilities and cross-community packages of compensations; engendering a public-private strategy for a comprehensive basin-wide treatment system, including working with industry (Kaiser and BKK in particular) to locate and help permit facilities of regional benefit; and, finally, encouraging the recycling of hazardous wastes to reduce the overall waste stream. The Authority served as a broad discussion forum and eventually took on the role of a regional planning agency for an integrated hazardous-waste management system. It has continued to play this role as each of its constituent members develops its Tanner plan. A counterpart in industry, the Coalition for Hazardous Materials Management, evolved out of these activities to lead in developing a regional business strategy for hazardous-waste and toxic-materials management.

The Project/Authority can be credited with developing the initial regional data base on hazardous wastes, a systematic siting study for treatment facilities and one or more residual repositories, fair-share allocation schemes, and proposals for a new approach to toxin liability and compensation formula. It clearly moved the discussion from siting per se to recycling, source reduction, and comprehensive planning, and did so by bringing the contending groups together formally and informally. Its early public outreach and the dialogue it fostered between local governments and among businesses and environmentalists in the region are probably its most notable accomplishments to date.

There are obviously significant differences between the experience of the Tanner Council and the Project/Authority in location, composition, leadership, and purpose. Of importance, also are their striking similarities. As with the Denver case, it required major policy gridlock and public pressure to wrest the participants from their normal adversarial roles played out within the conventional political arena. It took leadership from the public sector to initiate and legitimize an alternative approach, as well as the willingness of business and environmental, local and state adversaries to step back from their normal postures and give the new process a chance. (It also underscored the adverse effect the withdrawal of support from a political figure of the importance of a governor can have.) While Denver relied on third-party facilitators, the California programs were managed by the participants themselves. Still, in both instances, status plus technical and political support was accorded all, and a network of interest representation and concertation was fostered. Beginning with a common search for information, then new ideas, then major ways of reconceptualizing the problem, the process was drawn out over two years or more. Not only did this allow time for issues to be thoroughly reviewed and a general approach developed, but it fostered a new level of understanding and trust among the participants. By the end of the process, they had evolved into far more harmonious groups, able to emphasize their shared values rather than return to the stalemates over their differences.

4. CONDITIONS OF COOPERATIVE DECISION MAKING

The Denver and California cases illustrate that the way out of the classic LULU syndrome is not necessarily via a direct line or by doggedly pursuing more of the same in the policy arena. Their central features are outlined in the chart below. As suggested by the newly emerging catastrophe theory, getting across the chasm from where we are to where we want to be may require a fundamental rethinking of goals and new political institutions for realizing their achievement.

In the context of LULUs, "crisis" is a matter of perception and refers to the demand on and by public leaders to take bold action to remedy a problem that, for whatever reason, has reached a point of policy gridlock. "Political legitimation" refers to the creation of a formal process or organization with public authority to address a controversial public issue by political officials who are (temporarily at least) unwilling to tackle the problem in traditional ways. This may take the form of a granted commission, a formal request for investigation (always backed by the promise of funding), or actual devolution of government authority (based on statute) granting the right to develop and administer programs to new organizations.

"Functional representation" typically gives parity to each designated interest at the negotiating table. In the Denver case, on the Roundtable proper, the Denver Water Board and the environmentalists were given two representatives each, while other constituencies (e.g., suburban water districts, agricultural interests) were allotted a single representative. "Regional representation" typically involves the affected governmental units, which are geographically defined. One way to determine which groups consider an issue vital is to examine the funding of the mediating organization. The Southern California Authority was funded initially by federal and state monies, but this has been complemented with dues from the cities and counties of the region; the Denver Roundtable was funded initially by foundation grants, later supplemented by functional groups (e.g., development, banking); and the Tanner Council was funded by the legislature and some foundation support.

"Representative structure" highlights the internal organization of each entity. The Denver Roundtable and the Southern California Authority each organized along task lines, separating technical, educational, and planning activities. Typically such differentiation ultimately is hierarchical, as a single committee maintains final decision-making authority for the project as a whole. The Tanner Council operated largely as a single group, though industrial and environmental interests spent a good deal of time negotiating on the side.

TABLE 3.1
CONDITIONS CONTRIBUTING TO SUCCESSFUL LULU SITING

Case	Crisis	Political Legitimation	Interest Representation	Representative Structure	Iterative Bargaining	Resource Sharing	Development of Trust
Denver Roundtable	yes-coming	Lamm	regional/ fonctional	layered, sub-committees	phased agreements	SEIS review subsidy to envrionmentalists	ACCORD mediation, subsidy, sub-committees
Tanner Council	yes-existed	Tanner	functional/ regional	integrated	work papers, final draft	shared reports, selection of experts	2-year dialogue, retreats, European trip
Southern California Authority	yes-existed	Bradley	functional/ regional	layered, sub-committees	phased agreements	shared data, siting study, Kaiser siting contract, state and EPA funding	dialogue, sub-committees, pemanent Authority

Note: While the chart highlights the presence of the seven conditions, it should be noted that there were events going on outside the groups that pulled the members apart. Probably the most notable of these was the toxins initiative battle (Proposition 65) that took place in California in 1986, pitting business and environmental interests in a bitter public confrontation. While the low cooperative policy making was real, it does not seem to have had a crippling effect on the Tanner planning process and activities of the Authoritiy.

Though the development of trust is shown as a distinct condition in the chart, in practice it is the glue that holds the entire process together. Unless it can be fostered, little of lasting substance will come out of the process. Few will give more than pro forma attention to the enterprise and no one will participate in genuine dialogue and rethinking of the sort required to break out of the LULU cycle.

5. LULUs AND POLICY DEMOCRACY

The implications of these new decision processes are rather striking. The forums foster an environment where leaders learn non-adversarial modes of policy making and begin to view themselves as part of a policy-making community, not merely as opponents seated across the table. This is clearly indicated by findings in California that participants judge the process of collective policy making as successful even when they fail to achieve their desired policy outcomes[24]. Such processes call for persons who are by temperament and training consensual and cooperative, ecological in the sense of appreciating interdependencies, trusting and sharing, future oriented, and more global in their thinking. There is little room for the dogmatic ideologue or the person who sees the world in zero-sum terms of either complete victory or defeat.

Inviting participation from the divergent interests in a policy domain is one of the keys to the success of the process. At the same time, it raises serious questions about the democratically representative nature of the group, and to whom the members are accountable. Is it to the general public? Their own interest sector? Or, the body itself? The new forums also raise issues of power and authority. Are their agreements and understandings binding on the broader political community? To the extent that understandings and policies of the forums do become accepted policies of the community, how are they to be made part of the ongoing public-policy process? For example, what mechanisms are used to make water conservation in Denver or "fair-share" allocation of hazardous-waste facilities in Southern California a reality?

These are the challenging issues of "policy democracy," which will need to be addressed should these new forums become a common avenue

---

[24] Mazmanian, Stanley-Jones, and Green 1988: Ch. 6.

for political decision making. At present, they are of interest because they are unique in providing politically and institutionally viable mechanisms for breaking out of the deadlock of LULUs.

REFERENCES

Bacow, Lawrence, and Michael Wheeler. 1984. *Environmental Dispute Resolution*. New York: Plenum Press.

Baum, Andrew. 1988. "Disasters, Natural & Otherwise." *Psychology Today* (April).

Bingham, Gail. 1986. *Resolving Environmental Disputes: A Decade of Experience*. Washington, D.C.: Conservation Foundation.

Bingham, Gail, and Timothy Mealey, eds. 1991. *Negotiating Hazardous Waste Facility Siting and Permitting Agreements*. Washington, D.C.: Conservation Foundation.

Carpenter, Susan, and W.J.D. Kennedy. 1988. "The Denver Metropolitan Water Roundtable: A Case Study in Reaching Agreements." *Natural Resources Journal* 28: 21-36.

Crosby, Ned. 1987. "Citizen Panels: A New Democratic Process for Risk Management." Presented at the annual meeting of the American Society for Public Administration, Boston.

Fisher, Roger, and William Ury. 1981. *Getting to YES: Negotiating Agreement without Giving In*. Boston: Houghton Mifflin Company.

Kraft, Michael, and Bruce Clary. 1991. "Citizen Participation and the NIMBY Syndrome: Public Response to Radioactive Waste Disposal." *Western Political Quarterly*, 44.

Legislative Commission on Toxic Substances and Hazardous Wastes. 1987. "Hazardous Waste Facility Siting: A National Survey." Legislative Commission on Toxic Substances and Hazardous Waste, State of New York (April).

Lipset, Seymour Martin, and William Schneider. 1987. *The Confidence Gap: Business, Labor, and Government in the Public Mind*, rev. ed. Baltimore: John Hopkins University Press.

Mazmanian, Daniel. 1988. "Toxics Policy in California: New Directions in Environmental Policy Making." *Environmental Impact Assessment Review* 8: 149-57.

Mazmanian, Daniel, and David Morell. 1988. "The Elusive Pursuit of Toxics Management." *The Public Interest* 90: 81-98.

Mazmanian, Daniel, Michael Stanley-Jones, and Miriam Green. 1988. "Breaking Political Gridlock: California's Experiment in Public-Private Cooperation for Hazardous Waste Policy." Claremont, Calif.: California Institute of Public Affairs.

Morell, David. 1984. "Siting and the Politics of Equity." *Hazardous Waste* 1: 555-71.

Morell, David, and Christopher Magorian. 1982. *Siting Hazardous Waste Facilities: Local Opposition and the Myth of Preemption.* Cambridge, Mass.: Ballinger Publishing Company.

O'Connor, Robert, and L. Gardner Shaw. 1988. "Technological Imperatives and Public Policy." Presented at the annual meeting of the Midwest Political Science Association, Chicago.

O'Hare, Michael, Lawrence Bacow, and Debra Sanderson. 1983. *Facility Siting and Public Opposition.* New York: Van Nostrand Reinhold Co.

O'Neill, Thomas. 1988. "LULUs, NIMBY and Three Paradoxes of Home Rule." *New Jersey Bell Journal*, pp. 2-12.

Otway, Harry, and Detlof Von Winterfeldt. 1982. "Beyond Acceptable Risk: On the Social Acceptability of Technologies." *Policy Sciences* 14: 247-56.

Payne, B.A., S. Jay Olshansky, and T.E. Segel. 1987. "The Effects on Property Values of Proximity to a Site Contaminated with Radioactive Waste." *Natural Resources Journal* 27: 579-90.

Popper, Frank. 1985. "The Environmentalists and the LULU." *Environment* (March).

Raiffa, Howard. 1982. *The Art and Science of Negotiation*. Cambridge, Mass.: Harvard University Press.

Reich, Robert, ed. 1988. *The Power of Ideas*. Cambridge, Mass.: Ballinger Publishing Company.

Rowland, C.K., S.C. Lee, and D.D. Goetz. 1988. "Longitudinal and Catastrophic Models of State Hazardous Waste Regulation," in C.E. Davis and J.P. Lester, eds., *Dimensions of Hazardous Waste Politics and Policy*. New York: Greenwood Press, 93-116.

Ury, William, Jeanne Brett, and Stephen Goldberg. 1988. *Getting Disputes Resolved: Designing Systems to Cut the Costs of Conflict*. San Francisco: Jossey-Bass Publishers.

Zeeman, E.C. 1976. "Catastrophe Theory." *Scientific American* 234: 65-83.

ENVIRONMENTAL DISPUTE RESOLUTION AND HAZARDOUS WASTE CLEANUPS: A CAUTIONARY TALE OF POLICY IMPLEMENTATION

Robert Nakamura[1]
Thomas Church
Phillip Cooper

1. INTRODUCTION

This paper describes an attempt by New York State to clean up toxic dump sites by replacing a litigation-oriented, regulatory approach with a system of alternative dispute resolution, or ADR, designed to encourage settlement and voluntary remedial action. It is a cautionary tale, the moral of which is the importance of examining implementation issues when choosing among various policy options, even when a policy choice is accompanied by a strong presumption of superiority over the existing alternatives. ADR, currently a buzzword in legal and environmental circles, carries such presumptive efficacy. It has much to recommend it - particularly, say its advocates, when it is contrasted to the costs and delays endemic to more traditional systems of regulation and adjudication. Our case study is not meant to cast doubt on alternative dispute resolution as a means of resolving conflict, so much as to suggest that ADR, at least when applied as an implement of public policy, has its own distinctive set of assumptions and preconditions for success[2]. We thus conclude that lessons drawn from policy implementation in other contexts may help to establish some baseline requirements for use of ADR as a policy tool.

---

[1] This article was first published in: Journal of Policy Analysis and Management, Vol. 10, No.2,000-000 (1991) © 1991 by the Association for Public Policy Analysis and Management. Published by John Wiley & Sons, Inc. CCC 0276-8739/91/NNZZZZ-PP$04.00. We thank the editor for the copyright.

[2] The literature of policy tools or implements is growing. For recent examples, see Salamon (1989), Schneider and Ingram (1989), McDonnell and Elmore (1984), and Bardach (1980).

2. HAZARDOUS WASTE CLEANUP: THE POLICY ENVIRONMENT

Like other states with serious hazardous waste problems (and the federal Environmental Protection Agency at various stages in its history)[3] , New York has generally taken a hard-line approach to individuals and corporations legally liable for cleanup - the potentially responsible parties (PRPs). The basic tool remains a system of tort liability in which PRPs are coerced - by litigation or its threat - into paying the costs of environmental remediation .

Policy in this area has traditionally centered on the threat (or the actual use) of the legal process to compel privately funded cleanups. The Federal "Superfund" law[4] , and the various state "mini-Superfund" statues[5] , assign legal responsibility for cleanup to toxic waste generators, transporters, and property owners who can be linked to hazardous waste sites. Augmenting this statutory assignment of legal responsibility has been the courts' ready application of two common law tort doctrines to hazardous waste cases: strict liability - which allows a finding of legal responsibility without fault or negligence on the part of a PRP; and joint and several liability - which permits a court to require individual responsible parties to pay for the entire cost of a cleanup, regardless of the amount of their particular contribution to the waste on the site[6] . Administrative orders for cleanups with substantial fines for noncompliance represent an alternative legal lever. Should government be forced to undertake the cleanup itself, legislation typically provides regulatory officials with the capacity to engage in cost recovery actions against legally responsible parties, in which substantial additional penalties, including treble damage, can be levied[7] .

Not surprisingly, use of formal legal action by the states and the federal government has encountered substantial resistance from the targeted parties in the form of protracted litigation over the legality of the doctrinal tools applied (particularly the applicability of joint and several liability and the interpretation of other liability doctrine), and the appropriateness

---

[3] Mintz, 1988.
[4] CERCLA, 1980.
[5] Twenty states have enacted statutes, most modeled after the federal legislation.
[6] Wilkerson and Church, 1989.
[7] For a full description of the Federal Superfund apparatus, together with an assessment of program accomplishments, see Action (1990)

of the administrative procedures, factual evidence, proposed remedies, and allocation of costs in individual cases. Currently, Federal Superfund sites are covered by "joint and several," while the situation in New York's mini-Superfund is more ambiguous. The State contends that joint and several liability is applicable and PRPs claim that it is not. The resulting adversarial relationship between government and the PRPs closely approximates what Eugene Bardach and Robert Kagan (1982) described in their study of OSHA: a system in which the regulated population regards the actions of the government as unreasonable and unfair. As a result of this perception of "regulatory unreasonableness," individuals and corporations find themselves in a legal context in which they are treated at best as "amoral calculators" whose only concern is the bottom line of a profit and loss statement; at worst, they are regarded virtually as criminals[8]. This situation, in turn, provokes a stiffer adversary posture on their part, increasing the potential for expensive, time-consuming litigation. It also decreases the possibility of a voluntary cleanup based on negotiations, and can complicate relations between PRPs and the government in the complex series of joint activities usually necessary to remediate a toxic waste site.

Participants in these processes, frustrated by the glacial pace and high transaction costs that accompany the present system of regulation and litigation, have sometimes turned toward a new approach to address the problem: alternative dispute resolution. ADR stresses a more cooperative mode of interaction between government and PRPs, and among the PRPs themselves, in which common rather than divergent interests drive a process aimed at reaching a negotiated settlement in place of a litigated resolution of the problem[9].

This policy context can be described in more abstract terms: The disadvantages of the status quo - delays and high transaction cost - are seen as products of adversary legal and regulatory proceedings. Common interests in cleaning up a site and discharging legal obligations are overwhelmed by conflicts over what form the cleanup will take and how casts will be apportioned among the PRPs, and between PRPs and the government. Alternative dispute resolution promises a different system in which relationships are reordered into a more cooperative mode[10]. The

---

[8] Kagan and Scholz, 1984.
[9] Susskind and Cruikshank, 1987.
[10] Levin and Ferman, 1985.

ADR movement thus produces both an analysis of what is wrong - a system that encourages participants to act on conflicting interests - and a solution: a more cooperative system emphasizing participants' common goals.

3. ADR: A SOLUTION SEEKING A PROBLEM

As its title suggests, alternative dispute resolution is at least operationally defined more by what it is not than in terms of its own distinctive attributes. Indeed, ADR mechanisms sometimes appear to be a ragbag of miscellaneous techniques ranging from "policy dialogue," to informal and unstructured negotiation, to mediation and arbitration[11]. To add to the confusion, ADR methods are applied to conflicts as disparate as individual student programs in special education, management-labor negotiations, domestic or neighborhood quarrels, and insurance claim disputes. While definitional clarity is frequently forgotten in the boosterism that animates many ADR discussions, it would appear that the major characteristics common to these techniques are a reduction in both the level of conflict and informality of process over more traditional alternatives.

In the past decade, various ADR techniques, particularly mediation, have increasingly been applied in the sphere of environmental policy[12]. These techniques have been applied to land use disputes, planning and management of land and water resources, energy, air quality, and toxics[13]. Further, a number of specific problems relating to toxic waste cleanups have been successfully addressed through ADR by Clean Sites, Inc., a privately operated, public interest organization.

The ADR literature in the environmental area is primarily one of advocacy: written by proponents of, usually participants in, ADR activities. Much of what has been written is in textbook form, consisting of "how

---

[11] Rabe, 1988, p. 535.
[12] Bingham (1985) lists 160 environmental disputes addressed by ADR, although at least one proponent of ADR - Jay Hair, Executive Vice-President of the National Wildlife Federation - predicts that more than half of environmental disputes will be settled by ADR techniques by the end of this century (Hair, 1984). Alternative dispute resolution in the context of environmental policy even has its own acronym EDR, for Environmental Dispute Resolution.
[13] Bingham, 1985.

to" manuals for structuring mediation or conducting negotiation sessions. It is often difficult to separate advocacy from description and analysis in this literature[14]. The vast majority of this writing has come from lawyers, many of whom are actively involved in environmental mediation. The uncritical enthusiasm of much of this work has led one its few critics to label ADR the "new panacea"[15].

Despite this attention, we are aware of no systematic attempt to evaluate these ADR techniques in the literature of policy implementation and evaluation. Indeed, there does not even appear to be agreement as to what is, and is not, an ADR technique. The appellation has been applied to activities as disparate as mediated negotiation as an alternative to litigation, the "settlement of environmental policy issues," and the provision of "recommendations to the authorities"[16].

This contribution represents our preliminary attempt to add some order to the chaos by critically examining ADR techniques in one area of environmental policy that will almost certainly engage substantial energy and resources in the next decade, the cleanup of inactive toxic waste sites[17]. We investigate this subject by assessing the use of ADR as a policy tool in one failed effort to apply mediation to an inactive toxic waste site in upstate New York, the Phohl Brothers landfill in *Tonawanda*. While case study research is inevitably subject to the criticism of trying to see the

---

[14] Examples are Bacow and Wheeler (1984), Mernitz (1980), Susskind and Weinstein (1980), and Lake (1980). Each of these authors is in the business of environmental mediation, either as a teacher of techniques or as an actual mediator in environmental disputes. Not surprisingly, the thrust of these studies tends to be for increased usage of environmental mediation, rather than dispassionate analysis of the techniques. There are, however, a few exceptions. For work that is analytical, see especially Talbot (1983), Bingham (1985), and Amy (1987).

[15] Rabe, 1988, p. 590.

[16] Levinson, 1988, p. 575.

[17] The 1986 reauthorization of Superfund, the Superfund Amendments and Reauthorization Act (SARA), carried with it a substantially larger monetary ante than the original legislation. Over the five-year period of reauthorization (1986-91), EPA is committed to spending $8.5 billion dollars on cleanups of toxic waste sites. And the legislation was designed to encourage private cleanups far in excess of those directly supported from Superfund monies.

world in a grain of sand, we believe this set of events is instructive as ADR techniques are increasingly applied in policy contexts[18].

4. POLICY DESIGN: ADR AND THE PHOHL BROTHERS LANDFILL

This effort to use alternative dispute resolution in a cleanup of an inactive toxic waste site grew out of the Environmental Mediation Project, an idea put forward by the New York State Business Council. The Council's Public Policy Institute proposed to the State Department of Environmental Conservation (DEC) and to the New York State Attorney. General's office that it experiment with mediation techniques at a toxic waste site in the state to ascertain whether ADR might prove to be more effective, speedier, and less expensive than traditional adjudication. The experiment began in September 1985[19].

The basic strategy proposed by the Business Council was to bring PRPs together, with the aid of a mediator, to formulate a cleanup plan for the particular site selected, and to allocate the costs of the cleanup among themselves. It was also expected that the relationship between the PRPs and State environmental officials would be conducted through informal, nonconfrontational negotiations - perhaps also with the assistance of a mediator. All this would occur without the trappings of threatened adjudication and its attendant conflict, costs, and delays. Proponents of the experiment, the Business Council and its Public Policy Institute, assumed that mediation in this context would be quicker and cheaper than litigation, and that all participants would have sufficient incentives both to participate in the discussions and to agree voluntarily to a privately funded remediation plan. The PRPs would presumably save on legal costs and could discharge their obligations in a cost-effective fashion. For their part, State regulators would conserve their resources for investment in

---

[18] Our discussion of what occurred at the Phohl Brothers site is based on testimony delivered by the principal participants before the New York Legislative Commission on Toxic Substances and Hazardous Waste Hearing on March 16,1988, and on an examination of documentary material. Key participants were sent an earlier version of this paper for comments and corrections. Our discussion of the dynamics of Superfund is based, in part, on interviews we conducted with national and regional federal actors which was supported by a grant from Clean Sites, Inc.

[19] Public Policy Institute, 1988; Legislative Commission, 1988.

other areas, because most of the work involved in hammering out a settlement would be done by PRPs.

The process that produced the policy followed the well-known lines developed in the policy formulation literature. First, disparate dissatisfaction with the status quo had been building for some time[20]. Businesses, the largest of which were represented by the Business Council, were unhappy with the costs of the current cleanup system as well as with the risk and uncertainties associated with the doctrine of joint and several liability[21]. Regulatory agencies wanted to find ways to avoid the high administrative and economic costs involved in investigating and prosecuting complex cases, as well as the political costs of using the most powerful, but also most troublesome tool at their disposal—joint and several liability. Politicians, represented by Governor Cuomo, were under increasing pressure to get more sites cleaned up and saw the present system as both slow and expensive.

Moreover, it appeared that a "window of opportunity" had opened, due to a combination of mounting dissatisfaction with the current situation and development of a promising new "solution" in the form of EDR[22]. Among environmental lawyers, the EDR movement had been building strength for some time. A member of the Attorney General's office had taken a special interest in its application to environmental cleanup cases. Several key legislators had become aware of the successful efforts of Clean Sites, Inc., an independent, nonprofit organization established to mediate in Superfund cases, giving credibility to the mediation alternative to litigation. Finally, a few very large corporations faced potential liability in a number of inactive toxic waste sites and were looking for ways in which they could both limit their exposure and give the impression of a general willingness of big business to cooperate in cleaning up the environment.

During this opportune moment, a "policy entrepreneur" emerged to join together the problem and solution streams and to take the initiative

---

[20] Nakamura, 1984.

[21] Under joint and several liability, one defendant in a lawsuit could be held responsible for the entire costs of compensation if other responsible parties could not be located or were without funds to pay their share of the judgment This doctrine was understandably unpopular with major industrial concerns because it had at least the potential of making those with "deep pockets" liable for the whole cost of cleaning up a site that they had only partial responsibility for creating. See Wilkerson and Church (l9891.

[22] Kingdon, 1984.

for obtaining the political support necessary to forge agreement on a policy[23]. In this case, it was Peter Lanahan, then Executive Director of the Business Council's Public Policy Institute. Informal discussions were held with representatives from DEC, private industry, the Attorney General's office, the Department of Health, and the Environmental Planning Lobby Institute[24]. Lanahan took the initiative in selling the idea for a mediated approach. Members of the Business Council were told how the approach would save on litigation costs, on the bad publicity associated with protracted conflict, and on time, so that CEOs could get back to the business of running their corporations. The Governor, who had made his initial reputation as a mediator in a community government conflict issue, was recruited as an ally in a proposal promising a cooperative approach that would leave all participants better off. The Attorney General's Office and DEC were told that a less conflict-ridden, voluntary approach would allow them to clean up more sites with fewer workers than the traditional enforcement approach and would thus allow them to maximize the number of cleanups obtained from their scarce labor resources.

The product of these efforts was a joint announcement issued by the Governor, the Attorney General, DEC, and the Public Policy Institute in September 1985, inaugurating an experimental ADR policy. Which site would be selected for the experiment, the mechanics to be used in bringing about the agreement, and the ultimate cleanup method were to be developed as the experiment progressed.

At this point, the policy was formulated and endorsed by the policy makers. But, as the policy formulation literature indicates, such processes do not guarantee a good fit between the perceived problem and the proposed solution[25]. In this case, a number of important issues had to be resolved, including the design of the particular machinery to implement the policy[26], selection of a trial site, and the assignment of specific responsibilities to the key actors. The policy, as formulated, was a widely supported general idea in search of more precise machinery for implementation in a test case.

---

[23] For similar situations see Kingdom (1984); Pressman and Wildavsky (1973).
[24] Public Policy Institute, 1987.
[25] Kingdon, 1984; Nakamura, 1987.
[26] Bardach, 1982.

5. POLICY IMPLEMENTATION

Eugene Bardach (1977) has conceptualized the policy implementation process as assembling a machine that takes something in on one side - in this case, toxic waste dumps - and produces something on the other side - clean sites. Continuing with this metaphor for a moment, it is fair to say that the policy formulation process described above produced a set of tools to be used in building the machine, but said relatively little about how they were to be fitted together and by whom. With the benefit of hindsight, and by filling in with reasonable surmises where the policy is silent, we will briefly describe what was envisioned.

Site Identification. Everything else in the experiment is derived from this step. The selection of a site determines which individuals and businesses are identified as PRPs and the nature of what has to be cleaned up. The only explicit criterion for selection was that the site be a "multiple user hazardous waste site", because they are the most difficult to litigate. It appears that neither the number of PRPs (beyond the minimum required for a "multiple user" site) nor the nature of the site itself (beyond a concern that it constitute a serious health hazard) was systematically considered in the choice of an experimental site. The final determination was made by State regulatory authorities, primarily DEC. The Phohl Brothers landfill in the western upstate town of Cheektowaga was selected in March, 1986.

Identification of the PRPs. PRPs are, by definition, those who contributed or transported toxic materials to a site, or who have some form of proprietary interest in it. Depending on the site chosen, the universe of potential PRPs is small and well defined, or quite large and diffuse. The difficulty, of course, is that joint and several liability makes each PRP potentially liable for the entire cleanup. Assessing liability requires guessing about how courts will apportion blame in a trial. Moreover, adding to the uncertainty is that identification of the parties who contributed waste to a site can be extraordinarily difficult since dump site records are usually inadequate and frequently nonexistent. DEC defined the PRPs at the Phohl Brothers site as all those whose names were found on the records of the dump over a period of more than a decade of use. In this population were entities who dumped very small quantities of entirely harmless materials, as well as those whose activities involved much larger quantities of toxic materials. Given this operational definition, hundreds of very diverse parties received letters advising them of their potential legal exposure and inviting them to meet at a preliminary session in Cheektowaga.

Creation of PRP Committees and Administrative Structure. Once the PRPs were identified, it was envisioned that DEC and the Attorney General's staff would retire into the background. The policy's planners assumed that the PRPs would organize themselves into deliberative bodies which would make joint decisions. Using the Clean Sites model, these bodies might be divided into various types of PRP: big businesses, small businesses, local governments, etc. Each represents a particular set of interests with special problems. In turn, the various committees would send representatives to a more comprehensive, though much smaller, steering committee which would make decisions for the whole group and represent all PRPs to the government and the public.

Why would individual PRPs voluntarily participate in a process where participation might be viewed as an admission of responsibility, and where "success" would necessarily be an expensive cleanup bill for all involved[27]? The ADR literature suggested that PRPs would willingly use a forum which would facilitate agreement without the economic and political costs of litigation and which would give them a greater role in designing a cost-effective cleanup. There was also an expectation that DEC would proceed formally against recalcitrant PRPs if they failed to participate.

In fact, the vast majority of the PRPs identified by DEC avoided the meeting entirely. The small number who did attend were almost entirely representatives of major corporations. This group constituted itself as a steering committee in July 1986. The Committee consisted of representatives from Occidental Chemical, Westinghouse, General Motors, New York State Electric and Gas, Ford, American Standard, Curtiss-Wright, F. N. Burt, and the Phohl family. From the beginning there was conflict as to the role to be played by the mediator. However, the disagreement was at least temporarily resolved after discussions with DEC and officials from the State Attorney General's office.

Assessing What Needs to Be Done, Devising Plans, and Allocating Costs. This is the most complex step in any cleanup. It involves the need to sustain cooperation among PRPs', to resolve the difficult technical is-

---

[27] Public Policy Institute, 1986.

sues concerning the cleanup itself, and (perhaps most problematic of all) to apportion cleanup costs among the participants.

In order to bring about a successful cleanup, the following tasks needed to be accomplished by the PRPs:

(1) Development of a comprehensive site map (apparently a satisfactory one did not exist) showing the geographic extent of the problem area.

(2) Completion of interim remedial measures in order to limit further exposure of the population (e.g., build a fence, hire guards, etc.).

(3) Submission of an assessment of the dimensions of the problem and the range of potential solutions (the Remedial Investigation/Feasibility Study, or RI/FS). This step is expensive, requiring the hiring of consultants to conduct what is frequently a complex technological investigation. It is critical to all that follows, because it usually serves as the blueprint for all further action.

(4) Completion of the final remedial design, the plan for the actual cleanup.

(5) Supervision of the actual cleanup.

In the Phohl Brothers experiment the steering committee of PRPs did not progress beyond steps 1 and 2. They even refused to pay for building a fence and hiring guards for the site, despite the minimal costs involved, because of fears that the sharing of these minimal charges among the participating PRPs would serve as a precedent for the allocation of the much greater expenses to come. For its part, DEC set a series of deadlines for the various steps in the process and periodically threatened action against the PRPs, but it never moved to prosecution. Thus, DEC and the Steering Committee fell into an increasingly surly, adversarial relationship in which deadlines were set and missed and threats were routinely exchanged.

PRPs were uncertain and resentful; some sought to renegotiate various aspects of the process. First, they expressed fears that an agreement to pay any costs could prejudice any subsequent legal action against them.

For its part, the State made it clear that the PRPs' participation in the process would not foreclose the State from taking subsequent legal action against them if it saw fit. Second, the PRPs resented the fact that only those few parties who came forward appeared likely to bear the costs of the cleanup, while others (referred to in hazardous waste vernacular as those "hiding in the weeds") had apparently avoided such problems through nonparticipation. Third, the PRPs sought to extract some concessions for their cooperation in the form of a state contribution to the costs of the RI/FS and assurance of some protection against subsequent legal action. But so-called mixed funding arrangements between government and private parties are very complex and require the government to play a central role in negotiations - a part consistently avoided by both DEC and the Attorney General's office. Moreover, given the limited experience with waste site cleanups, it appeared to be legally (and politically) risky for government to grant waivers from future liability to the settling parties. It was at that point that the implementation of the policy stalled.

Implementing the Cleanup Plans. The next step in the process would have been to carry out the cleanup. As the implementation machine not stalled at the previous step, it would have faced another series of difficulties at this and the next stage. There was substantial dispute over the actual level of cleanup to be attained. DEC was under criticism from the legislature for its slowness in recommending standards for cleanups to the settling parties. Thus, the requirements for the cleanup (the determination of "how clean is clean?") and, presumably, its subsequent cost would have posed issues difficult to overcome during the formulation and implementation of the plan.

6. ANALYSIS OF IMPLEMENTATION OUTCOMES: HOW DOES THE IMPLEMENTATION LITERATURE INFORM THE ANALYSIS OF ADR ?

This attempt at using ADR techniques to achieve a cleanup of the Phohl Brothers site failed. What lessons can we take away from this failure? We should perhaps note at the outset that the policy idea *per se* does not seem to be at fault. We do know that ADR has been successfully used Clean Sites to clean up toxic waste sites by.

The ADR literature focuses primarily on use of ADR in a specific dispute, seldom in the context of a broad public policy problem. Thus it has not dealt with implementation issues, at least as they are understood in the field of policy analysis. It is our judgment that attention to these considerations in both the design and implementation of New York's ADR experiment might have produced a more successful result.

The implementation literature has gone through three generations of emphases: a focus on the politics of what happened to a particular policy initiative and its impact on goal attainment[28]; a concern with the organizational and political variables that explain successful implementation[29]; and a concern with the generic properties of policy implements[30]. While scholars often imply that the implementation literature is advancing along a continuum of theoretical sophistication, another useful way to think about this literature is to accept that each generation emphasizes different important features of the phenomenon being dealt with[31]. Evaluated that way, the literature provides a basis for constructing a mosaic of explanations producing a more comprehensive picture of what is involved in analyzing implementation in a given setting.

While, for students of implementation and proponents of ADR, the failure of New York's experiment with ADR was perhaps overdetermined, it is not failure *per se* in which we are interested. Rather, we seek to identify the choices facing policy makers and implementers as well as the junctures at which alternative courses of action were indicated. Further, we should also be concerned with sharpening the guidance to practitioners that might be derived from a good working knowledge of the implementation literature. What, then, is the "value added" to be derived from assessing the problems encountered at the Phohl Brothers experiment through the multiple lenses of the implementation literature, and how might that literature be reconceptualized to provide sharper policy guidance? We now turn to that discussion.

---

[28] Pressman and Wildavsky, 1986.
[29] Mazmanian and Sabatier, 1981, 1983.
[30] Salamon, 1981; Bardach, 1980; McDonnell and Elmore, 1987, Church and Heumann 1989.
[31] For a similar approach see Graham Allison's (1971) discussion of the Cuban missile crisis.

6.1. First Generation Explanations

Although varied, first generation explanations have some things in common. They focus on the particulars of a given case with an emphasis on why policy makers and other actors made the choices they did. (Why did EDA choose an economic development approach in Oakland? Why do street-level bureaucrats adopt the responses they do?) They turn our attention towards the relationship between individual priorities and motivations and the requirements of collective action. And these first generation explanations focus on the need for "fixers" at the micro-level to overcome or ameliorate the intrinsic communication and coordination difficulties arising from the complexity of joint action.

Why the Choice of the ADR Solution? The first generation literature stresses the role of particular policymaker motivations in shaping both individual preferences and subsequent investments in time and effort[32]. At a minimum, the initial agreement among policy makers that ADR was a good idea may not be indicative of a willingness to invest in making ADR work.

The initial decision that produced the promising plan was gained on a basis that was unrealistic and that encouraged participants to misallocate their energies or to underinvest their resources. DEC and the Attorney General's office were recruited on claims that ADR would constitute a less-resource intensive process to produce cleanups. Both agencies do their jobs in an atmosphere of heavy workloads, limited resources, and serious political demands for action[33]. Easy, effective, and low-cost cleanup of toxic waste sites was a seductive promise.

DEC's labor-saving approach created a number of problems. First, the agency did not do adequate groundwork on site selection and site mapping. That failure created an additional initial task for PRPs at a time when their cooperation was not assured, and emphasized to PRPs the uncertainty and organizational costs involved in the experiment. Second, the initial identification of PRPs was done in a quick and easy fashion that produced uncertainty about how large the universe of participants was. The perception of unfairness among those PRPs who did participate was

---

[32] Nakamura and Pinderhughes, 1978; Nakamura, 1984.
[33] DEC, for example, has fewer people in their enforcement division than there are on the legislative committee that heard its testimony regarding the failure of this experiment.

reinforced. Further work on PRP identification before commencing the experiment would have also reduced uncertainty about potential liabilities, which in turn would have increased PRPs' incentives to participate. Third, the role that DEC did take, one restricted to creating and enforcing performance deadlines, misconceived the agreement-building nature of the PRP deliberation process. While an alternative role of facilitator-negotiator-mediator-threatener would have been more labor intensive, it would almost certainly have contributed more to the process.

The Attorney General's office, for its part, was also attracted to the reduced need for prosecution assumed in the mediation approach. However, serious prosecution - or at least the clear threat of a willingness to prosecute - is necessary for several reasons. The threat to bring PRPs to court and compel them to pay for a costly cleanup that they had no hand in designing, together with the doctrine of joint and several liability that exposes each individual PRP to the possibility of paying the entire cleanup cost, fuels the process of cooperation. Without at least the threat of these eventualities, PRPs might be expected to have little interest in participating in a process that, at best, promises to be costly and time-consuming. In order to pose a credible threat, regulators must undertake some essential groundwork, including acquisition of reliable information on PRPs' past behavior. That task required an effort that neither DEC nor the Attorney General's staff seemed prepared to make. Even if the case had resulted in a cleanup agreement and ultimate remediation, success in future efforts would have required the State to pursue those PRPs who did not participate in the voluntary agreement. The PRPs who chose to become involved saw little evidence that the recalcitrants would actually be dragged out of the weeds.

The first lesson is, therefore, that policymakers and implementers did not invest the effort required to make ADR work. Their commitment was rather to create a new system in which the costs would be paid by others, primarily the PRPs.

The Structure of Individual Incentives. Bottom-up approaches to policy initiatives[34] posit a decentralized world with severe limitations on the part that can be played by the top. Analysts of this bent are subsequently more concerned with the degree to which incentives are structured to favor certain behaviors rather than others. Both cooperative and adversarial be-

---

[34] Lipsky 1978; 1980.

havior, from below, is explained in terms of what people find it in their interests to do.

This potential explanation of the failure of this initiative is one that economists would share. When behavior deviates from a preferred direction, economists look to the structure of incentives[35]. Clearly, those who formulated the ADR policy envisioned that incentives would drive the process. PRPs would participate in order to minimize litigation costs, to have a say in how clean and costly a cleanup should be, and to avoid the bad publicity and aggravation attending a lawsuit. These are, of course, rather negative incentives. Further, they fail to consider counterincentives. These perverse incentives include the fact that failure to participate almost certainly saves resources in the short run; "hiding in the weeds" is the cheapest immediate response to an invitation to become involved in sharing responsibility for a costly cleanup. The literature on negotiation in criminal and civil lawsuits suggests that serious negotiation seldom takes place until its alternative, the threat of a trial, is imminent[36]. Yet DEC and the Attorney General's office failed to take even the first steps toward a legal enforcement action against either the participants in the negotiation process or, perhaps more importantly, against nonparticipants.

Even the potential savings in litigation costs, when viewed from the perspective of a PRP lawyer, did not present the clear incentive to participate that the policy's designers apparently expected. While PRPs plainly wanted to reduce legal costs and minimize the bottom-line expenses of the entire cleanup, DEC offered no guarantee that PRPs would ultimately avoid litigation even if they did cooperate. Any breakdown in the negotiation process could land the entire dispute in court. The State made no promises about foregoing suits in the future, and third parties could still sue when a cleanup was underway, or even after completion. Moreover, the monetary incentives allegedly driving the process may have come into conflict with perceptions of fairness on the part of the participating PRPs. DEC's failure to pursue nonparticipants suggested that the "good guys" might very well bear the full brunt of State demands for action, a suspicion that may account for some of the stubbornness evidenced by participating PRPs. The literature on regulatory strategies cer-

---

[35] Schultze, 1977.
[36] See Heumann, 1978.

tainly suggests that corporate perceptions of governmental unreasonableness often produces intransigence rather than compliance[37].

At a minimum, this case study suggests that the mixture of positive and negative incentives to participate in the negotiation process, and to negotiate seriously, were insufficient to overcome the rather more direct costs related to serious participation and the potential benefits of withholding consent from a cleanup plan. If the desired behavior is not achieved by the present incentive structure, one solution is to add more in both directions. Thus, on the positive side, the suggestion (embodied in part in the new SARA amendments to the Federal Superfund legislation) that more State or federal money be used to get things underway, and reduce the total cleanup costs for PRPs, may make sense if speed and voluntary agreement are desired. Alternatively, the process might have moved more expeditiously with a more credible and immediate threat of the use of formal adversary procedures and the joint and several liability doctrine. In short, the incentive model is a balancing model and if the proper point is not reached, it is time to change the weights.

The Complexity of Joint Action Problem and the Role of "Fixers". When the State seeks to achieve its goals through the cooperative and coordinated action of numerous others not under its direct control, it places a premium on the need for "fixers". The problems with New York's experiment with EDR may thus have gone deeper than a mere misunderstanding of what was required for the policy to be successfully implemented. Two obvious design features stand out: a poor choice of implementers and a failure to build in a fixer role.

The implementation machine as designed, placed a large burden on DEC and that agency, by most accounts, did not do a very good job of shouldering it. DEC can be faulted for not doing some things it knew how to do, such as the groundwork on site selection. On the other hand, it may not have been the appropriate body to handle the negotiating aspects of the process. DEC's organizational identity is that of an enforcement agency. Agency representatives, testifying before the State legislature on the failure of the experiment, implied that they felt the agency was doing the PRPs a favor by letting them try to work out an agreement among themselves; they felt little responsibility to facilitate the process further. DEC officials noted at this hearing that the agency had a good record of

---

[37] Kagan and Scholz, 1984; Bardach and Kagan, 1982.

getting people to do things through legal action, and suggested that they had doubts as to the desirability of the ADR experiment. Such testimony suggests that the agency was not fully committed to making mediation work.

Bardach (1982) advises that when implementation capacity is needed, the choice is between using an existing agency, building a new one, or buying one off the shelf. In this case, the existing agencies were DEC's Environmental Law Division and the Attorney General's staff. These entities, staffed primarily by lawyers committed to a prosecutor's approach to "bad guy" polluters, might have been an inappropriate organization to spearhead an effort at mediating conflict. Building capacity outside existing agencies is difficult and conflicts with the desire to save on staffing. That leaves the alternative of buying it. Perhaps it would have made the most sense to employ the services of a third party to serve as the mediator. This option in itself would not have solved the other structural problems with the policy machine. Still, an experienced third party might have known how to do precisely those things called for by the policy machine design, assuming that a credible enforcement existed.

Finally, there is the need for a fixer. Fixers are people or organizations that have the motivation to make the policy work, including informational resources (knowledge about where the machine is broken and why), and power resources (the capacity to do something about it)[38]. Given a complex world with many points where the policy machinery might break down, successful policy implementations are often associated with fixers keeping the process going. While the foregoing is phrased in the jargon of the policy analysis, a restatement can be made in the context of the ADR literature. Neither DEC nor the Attorney General's staff had the desire or the ability to serve as a fixer in the dispute. Indeed, both were interested parties. Lanahan, the designer of the experiment (who left the employ of the Public Policy Institute shortly after the policy was adopted) might have played the role of a fixer. The same resources useful for the policy entrepreneur (contacts across participants) would have served a fixer well.

Quite clearly, the atmosphere of mistrust and uncertainty that characterized the breakdown points in the process would have been improved with a fixer playing a role in applying coercion or threats of unpleasant

---

[38] Levin and Ferrnan, 1985; Bardach, 1986.

consequences when required, and lobbying with the governmental actors to free resources or extract legal assurances when necessary in order to make an agreement more palatable to those who were, after all, ultimately to foot the bill.

6.2. Second Generation Explanations

The next generation of implementation studies is exemplified by Mazmanian and Sabatier (1981)[39]. These "top-down" approaches stress the role of organizational and other variables to explain the degree to which implementations are successful across cases. The emphasis is on the factors that promote effective central control (such as consistency of goals and commitment of policy makers and implementing agencies) and the adequacy of resources to overcome resistance from the bottom.

The top-down approaches would have anticipated difficulties for ADR in New York. Policymaker commitment, while broad, was also shallow. The implementing agency was not committed to carrying out the policy to the extent that it invested heavily in it. And while policymaker goals were consistent, and in some cases (e.g., minimizing legal costs) resonant with those of PRPs, there is a basic conflict of interests between those who have to pay and those who want them to pay.

6.3. Third Generation Approaches

Here the focus is "on the instruments common to different policies and on the conditions under which these instruments are most likely to produce intended effects"[40]. It is, therefore, knowledge about the generic properties of approaches that is brought to the analysis of implementation problems.

Shift of Implements. Following this vein of analysis, policy makers in this ADR initiative chose to replace a mandating[41] or regulatory[42] ap-

---

[39] See also Bullock and Lamb, 1984.
[40] McDonnell and Elmore, 1987, p. 133.
[41] McDonnell and Elmore, 1987.
[42] Levin and Ferman, 1985.

proach with one of "systems-changing"[43]. We can use this analysis to unpack the assumptions that underlay this choice. Systems-changing approaches are based on an analysis of the policy problem, which holds that the fault lies with the existing system of relationships, and which uses the authority of the State to reallocate responsibilities and obligations. It assumes, furthermore, that those with the reallocated responsibilities to act have or will develop both the motivation and capacity to deliver the expected public goods.

How well, then, was the policy chosen and implemented? Our previous discussion indicated that the policy's advocates hoped that voluntary agreement would follow the creation of discussion opportunities and the structuring of incentives. Their attention had been primarily directed at avoiding the costs and pitfalls of the dominant system of environmental cleanup.

In their haste, the policy's framers may have used an inadequate or incomplete understanding of what was required by ADR. This misunderstanding may be rooted, in part, in the advocacy nature of much of the ADR literature which often has had a clearer idea of what is to be avoided than what is required for action. The fault, however, is not entirely with ADR as an idea. Participants used the terms ADR and *mediation* interchangeably. They assumed that the parties, given sufficient incentives, would hire a mediator and that the process would proceed. In short, they apparently thought that effective mediation was a product of a process that they could set in motion and then leave alone. Elmore warns that in "systems-changing instruments, the central problem is how to keep existing institutional interests and arrangements from driving new ones out of existence before the new ones have a chance to form"[44].

Both the academic students of mediation[45] and practitioners (Clean Sites, Inc., for example) are quite clear in their contention that effective mediation occurs by explicit design. In their view, effective mediation has to be built in from the outset: careful groundwork in establishing lists of participants; getting potential participants sensitive to the costs of failure to agree; early involvement of mediators in helping groups to form and

---

[43] McDonnell and Elmore, 1987.
[44] Elmore, 1987, p. 179.
[45] Raiffa, 1982; Susskind and Cruikshank, 1987.

define themselves; the need to actively nurture cooperative relationships[46].

In short, theorists and practitioners treat mediation as a process that requires careful construction rather than as a natural product. In that sense the New York case may illustrate the pitfalls of not thinking systematically about what is required for the policy tool which actors thought they were adopting.

Generic Pitfalls in This Choice of Implements. Why was such a basic error committed? We already noted that motivations of policy makers concerned short-term organizational and political goals. But was the problem just shortsightedness? We think not. In experiences with other systems-changing approaches - school decentralization, the adoption of budgetary fads (program budgeting, management by objectives, and zero based budgeting), and governmental reorganizations - the tendency seems to have been to systematically underestimate the requirements of the new system to be put into place. It seems that the assumption behind systems-changing approaches - that it is current authority relationships that are at fault - disposes policy makers to stress the areas of their greatest agreement and to avoid the more vexing problems of precisely how to create the alternative system.

Fixing systems by incremental infusions of resources may be a less attractive solution than creating new relationships. Anthony Downs (1957), in his discussion of the issue cycle, posited a dynamic in which sharp public attention to a problem peaks and declines as information about the expense of solutions becomes more available. The adoption of systems-changing solutions promises better results with the same resources. They can be adopted quickly, precisely because their benefits are obvious and whatever costs they require are nonmonetary (changing the use of the regulatory power of the state) or off-loaded onto other actors (in this case PRPs). That, of course, says little about the willingness and capacity of these other actors to pay these costs; but that is not something that has to be determined in advance of adopting a systems-changing solution.

---

[46] For an insightful discussion of the problem of the dynamics required for effective negotiation, with a discussion of the subfield, see Burton (1990).

7. CONCLUSIONS

Our approach may be faulted for focusing on yet another policy failure, and it is fair to criticize the policy analysis literature for overemphasis on failures. Analyses of successes alone, on the other hand, may produce almost as much hubris as wisdom. New York's mistakes began with an uncritical reading of the promises and successes of ADR techniques in other contexts, without a careful assessment of what would be needed for it to succeed in their existing situation. We should not forget, however, that New York actors started with a relatively compelling analysis of what was wrong with the present system: an analysis that drew from their own experiences. And they experimented with an alternative approach which promised to avoid pitfalls that they knew too well. Where they erred was in misconceiving the requirements of the alternative system they hoped to establish.

The deficiencies in the design and operation of the New York experiment included failures in what might be termed ADR methodology. The consistently missing mediator, for example, and the failure of the governmental agencies involved to appreciate the difficulties of keeping such a system of negotiations running, are problems that would have been apparent to any experienced ADR practitioner.

Unlike other implementations of public policy, ADR does not operate directly on either the capacity or the motivation of the affected population to achieve a desired policy result[47]. A system of regulation, or benefaction, or inducement, can propel individuals and corporations to behave in ways that policy makers wish. But ADR, standing alone, can have no such impact. Its success or failure depends in large part on the perceived *alternatives* to a negotiated settlement and their relationship to what can be gained in negotiations[48].

Significantly, and unlike the situation in many mediated disputes, the governmental actors in this case study had substantial control over both the "carrots" that would accompany a negotiated resolution, and the "sticks" that would follow if negotiations broke down. The carrots included the possibility of a governmental contribution to the total costs of the cleanup; a release from present or (within legal limits) future liability;

---

[47] For a discussion of the capacity and motivation dimensions of public policy tools, see Church and Heumann (19891.
[48] Raiffa, 1982.

the promise of PRP participation in the remedial design to ensure that cost-effective and reasonable remedies were applied to the cleanup; and a potential for improved public relations. The sticks included the threat of imminent and costly litigation, public embarrassment, and the possibility of a "the-sky-is-the-limit" remedy imposed on PRPs by governmental officials under pressure from environmental groups and an irate citizenry. Yet New York officials made little use of their control over the ADR exercise. Rather, they seemed to take the position that all they needed to do was set the experiment in motion and then wait to reap its promised benefits.

We have attempted in this contribution to suggest how some of the broad lessons derived from the policy implementation literature may be used in future attempts to apply ADR in an explicit policy context. We should emphasize that our conclusion is not that ADR techniques are inappropriate in the environmental area, or in public policy disputes in general. Rather, we have tried to outline some additional considerations that should come into play when alternative dispute resolution is applied.

REFERENCES

Acton, Jan Paul (1989), *Understanding Superfund: A Progress Report* (Santa Monica, CA: RAND Institute for Civil Justice).

Allison, Graham T. (1971), *The Essence of Decision: Explaining the Cuban Missile Crisis* (Boston: Little, Brown).

Amy, Douglas J. (1987), *The Politics of Environmental Mediation* (New York: Columbia University Press).

Bacow, Lawrence and Michael Wheeler (1984), *Environmental Dispute Resolution* (New York: Plenum Press).

Bardach, Eugene (1977), The Implementation Game: *What Happens After a Bill Becomes a Law* (Cambridge, MA: MIT Press).

Bardach, Eugene (1980), "*Implementation Studies and the Study of Implements*", paper presented at the 1980 Annual Meeting of the American Political Science Association.

Bardach, Eugene and Robert Kagan (1982), *Going by the Book: The Problem of Regulatory Unreasonableness* (Philadelphia: Temple University Press).

Bingham, Gail (1985), *Resolving Environmental Disputes: A Decade of Experience* (Washington, DC: The Conservation Foundation).

Bullock, Charles and Charles Lamb (1984), "*A Search for Variables Important in Policy Implementation,*" in Bullock and Lamb (eds.) *Implementation of Civil Rights Policy* (Monterey, CA: Brooks/Cole).

Burton, Lloyd (1990), "*Ethical Discontinuities in Public-Private Sector Negotiations,*" Journal of Policy Analysis and Management 9(1), pp. 23-40.

CERCLA - Comprehensive Environmental Recovery, Compensation, and Liability Act of 1980, Public Law 94-510, codified at 42 U.S.C. 6901-6987.

Church, Thomas and Heumann, Milton (1989), "*The Underexamined Assumptions of the Invisible Hand: Monetary Incentives as Policy Instruments*," Journal of Policy Analysis and Management 8(4), pp. 641-657.

Downs, Anthony (1957), *An Economic Theory of Democracy* (New York: Random House).

Elmore, Richard (1987), "*Instruments and Strategy in Public Choice*," Policy Studies Review 7(1), pp. 174-186.

Hair, Jay (1984), "*Getting Ready to Win*," Address to Second National Conference on Environmental Dispute Resolution, Conservation Foundation, Washington, DC.

Heumann, Milton (1978), *Plea Bargaining* (Chicago: University of Chicago Press).

Kagan, Robert and Scholz, John (1984), "*The 'Criminology of the Corporation' and Regulatory Enforcement Strategies*," in Keith Hawkins and John Thomas (eds.) *Enforcing Regulation* (Boston: Kluwer/Nijhoff).

Kingdon, Roger (1984), *Agendas, Alternatives, and Public Policies* (Boston: Little, Brown).

Lake, Laura (ed.) (1980), *Environmental Mediation: The Search for Consensus* (Boulder, CO: Westview Press).

Legislative Commission on Toxic Substances and Hazardous Wastes (1988), "*Notice of Public Hearing*", March 16, 1988.

Levin, Martin and Ferman, Barbara (1985), *The Political Hand: Policy Implementation and Youth Employment Programs* (New York: Pergamon Press).

Levinson, Alfred (1988), "*Environmental Dispute Resolution and Policy making,*" Policy Studies Journal 16(3), pp. 575-584.

Lipsky, Michael (1978), "*Standing the Study of Implementation on its Head,*" in Walter Dean Burnham and Martha Weinberg (eds.) *American Politics and Public Policy* (Cambridge, MA: MIT Press).

Lipsky, Michael (1980), *Street Level Bureaucracy: Dilemmas of the Individual in Public Service* (New York: Russell Sage Foundation).

Mazmanian, Daniel and Sabatier, Paul (1981), *Effective Policy Implementation* (Lexington, MA: Lexington Books).

Mazmanian, Daniel and Sabatier, Paul (1983), *Implementation and Public Policy* (Glenview, IL: Scott, Foresman).

McDonnell, Lorraine M. and Elmore, Richard (1987), "*Getting the Job Done: Alternative Policy Instruments,*" Educational Evaluation and Policy Analysis 6(2), pp. 133-152.

Mernitz, Scott (1980), *Mediation of Environmental Disputes: A Sourcebook* (New York: Praeger Press).

Mintz, Joel (1988), "*Agencies, Congress and Regulatory Enforcement: A Review of EPA's Hazardous Waste Enforcement Effort, 1970-1987,*" Environmental Law 18, pp. 683-777.

Nakamura, Robert (1984), "*Coalition Formation and Policy Development: The Case of the Vanishing Coalition*", in Robert Eyestone (ed.) Policy Development (Greenwich, CT: JAI Press).

Nakamura, Robert (1987), "*The Textbook Policy Process and Implementation Process,*" Policy Studies Review 7(1), pp. 142-154.

Nakamura, Robert and Pinderhughes, Diane (1978), "*Changing Anacostia: Definition and Implementation,*" Policy Studies Journal 7 (Special Issue #3) pp. 1089-1100.

Pressman, Jeffrey and Wildavsky, Aaron (1973), *Implementation* (Berkeley, CA: University of California Press).

Public Policy Institute (1986), "*Clarification of the Points of Agreement for the Environmental Mediation Project,*" August 15, 1986.

Public Policy Institute (1987), "*Update and Analysis of the Environmental Mediation,* Project," March 1987.

Public Policy Institute (1988), "*Summary of Points of Agreement*".

Rabe, Barry G. (1988), "*The Politics of Environmental Dispute Resolution,*" Policy Studies Journal) 6(3) pp. 585-601.

Raiffa, Howard (1982), *The Art and Science of Negotiation* (Cambridge, MA: Belknap/Harvard University Press).

Salamon, Lester (1981), "*Rethinking Public Management: Third-Party Government and the Changing Forms of Government Action,*" Public Policy 29, pp. 255-273.

Salamon, Lester (ed.) (1989), *Beyond Privatization: The Tools of Government Action* (Washington: Urban Institute Press).

SARA-Superfund Amendments and Reauthorization Act of 1986, Public Law 99499, codified at 100 Stat. 1612 (1986).

Schneider, Anne and Ingram, Helen (1989), "*Behavioral Assumptions of Policy Tools,*" paper presented at 1989 Annual Meeting of Midwest Political Science Association.

Schultze, Charles W. (1977), *The Public Use of the Private Interest* (Washington, DC: The Brookings Institution).

Susskind Lawrence and Weinstein, Alan (1980), "*Towards a Theory of Environmental Dispute Resolution*," Boston College Environmental Affairs Law Review (9), pp. 311-357.

Susskind, Lawrence and Cruikshank, Jeffrey (1987), *Breaking the Impasse: Consensual Approaches to Resolving Public Disputes* (New York: Basic Books).

Talbot, Allan (1983), *Settling Things: Six Case Studies in Environmental Mediation* (Washington, D.C.: The Conservation Foundation).

Wilkerson, William R. and Church, Thomas W. (1989), "*The Gorilla in the Closet: Joint and Several Liability and The Cleanup of Toxic Waste Sites*," Law and Policy 11 (3), pp. 425-449.

VERHANDLUNGSLÖSUNGEN/MEDIATION: ERFAHRUNGEN AUS DEN USA UND ÜBERTRAGBARKEIT AUF DEUTSCHE VERHÄLTNISSE

W. Hoffmann-Riem/I. Lamb

1. GRENZEN EINSEITIGEN VERWALTUNGSHANDELNS

Die Verwaltung stösst in zunehmendem Masse auf die Grenzen ihres herkömmlichen Instrumentariums, wenn sie bestimmte Entscheidungen fällen und durchsetzen will: Vorhaben, die sich über den lokalen Bereich hinaus auf räumlich und zeitlich entfernt liegende Interessen auswirken - wie Abfalldeponien oder Verbrennungsanlagen, Fernstrassen oder Flughäfen -, sind gesellschaftlich umstritten. Bei fast jedem Vorhaben wird dieser Streit ausgetragen. Aber auch die in ihren Auswirkungen regional begrenzten "lulus", die "locally unwanted land uses", die ein Gefängnis, ein Musicaltheater oder ein Behindertenwohnheim sein können, stossen gelegentlich auf heftigen und erfolgreichen Widerstand der Anwohner. Bei der Beurteilung neuer technischer Anlagen wird es der Verwaltung häufig schon schwer fallen, die als Entscheidungsgrundlage notwendigen Informationen zu sammeln. Ist sie schliesslich zu einer Entscheidung gekommen, so bedeutet das noch nicht, dass diese auch durchgesetzt werden kann.

Für solche und ähnliche Problemfälle hat sich eine Vielzahl informeller Vorgehensweisen der Verwaltung herausgebildet. Durch Gespräche und Zusammenarbeit mit den Vorhabenträgern sollen beispielsweise Sachverhalte aufgeklärt, geeignete Instrumente gefunden oder die Realisierungschancen einer Entscheidung abgetastet werden. Da Mitarbeit aber umsonst kaum zu haben ist, münden solche Verhandlungen häufig in Tauschvorgänge. Die Ergebnisse werden in der Regel nicht rechtsverbindlich festgeschrieben, sondern "freiwillig" beachtet, da die Beteiligten sich von der Einhaltung Vorteile versprechen: Die Verwaltung ist insbesondere an der "freiwilligen" Beseitigung von Missständen interessiert, wenn die Durchsetzung hoheitlicher Massnahmen aufwendig oder rechtlich unsicher wäre. Der Adressat staatlicher Massnahmen kann mit Hilfe der Absprache manchmal die sonst einsetzbaren staatlichen Instrumente oder Sanktionen abmildern. In Sanierungsabsprachen werden gelegentlich sogar rechtswidrige Zustände für eine befristete Zeit geduldet, wenn eine Sanierung verbindlich zugesagt wird[1]. Auch können sich dauerhafte Netzwerke der Kommunikation und Interaktion bilden, die die Beteiligten nicht durch Nichtbeachtung einer unverbindlichen Absprache gefährden wollen. Es sind jedoch nicht nur bipolare Gespräche zwischen Verwaltung und Betreiber möglich. Zunehmend wird versucht, die von einem Vorhaben nachteilig Betroffenen in Verhandlungen einzubeziehen. Bestimmend dafür ist meist nicht das Ziel der Verwirklichung partizipativer Demokratie, wohl aber das Bemühen um eine Reaktion auf Möglichkeiten der Betroffenen, durch entsprechenden Widerstand Vorhaben zu verzögern oder ganz zu verhindern.

2. Zu Begriffen und Modellen von Verhandlungslösungen und Konfliktmittlung

Solche Aushandlungsprozesse bieten nur dann die Chance der Akzeptanzerhöhung, wenn die Träger der betroffenen Interessen sich in einen Versuch wechselseitiger Interessenoptimierung integrieren lassen. Das kann nur bei einem fairen Verfahren mit gleichmässig verteilten Durchsetzungschancen erwartet werden. Verhandlungsverfahren verlangen daher den Einbau verfahrensmässiger Sicherungen interessengerechter Ergebnisse. Damit unterscheiden sie sich von den in der Verwaltungspraxis vorkommenden informellen Abklärungen. Deren Vorteile sollen allerdings erhalten und nicht durch neue Formalisierungen ausgeschaltet werden.

Von mittlerunterstützten Aushandlungsprozessen (Konfliktmittlung/-Mediation) soll dann gesprochen werden, wenn ein neutraler Dritter eingeschaltet wird, um das Aushandeln eines Entscheidungsergebnisses unter Beteiligung der Verwaltung und der Betroffenen moderierend zu erleichtern. Die Mittlerrolle kann unterschiedlich ausgestaltet sein: vom blossen "Verfahrensmittler", der für den Verfahrensablauf verantwortlich ist, bis zum "Konfliktmittler", der zusätzlich die Problemlösung mitgestaltet, indem er beispielsweise Alternativen abklärt, Lösungsvorschläge erarbeitet

---

[1] Bohne, E. 1982, S. 38 ff.

oder die Realisierung des Verhandlungsergebnisses faktisch mitverantwortet[2].

3. VERHANDLUNGSLÖSUNGEN/MEDIATION IN DEN USA UND GRUNDSÄTZLICHE FRAGEN IHRER ÜBERTRAGBARKEIT

In den USA wurden Verhandlungsverfahren im Umweltbereich spätestens seit Beginn der 70er Jahre diskutiert und erprobt[3]. Zur Bewältigung der schwierigen Standortsuche für Sonderabfallentsorgungsanlagen sehen einige Bundesstaaten (Connecticut, Massachusetts, Rhode Island und Wisconsin) förmliche Verhandlungen zwischen dem Vorhabenträger und lokalen Verhandlungskomitees vor[4]. Die Verfahren sind so ausgestaltet, dass Verhandlungsanreize geschaffen werden, vor allem werden Massnahmen für einen Interessenausgleich vorgesehen. Die lokalen Verhandlungskomitees haben höchstens 13 Mitglieder. Diese erhalten in der Regel finanzielle Beihilfen für die Teilnahme, die vom Vorhabenträger kommen. Die Verhandlungen sind zeitlich gebunden. Kommt es zu Verhandlungsengpässen, können - so in Wisconsin und Massachusetts - Mittler herangezogen werden. Im Falle eines endgültigen Steckenbleibens sind schliesslich Schiedsverfahren vorgesehen.

Die amerikanischen Verfahren sind bisher mit sehr unterschiedlichem Erfolg beendet worden. So führten sie bis 1989 in Massachusetts noch zu keiner Ansiedlung; dagegen scheinen sie in Wisconsin - zum Teil mit Unterstützung eines Mittlers - relativ erfolgreich gewesen zu sein[5].

Aufgrund der praktischen Erfahrungen mit Verhandlungsverfahren wurde in der US-amerikanischen Diskussion folgender idealtypischer Ablauf erarbeitet[6]: Das Verfahren beginnt mit der Beauftragung eines Konfliktmittlers durch staatliche Stellen oder am Konflikt beteiligte Parteien - möglichst zu einem Zeitpunkt, in dem noch ausreichend Alternativen offenstehen und nicht eine bestimmte Entscheidung schon faktisch präjudiziert ist. Der Mittler stellt den Kreis der Verhandlungsteilnehmer zusammen, indem er Repräsentanten für die von dem Vorhaben betroffe-

---

[2] Hoffmann-Riem, W. 1989, S. 21
[3] Holznagel, B. 1989, S. 423 f.
[4] Zu Einzelheiten dieser Verfahren s. Holznagel, B. 1990, S. 129 ff.
[5] Gardner, J. 1990 a, S. 205 ff.; Holznagel, B. 1990, S. 151, 167 ff.
[6] Im folgenden dargestellt nach Holznagel, B. 1990, S. 119 ff.

nen Interessen zur Teilnahme zu bewegen sucht. Diese müssen ihn später in seiner Funktion als Konfliktmittler bestätigen. Anschliessend werden die wesentlichen umstrittenen Fragestellungen erarbeitet. Die Finanzierung muss geklärt werden, und die Beteiligten sollen sich einen Zeitplan und Verfahrensregeln für die Verhandlungen geben. Nach dieser Vorverhandlungsphase beginnen die Verhandlungen mit der Sammlung und Auswertung der notwendigen Informationen; eventuell werden Sachverständigengutachten vergeben. Diese Phase ist besonders wichtig zum Abbau von Informationsungleichgewichten zwischen den Beteiligten. Auf der Grundlage dieser Informationen wird versucht, über die Streitfragen zu einem Konsens zu kommen. Möglicherweise lässt sich ein angemessener Interessenausgleich mit Hilfe von Kompensationsmassnahmen erreichen. Wird zwischen den vertretenen Interessen ein Konsens erzielt, so unterzeichnen die Beteiligten eine Verhandlungsübereinkunft. Diese wird durch verschiedene Umsetzungsakte für alle Beteiligten verbindlich gemacht. Schliesslich kann der Konfliktmittler oder ein verwaltungsunabhängiges Sachverständigengremium mit der Überwachung beauftragt werden, ob und wie die Übereinkunft vollzogen wird.

Wie weit lässt sich nun dieses Verfahren auf die Bundesrepublik übertragen? Die Antwort darauf muss zuerst auf die unterschiedlichen Vorstellungen von Verwaltung und Verwaltungsrecht in beiden Rechtskreisen hinweisen. In der deutschen Verwaltungstradition werden die Entscheidungsinhalte in starkem Masse gerichtlich kontrolliert; entsprechend programmiert Verwaltungsrecht Entscheidungen inhaltlich vor. In den USA ist die gerichtliche Kontrolle dagegen vorrangig auf das Verfahren und nicht auf die Entscheidungsinhalte bezogen. Inhalte müssen also weniger stark rechtlich vorgegeben sein, die Verwaltung lässt sich stärker an politische und gesellschaftliche Entwicklungen anbinden[7]. In einem solchen Umfeld scheint es einfacher, Verhandlungsverfahren zur Entscheidungsfindung zu entwickeln. In den letzten Jahrzehnten tendierte das amerikanische Verwaltungsrecht jedoch zunehmend zur Materialisierung, während sich das deutsche auf eine verstärkte Prozeduralisierung hinbewegte. In beiden Rechtsordnungen ist die Verwaltung zudem gezwungen, für komplexe und politisch umstrittene Situationen praktikable Lösungen zu finden. Wegen dieser vergleichbaren Probleme und Verwaltungsrealitäten bietet es sich an, die amerikanischen Verhandlungsverfahren kritisch auf

---

[7] Grundsätzlich Scharpf, F. 1970.

Anwendungsmöglichkeiten in Deutschland zu überprüfen - unter Beachtung des anderen Hintergrundes des deutschen Verwaltungsrechts, aber auch unter Beachtung schon erfolgter praktischer Erfahrungen.

4. ERFAHRUNGEN MIT MITTLERGESTÜTZTEN VERHANDLUNGSVERFAHREN IN DER BUNDESREPUBLIK DEUTSCHLAND

Die deutsche Verwaltungspraxis nutzte schon bisher in einigen Fällen, in denen herkömmliche Verfahren oder auch informelle Absprachen ins Stocken gerieten, die Vermittlungsdienste neutraler Dritter. Nur so konnte beispielsweise die Hamburger Umweltbehörde erfolgreich einige Sanierungskonzepte mit den betroffenen Betrieben vereinbaren[8]. Allerdings fanden diese Verhandlungen im bipolaren Verhältnis zwischen Verwaltung und Anlagenbetreiber statt. Drittbetroffene waren nicht beteiligt. Sie konnten nur mittelbar durch politischen Druck auf die Umweltbehörde Einfluss ausüben.

Mittlerweile werden Verhandlungsverfahren und die oben beschriebenen US-amerikanischen Konfliktmittlungsverfahren in der Bundesrepublik erprobt[9].

Bekanntestes Beispiel dürfte die Konfliktmittlung zur Lösung des Streits um die Sonderabfalldeponie Münchehagen sein[10]. Die Deponie liegt in Niedersachsen, in der Nähe zu einer benachbarten Gemeinde und zur Staatsgrenze nach Nordrhein-Westfalen. Sie wurde bis 1983 betrieben. Während ihrer Nutzung und in der Zeit danach gab es Beschwerden von Anwohnern, Bürgerinitiativen und Umweltverbänden wegen Belästigungen durch Emissionen sowie wegen der Kontamination von Gewässern und Grundwasser. 1985 trat stark dioxinhaltiges Öl aus. Ausserdem fanden sich hohe PCB-Werte in Boden und Grundwasser nahe bei der Deponie. Es kam zu mehreren gerichtlichen Verfahren um die Deponie, die zum Teil noch nicht abgeschlossen sind, sowie zu Strafanträgen. Schliesslich wurde sogar eine Sonderkommission des Landeskriminalamts

---

[8] Funke, R. 1990 b, S. 209 ff.
[9] Für Fallbeschreibungen s. Forschungsschwerpunkt Technik - Arbeit - Umwelt 1991, S. 5 ff.; Striegnitz, M. 1990; S. 51 ff. und 1991; Wiedmann, P. u.a. 1990.
[10] Dazu und zum folgenden ausführlich Striegnitz, M. 1990, S. 51 ff., ders. 1991.

Niedersachsen eingesetzt. Die Beziehungen zwischen den Konfliktparteien wurden zunehmend angespannter. Ab 1986 brachte die Evangelische Akademie Loccum im Rahmen von Fachveranstaltungen die Konfliktpartner jedoch zusammen. So führte das Fachgespräch Hydrogeologie, das als Konfliktmittlungsverfahren über die zugrundeliegenden sachlich-wissenschaftlich-technischen Aspekte organisiert war, zu einem weitgehenden Konsens über den Kenntnisstand und zur Identifizierung der offenen Fragen[11]. Dagegen verliefen die Erfahrungen zur Konfliktmittlung mit dem ersten "Münchehagen-Ausschuss" enttäuschend. Beklagt wurden vor allem der ungenügende Informationsfluss und die Kompetenzlosigkeit des Ausschusses. Aufgrund dieser Erfahrungen wurde Mitte 1990 der Ausschuss vollständig neu organisiert. Er besteht aus dem Münchehagen-Plenum, in dem ein möglichst umfassendes Spektrum aller Interessen vertreten sein soll. Stimmberechtigte Mitglieder sind die Interessenvertreter, während die Vertreter technischer Ämter nur Rederecht haben. Die Vertreter der durch die Deponie nachteilig betroffenen Gruppen (Gemeinden, Anwohnerinitiativen und Umweltgruppen) haben im Plenum eine - wenn auch knappe - Mehrheit. Die Treffen des Plenums sind öffentlich. Das Plenum schafft die Verbindung zur Öffentlichkeit und dient zur Identifikation von Konflikten. Für die eigentliche Konsensfindung ist der Vermittlungsausschuss zuständig - ein Unterausschuss des Plenums. Seine 16 Mitglieder repräsentieren die wesentlichen Konfliktparteien. Abstimmungsberechtigt sind insgesamt 12 Personen, darunter Vertreter zweier Bürgerinitiativen, des BUNDs, einer Anwohnergemeinschaft, des niedersächsischen Umweltministeriums, der Bezirksregierung Hannover, der Landkreise Nienburg und Minden-Lübbecke, der Städte Rehburg-Loccum und Petershagen sowie die beiden örtlichen Landtagsabgeordneten von CDU bzw. SPD. Die Mehrheitsverhältnisse entsprechen denen im Plenum. Der Ausschuss tagt hinter verschlossenen Türen. Als Konfliktmittler wurde ein Mitarbeiter der Evangelischen Akademie Loccum gewählt. Bis Ende 1991 einigte sich der Ausschuss immerhin über einige umstrittene technische Fragen, über die Rechtsform der Abwicklung der Sicherungsarbeiten, über Zielsetzung, Begründung und Dimensionierung eines ökologischen Landschaftsgürtels sowie über die weitere Behandlung juristischer und technischer Streitpunkte, insbesondere auch über Design

---

[11] Striegnitz, M. 1990, S. 59 f.

und Durchführung einiger Untersuchungen, die von grosser Bedeutung für die weitere Arbeit sind[12].

Ein weiteres Mediationverfahren begann im Kreis Neuss zur Implementation des von der Kreisverwaltung entwickelten Abfallwirtschaftskonzepts. Das Verfahren soll zugleich als wissenschaftlich begleitetes Experiment der Überprüfung von Erfolg oder Misserfolg mittlergestützter Verhandlungen dienen[13]. Als Mittler wurde ein ehemaliges Mitglied des Sachverständigenrates für Umweltfragen gewonnen. In ersten Gesprächen mit Vertretern betroffener Interessen wurde die Bedeutung verfahrensmässiger Sicherungen für faire Beteiligungsmöglichkeiten deutlich. Ausserdem wurde vor allem von den Vertretern von Umweltinteressen ein frühzeitiger Einbezug gewünscht, um so tatsächliche Einflussmöglichkeiten auf das Entscheidungsergebnis zu erhalten. Nur so liess sich der Befürchtung begegnen, solche Verfahren würden von der Verwaltung eingesetzt, um Akzeptanz für schon unumstösslich bestehende Entscheidungen manipulativ herzustellen.

5. EINPASSUNG IN DIE BUNDESDEUTSCHE RECHTSORDNUNG

Wie die zahlreichen informellen Abklärungen, aber auch die Beispiele schon erfolgter Verhandlungs- und Konfliktmittlungsverfahren zeigen, lassen sich Verhandlungen und auch der Einsatz von Konfliktmittlern in die deutsche Verwaltungspraxis einfügen. Solche Konzepte dürfen jedoch die rechtsstaatliche Gesetzesbindung nicht aufheben. Vielmehr ist anzustreben, dass sie bisher praktizierte Formen informeller Vorabklärungen aus der Grauzone und dem Verdacht der Kungelei herausholen und sie verstärkter Tranzparenz und Kontrolle unterwerfen.

Im Rahmen nichtförmlicher Verwaltungsverfahren, die nach §10 des bundesdeutschen Verwaltungsverfahrensgesetzes vom 25. Mai 1976 (VwVfG) einfach und zweckmässig durchzuführen sind, sind Verhandlungen und allgemein informelle Verhaltensweisen grundsätzlich zulässig. Entscheidungen in besonders komplexen Problemlagen, wie bei der Ansiedlung von Abfallbeseitigungsanlagen, werden jedoch in förmlichen Verwaltungsverfahren, insbesondere in Planfeststellungsverfahren, erlas-

---

[12] Striegnitz 1992
[13] Dazu Forschungsschwerpunkt Technik -Arbeit - Umwelt 1991, S. 5 ff.

sen. Aushandlungen dürfen grundsätzlich informell vor oder neben diesem förmlichen Verfahren ablaufen, wenn sie nicht im konkreten Fall die Sicherungen des förmlichen Verfahrens unterlaufen. Wie weit lassen sie sich aber in das förmliche Verfahren integrieren? Dafür bietet sich das gesetzlich vorgesehene Anhörungsverfahren mit dem Erörterungstermin an[14]. Der Erörterungstermin wurde vom Gesetzgeber dafür vorgesehen, zu einer Einigung über die Einwendungen zu kommen[15]. Da solche Einigungen ohne Verhandlungen regelmässig nicht zu erreichen sein dürften, sind damit auch Aushandlungsverfahren mittelbar legitimiert. Bei der Integration in den Erörterungstermin stellt sich jedoch ein anderes Problem. Er ist im Planfeststellungsverfahren erst in einem späten Stadium zwingend vorgesehen, wenn in der Regel wesentliche Entscheidungen schon gefallen sind und zumindest faktisch binden. Häufig fanden schon Vorabklärungen zwischen einzelnen Beteiligten statt, insbesondere zwischen Vorhabenträger und Behörde. Daraus ergibt sich für die erst spät am Verfahren Beteiligten schnell das Gefühl der Einflusslosigkeit. Dieses führt leicht zum Scheitern von Verhandlungen. Sollen Verhandlungen erfolgreich sein, müssen die Beteiligten mit ihrem Einsatz auch tatsächlich Einfluss auf das Ergebnis nehmen können.

Der Einsatz eines Mittlers kann die Verwaltung von der Verhandlungsleitung entlasten. Das bedeutet nicht nur für die Verwaltung verringerten Arbeitsaufwand, sondern erhöht die Chancen der Konfliktlösung. Zwar ist die Rolle der Verwaltung im deutschen Verwaltungsrechtssystem als neutraler und objektiver Sachwalter des öffentlichen Interesses konzipiert. Es muss hier nicht eingehend diskutiert werden, wie weit sie diese Anforderungen erfüllt. In der Einschätzung der von Anlagenansiedlungen Betroffenen gilt die Verwaltung jedenfalls häufig als industrienah[16]. Bei einer solchen Einschätzung wird einer Verhandlungsleitung durch die Verwaltung wenig Vertrauen entgegengebracht werden. Soweit die Verwaltung - wie es häufig der Fall ist - eine bestimmte Entscheidung erreichen bzw. durchsetzen will, gerät sie zudem in die Rolle einer Konfliktpartei. Deutlich wird dies oft in Fällen, bei denen ein öffentliches Interesse an der Anlagenansiedlung besteht, wie bei der Abfallentsorgung, dieses Interesse aber in Konflikt mit anderen öffentlichen Interessen (z.B. Gesundheitsschutz der Anwohner) gerät, die von den Betroffenen ver-

---

[14] § 73 VwVfG.
[15] Arg. § 74 II 1 VwVfG.
[16] Vgl. die Fallstudien bei Wiedmann, P. M., u.a. 1990, S. 87.

teidigt werden. Auch wenn der Interessenausgleich ureigenste Aufgabe der Verwaltung ist, wird sie leicht von den anderen Beteiligten für parteiisch gehalten. Die Doppelfunktion als Partei und neutraler Verhandlungsleiter kann auch nach der Selbsteinschätzung von Behörden aufgrund ihrer Erfahrungen in Verhandlungsverfahren zu Problemen führen[17].

Die Probleme mit dieser Doppelfunktion könnten durch die Heranziehung eines bisher nicht am Streit beteiligten Dritten als Mittler verringert werden. Bei mittlergestützten Verhandlungen muss besonders beachtet werden, dass weder der Mittler noch allgemein die an der Aushandlung Beteiligten die Rechtsmacht haben, die Verwaltungsentscheidung zu ersetzen. Problematisch ist der Einbau eines neutralen Vermittlers in Verwaltungsverfahren, soweit damit die gesetzlich vorgesehene Verfahrenshoheit der Verwaltung beeinträchtigt wird. Das könnte der Fall sein, wenn der Mittler in förmlichen Verwaltungsverfahren z.B. die Verhandlungsleitung im Erörterungstermin übernähme. Es ist nämlich sehr zweifelhaft, ob die Verwaltungsverfahrensnormen die Beleihung eines neutralen Dritten mit den hoheitlichen Aufgaben zulassen, die das Gesetz für den Verhandlungsleiter vorsieht: Der Verhandlungsleiter muss gleichzeitig eine Grundlage für den Planfeststellungsbeschluss schaffen, falls keine Einigung zustande kommt. Doch scheint ein Einbau des Konfliktmittlers in den Erörterungstermin auch wenig sinnvoll, zum einen wegen des späten Zeitpunkts des Termins, zum andern, weil die Aufgabe, den Planfeststellungsbeschluss vorzubereiten, möglicherweise zu Rollenkonflikten führt, die sich auf die Glaubwürdigkeit des Mittlers auswirken können. Auch bei den bisherigen informellen oder formalisierten Ansätzen zur Konfliktmittlung wie in Münchehagen wurde die Integration in das Verwaltungsverfahren nicht versucht. Genauso sind die mittlergestützten Verhandlungsverfahren in den USA von dem dortigen "Erörterungstermin" abgekoppelt.

Einen Weg zur Erprobung mittlergestützter Verfahren zeigt das Gesetz zur Einführung der Umweltverträglichkeitsprüfung vom 12.2.1990 auf. Es verweist in § 5 ausdrücklich darauf, dass auch Dritte in dem Verfahren zur Erörterung des Untersuchungsrahmens herangezogen werden können; also schon in einem relativ frühen Stadium der Umweltverträglichkeitsprüfung. Ein solcher Dritter könnte ein Konfliktmittler sein. Die

---

[17] Vgl. Wiedmann, P. M. u.a. 1990, S. 117 und 119 für einen österreichischen Fall; s. dazu auch Ahrens, A. 1990, S. 51; Zieschank, R. 1991, S. 33; für eine andere Einschätzung aber Brohm, W. 1991, S. 1032 f.

Umweltverträglichkeitsprüfung greift aber selbst erst spät. Schon in früheren Stadien, so bei der nicht verfahrensrechtlich geregelten Standortwahl für Abfallentsorgungsanlagen, sollten Aushandlungsverfahren mit den Betroffenen einsetzen[18].

Schliesslich enthält der im Auftrag des Umweltbundesamtes erstellte "Professorenentwurf" eines Allgemeinen Teils eines Umweltgesetzbuches Möglichkeiten zum Einsatz von Konfliktmittlung. Ausgangspunkt ist das in § 6 geregelte Kooperationsprinzip. So können nach § 54 IV, der den Erörterungstermin im Bewilligungsverfahren regelt, die Länder vorsehen, dass die zuständige Behörde Vorbereitung und Durchführung einem unbeteiligten Dritten als Verfahrensmittler anvertrauen kann. In § 73 II des Entwurfes wird für nachträgliche Erhöhungen der Anforderungen an die Umweltverträglichkeit die Möglichkeit geregelt, dass Behörde und Verantwortlicher unter Mitwirkung Dritter konsensual ein Konzept zur Erzielung besserer Umweltverträglichkeit erarbeiten. Mit solchen Regelungen wären Verhandlungs- und Konfliktmittlungsverfahren ausdrücklich gesetzlich legitimiert[19].

6. DIE BETEILIGUNG AN VERHANDLUNGSVERFAHREN

Ein besonderes Problem ist die Auswahl derer, die an den Verhandlungen teilnehmen dürfen. Ausgangspunkt sind die Regeln über die Beteiligung im Verwaltungsverfahren[20]. An ihm sind der Antragsteller, der Adressat eines Verwaltungakts oder der Partner eines öffentlich-rechtlichen Vertrags immer beteiligt. Bei allen anderen differenziert das VwVfG danach, ob sie einen Rechtsanspruch auf Beteiligung haben[21]. Werden ihre Interessen durch den Ausgang des Verfahrens nur "berührt", haben sie einen Anspruch auf fehlerfreie Ermessensentscheidung über ihre Beteiligung[22]. Schliesslich gibt es eine dritte Gruppe der "nur" Einwendungsberechtigten mit dem Recht auf Teilnahme am Erörterungstermin[23]. Wenn das Ergebnis mittlerunterstützter Verhandlungen also im weiteren Verwaltungsver-

---

[18] Gassner, H./Siederer, W. 1990, S. 53.
[19] Kloepfer, M. u.a. 1990, S. 334 f.
[20] S. §13 VwVfG
[21] S. z.B. § 13 II VwVfG.
[22] § 13 II 1 VwVfG
[23] Vgl. § 73 IV VwVfG.

fahren Bestand haben soll, so müssen alle möglicherweise von § 13 II VwVfG erfassten Personen an den Verhandlungen teilnehmen. Ausserdem sollten alle staatlichen Stellen, die ein Interesse an oder gar ein Mitspracherecht bei der Entscheidung haben, beteiligt werden. So sind beispielsweise bei der Konfliktmittlung über Münchehagen auch die technischen Ämter oder das Umweltministerium dabei.

Der Kreis der Beteiligten im Verhandlungsverfahren kann und wird im Interesse der Verfahrenseffizienz aber über den Kreis der im Verwaltungsverfahren zu Beteiligenden hinausgehen. Um ihn zu bestimmen, muss nach den Zwecken der Beteiligung gefragt werden. Drei Punkte scheinen besonders wichtig: Die Beteiligung dient der Verbesserung der Informationsgrundlage für die zu fällende Entscheidung. Sie dient dem vorgezogenen Rechtsschutz; späteres Einlegen von Rechtsmitteln soll möglichst überflüssig gemacht werden. Schliesslich dient sie der Akzeptanzerhöhung. Daraus lassen sich Rückschlüsse auf den Kreis der Beteiligten ziehen. Während es für die Rechtsschutzfunktion ausreichen kann, diejenigen zu beteiligen, die in ihren rechtlich geschützten Interessen betroffen sind, verlangt Akzeptanzverbesserung, dass sinnvollerweise auch beteiligt wird, wer faktisch Widerstandspotential aktivieren kann. Soll die Informationsgrundlage für die Entscheidung verbessert werden, so müssen vielfältige Interessen, die von der Entscheidung betroffen sein könnten, ihre Positionen einbringen. Auch "sachverständige Interessen", z.B. aus Instituten, die Industrie oder Umweltverbänden nahestehen, können dafür hilfreich sein.

Die erwünschte Akzeptanzerhöhung durch Verhandlungen lässt sich aber nur erreichen, wenn die Beteiligten eine reelle Chance zur Wahrung und Durchsetzung ihrer Interessen haben. Haben sie den Eindruck, ihre Teilnahme diene nur dazu, nach aussen den "Tisch abzurunden", über den sie dann gezogen würden, so wird dies nicht zur Akzeptanz des Ergebnisses und langfristig statt dessen zur Verweigerung der Teilnahme an Verhandlungen führen[24]. Um dies zu verhindern, müssen alle Verhandlungsteilnehmer vergleichbare Verhandlungsmacht haben.

Eine wichtige Bedingung dafür ist der freie Zugang zu Informationen für die Verhandlungsteilnehmer, d.h. im weitesten Sinne die Sicherung von Transparenz. Dabei ist selbstverständlich der legitime Vertraulich-

---

[24] Zu den Bedenken von Umweltverbänden bei Verhandlungsverfahren s. auch Führ, M. 1990, 52.

keitsbedarf gegen die Vorteile der Transparenz abzuwägen. Besteht ein schutzwürdiges Interesse daran, Informationen nicht an die allgemeine Öffentlichkeit zu lassen, so wird Beteiligtentransparenz sich als ein Mittelweg zwischen Geheimnisschutz und Informationsgleichgewicht anbieten. Allerdings wird der Vertraulichkeitsschutz von Informationen in der deutschen Rechtsordnung relativ hochgehalten. In anderen Ländern wie den USA oder Schweden wird deutlich weniger Bedarf an "Geheimniskrämerei" anerkannt[25]. Ein Blick dorthin lässt vermuten, dass der Staat oder gar die privaten Unternehmen nicht unter etwas grösserer Transparenz von Verwaltungsvorgängen leiden oder gar zusammenbrechen müssen. Häufig scheint die Berufung auf Vertraulichkeitsbedarfe auch ein Schutzschild der Verwaltung gegenüber möglicher Kontrolle und Kritik zu sein. Ob die Umsetzung der Umweltinformationsrichtlinie der Europäischen Gemeinschaft insoweit eine Änderung mit sich bringt, scheint angesichts der dort vorgesehenen Ausnahmeregelungen ebenfalls eher zweifelhaft. Ohne Transparenz der Entscheidungsgrundlagen lässt sich chancengleiche Teilnahme am Verhandlungsverfahren jedenfalls nicht erreichen.

Für die Verfahrenschancengleichheit sollten ausserdem die Tausch- und Drohpotentiale der beteiligten Interessen gleichwertig sein. Aussicht auf Verhandlungserfolg hat in der Regel nur, wer etwas zu bieten hat, was die andere Seite zum Eingehen auf seine Interessen veranlasst. Damit werden nicht nur tatsächliche Widerstandspotentiale zu Tauschmitteln, sondern auch Rechtsansprüche und Rechtsschutzmöglichkeiten. Die Anerkennung der Tauschfähigkeit von Rechtspositionen stösst allerdings auf erhebliche rechtliche und rechtspolitische Ablehnung[26]. Ein wichtiger Einwand betrifft die ungleichmässige gesellschaftliche Verteilung von Tauschmacht. Sie kann in Tauschprozessen reproduziert und versteinert werden. Verfahrensmässig abgesicherte Tausch- und Drohmacht sollte deswegen für alle schutzbedürftigen Positionen verfügbar sein - auch wenn diese in der Rechtsordnung nicht mit subjektiven Rechten gekoppelt sind. Sie sollte nicht allein von dem Zufall abhängig sein, ob sich am jeweiligen Ort im Widerstand geübtes "Potential" befindet. Insbesondere objektiv-rechtliche Pflichten oder gar die Belange zukünftiger Generationen laufen Gefahr, bei Verhandlungen zu kurz zu kommen. Zwar ist ihre

---

[25] S. Gurlit, E. 1989.
[26] Dazu Winter, G. 1985.

Sicherung in der deutschen Verwaltungsrechtsordnung grundsätzlich Teil der Allgemeinwohlverpflichtung der Verwaltung, doch ist diese in das Verfahren mit so vielfältigen und sich zum Teil widersprechenden Aufgaben eingebunden, dass die "Auslagerung" auf andere Interessenwahrer zu ihrer Ergänzung sinnvoll erscheint. Wichtig kann deshalb die Beteiligung von altruistisch orientierten Verbänden wie z.B. den Naturschutzverbänden sein. Die Verhandlungschancen altruistischer Verbände und damit die Durchsetzungschancen solcher Allgemeininteressen könnten durch die Einräumung von Beteiligungsrechten im Verwaltungsverfahren und von Verbandsklagerechten erheblich gestärkt werden. Damit erhielten sie die notwendige Tausch- und Drohmacht. Auch unter diesem Aspekt sollte über Änderungen im bestehenden Rechtsschutzsystem diskutiert werden.

Bei der Lösung von Problemen im Zusammenhang mit der Beteiligung kann der Einsatz eines Verfahrensmittlers hilfreich sein. Mittler können die zerstrittenen Parteien vielleicht überhaupt erst an einen Tisch bringen - wie dies Mitarbeiter der Evangelischen Akademie Loccum im Fall Münchehagen taten. Eine wesentliche Aufgabe wird für sie in der Regel in der Ermittlung der relevanten Interessen liegen und in dem Versuch, sie zur Beteiligung zu bewegen. Bei dieser Aufgabe können sie die Verwaltung sinnvoll ergänzen - vor allem in Fällen, in denen diese schon so weit in die Entscheidung verstrickt ist, dass sie von einigen Betroffenen nicht mehr als neutral angesehen wird, sondern als Partei und als Gegner, den es zu bekämpfen gilt. Der Konfliktmittler kann gerade in solchen Fällen helfen, Verständigungsbarrieren zwischen den Beteiligten abzubauen. Ausserdem können Mittler den Abbau von Informationsdefiziten unterstützen und auf die Herstellung gleicher Verhandlungsmacht achten. Da die Verfahrensherrschaft der Verwaltung kein Selbstzweck ist, sondern nur ein Instrument zur Erzielung einer recht- und zweckmässigen Problemlösung, ist ihr Abbau normativ insoweit zu rechtfertigen, als dadurch die Chancen einer Konfliktlösung tendenziell verbessert werden.

7. INHALTLICHE ERFOLGSVORAUSSETZUNGEN FÜR VERHANDLUNGSVERFAHREN

Neben den verfahrensmässigen Sicherungen muss für angemessene inhaltliche Rahmensetzungen des Interessenausgleichs gesorgt werden. Ausgangspunkt für folgende Überlegungen soll eine Unterscheidung zwischen Interessen und Positionen sein[27]. Position ist das, was konkret durchgesetzt werden soll, z.B. den Bau einer Abfallverbrennungsanlage zu verhindern. Hinter dieser Position können ganz unterschiedliche Interessen liegen: beispielsweise Angst vor Wertminderung eines Grundstücks, Sorge um Dioxinbelastung in Nahrungsmitteln oder Muttermilch, Verhinderung einer auf Verbrennung und nicht auf Vermeidung setzenden Abfallpolitik ... Bei Verhandlungen soll nach Wegen gesucht werden, die es ermöglichen, bei Anerkennung und Wahrung der Interessen die Positionen zu verändern. Es muss also zunächst abgeklärt werden, wie weit Interessen (nicht Positionen) deckungsgleich sind. Weiter müssen alternative Positionen herausgearbeitet werden. Ziel darf nicht sein, ein Interesse einseitig zu Lasten anderer durchzusetzen. Vielmehr geht es darum, möglichst alle Interessen in einen Prozess der verbesserten Interessendurchsetzung zu integrieren. Es müssen win-win-Situationen vorliegen, d.h. jedes Interesse muss irgendwie gewinnen können. Win-win-Situationen sind allerdings beim Bau von Entsorgungsanlagen nur schwer zu erreichen, da zumindest die Betreiber und die für die Abfallentsorgung zuständigen Behörden einerseits, sowie die Anlagenanwohner andererseits Interessen haben, die sich kaum in Ausgleich bringen lassen[28].

Um Veränderungen in den Positionen überhaupt möglich zu machen, müssen Entscheidungsalternativen bestehen. Deshalb müssen Verhandlungslösungen in einem möglichst frühen Entscheidungsstadium versucht werden. In diesem Bereich kann der aktive Konfliktmittler viel Einfluss nehmen. Zwar sieht das deutsche Verwaltungsrecht vor, dass der Antragsteller in seinem Antrag die Modalitäten des Vorhabens selbst bestimmt. Formal scheint also wenig Spielraum für Alternativen zu bestehen. In der Praxis verhandeln aber in schwierigen Fällen Antragsteller und Verwaltung informell über Genehmigungsvoraussetzungen und Modifikationen. Diese Verhandlungen lassen sich für sonstige Beteiligte öffnen.

---

[27] Vgl. Fisher, R./Ury, W. 1983, S. 41 ff.
[28] Wiedmann, P. M. u.a. 1990, S. 90.

Doch nicht nur die informellen zweiseitigen Abklärungen reduzieren den Alternativenspielraum. Die Verwaltungspraxis neigt dazu, schwierige Entscheidungen in kleine Häppchen aufzuteilen und Stück für Stück abzuschichten. Diese Vorgehensweise ist in der Rechtsordnung angelegt. Beispielsweise lassen sich Standort- und Anlagengenehmigung trennen, gibt es Vorbescheid, Teilgenehmigung und Endentscheidung. Durch solche abgeschichteten Vorentscheidungen werden Zwangspunkte geschaffen, die bei oberflächlicher Betrachtung den verbleibenden Konfliktstoff einschränken. Wie weit empfehlen sich diese Strategien segmenthafter Entscheidungszersplitterung aber weiterhin? Sie verbauen schnell den Weg zu einem umfassenden Interessenclearing in einem Akt. Die Interessen der erst später am Verfahren Beteiligten fallen im Zeitpunkt der Schaffung von Zwangspunkten leicht unter den Tisch. Auch hier lässt sich auf die Erfahrungen mit den informellen Abklärungen zwischen Verwaltung und Antragsteller zurückgreifen. Sie sind meist keineswegs auf Teile des Vorhabens begrenzt, sondern umfassen es vollständig und erstrecken sich zum Teil noch auf andere Vorhaben.

Das Offenhalten von Entscheidungsalternativen hat auch den Sinn, Verbundlösungen und Kompensationen zu ermöglichen. Beide sind notwendig, wenn win-win-Situationen geschaffen werden sollen. So lassen sich vielleicht Nachteile ausgleichen, wenn unterschiedliche Vorhaben miteinander verkoppelt werden. In diesem Bereich lässt das US-amerikanische Recht wesentlich weitere Möglichkeiten zu als die deutsche Rechtsordnung. Das deutsche Verwaltungsrecht verbietet weitgehend die Koppelung von Entscheidungen, die nicht im sachlichen Zusammenhang zueinander stehen[29]. Dieses Koppelungsverbot soll verhindern, dass die Verwaltung ihre Macht missbraucht und Hoheitsakte "verkauft". Werden solche Risiken jedoch durch die verfahrensmässige Absicherung von Verhandlungen und durch den Einsatz von Konfliktmittlern verringert, so könnte über eine Lockerung des Koppelungsverbotes im Wege der Gesetzesauslegung aber auch durch Gesetzesänderung diskutiert werden.

Neben der Verkoppelung verschiedener Entscheidungen bieten sich Kompensationszahlungen als Mittel zur Herstellung eines angemessenen Interessenausgleichs an. Zum Teil sind diese schon von der Rechtsordnung vorgesehen wie in den Fällen der Schadensersatz- und Entschädi-

---

[29] S. dazu §§ 36 Abs. 3, 56 Abs. 1 Satz 2, Abs. 2 VwVfG.

gungsnormen. Zum Ausgleich kann der private Vorhabenträger[30] oder der Staat[31] verpflichtet sein. In einigen Fällen gewähren gesetzliche Regelungen auch dann Kompensationen, wenn der nachteilig Betroffene keinen Entschädigungsanspruch hat, Kompensationen aber sachgerecht erscheinen[32]. Kompensation bedeutet keineswegs nur Geldzahlung. Denkbar sind Ersatzmassnahmen[33], begünstigende Infrastrukturleistungen (Anschluss an das Nahverkehrsnetz), der Verzicht auf zukünftige Belastungen durch weitere Anlagen, Risikoversicherungen und vieles mehr. Es ist gerade die Funktion von Verhandlungen, gegebenenfalls mit Hilfe des Konfliktmittlers, nach geeigneten Formen des Ausgleichs für Nachteile zu suchen. Dabei sind Kompensationszahlungen grundsätzlich zulässig, soweit sie nicht gegen das Koppelungsverbot verstossen oder sittenwidrig sind. Bei Kompensation durch den Staat müssen allerdings die gesetzlichen Bindungen beachtet werden. So benötigt er nach dem Haushaltsrecht eine Ermächtigung zur Zahlung. Für Kompensationen privater Vorhabenträger gibt es keine besonderen gesetzlichen Beschränkungen.

Politisch sind Kompensationen allerdings umstritten. Es wird der Verdacht geäussert, die Aussicht auf Kompensationen stimuliere Widerstand, der andernfalls gar nicht aufgekommen wäre. Doch kann die Verwaltung immer auch einseitig entscheiden und muss sich nicht auf Verhandlungen über Kompensationen einlassen, die ihr ungerechtfertigt erscheinen. Andererseits werden Kompensationen zum Teil als Mittel zur Korrumpierung von Widerstandspotential angesehen. In diesen Fällen wird deutlich, dass Widerstand gegen eine Anlage von sehr unterschiedlichen Interessen geleitet sein kann, von denen einige durch Kompensationszahlungen ausgeglichen werden können, andere nicht. Politischen Protest erzeugen Fallkonstellationen wie im Bergkamen-Fall. Dort entstand der Eindruck, Widerstand im Namen des Allgemeinwohls werde durch individuelle "Schmiergeld"-Zahlungen abgekauft[34].

Kompensationen sind jedoch grundsätzlich auch dann möglich, wenn nicht-individuelle Interessen des Gemeinwohls und vor allem zukünftiger Generationen ausgeglichen werden sollen. So wurden für die Ansiedlung

---

[30] Z.B. § 14 Satz 2 BImSchG.
[31] Z.B. § 9 Abs. 9 FStrG.
[32] Z.B. § 8 Abs. 4 S. 2 AbfG, § 17 Abs. 4 FStrG, § 74 Abs. 2 Satz 3 VwVfG.
[33] Z.B. § 8 Abs. 2 NatSchG.
[34] S. etwa Frank, G. 1980, S. 290 ff.; andererseits aber BGHZ 79, S. 131 ff.

eines Daimler-Benz PKW-Werkes in Rastatt ökologische Ausgleichsmassnahmen in Form eines neu anzulegenden Naturschutzgebietes zugesagt. Die Verbände versprachen im Gegenzug, Rechtsmittel gegen die Unternehmensansiedlung nicht zu unterstützen[35]. Ein Verzicht auf Rechtsmittel erscheint zulässig, da auch von Anfang an darauf verzichtet werden könnte, Rechte überhaupt geltend zu machen. Bei Zahlung von hinreichenden Kompensationen entfällt bei den Rechts- bzw. Interessenträgern nach ihrer Ansicht die Beeinträchtigung, so dass sie keinen Grund zur Geltendmachung von Abwehransprüchen mehr sehen und deswegen darauf verzichten.

Kompensationen können ausserdem zu der umweltpolitisch erwünschten Internalisierung externer Kosten führen. Die Ausgleichspflicht für soziale Folgekosten eines Vorhabens schafft möglicherweise einen Anreiz, die Anlage so zu gestalten, dass diese Kosten erst gar nicht entstehen. Dafür müssen die Kompensationen aber vom Vorhabenträger finanziert werden und nicht - wie im Falle Rastatt - vom Staat.

8. DIE LETZTVERANTWORTUNG DER VERWALTUNG UND DIE UMSETZUNG DES KONSENSES

Die Umsetzung des Verhandlungsergebnisses findet in dem Spannungsfeld zwischen Letztverantwortung der Verwaltung und Vertrauen der Beteiligten auf Einhaltung und Durchsetzung statt. Die verfassungsrechtlich gebotene Verantwortung der Verwaltung für hoheitliche Entscheidungen verlangt, dass sie den gefundenen Konsens auf seine Recht- und Zweckmässigkeit hin überprüft. Diese Entscheidungsverantwortung darf auf niemanden sonst - auch nicht auf den Konfliktmittler - übertragen werden.

Die Fähigkeit der Verwaltung zur einseitig-hoheitlichen Entscheidung verschafft ihr in den Verhandlungen im übrigen Macht, da sie mit einer einseitigen Entscheidung "drohen" kann. Diese Macht kann sie einsetzen, um auf ein Ergebnis hinzuwirken, das sich ohne Bedenken in Hoheitsakte umsetzen lässt.

Das Vertrauen der Beteiligten kann durch faktische Vorausbindungen der Verwaltung geschützt werden. Vorausbindungen des Planungsverhaltens der Verwaltung sind dann zulässig, wenn sie sachlich gerechtfertigt

---

[35] Dazu Benz, A. 1990, S. 45 ff.

sind, unter Wahrung der (planungs-)rechtlichen Zuständigkeitsordnung getroffen werden und inhaltlich nicht beanstandet werden können[36]. Der Einsatz eines Mittlers erhöht die Wahrscheinlichkeit, dass diese Voraussetzungen erfüllt sind, aber er garantiert sie nicht. Deswegen dürfen diese für das bisherige informelle Verfahren entwickelten Kriterien bei mittlergestützten Verhandlungsverfahren nicht aufgegeben werden. Auch die Möglichkeiten zu faktischen Bindungen ändern nichts an der Pflicht der Verwaltung, das Ergebnis der Verhandlungen zu überprüfen. Erst wenn sie es für recht- und zweckmässig hält, darf sie sich faktisch binden.

Verhandlungen können weiter durch den Abschluss von öffentlich-rechtlichen Verträgen beendet werden. Ausserdem gibt es Verhandlungsergebnisse, vor allem Kompensationen, die sich unmittelbar zwischen Antragsteller und belasteten Dritten privatvertraglich vereinbaren lassen.

Das Risiko, dass gegen den Konsens neue Oppositionen entstehen oder Splittergruppen (vor allem von Bürgerinitiativen) den Konsens nicht mittragen, besteht allerdings auch weiterhin. Um es zu verringern, bieten sich Öffentlichkeitsarbeit und Transparenz bei den Verhandlungen an[37]. Ausserdem werden die tatsächlichen und rechtlichen Durchsetzungschancen des Verhandlungsergebnisses wohl erhöht sein, wenn die Verhandlungen zu einem von vielen (wenn auch nicht von allen) weitgehend als fair akzeptierten Ergebnis führen.

9. SCHLUSSBEMERKUNG

Verhandlungsverfahren sind kein Allheilmittel. Möglicherweise können sie bisherige Verfahren ergänzen und durch Kooperation mit den Betroffenen zu angemessenen Problemlösungen führen. Sie sind vielleicht ein Weg, um die Alles-Oder-Nichts-Positionen zu überwinden, die in manchen Entscheidungsprozessen überwiegen und die späteren Blockaden der Entscheidungsdurchsetzung provozieren. Ergebnis von Verhandlungen kann übrigens auch sein, dass ein Vorhaben nicht verwirklicht wird. Es darf nicht vergessen werden, dass auch die Antragsablehnung eine Möglichkeit ist, für die sich die Verwaltung entscheiden kann - vorausgesetzt, dies ist rechtlich zulässig. Bei der Suche nach Konsens sollte vermieden

---

[36] Vgl. BVerwGE 45, S. 309, 320 ff. - Flachglas.
[37] Wiedmann, P. M. u.a. 1990, S. 74 f.

werden, diejenigen auszusondern, die sich nicht in den Konsens einbinden lassen wollen. Die Gesellschaft hat Mechanismen, um auch ohne Konsens zu arbeiten - sie kennt keinen Konsenszwang. Dabei darf sie nicht diejenigen negativ sanktionieren, die sich nicht in einen von anderen erzielten Konsens einbezogen wähnen. Konsens kann in einer Gesellschaft nur dann ein erstrebenswertes Ziel sein, wenn diese Gesellschaft zugleich den Konflikt akzeptiert: als produktives Durchgangsstadium zur Interessenbewältigung.

LITERATURVERZEICHNIS

A. Ahrens, *Beteiligung bei der Technologie-Erprobung*, Informationsdienst Umweltrecht 1990, S. 49 ff.

A. Benz, *Verhandlungen ohne Vermittlung*, Informationsdienst Umweltrecht 1990, S. 45 ff.

E. Blankenburg/K. Lenk(Hrsg.), *Organisation und Recht*, Opladen 1982.

E. Bohne, *Informales Verwaltungshandeln im Gesetzesvollzug*, in: E. Blankenburg/K. Lenk (Hrsg.) 1982, S. 20 ff.

W. Brohm, *Beschleunigung der Verwaltungsverfahren - Straffung oder konsensuales Verwaltungshandeln*, Neue Zeitschrift für Verwaltungsrecht 1991, S. 1025 ff.

R. Fisher/W. Ury, *Getting to YES, Negotiating Agreement without Giving*, 1983.

G. Frank, *Die Kommerzialisierung von Grundrechtspositionen des Bürgerprotestes*, Publizistik 1980, S. 290 ff.

M. Führ, *Mitbestimmungsmodell für Umweltentscheidungen?*, Informationsdienst Umweltrecht 1990, S. 52.

R. Funke, *Konfliktbewältigung aus Anlass von Genehmigungsverfahren*, in: W. Hoffmann-Riem/E. Schmidt-Assmann (Hrsg.) 1990 b, S. 209 ff.

J. Gardner, *Massachusetts Siting Act and Experience to Date*, in: W. Hoffmann-Riem/E. Schmidt-Assmann (Hrsg.) 1990 a, S. 205 ff.

H. Gassner/W. Soederer, *Einstiegschance nur über konsensuales Standortauswahlverfahren*, Informationsdienst Umweltrecht 1990, S. 53.

E. Gurlit, *Die Verwaltungsöffentlichkeit im Umweltrecht*, 1989.

W. Hoffmann-Riem, *Konfliktmittler in Verwaltungsverfahren*, 1989.

W. Hoffmann-Riem/E. Schmidt-Assmann (Hrsg.), *Konfliktbewältigung durch Verhandlungen*, Bd. 1: Informelle und mittlerunterstützte Verhandlungen in Verwaltungsverfahren, 1990 (1990 a).

W. Hoffmann-Riem/E. Schmidt-Assmann (Hrsg.), *Konfliktbewältigung durch Verhandlungen*, Bd. 2: Konfliktmittlung in Verwaltungsverfahren, 1990 (1990 b).

B. Holznagel, *Der Einsatz von Konfliktmittlern im amerikanischen Umweltrecht*, Die Verwaltung 1989, S. 421 ff.

B. Holznagel, *Konfliktlösung durch Verhandlungen*, 1990.

M. Kloepfer/E. Rehbinder/E. Schmidt-Assmann, *Umweltgesetzbuch - Allgemeiner Teil*, Forschungsbericht im Auftrag des Umweltbundesamtes, 1991.

Mitteilungen des Wissenschaftszentrums Berlin, *Forschungsschwerpunkt Technik - Arbeit - Umwelt, Mediation in der Umweltpolitik - Das Konzept zur Abfallwirtschaft im Kreis Neuss*, September 1991, S. 5 ff.

F. Scharpf, *Die politischen Kosten des Rechtsstaats. Eine vergleichende Studie der deutschen und amerikanischen Verwaltungskontrollen*, 1970.

M. Striegnitz, *Mediation: Lösung von Umweltkonflikten durch Vermittlung - Praxisbericht zur Anwendung in der Kontroverse um die Sonderabfalldeponie Münchehagen -*, Zeitschrift für angewandte Umweltforschung 1990, S. 51 ff.

M. Striegnitz, *Consensual Approaches to Solving Clean-Up Issues, case example presented to the international workshop Innovative Approaches to Siting*, Montebello, Canada, April 27-30, 1991, Manuskript.

M. Striegnitz, *Rückblick auf die Arbeit des Münchehagen-Ausschusses seit November 1990*, Vorlage zu TOP 4 der 7. Sitzung des Münchehagen-Ausschusses - Plenum - am 14. Januar 1992

P.M. Wiedemann/S. Femers/L. Hennen, *Bürgerbeteiligung bei entsorgungswirtschaftlichen Vorhaben - Analyse und Bewertung von Konflikten und Konfliktlösungsstrategien*, Arbeit zur Risiko-Kommunikation, Heft 18, Jülich, November 1990.

G. Winter, *Bartering Rationality in Regulation*, 19 Law and Society Review 1985, S. 219.

R. Zieschank, *Mediationsverfahren als Gegenstand sozialwissenschaftlicher Umweltforschung*, Zeitschrift für Umweltrecht 1991, S. 27 ff.

INNOVATIVE KONFLIKTREGELUNG IN DER UMWELTPOLITIK DURCH MEDIATION: ANREGUNGEN AUS DEM AUSLAND FÜR DIE BUNDESREPUBLIK DEUTSCHLAND

Helmut Weidner

1. MEDIATIONSVERFAHREN IM AUSLAND, INSBESONDERE IN DEN USA

In allen demokratischen Industriegesellschaften nehmen die Umweltkonflikte zu, ihre Regelung gehört inzwischen zum Alltagsgeschäft der Umweltpolitik. Einige Bereiche haben sich jedoch in den letzten Jahren als besonders resistent gegen staatliche Steuerungsversuche mit dem konventionellen Politikinstrumentarium erwiesen. Das gilt vor allem für grosstechnische Entwicklungsvorhaben, von deren Realisierung unabsehbare Umwelt- und Gesundheitsgefährdungen befürchtet werden. Da diese Einrichtungen und Infrastrukturmassnahmen häufig eine Schlüsselfunktion für die Industriegesellschaft haben (etwa Flughäfen, Autobahnen, Kraftwerke, Mülldeponien und -verbrennungsanlagen), führen ökologisch motivierte Proteste nahezu regelmässig zu Grosskonflikten, in die eine Vielzahl staatlicher, kommunaler, wirtschaftlicher und umweltengagierter Akteure und Institutionen verwickelt ist. Ihre unterschiedlichen Ziele und Interessen resultieren oftmals in Handlungsblockaden und schier unüberwindlich scheinenden Kommunikationsbarrieren. Angesichts der Konfliktdimensionen und ihrer politischen Kosten werden sachlich notwendige Entscheidungen nicht gefällt, aufgeschoben, unangemessen verändert oder den Gerichten überlassen. Gerichtsentscheidungen sind mit hohem zeitlichen und finanziellen Aufwand für alle Beteiligten, mit späteren Vollzugsdefiziten und nachhaltiger Verbitterung der unterelegenen Gruppen verbunden. Die Sicherstellung einer ökologischen und ökonomischen Daseinsvorsorge in sozialverträglicher Weise ist prominente Staatsaufgabe, doch offensichtlich sind staatliche Institutionen hierzu immer weniger in der Lage. Als Ursache für dieses Dilemma wird von Sozial- und Wirtschaftswissenschaftlern überwiegend das konventionelle staatliche Steuerungsinstrumentarium ausgemacht, das vorzugsweise mit unter frühindustriellen Bedingungen entwickelten polizeirechtlichen Methoden (Ge- und Verboten) arbeitet und in einer Allzuständigkeitsvorstellung des Staates wurzelt, die in modernen komplexen Gesellschaften etliche Kritiker an bürokratische Allmachtsphantasien gemahnt. Des weiteren wird auf den immensen Verlust an Vertrauen in den Willen und die Fähigkeit von Politik und Verwaltung zu ökologiegerechten Massnahmen verwiesen. Vertrauen ist offensichtlich in der Umweltpolitik eine sehr knappe, von Politik und Verwaltung sehr unpfleglich behandelte und deshalb derzeit kaum oder gar nicht nachwachsende Ressource geworden. Wieder einmal waren es im internationalen Vergleich die umweltpolitisch wohl innovativsten - im Vollzug hingegen weniger leistungsfähigen - USA[1], wo schon vor geraumer Zeit (in den siebziger Jahren) neuartige Konfliktregelungsverfahren entwickelt und praktiziert worden sind, um eine neue Vertrauensbasis zwischen Politik, Verwaltung, Wirtschaft und Umweltbewegung zu schaffen und unproduktive Konflikte zu vermeiden. Sie firmieren dort unter der Bezeichnung "alternative Streitbeilegungsverfahren" (Alternative Disputes Resolution; kurz: ADR). Hierunter werden nicht-förmliche Verfahren verstanden, die konventionelle (administrative, legislative und judikative) Entscheidungsverfahren ergänzen, nicht aber ersetzen. Den zahlreichen Formen alternativer Verfahren ist eines gemein: Sie sollen Streitigkeiten auf dem Verhandlungswege beilegen. Die Teilnahme an ihnen ist freiwillig. Aufgehoben ist die hierarchische Struktur konventioneller Verfahren: Verwaltungsvertreter etwa verfügen hierbei nicht über herausgehobene Steuerungs- und Entscheidungskompetenzen, haben jedoch aufgrund ihrer formalen Kompetenzen eine zentrale Rolle inne, so dass sie als primus inter pares bezeichnet werden können. Im Unterschied zu einseitig hoheitlichen oder gerichtlichen Entscheidungen werden bei Verhandlungslösungen konsensuale Lösungen angestrebt; ein unnötiger Verschleiss noch vorhandener Gemeinsamkeiten zwischen den Streitparteien soll vermieden werden. Die Beteiligten geben sich ihre Verfahrensregeln selbst. Die Beschlüsse binden durch eine Art Selbstverpflichtung der Beteiligten, es werden aber auch vertragsrechtliche Fixierungen praktiziert.

---

1 Vgl. zu den USA L. Susskind und J. Cruikshank, *Breaking the Impasse*. Consensual Approaches to Resolving Public Disputes, New York 1987.

Alternative Streitbeilegungsverfahren gibt es auf allen umweltpolitisch relevanten Ebenen: In *Politikdialogen* werden politische Strategien oder Verhaltensregeln für Wirtschaftsbranchen ausgehandelt; aus *Normdialogen* gehen öffentlich-rechtlich bindende Regelungen (z. B. Umweltstandards) hervor; *Informationsaustauschverfahren* dienen der Herstellung einer gemeinsamen und konsentierten Wissensbasis. Die Mehrzahl aller Verfahren findet jedoch in den USA, Kanada, Japan wie auch in Europa zu konkreten Planungs- und Bauvorhaben statt.

Im weiten Spektrum von unterschiedlichen Organisationsformen alternativer Streitregelungsverfahren (siehe Kasten: Formen alternativer Streitbeilegungsverfahren) hat sich eine Form als besonders erfolgreich herauskristallisiert: das *Mediationsverfahren* (oder Konfliktvermittlerverfahren, auch -mittlerverfahren). Im folgenden wird der Terminus Mediation beibehalten; er hat sich offensichtlich gegen deutschsprachige Umschreibungen durchgesetzt.

Formen alternativer Streitbeilegungsverfahren

1. Verhandlung ohne Unterstützung
2. Unterstützter Politikdialog
3. Gemeinsame Problemlösungsverhandlungen
4. Passive oder aktive Mediation
5. Nicht bindende Schlichtungs- oder Schiedsspruchverfahren
6. Bindende Schlichtungs- oder Schiedsspruchverfahren
7. Richterliche Entscheidung

Mediationsverfahren folgen dem Grundmuster Konfliktregelung durch Verhandlungslösungen[2]. In den Verhandlungen sollen Streitigkeiten zwischen zwei oder mehreren Parteien mit Hilfe einer neutralen, vermittelnden Person (Mediator) beigelegt werden. Der Mediator darf hierbei keine eigenen Interessen verfolgen; er soll für alle Lösungen offen sein, die von den Beteiligten gemeinsam erkundet und entwickelt wurden. Er hat, anders als ein Schiedsmann oder Schlichter, keine Autorität, den Streitenden ohne deren gemeinsames Einverständnis eine Konfliktlösung aufzu-

---

2 So der Titel von zwei einschlägigen Sammelbänden, hrsg. von W. Hoffmann-Riem und E. Schmidt-Assmann (Baden-Baden 1990). Vgl. auch den Beitrag von Hoffmann-Riem in diesem Band.

zwingen; er macht in aller Regel auch keinen eigenproduzierten Lösungsvorschlag. Seine Hauptaufgabe liegt in der Gestaltung eines fairen Verfahrens, das eine für alle am Konflikt beteiligten Personen und Institutionen akzeptable und tragfähige Problemlösung ermöglicht, wobei der Mediator bestrebt sein soll, möglichst alle für den Konflikt relevanten Gruppen, besonders artikulationsschwache und solche, die in förmlichen Verfahren keine oder nur schwache Beteiligungsrechte haben, in das Verfahren einzubeziehen.

Das Verfahren basiert auf dem freien Gebrauch der Vernunft, verbunden mit der Hoffnung auf sachlich vernünftige, zumindest kompromissfähige Ergebnisse. Es lässt Konflikte zu, allerdings nur in einer Form, die nicht dialogzerstörend wirkt. Im Grunde ist es ein Verfahren, in dem unter den Beteiligten Konsens über den Umgang mit Konflikten sowie eine Hoffnung auf Kompromisse in der Sache besteht. Der Mediator wirkt als Hüter dieser Idee.

Mediationsverfahren zur Regelung von Umweltkonflikten sind vermutlich in systematischer Weise zuerst in Japan[3] eingesetzt worden, wo die konsensorientierte politische Kultur generell versöhnliche Streitbeilegungsverfahren unterstützt. Es gibt kaum ein grösseres umweltrelevantes Vorhaben, in dem nicht Verhandlungslösungen angestrebt werden. Ihre grosse Bedeutung für die relativ erfolgreiche japanische Umweltpolitik zeigt sich auch darin, dass es dort gegenwärtig über 35'000 Umweltschutzvereinbarungen zwischen Firmen und Kommunen sowie Bürgergruppen gibt, in denen für den Einzelfall massgeschneiderte Umweltschutzmassnahmen festgelegt werden. Darüber hinaus wurde aufgrund der ausserordentlich heftigen Umweltkonflikte in den sechziger Jahren bereits in Japans Umweltbasisgesetz von 1967 die Grundlage zu spezialgesetzlichen Regelungen für aussergerichtliche Streitregelungsverfahren gelegt. Darin wird die Regierung verpflichtet, Mediations-, Schlichtungs- und Schiedsverfahren einzurichten. Im Jahr 1970 trat, als ein erster Schritt, das Gesetz zur Beilegung von Streitigkeiten in Zusammenhang mit Umweltschäden in Kraft. Insgesamt werden die Verfahren zur Streitbeilegung hinsichtlich ihrer Effekte positiv bewertet. Sie gelten als flexibel und bürgernah. Ausgangspunkt der Karriere des Mediationsverfahrens als ein nunmehr auch in europäischen Ländern vieldiskutiertes Umwelt-

---

[3] Vgl. zum Beispielfall Japan die einschlägigen Beiträge in S. Tsuru und H. Weidner (Hg.), *Environmental Policy in Japan*, Berlin 1989.

politikinstrument sind dagegen die USA. Hier wurde es erstmals 1973 auf Betreiben der Wissenschaftler Gerald W. Cormick und Jane E. McCarthy zur Regelung der heissumstrittenen Planung von Flutsicherungsmassnahmen am Snoqalmie River im Staate Washington angewendet - mit so durchschlagendem Erfolg, dass diesem Pionierverfahren zahlreiche weitere folgten. Inzwischen wird in den USA gar von einem Mediationsboom gesprochen. Damit verbunden ging eine Professionalisierung der Mediatortätigkeit einher; in nahezu allen US-Bundesstaaten wurden private und halbstaatliche Mediationsinstitute gegründet, die Mediatoren ausbilden sowie ihre Dienste bei Umweltkonflikten anbieten. Mehrere Fachzeitschriften (z. B. Negotiation Journal) und Informationsdienste (z. B. Consensus, Resolve) widmen sich überwiegend alternativen Konfliktregelungsverfahren.

Eine beträchtliche Schar von Befürwortern und Unterstützern von Mediationsverfahren - nahezu alle grossen Umweltorganisationen und Stiftungen (etwa die Rockefeller-, Ford-, Hewlett-Foundation), viele Regierungsinstitutionen, Sozialwissenschaftler und Privatunternehmen gehören dazu - hebt besonders die Vorteile gegenüber konventionellen Politikinstrumenten hervor: Sie führten zu faireren, effektiveren, effizienteren, flexibleren, schnelleren und für alle Konfliktparteien zufriedenstellenderen Ergebnissen. Anders als bei Gerichtsverfahren und ihren Gewinner-Verlierer-Lösungen würden Jeder-gewinnt-Lösungen[4] ermöglicht. Die bislang umfassendste empirische Untersuchung im Umweltbereich von Gail Bingham zeigt tatsächlich eine beeindruckend positive Bilanz auf: In 78 Prozent von 132 untersuchten grossen Streitfällen wurde ein Konsens von zuvor zutiefst zerstrittenen Gruppen erreicht; ein Grossteil dieser Gentlemen's Agreements wurde später auch realisiert. Gleichwohl gibt es kritische Stimmen. In eher fundamentalistischer Weise weisen einige von ihnen darauf hin, dass es in Umweltfragen um grundsätzliche, prinzipiell nicht verhandlungs- und kompromissfähige Werte gehe. Andere zeigen anhand von Einzelfällen Schwachstellen auf, so etwa den teilweise grossen Zeitbedarf zur Erzielung eines breiten Konsenses oder die erhebliche Benachteiligung von Umweltgruppen gegenüber den in taktischem Verhandlungsverhalten geschulten und erfahrenen Behörden- und Unternehmensvertretern. Es wird auch auf die mit den Professionalisierungsten-

---

4 G. Bingham, *Resolving Environmental Disputes*. A Decade of Experience, Washington, D.C. 1986.

denzen verbundenen ökonomischen Eigeninteressen von Mediatoren und Mediationsinstituten verwiesen, was zu einer einseitig-positiven Berichterstattung über die Verfahren führe, um die Nachfrage zu stimulieren. Diese Probleme werden aber in der Wissenschaft durch entsprechende Unterstützungsmassnahmen und infolge von sozialem Lernen für heilbar gehalten, und manch' ein Wertkonflikt[5] hat sich im Dialog tatsächlich als ein verhandlungsfähiger Interessenkonflikt erwiesen. Die Befürworter von Mediationsverfahren überwiegen jedenfalls in den USA ganz eindeutig.

Die Praxis scheint sich ohnehin wenig um theoretische Streitigkeiten zu scheren: Die Anwendung von Mediationsverfahren steigt in den USA stetig, und in den europäischen Ländern wächst seit einigen Jahren das Interesse hieran. Einige wenige solcher Verfahren hat es in Europa bereits gegeben. Damit ist hier im Jahr 1992 - mit rund zwanzigjähriger Verspätung - in Sachen Mediation von Umweltkonflikten in etwa der praktische Stand der USA von 1973 erreicht worden. In Österreich, der Schweiz und in den Niederlanden, also Ländern mit einer partizipativen[6] politischen Kultur, werden besonders bei Konflikten über Standorte und Techniken zur Abfallbeseitigung Mediationsverfahren eingesetzt. In der vergleichsweise staatsfixierten und formalrechtlich ausgerichteten Bundesrepublik Deutschland gibt es bislang nur zwei bedeutende Mediationsverfahren im Umweltbereich. Beide haben mit Müllproblemen zu tun und werden von der interdisziplinären (Politikwissenschaft, Psychologie, Soziologie, Ingenieurswissenschaft) Projektgruppe Mediationsverfahren im Umweltschutz des Wissenschaftszentrums Berlin für Sozialforschung (WZB), Abteilung Normbildung und Umwelt, mit finanzieller Unterstützung des Bundesministeriums für Forschung und Technologie untersucht. Sie stehen im Zentrum der folgenden Ausführungen.

---

[5] Zum Stand der Mediationspraxis in den USA liegt eine schier unübersehbare Fülle von Publikationen vor. Einen Überblick geben aus befürwortender Sicht L. S. Bacow und M. Wheeler, *Environmental Dispute Resolution*, New York 1984; L. Susskind und J. Cruikshank, *Breaking the Impasse*, New York 1987; G. Bingham, *Resolving Environmental Disputes*, Washington, D.C. 1986; aus eher ablehnender Sicht: J. Amy, *The Politics of Environmental Mediation*, New York 1987.

[6] Vgl. für die Schweiz die Beiträge von M. Rey und P. Knoepfel in diesem Band sowie P. Knoepfel und M. Rey, *Konfliktminderung durch Verhandlung: Das Beispiel des Verfahrens zur Suche eines Standorts für eine Sondermülldeponie in der Suisse Romande*, in: W. Hoffmann-Riem und E. Schmidt-Assmann, a.a.O., Bd. II, S. 257-286.

2. MEDIATIONSVERFAHREN IN DER BUNDESREPUBLIK DEUTSCHLAND

Seit mehr als zwanzig Jahren wird eine systematische (rechtlich-institutionell ausdifferenzierte) Umweltpolitik in der Bundesrepublik Deutschland betrieben. Die Bilanz fällt heute insgesamt, trotz unbestrittener Erfolge in Einzelbereichen, ernüchternd aus[7]. Der im internationalen Vergleich sehr grosse Finanzaufwand könnte, so ist seit Jahren aus Wissenschafts- und Wirtschaftskreisen zu hören, mit flexibleren, marktwirtschaftlichen Instrumenten effizienter eingesetzt werden. Einer der führenden deutschen Umweltökonomie-Experten, Professor Karl-Heinrich Hansmeyer, attestiert Politik und Verwaltung, sie sehen ihr umweltpolitisches Heil überwiegend in einer Perfektionierung ordnungsrechtlicher Eingriffe. Denselben Sachverhalt formuliert der Ministerialbeamte Professor Ernst-Hasso Ritter noch drastischer: Die ordnungsrechtliche Umweltpolitik mit der Pickelhaube sei an ihren Grenzen angelangt, und der Umweltpolitologe Professor Martin Jänicke spricht gar von einem Staatsversagen im Umweltschutz. Die umweltpolitische Programmatik der Bundesregierung steht der Anwendung flexibler, kooperativer Regelungsformen im Prinzip nicht entgegen. So nennt sie neben dem Vorsorge- und Verursacherprinzip ausdrücklich das Kooperationsprinzip als Leitziel staatlichen Handelns. Doch nach wie vor - nahezu unberührt von Regierungswechseln - atmen umweltpolitische Regelungen den Geist eines bürokratisch-hierarchischen Staatsverständnisses.

Der staatliche "Regelungswahn" lässt für den Vollzug verantwortliche Institutionen immer häufiger und heftiger gegen ein hierdurch programmiertes Vollzugsdefizit im Umweltschutz protestieren. Vor einiger Zeit hat beispielsweise der Sonderausschuss Umweltschutz des Städtetages Nordrhein-Westfalen eine Resolution gebilligt, in der protestiert wird gegen eine Gesetzgebungs- und Verordnungspraxis, die noch immer versucht, den wachsenden Problemen des Umweltschutzes fast ausschliesslich mit immer mehr immer schwerer vollziehbaren ordnungsrechtlichen Vorschriften zu begegnen, an deren effektive Umsetzbarkeit auch die gesetzgebenden Organe selbst längst nicht mehr glauben. Abgelehnt wird

---

[7] Vgl. H. Weidner, *Umweltpolitik - Auf altem Weg zu einer internationalen Spitzenstellung*, in W. Süss (Hrsg.), Die Bundesrepublik in den achtziger Jahren, Opladen 1991, S. 137-152.

insbesondere eine symbolische Umweltrechtspolitik, die der Öffentlichkeit wider besseres Wissen den Eindruck vermitteln soll, dass die Belastung der Umwelt durch ein ständig weiter ausgebautes, von den Ordnungsbehörden zu vollziehendes Umweltordnungsrecht wirksam kontrolliert werden kann. Die Resolutionsverfasser erklären überdies offen, dass sie sich zu einer wirksamen und flächendeckenden Umsetzung der ihnen anvertrauten Umweltgesetze und Verordnungen nicht in der Lage sehen. Das Umweltrecht müsse aufhören, dem Bürger Anforderungen vorzuspiegeln, die in der Praxis nicht umsetzbar sind[8]. Auf der dezentralen Verwaltungsebene, wo Umweltpolitik vollzogen wird, ist ausserdem eine zunehmende Experimentierfreude an neuen Verfahrensformen feststellbar. Hier kommt, neben innovationsförderlichem Problemdruck, der Umstand zum Tragen, dass ein neuer, effektorientierter Typ von Umweltadministratoren in den Landes- und Kommunalverwaltungen Fuss fasst, der sich auch nicht vor einer engeren Kooperation mit Umweltgruppen scheut. Bislang wirkt zwar noch das über Jahre gewachsene gegenseitige Misstrauen nach - Umweltgruppen fürchten, über den Tisch gezogen zu werden; Unternehmer und Beamte bezweifeln die Dialog- und Kompromissfähigkeit von Umweltorganisationen -, doch gibt es bereits etliche Fälle konsensorientierten Umweltverhandelns im Schatten formaler Verfahren, in denen auf juristische und politische Konfliktrituale, auf Diskriminierungen und Manipulationstechniken weitgehend verzichtet wird.

Umweltbezogene Entscheidungsverfahren, die in ihrer Grundstruktur eher auf Kompromiss als auf Konflikt angelegt sind, wo es unter Anerkennung einer möglichen Vielfalt gleichberechtigter Interessen, Problemanalysen und -lösungsstrategien darum geht, im fairen Dialog einen gangbaren Weg aufzuzeigen, der allen Sichtweisen möglichst weitgehend gerecht wird, finden gegenwärtig in nahezu allen Umweltbereichen statt; Abfall(entsorgungs)probleme machen die Mehrzahl der Fälle aus.

Um nur einige Beispiele zu nennen, bei denen neue Formen der Konfliktregelung versucht werden: Standortsuche für eine Siedlungsabfalldeponie im Raum Hildesheim und für eine Sondermülldeponie im Regierungsbezirk Arnsberg; Gefährdungsabschätzung, Sicherung und Sanierung eines bewohnten Altlastgebietes in Wuppertal, Essen und Hamburg;

---

[8] Die Resolution wurde am 7. Juni 1991 auf einer Sitzung in Köln gebilligt. Vgl. *Informationsdienst Umweltrecht* (IUR), Nr. 4/1991, S. 219.

Absicherung und Sanierung der Mülldeponie Vorketzin (Brandenburg); Sanierung einer Schlammdeponie in Bielefeld; Änderung einer Müllverbrennungsanlage in Bielefeld-Herford; Einrichtung eines Verkehrsforums zur Erarbeitung eines langfristigen Verkehrsleitbildes für Heidelberg; Entwicklung eines Sonderabfallkonzeptes für Niedersachsen; Einrichtung eines Arbeitskreises Abfallwirtschaft im Landkreis Osnabrück; Planung einer Hafenschlickdeponie in Hamburg; Sanierung von umweltbelastenden Quellen und Einrichtung von Umweltschutzanlagen in Unternehmen (Hamburg, Seelze bei Hannover); Prüfung der Umweltverträglichkeit der Produktion eines Pestizides in der Firma Hoechst und ein Diskurs zur Technikfolgenabschätzung des Anbaus von Kulturpflanzen mit gentechnisch erzeugter Herbizidresistenz[9].

In den genannten Fällen, die im Zusammenhang mit Raumordnungs-, Umweltverträglichkeitsprüfungs-, Planfeststellungs-, Genehmigungs- und sonstigen förmlichen Verfahren stehen, finden Gespräche in Arbeitsgruppen statt, werden Moderatoren, besondere Beauftragte oder Beratungsbüros mit der Aufgabe der Information und Kompromissfindung betraut.

Richtige Mediationsverfahren, in denen neutrale Vermittler (Mediatoren) einen problemlösungsbezogenen Dialog zwischen vielen Konfliktparteien in einer Weise managen, die auch vor den in den USA entwickelten Standards Bestand haben und wo es um sachlich und politisch-gesellschaftlich grossdimensionierte Konfliktfälle geht, gibt es in der Bundesrepublik Deutschland nur zwei: die Mediationsverfahren in Münchehagen (Niedersachsen) und im Kreis Neuss (Nordrhein-Westfalen). Beide haben mit Abfallproblemen zu tun, beide werden vom interdisziplinären Forschungsteam Mediationsverfahren[10] des Wissenschaftszentrums Berlin für Sozialforschung (WZB) untersucht.

---

[9] Diese und weitere Fälle verhandlungsorientierter Verfahren zu Umweltkonflikten werden im Rahmen des Mediationsprojektes des Wissenschaftszentrums Berlin für Sozialforschung (WZB) dokumentiert und ausgewertet. Ein allgemeiner Überblick zum Forschungsprogramm findet sich in W. van den Daele, *Zum Forschungsprogramm der Abteilung »Normbildung und Umwelt«*, Wissenschaftszentrum Berlin für Sozialforschung, FS II 91-301, Berlin 1991.

[10] Vgl. H.-J. Fietkau und H. Weidner, *Mediationsverfahren in der Umweltpolitik. Erfahrungen in der Bundesrepublik Deutschland*, in: Aus Politik und Zeitgeschichte, B 39-40/1992 (Beilage zur Wochenzeitung Das Parlament), S. 24-34.

2.1. Mediationsverfahren in Münchehagen

Anlass für die Einrichtung des Mediationsverfahrens in Münchehagen waren jahrelange Kontroversen um die dortige Sonderabfalldeponie wegen des Verdachts illegaler Abfallablagerungen, Wasserkontaminationen und Gesundheitsbelastungen. Im Verlauf der skandalreichen Geschichte hatten sich die Kontrahenten - Vertreter des Landes, verschiedener Städte, Kommunen und Landkreise sowie mehrere Bürgerinitiativen - zutiefst zerstritten.

In dieser Situation wurde Meinfried Striegnitz, ein Mitarbeiter der nahe gelegenen Evangelischen Akademie Loccum, aktiv. Er organisierte und moderierte mehrere Gespräche zwischen den Streitparteien. Die grundsätzlich positiven Erfahrungen mündeten Ende 1990 in ein Mediationsverfahren, wobei der Akademiemitarbeiter von der niedersächsischen Umweltministerin zum offiziellen Mediator bestellt wurde. Die Finanzierung des Verfahrens trägt das Land Niedersachsen. Ziel des Verfahrens ist die Verständigung der Konfliktparteien auf eine allseits akzeptierte Sanierungsmethode.

Das Verfahren ist noch nicht abgeschlossen, die bisherigen Erfahrungen sind jedoch, ganz besonders angesichts seiner Pionierfunktion, sehr vielversprechend. So wurde durch das Verfahren die sachliche und konstruktive Zusammenarbeit der ehemals zerstrittenen Parteien erreicht. Für einige hochkontrovers diskutierte Probleme konnten einvernehmliche Lösungen gefunden werden. Erste Ergebnisse einer Untersuchung des Verfahrens durch das WZB (halbstrukturierte Interviews mit allen Verfahrensbeteiligten) zeigen eine überwiegend positive Beurteilung durch nahezu alle Beteiligten. Besonders hervorgehoben wurde von den Befragten die positive Funktion des Mediators bei der Verbesserung der allgemeinen und sachbezogenen Kommunikation zwischen den Konfliktbeteiligten und zur Förderung des Problemlösungsprozesses.

Es bestehen begründete Hoffnungen, bis Ende 1993 zu einer Vereinbarung über ein Gesamtsanierungskonzept zu kommen, nachdem im August 1992 zwischen allen Beteiligten Übereinstimmung in den generellen Sanierungszielen, über Sicherheitsmassnahmen und diesbezügliche Bewertungskriterien erzielt worden war.

2.2. Mediationsverfahren im Kreis Neuss

Das zweite grosse Mediationsverfahren findet seit 1991 im Kreis Neuss (Nordrhein-Westfalen) zum Abfallwirtschaftskonzept des Kreises statt. Es wurde von der Projektgruppe Mediationsverfahren[11] des Wissenschaftszentrums Berlin für Sozialforschung (WZB) mitinitiiert, die auch die Begleitforschung unternimmt. Besonders umstrittene Punkte des Abfallwirtschaftskonzeptes sind der geplante Bau einer Müllverbrennungsanlage, die Möglichkeiten zur Vermeidung und Verminderung von Haus- und Gewerbemüll sowie die Standorte für neue Anlagen zur Behandlung und Deponierung von Abfällen.

Mit diesem Forschungsvorhaben wird wissenschaftliches Neuland betreten. Ergebnisse sozialwissenschaftlicher (Evaluations-)Forschung zu Mediationsverfahren liegen für die Bundesrepublik bislang nicht vor. Die am weitesten fortgeschrittene nordamerikanische Forschung ist wegen anderer rechtlicher Rahmenbedingungen und einer anderen politischen Kultur in ihren Ergebnissen nur bedingt auf deutsche Verhältnisse übertragbar. Sie ist aber auch methodisch insofern noch defizitär, als sie überwiegend Mediationsverfahren retrospektiv analysiert. Nur eine prozessbegleitende Forschung, wie sie exemplarisch derzeit durch das Forschungsteam des WZB in Neuss erfolgt, ermöglicht es unseres Erachtens, zu Ergebnissen zu kommen, die nicht durch unzulängliche Erinnerungen der Beteiligten getrübt sind und die aufgrund der Unmittelbarkeit der Beobachtungen keine Verkürzungen hinnehmen müssen, die sich bei einer Analyse von Dokumenten (Protokollen) zwangsläufig ergeben. Im Rahmen der Untersuchung fand eine Protokollierung (nahezu) aller Vorgespräche statt, die dann zur Einrichtung des Verfahrens führten. Die grossen Mediationssitzungen werden per Tonband und Video aufgezeichnet, die kleinen Sitzungen werden protokolliert[12]. Darüber hinaus werden jeweils zu den grossen Sitzungen schriftliche Befragungen aller Teilnehmer vorgenommen. Diese forschungspraktisch sehr aufwendigen prozessbe-

---

[11] Im Rahmen des Forschungsprojektes werden ausserdem Mediationsverfahren im europäischen und aussereuropäischen Ausland untersucht (Niederlande, Österreich, Schweiz, USA, Kanada, Japan).

[12] Vgl. hierzu K. Pfingsten und H.-J. Fietkau, *Mediationsverfahren: Leitgedanken und methodische Erfassungsmöglichkeiten*, Wissenschaftszentrum Berlin für Sozialforschung, FS II 92-305, Berlin 1992.

gleitenden Analysen laufen zur Zeit; über ihre Resultate kann detailliert erst zu einem späteren Zeitpunkt berichtet werden.

Im September 1991 hat der Kreistag Neuss ein Abfallwirtschaftskonzept beschlossen. Es soll sowohl die vom Gesetz geforderte Entsorgungssicherheit langfristig gewährleisten als auch den Vorrang von Vermeiden und Verwerten vor dem Beseitigen des Abfalls in die Praxis umsetzen. Der verbleibende Müll soll verbrannt, die Verbrennungsrückstände sollen deponiert werden. Verschiedene Aspekte dieses Konzepts werden in der Bevölkerung zum Teil kontrovers diskutiert, vor allem die Notwendigkeit und Kapazität einer Müllverbrennungsanlage und die Standorte für neue Anlagen zur Sortierung, Verwertung (Kompostierung, Behandlung, Verbrennung) und Deponierung.

Zu diesem Abfallwirtschaftskonzept initiierte das Projektteam Mediationsverfahren des WZB in Kooperation mit der Kreisverwaltung ein Mediationsverfahren. Die Suche nach einem Mediator gestaltete sich schwierig und zeitaufwendig, da es für diese Tätigkeit in der Bundesrepublik bislang noch keine spezialisierten Personen gibt. Auf Mitarbeiter von Unternehmensberatungsfirmen wurde bewusst verzichtet, da solche Firmen - die verstärkt in dieses Aufgabenfeld drängen und mittlerweile Mediatordienste anbieten - ihre Aufgabe noch sehr im Sinne einer erweiterten Öffentlichkeitsarbeit, teilweise auch bloss als neue Managementtechnik des Unternehmens- und Verwaltungshandelns (ihrer Auftrag- und Geldgeber) sahen. Gleichfalls wurden Juristen nicht angesprochen, um in ein neuartiges Konfliktregelungsverfahren, das auch und besonders wegen einer rechtlichen Überregelung ("Verjuristifizierung") in der Umweltpolitik notwendig geworden ist, nicht juristische Problemsichten und -regelungsansätze dominant werden zu lassen - in den USA beispielsweise ist bereits eine Tendenz zur Verrechtlichung informaler Verhandlungsprozesse deutlich erkennbar. Das bedeutet nicht, dass wir rechtlichen Aspekten nur einen untergeordneten Stellenwert beimessen. Im Gegenteil, sie sind im Verfahren selbst und hinsichtlich der Fragen einer Verkopplung der Ergebnisse des Mediationsverfahrens mit den rechtlich vorgeschriebenen Verfahren von zentraler Bedeutung, wofür gründliche Rechtsexpertisen unabdingbar sind. Dazu braucht es unserer Meinung nach aber nicht unbedingt einen Juristen als Mediator.

Als Mediator konnte schliesslich Professor Dr. Georges Fülgraff (ehemals Präsident des Bundesgesundheitsamtes, Staatssekretär im Bundesgesundheitsministerium und Mitglied im Sachverständigenrat für Umweltfragen) gewonnen werden. Bei der Suche und Auswahl des Mediators orientierten wird uns an folgenden Kriterien, die von einem Mediator erfüllt werden sollten: Neutralität, fachliche und soziale Kompetenz, politische Erfahrung und allgemeine Reputation. Sowohl für die Durchführung des Verfahrens als auch für die Person des Mediators fand sich weitgehende Zustimmung im Kreis. Zur organisatorischen Betreuung des Verfahrens vor Ort wurde vom WZB eine Mediationsgeschäftsstelle im Kreis (Technologiezentrum Glehn) eingerichtet.

Nach längeren Vorverhandlungen und zahlreichen bi- und multilateralen Vorgesprächen des Mediators mit den möglichen Verfahrensteilnehmern fand im März 1992 in Grevenbroich, dem Sitz der Kreisverwaltung, die erste gemeinsame ("grosse") Mediationssitzung statt. An ihr nahmen über 60 Personen teil, die rund 30 Organisationen und Institutionen aus Politik, Verwaltung, Naturschutzorganisationen, Bürgerinitiativen und Wirtschaft repräsentierten. Mit dieser Sitzung wurde das Mediationsverfahren eingeleitet. In einer zweiten grossen Sitzung im Mai 1992 konnte ein erstes Ergebnis in der Sache erreicht werden: Es wurde quasi ein Moratorium beschlossen. Danach sollen keine Festlegungen, insbesondere durch das Handeln der Verwaltung, erfolgen, bis nach dem Vorliegen einer Reihe von Gutachten (deren Bearbeiter das Vertrauen der Bürgerinitiativen geniessen) die Diskussion auf eine sachlichere Basis gestellt werden kann.

Neben den Vollversammlungen fanden verschiedene kleinere Sitzungen statt, an denen Vertreter der Kreisverwaltung, der Bürgerinitiativen und der Umweltverbände sowie externe Gutachter teilnahmen. Hierbei wurde Konsens über einen Fragenkatalog zu einem Gutachten über das Abfallwirtschaftskonzept, den Auftragnehmer (Öko-Institut Darmstadt) und über Immmissions- und Gesundheitsbelastungsuntersuchungen an drei möglichen Standorten einer Müllverbrennungsanlage erzielt.

Über den Verlauf des Mediationsverfahrens gibt die im folgenden aufgeführte Kurz-Chronologie Aufschluss.

Kurz-Chronologie des Mediationsverfahrens im Kreis Neuss

Dezember 1990
Der Umweltdezernent des Kreises Neuss, Dr. R. Fonteyn, deutet Interesse an, ein Mediationsverfahren zu Abfallproblemen im Kreis Neuss mit

dem Wissenschaftszentrum Berlin für Sozialforschung (WZB) durchzuführen.

Februar 1991
Das Mediationsvorhaben wird mit dem WZB in der Kreisverwaltung diskutiert, und wir kommen überein, ein solches Vorhaben gemeinsam auf den Weg zu bringen.

Juni 1991
Auf dem Abfallforum des Kreises Neuss stellen wir unser Mediationsvorhaben vor und schlagen den von uns ins Auge gefassten Mediator Professor Dr. Georges Fülgraff vor. Das Vorhaben und der Mediator stossen auf Zustimmung.

August 1991
Der Mediator übernimmt seine Aufgabe.

September 1991
Der Kreistag des Kreises Neuss beschliesst ein neues Abfallwirtschaftskonzept. Es soll sowohl die vom Gesetz geforderte Entsorgungssicherheit langfristig gewährleisten als auch den Vorrang von Vermeiden und Verwerten vor dem Beseitigen des Abfalls in die Praxis umsetzen. Der verbleibende Müll soll verbrannt, die Verbrennungsrückstände sollen deponiert werden.

Oktober 1991
Einrichtung eines Mediationsbüros im Kreis Neuss durch das WZB.

13. November 1991
Zwischen dem Kreis Neuss und dem WZB wird eine Kooperationsvereinbarung zum Mediationsverfahren abgeschlossen.

November 1991 - Januar 1992
Vorbereitungsgespräche zur ersten Mediationssitzung: Mit allen potentiellen Akteuren finden insgesamt 21 Vorgespräche durch den Mediator und das Projektteam Mediation des WZB statt. Im allgemeinen zeigt sich Zustimmung zum Verfahren und Bereitschaft, daran teilzunehmen.

28. März 1992
Erste gemeinsame Mediationssitzung in Grevenbroich (Kreis Neuss). An ihr nehmen über 60 Personen teil, die rund 30 Organisationen und Institutionen aus Politik, Verwaltung, Naturschutzorganisationen, Bürgerinitiativen und Wirtschaft repräsentieren. Mit dieser Sitzung wird das Mediationsverfahren eingeleitet. Ein erstes Ergebnis besteht in der Absicht, zum vorliegenden Abfallwirtschaftskonzept eine Stellungnahme von Gutachtern einzuholen, die das Vertrauen der Bürgerinititativen geniessen. Erst nach Abschluss des Gutachterprozesses (einschliesslich der daran anschliessenden Diskussion) sollen weitere Massnahmen erfolgen.

8. Mai 1992
Einzelfragen zum vereinbarten Gutachten werden vom Mediator mit den Bürgerinitiativen und Umweltorganisationen erörtert. Es wird ein Fragenkatalog entwickelt. Die begutachtende Einrichtung wird ausgewählt.

26. Mai 1992
Zweite grosse Mediationsrunde. Die etwa 40 Teilnehmer erörtern die Vorschläge der Verwaltung zur weiteren Gutachtenvergabe. Auch hierüber wird Übereinkunft erzielt.

3. Juli 1992
Abstimmungsgespräch über ein Immissionsgutachten zwischen der Kreisverwaltung, den Bürgerinitiativen und Gutachtern. Es wird ein Gutachten in Auftrag gegeben, das die Immissionsbelastungen beschreiben soll, wie sie derzeit an drei möglichen Standorten für die Müllverbrennungsanlage (MVA) herrschen.

10. Juli 1992
Abstimmungsgespräch über eine Gesundheitsuntersuchung zwischen der Kreisverwaltung, den Bürgerinitiativen und Gutachtern. Es wird ein Gutachten in Auftrag gegeben, das den Gesundheitszustand der Bevölkerung beschreiben soll, wie er derzeit an den drei möglichen Standorten der MVA gegeben ist.

November 1992[13]

Dritte grosse Mediationsrunde, in der die Gutachten diskutiert und Entscheidungen über das weitere Vorgehen zur Umsetzung des Abfallwirtschaftskonzeptes (insbesondere zur MVA) getroffen werden.

Der bisherige Verlauf des Mediationsverfahrens wird von den Teilnehmern überwiegend positiv beurteilt. Diese Sicht wird auch von vorläufigen wissenschaftlichen Auswertungen des Verfahrens gestützt. Es ist deutlich zu sehen, dass die vormals stark zerstrittenen Kontrahenten einen sachlichen Umgangston miteinander anstreben und unterschiedliche Sichtweisen der zukünftigen Lösung der Abfallproblematik rational und produktiv mit dem Ziel diskutieren, eine einvernehmliche Lösung für die zukünftige Abfallkonzeption des Kreises zu finden.

Die Auswertung der schriftlichen Befragung zur zweiten Mediationssitzung durch meinen Kollegen H.-J. Fietkau ergab u. a.:

- Die meisten Verfahrensbeteiligten haben keine Vorerfahrung mit Mediations- oder ähnlichen Verfahren. Sie bewegen sich auf unvertrautem Gebiet.

- Der Mediator wird von den Teilnehmer/innen sehr positiv beurteilt. So wird er z. B. recht einvernehmlich als kompetent, fair und sicher wahrgenommen.

---

[13] Aber neue Konflikte sind hier wie andernorts vorprogrammiert: Es ist deutlich zu sehen, dass auch die von Umweltgruppen üblicherweise als Alternative zur Müllverbrennung bevorzugten "kalten Verfahren" (biologisch-mechanische Abfallbehandlung) in den Standortgemeinden zunehmend kritisiert und abgelehnt werden - mit ähnlichen Argumenten wie bei der Müllverbrennung (hohe Gesundheitsrisiken, Umweltbelastungen und -schäden). Es wird also weiterhin reichlich Konfliktstoff in der Abfallpolitik für alternative Konfliktregelungsverfahren geben. Ob es angesichts des grossen Aufwandes, den solche Verfahren für alle Beteiligten mit sich bringen, ein weltpolitisch vernünftiger und sozialverträglicher Weg wäre, quasi zu jedem Komposthaufen ein Mediationsverfahren durchzuführen, darf bezweifelt werden. Mediationsverfahren sollten eher als zusätzliches Regulierungsinstrument und generell für grössere Umweltkonflikte vorgehalten werden. Die Regelung relativ "normaler" Interessenkonflikte sollte Aufgabe des politisch-administrativen Normalprozesses bleiben, den es entsprechend zu verbessern gilt.

- Fast die Hälfte der Beteiligten hält eine gemeinsam getragene Problemlösung für denkbar. Die anderen Teilnehmer/innen sind hier eher unsicher oder skeptisch.

- Etwa ein Drittel der Mediationsteilnehmer/innen gibt an, dass die gemeinsame Mediationssitzung ihre Einstellung zum Sachproblem und/oder den anderen Verfahrensbeteiligten verändert habe.

- Ungefähr die Hälfte der Teilnehmer/innen hält es für möglich, dass es durch das geplante Abfallwirtschaftskonzept zu negativen Auswirkungen kommt. Mögliche Risiken werden in bezug auf die Gesundheit der Bevölkerung, das politische Klima, die ökologische Situation und die Lebensqualität vor Ort gesehen.

- Von der Mehrheit wird das Abfallwirtschaftskonzept vor allem im Hinblick auf die Wirtschaftskraft der Region als nützlich bewertet, nicht so sehr für die anderen Bereiche (Gesundheit, Ökologie, Politik, Lebensqualität).

- Fast die Hälfte der Verfahrensbeteiligten glaubt an die Verfügbarkeit von Alternativen, die eine Realisierung des wirtschaftlichen Nutzens auch auf andere Weise ermöglichten.

- Eine von den Teilnehmer/innen vorgenommene Ordnung verschiedener (vorgegebener) Verfahrensziele nach ihrer Wichtigkeit ergab die folgenden *durchschnittlichen* Prioritäten: 1. eine Lösung, die Bestand hat; 2. eine faire Lösung; 3. ein einvernehmliches Ergebnis; 4. eine Lösung, die die Öffentlichkeit gutheisst; 5. ein Ergebnis, das problemlos umgesetzt werden kann; 6. eine schnelle Lösung.

Der Verlauf des Mediationsverfahrens ist bislang ermutigend hinsichtlich der Frage, ob solche Formen der Konfliktregelung in der Bundesrepublik Deutschland eine Chance haben könnten. Gleichwohl sind verständlicherweise bei dieser so komplexen und in der Bundesrepublik generell hochstrittig diskutierten Thematik noch zahlreiche Fragen offen und Probleme zu lösen, so dass im Kreis Neuss eine schnelle Entscheidung nicht zu erwarten ist. Es wären auch weit überzogene Ansprüche, von diesem in der Bundesrepublik ersten Mediationsverfahren zu einem

Abfallwirtschaftskonzept einen reibungslosen Verlauf zu erwarten. Es handelt sich bei diesem Pionierverfahren um ein soziales Experiment, das ein hohes Mass an institutionellem und individuellem Lernvermögen verlangt.

Die Teilnehmer in Neuss haben es wie alle Pioniere, die umweltpolitisches Neuland betreten, besonders schwer; nachfolgende Mediationsverfahren werden hiervon profitieren.

3. FAZIT

Die traditionellen Instrumente der Umweltpolitik stossen in allen demokratischen Industrieländern zunehmend an Grenzen der Problem- und Konfliktregelung. Informale, konsensorientierte Verfahren mit Verhandlungscharakter, insbesondere Mediationsverfahren, sind in relevanten Fällen offensichtlich besser zur Konfliktregelung geeignet. Gleichwohl, so zeigen bisherige Erfahrungen, haben auch Mediationsverfahren ihre Grenzen: Sie sind einerseits offensichtlich nicht zur Regelung von fundamentalen Wertkonflikten geeignet; zum anderen ist zu beachten, dass die Grenzen der Belastbarkeit von nicht-staatlichen Umweltorganisationen und Bürgerinitiativen durch solche sehr zeitaufwendigen Verfahren recht schnell erreicht werden können. Es handelt sich hierbei nicht nur um zeitliche und finanzielle, sondern ganz besonders um psychische Grenzen, sind doch die Vertreter von Umweltgruppen ausserordentlich hohen psychischen Belastungen ausgesetzt, wenn sie die kompromissorientierten Verfahrens(teil)ergebnisse ihren Organisationen vermitteln und sie zur entsprechenden Selbstverpflichtung bewegen sollen - ganz zu schweigen von dem sozialen Druck, dem sie als "Kompromissler" in ihrer Lebensumwelt dann meist ausgesetzt sind. Insofern werden diese Verfahren in der Umweltpolitikarena wohl weitgehend auf wichtige lokale, regionale, also von den Beteiligten überschaubare Konfliktfälle beschränkt bleiben.

Mediationsverfahren - wie allgemein alternative Konfliktregelungsverfahren - haben meines Erachtens das Potential, das bestehende Instrumentarium zur Regelung von Umweltproblemen sinnvoll zu bereichern. Es wäre aber ein überzogener Anspruch, von ihnen zu erwarten, dass sie einen Königsweg in der Umweltpolitik ebnen könnten. Einen solchen alleinseligmachenden Weg wird es im hochkomplexen Gebiet der Umweltpolitik wohl nicht geben; das zeigen sämtliche bisherigen praktischen Erfahrungen in allen Ländern, besonders auch die mit den zeitweilig hochpräferierten ökonomischen Anreizinstrumenten. In (bescheidener) Anerkenntnis dessen, dass nicht die Suche nach *dem* bestgeeigneten Superinstrument, sondern die pragmatische Entwicklung einer grösseren Instrumentenvielfalt - die eine flexible Reaktion auf die Problemvielfalt erlaubt - der erfolgversprechendere Ansatz ist, sollten Umweltsozialwissenschaftler bei der kritischen Evaluation von Mediationsverfahren und bei ihren theoretischen Überlegungen zu Umweltpolitikinstrumenten die Evaluationskriterien und Erwartungen nicht allzu hoch schrauben. Sie sollten sich hierzu auch nicht von den unkritischen Befürwortern von Mediationsverfahren, besonders jenen, die an der Zunahme dieser Verfahren ein geschäftliches Interesse haben und die Möglichkeiten dieser Verfahren in viel zu rosigen Farben schildern, verleiten lassen. Es bleibt dann immer noch genug übrig für ihr Kritikgeschäft.

In der Bundesrepublik Deutschland liegen bislang nur in geringem Umfang Erfahrungen mit Mediationsverfahren im Umweltschutz vor. Allerdings ist es möglich, an ausländische Konzepte, die insbesondere in den USA, Japan und Kanada entwickelt wurden, anzuknüpfen. Mediationsverfahren finden hierzulande zunehmend Aufmerksamkeit in der Wissenschaft. Vor allem Juristen haben sich dieser Verfahrensmöglichkeit analytisch und normativ angenommen. Inzwischen blicken auch die Sozialwissenschaften verstärkt auf Mediationsverfahren. Die wissenschaftlichen Betrachtungen, die in der Bundesrepublik vorliegen, sind jedoch oft rein spekulativer Natur; sie entbehren notgedrungen der konkreten Erfahrung. Ob und wie Mediationsverfahren unter den rechtlichen Rahmenbedingungen und in der politischen Kultur der Bundesrepublik Deutschland erfolgreich durchgeführt werden können, ist derzeit noch offen. Dazu ist zunächst vor allem (theoriegeleitete) empirische Kärrnerarbeit angesagt.

Literaturverzeichnis

J. Amy, *The Politics of Environmental Mediation*, New York 1987.

L. S. Bacow und M. Wheeler, *Environmental Dispute Resolution*, New York 1984.

G. Bingham, *Resolving Environmental Disputes. A Decade of Experience*, Washington, D.C. 1986.

H.-J. Fietkau und H. Weidner, *Mediationsverfahren in der Umweltpolitik. Erfahrungen in der Bundesrepublik Deutschland*, in: Aus Politik und Zeitgeschichte, B 39-40/1992 (Beilage zur Wochenzeitung Das Parlament), S. 24-34.

W. Hoffmann-Riem und E. Schmidt-Assmann (Hg.), *Konfliktbewältigung durch Verhandlungslösungen,* Baden-Baden 1990.

P. Knoepfel und M. Rey, *Konfliktminderung durch Verhandlung: Das Beispiel des Verfahrens zur Suche eines Standorts für eine Sondermülldeponie in der Suisse Romande*, in: W. Hoffmann-Riem und E. Schmidt-Assmann, a.a.O., Bd. II, S. 257-286.

K. Pfingsten und H.-J. Fietkau, *Mediationsverfahren: Leitgedanken und methodische Erfassungsmöglichkeiten*, Wissenschaftszentrum Berlin für Sozialforschung, FS II 92-305, Berlin 1992.

L. Susskind und J. Cruikshank, *Breaking the Impasse. Consensual Approaches to Resolving Public Disputes*, New York 1987.

S. Tsuru und H. Weidner (Hg.), *Environmental Policy in Japan*, Berlin 1989.

W. van den Daele, *Zum Forschungsprogramm der Abteilung "Normbildung und Umwelt"*, Wissenschaftszentrum Berlin für Sozialforschung, FS II 91-301, Berlin 1991.

H. Weidner, *Umweltpolitik - Auf altem Weg zu einer internationalen Spitzenstellung*, in W. Süss (Hrsg.), Die Bundesrepublik in den achtziger Jahren, Opladen 1991, S. 137-152.

LES DIFFICULTES DE LA NEGOCIATION INSTITUTIONNALISEE, LE PARC NATIONAL DES PYRENEES OCCIDENTALES OU LA COOPERATION CONTRARIEE

Patrice Duran

1. INTRODUCTION

On s'accorde aisément à reconnaître aujourd'hui les mérites d'une gestion publique partenariale par une sorte de glissement d'un Etat-tuteur vers un Etat-partenaire. Une telle évolution n'est pas tant dictée par une volonté d'approfondissement de la démocratie que par les nécessités mêmes de l'action publique. Le recours à l'accord et au contrat se justifie donc pleinement par un souci d'efficacité dès lors que l'on est conduit à reconnaître qu'il ne peut y avoir de gestion purement technique des problèmes de société. La nature plus transversale et plus collective des problèmes publics interdit de plus en plus le seul usage de la contrainte, et l'Etat est amené du même coup à solliciter l'accord des gens qu'il est censé diriger[1]. Si aucun acteur n'a véritablement de capacité à gérer de manière autonome de tels problèmes, il est clair que la recherche de l'assentiment devient essentielle, et que la logique de l'ajustement mutuel doit l'emporter sur l'injonction autoritaire. La preuve en est que, même lorsque l'Etat intervient de manière autoritaire par la loi, il est bien souvent conduit à en négocier la mise en oeuvre avec les intéressés afin de réduire au maximum les résistances possibles. Cependant, la reconnaissance d'une réalité selon laquelle "gouverner, c'est gérer de l'action collective"

---

[1] Ceci n'est bien sûr pas sans conséquence au niveau du droit. Cf. l'article désormais classique de P. Amselek, "L'évolution générale de la technique juridique dans les sociétés occidentales", *Revue de droit public*, mars-avril 1982. On consultera également, C.-A. Morand, "La contractualisation du droit dans l'Etat providence", in C.-A. Morand (sous la direction de), *L'Etat propulsif*, Publisud, 1990.

ne rend pas les choses plus faciles, car les processus sociaux échappent - heureusement - à toute régulation excessivement volontariste[2].

Les questions relatives à l'environnement constituent à n'en pas douter une illustration convaincante d'une telle évolution, en même temps qu'elles fournissent un champ privilégié pour la réflexion sur l'action collective dès lors que l'on est conduit à voir dans l'*environnement* l'existence d'un bien public. La protection des ressources naturelles se situe de nos jours en bonne place sur l'agenda politique par l'attention qui lui est accordée comme par l'intensité des débats suscités, car aucune solution à la question de la coopération et de son coût ne s'impose vraiment. Longtemps la discussion sur les biens publics s'est résumée à une opposition simple du *marché* et de la *hiérarchie*. Les adeptes de la privatisation trouvaient dans l'affirmation des droits de propriété et dans les mécanismes du marché les principes d'allocation des biens collectifs, quand les partisans d'une régulation centralisée voyaient dans l'intervention de l'administration publique le moyen le plus sûr à la gestion de problèmes caractérisés par une interdépendance assez forte des personnes dans l'utilisation des ressources communes et en conséquence par un degré élevé d'opportunisme possible de leur part[3]. Au-delà de l'irréductibilité des positions, les deux écoles partagent pourtant en commun une représentation pessimiste de l'action collective: tout changement institutionnel dans le sens d'une solution privée ou publique doit en effet nécessairement venir de l'extérieur et s'imposer aux individus, car le propre des problèmes liés à l'usage des ressources communes est de ne pouvoir être résolu par les acteurs eux-mêmes[4]. Il ressort cependant de la pratique que, si certains problèmes fondamentaux ne peuvent être solutionnés autrement que par l'appel à la puissance publique, il n'est pas non plus exclu d'envisager une participation des acteurs concernés dans le cadre d'un processus de régulation conjointe. Mais si s'impose la nécessité d'une approche négociée des problèmes de gouvernement et plus particulièrement de ceux touchant à l'environnement, demeure la question de sa

---

[2] Sur cette question, nous renvoyons à notre article, "Le savant et la politique, pour une approche raisonnée de l'analyse des politiques publiques", *L'Année sociologique*, 40, 1990.

[3] On se reportera avec profit à C. Hood, *Administrative Analysis, An Introduction to Rules, Enforcement and Organizations*, Wheatsheaf books limited, 1986; ainsi qu'à A. Wolfelsberger, *Les biens collectifs*, Paris, PUF, 1975.

[4] Pour une critique de cette position, cf. E. Ostrom, *Governing the Commons, The Evolution of Institutions for Collective Action*, Cambridge University Press, 1990.

forme. De ce point de vue, l'institution française des parcs nationaux apparaît comme une alternative d'action visant à atténuer le caractère excessif des positions précédemment évoquées, et à réaliser sous la forme juridique d'un *établissement public à caractère national* un habile compromis entre négociation et organisation, entre autorité de l'Etat et participation démocratique, par l'intégration dans une institution unique de l'ensemble des parties prenantes à la gestion d'un territoire donné. Tentative de solution à des problèmes de choix collectifs par la création institutionnelle, les parcs relèvent manifestement d'un mode de raisonnement qui s'inspire encore des théories de la contrainte en matière de gestion des biens collectifs sans que pour autant la recherche active d'un consentement soit exclue. Ceci est aussi clairement la résultante d'une philosophie politique selon laquelle la protection de l'environnement, si elle est devenue une obligation d'Etat, est avant tout considérée comme un devoir des citoyens: "il est du devoir de chacun de veiller à la sauvegarde du patrimoine naturel dans lequel il vit" (art. 1, al. 2 de la loi du 10 juillet 1976 relative à la protection de la nature).

La protection du domaine naturel est encore une préoccupation récente. Jusqu'en 1960, la France ne disposait en ce domaine que de la loi de 1930 sur la protection des monuments naturels et des sites, complétée en 1957 dans un but scientifique afin que des éléments de flore et de faune menacés de disparition puissent être constitués en réserves naturelles bénéficiant d'une protection spéciale. En vertu de la loi du 22 juillet 1960 (complétée par le décret n° 61-1195 du 31 octobre 1961), relative à la création des parcs nationaux, les objectifs poursuivis par le classement d'un territoire en parc national sont "la conservation de la faune, de la flore, du sous-sol, de l'atmosphère, des eaux et en général du milieu naturel". Il importe de "préserver ce milieu contre tout effet de dégradation naturelle et de le soustraire à toute intervention artificielle, susceptible d'en altérer l'aspect, la composition et l'évolution". La création des parcs nationaux à partir de 1960 correspond pourtant en pratique à une volonté nouvelle de préserver des milieux naturels entiers à des fins scientifiques, éducatives, et biologiques sans que soient pour autant perdues de vue les exigences de développement local, en particulier au moment où la croissance d'une France urbaine conduisait à s'interroger dans le cadre de l'aménagement du territoire sur les déséquilibres et les inégalités produits par un développement incontrôlé. Par leur participation à la gestion d'enjeux aussi complexes que la protection de la nature et le développement local, les parcs se trouvent ainsi au coeur d'un réseau complexe où les acteurs individuels et collectifs qui interviennent sont diversifiés, leurs objectifs ne sont pas toujours explicites, leurs modes d'action et leurs stratégies sont différenciés, mais où ils demeurent très largement interdépendants. Personne ne peut en effet être totalement propriétaire d'enjeux tels que la sauvegarde du patrimoine naturel ou le développement local, qui nécessitent une approche collective, dont la création des parcs constitue une des modalités possibles. Ces derniers correspondent d'une certaine manière à un *mécanisme d'institutionnalisation d'intérêts socio-politiques spécifiques* - qu'il s'agisse de l'Etat dans ses différentes composantes, des collectivités territoriales, de groupes professionnels, de scientifiques, ou d'associations de défense - autour d'enjeux communs, dont le traitement suppose le maintien d'un minimum de conformité et de compatibilité entre les conduites des protagonistes. La gestion de telles organisations ne peut donc qu'être fonction de leur capacité à accommoder des exigences souvent contradictoires, au point que l'on peut s'interroger sur leur capacité à développer une stratégie autonome, à quelles conditions, et à quel prix.

C'est à travers l'exemple plus précis du Parc National des Pyrénées Occidentales (PNPO) que nous voudrions tester la validité et la pertinence d'une solution à la négociation par l'*organisation*[5]. Le PNPO, créé par un décret du 23 mars 1967, est, comme ses homologues, un établissement public à caractère administratif, et à ce titre il conduit une mission de service public dans les domaines de la *protection de la nature*, de l'*observation scientifique*, de l'*accueil du public*, et du *développement local*. Malheureusement, en dépit des vertus affichées, il est une "invention" fragile et contestée, car cette institution "hybride" n'a pas véritablement réussi à s'imposer dans le double registre qui était le sien, de l'affirmation de la légitimité propre à une autorité publique, et de la participation de ses membres à l'élaboration d'un projet collectif en matière de gestion du territoire. Le Parc National des Pyrénées Occidentales est aujourd'hui confronté à de multiples interrogations quant à ses mis-

---

[5] Nous nous appuierons ici sur notre propre travail d'évaluation du Parc National des Pyrénées Occidentales qui constitue la première étude du genre en France. Les investigations réalisées allaient bien au-delà de notre propos dans cet article, aussi nous n'en retiendrons que les aspects les plus directement liés au thème de la négociation. Cf. P. Duran, *Le territoire de l'environnement, le cas du Parc National des Pyrénées Occidentales*, Ministère de l'Environnement/PNPO, 1991.

sions, son fonctionnement, et par conséquent son devenir. Il est en effet une organisation faible qui combine un relatif malaise de son personnel et une certaine usure des hommes avec trop de flou et d'approximation dans la conduite de ses missions en l'absence d'un réel soutien de ses partenaires. Critiqué de toutes parts, il est accusé par les uns de ne pas répondre aux exigences primordiales de protection de la nature, par les autres de ne pas tenir ses promesses en matière de développement. Du même coup, les perspectives d'évolution s'avèrent difficiles à penser de manière dynamique, ce qui ne permet guère bien souvent d'intégrer autrement que de manière défensive un changement que l'on perçoit pourtant comme nécessaire, si l'on veut éviter la marginalisation progressive de l'institution.

Le PNPO symbolise en fait l'échec d'un *apprentissage institutionnel* d'une gestion collective de l'environnement probablement par sous-estimation des difficultés inhérentes à l'action collective[6]. Pas plus qu'on ne change la société par décret, on ne décrète la négociation et la participation par l'organisation. Certes, l'organisation est une des solutions possibles à l'action collective, mais il convient de ne pas confondre le cadre de l'action avec l'action elle-même, même s'il faut manifestement en penser l'interdépendance[7]. La seule imposition de règles communes ne suffit pas à créer de la communication, pas plus que la formalisation et la codification des positions et des procédures ne rendent les comportements prévisibles. La panoplie "rationnelle" des rôles, des règles et des procédures qui constitue le dessin de l'organisation ne doit pas faire oublier la capacité des membres à en déplacer les buts et en subvertir les règles de fonctionnement[8]. Ceci montre à l'évidence que si l'existence d'une organisation peut être un élément favorable à une participation à l'action collec-

---

[6] Nous empruntons cette notion à M. Crozier, "Pour une analyse sociologique de la planification française", *Revue française de sociologie*, 6, 1965. Dans cet article, Crozier montrait comment par la participation à la planification pouvait être l'occasion d'un apprentissage institutionnel d'un autre modèle d'action collective que celui de l'organisation. Pour une critique sévère d'une telle illusion par un des proches mêmes de Crozier (dont nous reprendrons nous-mêmes certains des arguments), voir P. Gremion, "La théorie de l'apprentissage institutionnel et la régionalisation du cinquième plan", *Revue française de science politique*, XXIII, 2, 1973.

[7] Cf. sur cette importante question, M. Crozier, E. Friedeberg, *L'acteur et le système*, Paris, Seuil, 1977.

[8] Voir par exemple J. G. March, J. P. Olsen, *Ambiguity and Choice in Organizations*, Norway, Universitetsforlaget, 1976; K. E. Weick, "Educational Organizations as Loosely Coupled Systems", *Administrative Science Quarterly*, 21, 1976.

tive, elle n'est pas non plus une condition suffisante[9]. La simple *internalisation* de l'environnement ne pouvait mécaniquement produire de l'intégration. Celle-ci est toujours la résultante d'un processus interactif complexe de création et de recréation de significations à travers lesquelles les acteurs en présence construisent les possibilités de leur accord[10]. La question qui se pose ici est bien de se demander pourquoi l'institution "parc" n'a pu être le véhicule pleinement satisfaisant d'un tel processus de structuration.

Le sentiment d'un échec a conduit l'ensemble des acteurs présents au sein du conseil d'administration de l'établissement à s'engager dans une réflexion précise sur les conditions de fonctionnement du parc afin de promouvoir les changements susceptibles de s'imposer. Cette mobilisation collective, même si chacun des partenaires y voyait l'occasion de vérifier ses propres thèses, ne pouvait en effet se développer sans une clarification première qui a pris en l'occurrence la forme d'une demande de diagnostic. L'action nécessite toujours une bonne intelligence des situations. De fait, la demande d'analyse était partie prenante d'un processus collectif de changement dont celle-ci constituait une pièce essentielle, en particulier par l'apprentissage que pouvait permettre l'appropriation d'un diagnostic qui est l'affaire de tous. Au fond, les difficultés de la négociation institutionnalisée amenaient à voir dans une évaluation un principe de collaboration pour la redéfinition d'une coopération future. En ce sens la démarche d'intervention était donc tout à la fois rétrospective et prospective dans la mesure où elle constituait de manière dynamique un outil de connaissance et une méthodologie du changement. Notre investigation visait dans un premier temps à:

- dégager les problèmes concrets et les enjeux réels des acteurs, ainsi que les conceptions implicites qui structurent leurs modes de raisonnement; la centralité du thème de la coopération nous a en effet amené à insister sur: les attentes et les orientations subjectives des acteurs, c'est-à-dire la façon dont ils définissent les problèmes qui sont les leurs; leur type d'implication pour mesurer leur degré d'engagement

---

[9] Nous partageons amplement ici les vues de P. Mann, *L'action collective, mobilisation et organisation des minorités actives*, Paris, Armand Colin, 1991.
[10] Cf. en particulier S. Ranson, B. Hinings, R. Greenwood, "The Structuring of Organizational Structures", *Administrative Science Quarterly*, 25, 1980.

vis à vis du parc; et enfin les sources éventuelles d'incitations positives et négatives à participer.
- mieux cerner la structure de leurs tâches, et considérer leurs activités telles qu'ils les perçoivent et les conduisent en tenant particulièrement compte des contraintes qui s'imposent à eux.

- En second lieu, il s'agissait de se centrer sur les relations entre les personnes et entre les services, et de mettre au jour les difficultés, les tensions, et les conflits qui se produisent le plus fréquemment, comme les solutions qui y sont généralement apportées. Il convenait ensuite de recomposer les stratégies des divers acteurs. Ceci avait pour but de recomposer le système d'action constitutif du PNPO et de découvrir les jeux et les régulations sur lesquels repose son fonctionnement.

Cependant, la nature collective des problèmes à résoudre implique manifestement celle de leur traitement. Ainsi la réappropriation par les membres concernés s'est-elle effectuée à travers la mise en place d'une démarche formalisée d'apprentissage collectif qui fait du dispositif un lieu de négociation itératif et interactif. L'ensemble de l'opération a été accompagnée par un comité de pilotage regroupant les représentants des différents intérêts en présence et la création plus contingente de groupes thématiques à composition pluraliste.

Le parc est à l'évidence arrivé à la croisée des chemins. Issue d'une interrogation historiquement datée sur les problèmes d'environnement et de protection de la nature, on est en fait en droit de se demander aujourd'hui ce que peut être le futur d'une telle institution. Toute institution étant une solution à un problème, la question est donc de savoir si l'adéquation de l'un et de l'autre demeure pertinente, et sinon quelles sont les solutions à envisager.

2. Une institution en miettes

Une organisation dans sa réalité est toujours le résultat de la combinaison particulière d'hommes, de structures, et d'enjeux spécifiques. Or, de ce point de vue, le parc reproduit assez fidèlement les caractéristiques des organisations publiques que March et Olsen qualifiaient d'*anarchies organisées*[11] à savoir:

* *des buts abstraits, flous, mal définis et faiblement cohérents*. La protection de la nature, tout comme du reste le développement local, ne va pas de soi, et est susceptible de multiples interprétations. La question qui se pose ici est donc moins celle des orientations de l'action que celle de leurs définition, articulation, et opérationnalisation en termes d'objectifs d'action et de procédures.

* *des technologies ambiguës*. Compte tenu du point précédent, il n'est pas facile de déterminer avec une grande précision les compétences et les savoir-faire nécessaires à l'accomplissement des missions, ce qui introduit des difficultés d'organisation et d'évaluation du travail.

* *un mode de participation instable et fluctuant de ses partenaires*. Le degré d'implication des acteurs concernés par l'action du parc demeure encore très aléatoire, sujet à d'importantes variations qui sont source d'incertitude. Leur mobilisation est insuffisante, et l'établissement d'une coopération stable fait cruellement défaut, qui montre la fragilité des liens établis avec l'environnement.

Ces différents points induisent une image faible et statique du PNPO, et conditionnent une perception de l'avenir, qui, sans être totalement pessimiste, demeure largement indéterminée. L'ambiguïté et le caractère apparemment contradictoire des missions du parc tiraillé entre protection et développement, tout comme la méconnaissance de son fonctionnement réel aboutissent, au plan externe au maintien de jugements, qui, sans être toujours hostiles ou négatifs, restent généralement superficiels et exagérément critiques.

---

[11] J. G. March, J. P. Olsen, "The Garbage Can Model of Organizational Choice", *Administrative Science Quarterly*, 17, 1, 1972.

La grande difficulté du PNPO - et à des degrés divers de l'ensemble des parcs - est d'avoir voulu combiner sous la forme unitaire d'une seule institution une pluralité d'enjeux et une multiplicité de partenaires. Cette situation d'"anarchie organisée" s'explique par un enchevêtrement des enjeux et une hétérogénéité des acteurs du fait même qu'un territoire ne se laisse jamais appréhender de manière unique et qu'il abrite des locataires souvent bien différents.

2.1. Le parc national, une ambiguïté originelle

Les parcs nationaux sont, dès leur origine, au coeur d'une symbolique complexe qui a conduit à les considérer comme des "cathédrales du silence", des "conservatoires de la nature", mais aussi comme le "jardin des français", ou tout simplement selon l'expression d'un guide de montagne des "jardins pour tous". Mais au-delà des formules naïves ou racoleuses qui en ont accompagné la naissance, s'exprime la réalité qui est celle d'une époque dans laquelle les pouvoirs publics ont tenté la réconciliation de la protection de la nature et de l'aménagement.

Les préoccupations d'aménagement ont en effet marqué les années 60. Non seulement il faut mieux planifier le développement d'une société industrielle et urbaine, mais il convient d'y intégrer un souci écologique et paysager qui réponde aux attentes des citadins. Au fond, la création des parcs nationaux en France vise dans la pratique (et en dépit de la pureté des intentions affichées par la loi) à répondre à un triple objectif:

* préservation de richesses naturelles devenues rares;

* réponse aux aspirations de nature d'une population citadine;

* contribution, enfin, à l'aménagement local, et plus particulièrement des zones fragiles.

Peu de place, on le voit, est faite aux préoccupations scientifiques. La période est de fait surtout marquée par la crise d'une société rurale dans un contexte général de restructuration de l'agriculture à laquelle est allouée de nouvelles fonctions, paysagère et environnementale, susceptibles de fournir des alternatives de développement à des zones agricoles marginales. Ainsi dans la ligne du Plan MANSHOLT, le rapport VEDEL[12] prévoyait-il de mener dans ces zones, outre le reboisement et la sylviculture, "des actions sur le plan communautaire, destinées à favoriser la détente et la santé publique, par l'encouragement et la création de parcs naturels et de zones de détente. Il est entendu que des actions concentrées et parallèles doivent être entreprises dans le secteur des activités touristiques". Ces lignes, même si elles ont suscité bien des réserves et des polémiques par la crainte de voir se développer une "France sans paysans", illustrent la problématique qui va imprégner les parcs nationaux à la fin des années 60, et le PNPO tout particulièrement.

Les parcs nationaux se sont ainsi trouvés au carrefour de problèmes multiples qu'ils avaient à charge d'intégrer au sein d'une institution unique: à la fois conduire l'avenir par le développement de l'industrie touristique, gérer le présent de l'exode rural, et assumer le passé par la revalorisation des activités agro-pastorales, à travers un enjeu nouveau de sauvegarde du patrimoine naturel.

Le montage institutionnel des parcs[13] correspond à la fois à une réalité spatiale et à une volonté des pouvoirs publics de répondre à une série de problèmes que l'on perçoit liés les uns aux autres dans le langage de la planification et de la programmation d'une époque caractérisée par un effort de rationalisation de l'intervention publique. Ainsi, autour du parc proprement dit où les activités humaines sont strictement réglementées, est constituée une zone périphérique. Celle-ci n'est soumise à aucune des servitudes de protection de la nature du parc, mais elle est considérée comme une sorte de zone tampon entre le monde extérieur et la pleine nature. Elle doit permettre un ensemble de réalisations et d'améliorations d'ordre social, économique et culturel tout en assurant une protection plus efficace de la nature dans le parc lui-même. Cette zone est la base d'accueil ou de séjour où peuvent rayonner tous ceux qui désirent profiter du parc. Ce doit être également pour les populations locales une zone d'expansion économique incitant les hommes à demeurer sur place. L'adjonction d'une zone périphérique est bien la traduction d'une volonté d'aménagement et de développement, en même temps qu'elle est

---

[12] Le rapport VEDEL, intitulé "Perspectives à long terme de l'agriculture française (1968-1985)", fut remis le 20 juin 1969 à J. Duhamel, ministre de l'Agriculture.

[13] Pour plus de précisions, voir F. Constantin, "Environnement et ressources naturelles, les parcs nationaux", *Jurisclasseur de droit rural*, fascicule B-2, 1984; ou encore M. Prieur, *Droit de l'environnement*, Paris, Dalloz, 2ème édition, 1991.

l'expression d'un type d'habitat et d'une imbrication corrélative des espaces sociaux. Ainsi que d'autres l'ont souligné, le cas du PNPO montre à quel point l'interdépendance pour l'exploitation des pâturages entre communes du piedmont et communes d'altitudes est problématique, qui explique l'extension particulière de la zone périphérique pour tenir compte de l'enchevêtrement foncier. L'instauration d'une zone périphérique relève donc d'une triple logique: *spatiale*, par la prise en compte nécessaire des habitants et de leurs modes de vie; *économique*, par l'affirmation d'une logique de développement; *politique*, comme instrument de compensation à la réticence des collectivités locales à accepter les contraintes du parc.

Dès le départ, on constate donc l'étroite association des perspectives d'aménagement, de développement, et de conservation dont le parc devrait réaliser l'intégration. Tout concourt du reste à faire des parcs des "zones aménagées" tant en zone centrale qu'en zone périphérique. Mais la réconciliation du rural et de l'urbain, de l'aménagement et de la protection s'est perdue dans l'expression de multiples clivages et dans l'addition de missions qui ont fini par s'opposer. La formalisation d'une zone périphérique et son inclusion avec la zone centrale dans une institution unique ont échoué dans leur tentative de prise en compte simultanée d'enjeux connexes. Faute de construire un espace intégré d'expression des intérêts, on a aménagé l'occasion de leur opposition. C'est là, selon nous, l'erreur de départ.

Faute de réussir à les articuler, on s'est en fait contenter de procéder à une énumération des missions auxquelles devaient répondre les parcs comme autant de problèmes distincts qui leur étaient posées. Ils ont eu ainsi à inventer les solutions concrètes à la mise en oeuvre d'objectifs ambitieux qui dépassaient de beaucoup les moyens dont ils pouvaient disposer en compétences comme en autorité.

2.2. Un milieu peu porteur

Le parc, dans la conduite de ses missions, se trouve confronté à un ensemble d'acteurs hétérogènes et mal intégrés qui constituent autant d'intérêts spécifiques et d'interprétations divergentes de la réalité, et au sein duquel les différences sont importantes au plan culturel comme au plan du pouvoir et de l'influence.

La situation géographique du parc n'est bien sûr pas sans incidence sur une telle diversité. En effet, le PNPO s'étend sur deux départements, Hautes-Pyrénées et Pyrénées Atlantiques, correspondant chacun à deux Régions distinctes, Région Midi-Pyrénées pour le premier, Aquitaine pour le second. Le parc couvre sans interruption la frontière espagnole sur 105 kilomètres de longueur. La zone de parc, dite aussi zone centrale, couvre 45.707 hectares (15.120 ha en Pyrénées Atlantiques; 30.587 ha en Hautes-Pyrénées); inhabitée, elle est seulement fréquentée l'été par les bergers. S'y rajoute une réserve naturelle attenante au parc, la Réserve Naturelle du Néouvielle, d'une superficie de 2.300 hectares. La zone périphérique s'étend sur 206.352 hectares comprenant 86 communes (94.192 ha en Pyrénées Atlantiques; 112.160 en Hautes-Pyrénées). Le chevauchement de deux circonscriptions politiques et administratives rajoute encore à la complexité en multipliant par deux le nombre des interlocuteurs potentiels qu'il s'agisse des services de l'Etat ou des collectivités locales.

A la diversité des acteurs correspond aussi la fragmentation du territoire et des cultures. Le clivage entre les Hautes Pyrénées et les Pyrénées Atlantiques est nette, car le positionnement géographique du parc n'est pas le même dans l'un ou l'autre département. Dans les Hautes Pyrénées, les relations avec l'environnement sont plus stables, et ne suscitent plus guère de vrais conflits. La hauteur même des montagnes, alliée à la protection que constitue le parc espagnol d'Ordesa auquel il est adossé, est une limite naturelle à toute forme d'envahissement. Dans les Pyrénées Atlantiques, le tracé même du parc a été moins heureux, résultat de marchandages nébuleux entre l'Etat, les collectivités locales, et les organisations de chasse, qui comprend les deux pénétrantes fortes que sont la route du Pourtalet et le col du Somport. Il était inévitable qu'elles deviennent au centre de multiples débats, d'autant que la pression espagnole du fait d'un essor économique rapide est très forte dans cette partie des montagnes tant en matière d'urbanisation que d'infrastructures routières. Ainsi la réalité des contextes géographiques, par la spécificité des problèmes qu'ils induisent, n'est pas sans influencer les enjeux et les stratégies. Si les différences entre les départements sont nettes, il en est aussi de même au niveau des régions. Si la région Midi-Pyrénées est très engagée dans la gestion de la montagne, l'Aquitaine est largement dépourvue d'une culture montagnarde qui la pousse à s'engager autrement qu'à la marge auprès du PNPO, et ceci se traduit très concrètement par des difficultés réelles pour obtenir de celle-ci la signature d'une convention pluriannuelle d'exécution du contrat de plan Etat-région pour ce qui concerne le traitement de la zone périphérique à l'instar de ce qui a déjà été fait en Midi-Pyrénées.

Il est facile de comprendre les oppositions historiques des collectivités locales à une telle main mise sur une partie conséquente de leur territoire. A l'origine du Parc, l'Etat a du faire de nombreuses promesses financières afin que des compensations puissent accompagner sa création et atténuer les effets éventuellement négatifs de la présence du parc, ne serait-ce qu'à cause de l'insuffisance dans les années 60 des dispositifs d'aide aux zones fragiles de montagne. Mais il s'est avéré difficile de pérenniser cette vocation distributrice. Depuis la mise en place du parc, bien des politiques spécifiques de développement ont été mises en oeuvre, de même que des formes de financement de multiple nature ont été créées (en particulier d'origine européenne), sans compter que la décentralisation a établi d'autres canaux de gestion du tissu territorial qui ne passent plus seulement par le recours à l'Etat. En conséquence le parc dispose aujourd'hui de peu d'atouts pour mobiliser directement son environnement. Il est bien clair que les crédits dont il dispose pour le développement local de la zone périphérique (environ 8 millions de francs) représentent bien peu en termes de possibilités d'action.

Les communes sont, parmi les collectivités locales, les premières concernées par l'activité du parc. Mais leurs élus qui doivent faire face à des exigences nombreuses n'ont pas trouvé auprès du parc le support financier et l'assistance qu'ils espéraient du fait de leur faiblesse et de leur extrême fragilité. Si des oppositions historiques ont marqué les relations avec le parc et favorisé le développement d'attitudes de méfiance plutôt que de collaboration, l'hostilité n'est pourtant plus de mise de manière générale, excepté dans les situations de tension où l'appel à la mémoire et aux promesses non-tenues constitue une stratégie de mobilisation collective. Les attitudes de l'ensemble des élus se révèlent assez neutres, manifestant une implication plutôt faible à l'égard du parc, ce manque d'enthousiasme n'étant lui-même que la conséquence de l'image figée et faiblement attractive du parc actuellement.

Quant aux services de l'Etat, ils ne représentent guère des alliées potentiels. A l'évocation du parc, ils marquent généralement un intérêt poli, et leur désir de coopérer est souvent plus symbolique que réel, expression d'une certaine forme de condescendance, parfois voisine de la compassion, car ils ne perçoivent pas l'intérêt qu'ils auraient à collaborer avec lui. La présence du parc ne s'étant pas révélée très menaçante pour leur autonomie, une certaine indifférence s'est installée. Les services de l'Etat, qu'il s'agisse des administrations techniques ou des offices (Office National des Forêts, Office National de la Chasse), ne peuvent constituer des appuis directs pour le parc, car leur vocation les incite surtout à se rapprocher de leur clientèle naturelle que sont les collectivités territoriales. Leur implication auprès du parc ne peut donc qu'être prudente, dépendante de leur propre logique de marché que l'action de ce dernier peut éventuellement contrecarrer. Par sa présence, le parc les oblige souvent à tenir compte de problèmes environnementaux qui compliquent leurs interventions, et assurent la présence d'associations de défense susceptibles de venir s'intercaler dans les relations privilégiées qu'ils entretiennent généralement avec les collectivités locales. Quant aux préfets, leur mission est plus celle d'une harmonisation des intérêts en présence que de leur opposition. Ils sont par là même hostiles à ce qui peut créer des problèmes d'intégration. Pour eux, le parc n'est pas très important, mais il est surtout une source potentielle de conflits. Ceci explique leur satisfaction à l'élection récente d'un élu à la tête du conseil d'administration du parc en remplacement d'un haut fonctionnaire de l'Etat qui en occupait par tradition la présidence symbolisant ainsi le caractère national de l'institution.

Les associations de protection de la nature sont incontestablement les plus naturellement concernées par les missions du parc, mais elles souffrent de la marginalisation plus générale du mouvement associatif dans le système politique et administratif français. Leurs difficultés essentielles viennent largement de leur faible capacité à pénétrer un milieu local qui leur est souvent hostile du fait de leur recrutement, en dépit parfois de préoccupations très proches en matière de protection de la nature. Leurs stratégies, que certains considèrent comme maximalistes, ne sont bien souvent que la conséquence de leur éviction des instances réelles de décision.

Quant aux scientifiques, ils représentent eux-mêmes un milieu cloisonné, en même temps qu'ils sont porteurs de raisonnements spécifiques liés à des problématiques elles-mêmes spécifiques. Ils ne peuvent avoir vocation à la synthèse, et ne disposent de ce fait que d'une parcelle de légitimité qui ne peut être considérée comme plus prépondérante que d'autres.

Nous pourrions envisager encore d'autres catégories d'acteurs, mais cette rapide évocation montre à quel point les oppositions peuvent être faciles entre des acteurs qui ne sont guidés ni par les mêmes préoccupations, ni par les mêmes modes de raisonnement. Pour les deux premiers, la protection de l'environnement constitue un enjeu parmi d'autres, et il leur faut agir dans une logique qui est par nature davantage celle du court terme que celle du long terme. L'urgence du développement peut leur masquer bien souvent l'importance des questions d'environnement. A l'inverse, les derniers ont des préoccupations plus homogènes, qui les amènent à un raisonnement plus centré sur le long terme, mais leur absence de représentativité en termes de territoire en fait des acteurs faibles.

Ainsi le parc se trouve placé dans une situation où les acteurs les plus susceptibles de soutenir son action sont aussi les moins pertinents dans le contexte local qui est le sien. Or, le problème du parc est avant tout de réussir son intégration dans le territoire auquel il appartient, la zone périphérique lui en fait l'obligation; il lui faut donc chercher à établir des liens avec les acteurs qui en sont les plus représentatifs. Pour l'instant, il a bien du mal à les mobiliser activement, et à être le lieu de réconciliation des multiples logiques en présence. De là découle la fragilité d'un montage institutionnel peu propice à l'affirmation de buts collectifs.

De telles attitudes de retrait nuisent à la prise en compte d'enjeux communs, par suite aussi d'une idée de protection de la nature qui tend par son flou à opposer les acteurs plus qu'à les rassembler. D'autant que, comme nous l'avons précédemment souligné, il s'agit pour beaucoup d'un enjeu parmi d'autres avec lesquels il rentre, sinon en contradiction, au moins en concurrence.

3. LOGIQUE DE BOUC EMISSAIRE ET FONCTION TRIBUNICIENNE

Si le parc souffre manifestement d'un manque d'identité qui l'empêche de se positionner de manière dynamique, c'est bien parce qu'il manque tout particulièrement d'une assise institutionnelle stable, comme d'une articulation de ses missions autour d'enjeux clairement explicités. Mais de telles faiblesses sont plus la conséquence que la cause du jeu des acteurs en présence. Du même coup, le PNPO se définit concrètement moins par les fins qu'il affiche officiellement que par la nature des rapports qui se nouent entre ses membres, lesquels conditionnent de fait les objectifs qu'il est capable de réaliser.

3.1. Le bricolage institutionnel et l'improbable consentement

En sa qualité d'établissement public, le parc a ses propres organes de décision et d'exécution, à savoir un conseil d'administration (CA) et une direction, assistés par une commission permanente et un conseil scientifique consultatif. La recherche active du consentement explique cependant l'importance de la question de la représentation des intérêts. Là encore le couplage zone périphérique/zone centrale produit des effets particulièrement déterminants dans la mesure où en découle la très forte hétérogénéité de la représentation. En se voulant la duplication de son propre environnement, le parc devient tributaire des variations qu'y s'y produisent, et donc de sa capacité à les intégrer. Or, le parc a été pensé à une époque où l'Etat affirmait une autorité incontestable sur les autres collectivités. L'affirmation d'une telle autonomie de volonté se trouve aujourd'hui très fortement amoindrie par la décentralisation qui a considérablement renforcé le poids des scènes locales, non seulement politiquement, mais également dans leur légitimité à fixer leurs propres finalités. Désormais, selon la formule de Léon Duguit, il devient effectif que "l'Etat n'a pas le monopole du bien public". La mise en oeuvre de la décentralisation et de son principe de libre administration des collectivités locales ne pouvait qu'altérer le fonctionnement de l'institution, et générer le sentiment d'une contradiction entre un statut juridique assurant à l'Etat une supériorité hiérarchique et une réalité réservant aux collectivités décentralisées une responsabilité et une légitimité considérablement accrues. De fait, la distinction des zones détermine tant la structure de la représentation que la nature des enjeux, donc du débat.

3.2. Logique juridique et raison pratique

La nature juridique de l'établissement est en elle-même productrice d'un certain nombre d'effets qui ne manquent pas d'avoir des répercussions sur son fonctionnement. Le rattachement à la collectivité nationale, tout d'abord, est la manifestation d'un intérêt supérieur qui s'impose logiquement aux autres collectivités. Depuis longtemps déjà l'Etat a choisi d'intervenir dans des domaines sensibles telles que, par exemple, la protection des sites ou l'urbanisme en montagne afin de préserver la qualité de l'environnement. L'Etat garde a donc en droit la pleine maîtrise des dispositions réglementaires visant à assurer l'activité du parc. Il ne fait qu'associer à son action les partenaires qu'il entend se donner dans la gestion de ses propres compétences. En conséquence, toute remise en cause du pouvoir de l'Etat ne pourrait procéder que d'une intervention externe à l'établissement, car elle devrait alors avoir pour objectif de modifier les fondements législatifs à l'existence des parcs, ce que seule la loi bien sûr peut réaliser. Il faut rappeler que de ce point de vue la présence des collectivités décentralisées en nombre important au sein du conseil d'administration ne procède d'aucune obligation juridique, même si elle apparaît logique et nécessaire, compte tenu de la place occupée par elles dans la gestion du territoire, et de ce qu'elles sont aussi propriétaires d'une partie du territoire. Ce n'est que par exception en effet que des collectivités décentralisées sont autorisées à participer à la gestion d'un établissement public national. Il est à noter d'ailleurs que cette situation est commune à d'autres institutions liées à la gestion de l'environnement telles que les agences de bassin ou le Conservatoire du littoral qui montre bien que l'inscription sur un territoire implique la participation des collectivités concernées[14]. De fait, la formule de l'établissement public permet à l'Etat d'organiser, sous son contrôle, la coopération entre lui-même, les collectivités territoriales, et des représentants d'intérêts divers, et c'est à ce titre qu'elle a été retenue. En effet, les finalités de l'établissement auraient pu conduire à ce que le CA soit composé de membres connaissant, en qualité d'experts, les questions liées à la protection de la nature. La réalité des choix effectués par le pouvoir réglementaire, et qui s'explique par la nature même des enjeux (en particulier leur très forte territorialisation), a entraîné que les membres sont en fait essentiellement à un titre ou à un autre des "usagers" de la nature.

Mais la situation actuelle issue de la décentralisation a accentué l'ambiguïté du dispositif. Certes les collectivités locales, quels que soient par ailleurs les effets de la décentralisation, ne peuvent remettre en question la réglementation que le parc est chargé d'appliquer, ni même les princi-

---

[14] On peut du reste voir dans ces mécanismes des pratiques de cooptation proches de ce que P. Selznick décrivait dans son ouvrage bien connu, *TVA and the Grass Roots*, New York, Harper, 1966.

pes de son fonctionnement qui relèvent de l'Etat seul. Ce sont là les limites à l'action du Conseil d'administration en matière de changement, puisqu'il ne peut contester le cadre de son intervention. Dans la réalité cependant la décentralisation a introduit une nouvelle donne qui a invité les parcs nationaux à définir une autre répartition des pouvoirs plus propice aux collectivités locales.

Ceci s'est traduit par l'élargissement du Conseil d'administration à de nouveaux représentants des collectivités locales qui sont désormais en nombre suffisant pour être sûr de faire entendre leur voix, et qui ont pu de ce fait faire élire l'un d'eux à la tête du Conseil. L'ambivalence des parcs nationaux découle manifestement de l'introduction de la notion peu claire de zone périphérique. Si l'on peut concevoir que l'Etat demeure le patron pour ce qui est de la gestion de la zone centrale, la question est plus délicate pour ce qui relève d'une zone dans laquelle les collectivités locales sont devenues pleinement responsables de leur propre développement. Pour des raisons symboliques, les collectivités locales rechignent donc à se retrouver sous la coupe de l'Etat, fut-ce dans un établissement public au sein duquel elles sont fortement représentées, et à plus forte raison quand c'est pour ne pas en retirer des avantages substantiels. Or, si l'on demande aujourd'hui à ces mêmes collectivités de s'engager davantage, voire financièrement, pour pallier une "présence" de l'Etat de plus en plus timide, il est certain que le statut actuel peut poser problème, car il est vécu sous le mode de la contradiction, sinon en droit, au moins en pratique. Il n'est peut-être pas sûr cependant que l'hostilité au parc serait du même ordre s'il disposait de réelles ressources, et si son utilité était bien ressentie, car les modalités actuelles de son fonctionnement ne font pas de l'Etat un tuteur très autoritaire, et ce d'autant qu'il ne dispose d'aucune majorité de fait au conseil d'administration.

3.3. La recherche du consensus

Le conseil d'administration (CA) est un organe fondamental non seulement dans la hiérarchie administrative de l'institution, mais surtout dans la mesure où il représente l'ensemble des partenaires du parc. Compte tenu de l'espace occupé par le parc et de la multiplicité des intervenants, on comprend assez bien le caractère pléthorique et disparate d'une telle assemblée: celle-ci rassemble en effet, outre des élus locaux, des représentants des associations cynégétiques départementales, des Chambres départementales d'agriculture et d'industrie, des professionnels de la montagne (agriculteurs, guides), des fonctionnaires des administrations centrales concernées, des personnalités scientifiques, des représentants d'associations de protection de la nature (soit un total de 62 personnes pour le PNPO!). Le CA se veut donc remplir une *fonction d'intégration* en permettant de rassembler dans un même lieu la majeure partie des acteurs concernés par la gestion d'un même espace géographique. Mais il la remplit mal. Cette participation "obligée" est loin de correspondre à un engagement positif des différents membres, ni même à un intérêt clairement ressenti. Ceci explique la méfiance de beaucoup comme la faiblesse de leur participation. Au fond, peu entendent se lier les mains par une participation réelle, et c'est plutôt la réserve qui domine jusqu'ici. La situation du CA n'est en fait que l'illustration de ce que nous avons précédemment mis en valeur à propos de l'environnement. La reconnaissance institutionnelle des partenaires n'a pas produit l'apprentissage espéré d'une communauté d'intérêts. Ceux-ci demeurent multiples, et de surcroît le parc ne représente pas le même enjeu pour tous. Pour une bonne partie des membres, la collaboration avec le parc ne constitue qu'un aspect secondaire de leur propre activité, ce qui explique la timidité de leurs interventions. D'autres ont simplement du mal à coopérer sur un enjeu qu'ils ne perçoivent pas clairement, et qui demeure abstrait et lointain faute de représentation plus précise des missions du parc. Ceci est tout particulièrement vrai pour les collectivités locales qui se sentent obligées à une coopération dont elles ne ressentent pas toujours la nécessité ni l'utilité, et dans des conditions qu'elles n'ont pas elles-mêmes fixées puisqu'elles le sont par l'Etat. Pour cette raison, le CA devient souvent le lieu symbolique d'une relation à l'Etat, doublement présent en la personne du Commissaire de la République, commissaire du gouvernement, et dans celle du directeur du parc, nommé par arrêté du ministre chargé des parcs nationaux.

En un sens, le CA perd sa vocation initiale d'instance administrative pour devenir une *tribune* à partir de laquelle de petites collectivités interpellent l'Etat sur une question plus vaste qui est celle de leur propre développement, quand d'autres le somment d'imposer une protection autoritaire de la nature. La "dramatisation" y est d'autant plus facile que la taille du public s'y prête, et que les acteurs sont d'autant moins liés au parc que celui-ci est une institution faible, distributrice de maigres ressources. Le CA remplit d'une certaine manière une fonction latente d'expression des intérêts.

La vie du CA se résume ainsi à une opposition simple entre "protecteurs" et "développeurs". Une fois encore la disjonction des zones empêche l'émergence d'un enjeu commun, car elle rend possible, conforte même, la segmentation des enjeux. Au titre de la zone périphérique, les collectivités locales sont habilitées à questionner l'Etat sur leur développement, quand, au titre de la zone centrale, les partisans d'une protection ferme de la nature placent délibérément le débat sur le terrain d'une écologie sans concession. Chacun trouve dans l'architecture de l'institution la justification du bien-fondé de sa position. Le débat s'oriente plus vers une guérilla quasi permanente dans laquelle s'affrontent des positions de principe que vers la recherche de solutions pratiques, car au fond, personne n'ayant un intérêt véritable au compromis, les enjeux se recoupent rarement. La coopération s'impose d'autant moins que, comme nous l'avons dit, les bénéfices sont diffus et les coûts peu élevés, ce qui définit une structure de participation caractérisée par la faiblesse des processus de coopération.

Les communes n'ont qu'un intérêt limité à la part d'espace qui les concerne, leur interdépendance est pratiquement nulle; nous ne sommes pas en effet dans une situation d'utilisation commune d'une ressource commune comme dans le cas de la "Tragedy of the Commons"[15]. Elles ne sont pas non plus en compétition pour l'obtention des crédits de développement; non seulement la maigreur de ces derniers, mais une pratique de saupoudrage a également tendu à éviter toute concurrence. Pour ces raisons, le CA sert surtout aux communes les plus faibles et les plus hostiles au parc à faire entendre leurs voix, et au nom d'une solidarité négative de défense, elles sont supportées par l'ensemble des autres élus pour former un front uni, leur légitimité politique n'étant plus garante de leur supériorité. Quant aux conseillers généraux, trop dépendants électoralement des communes, ils se gardent bien d'avoir une attitude opposée à ces dernières, alors même qu'ils pourraient faire valoir un intérêt propre.

La constitution du CA aboutit à réduire de fait le rôle des élus à une dimension essentiellement corporatiste de défense d'intérêts "particularistes", purement locaux et à court terme, quand par suite d'une inversion particulièrement significative des logiques, les représentants des milieux

---

[15] Cf. G. Hardin, "The Tragedy of the Commons", *Science 162*, 1968.

écologiques ont à prouver qu'ils ne représentent pas des intérêts particuliers, et se situent dans le cadre plus général et plus global d'une rationalité à long terme au nom d'intérêts aisément "universalisables" de sauvegarde du patrimoine naturel. Dès lors une telle situation ne peut manifestement permettre l'émergence d'attentes partagées en l'absence de réactions et de références semblables[16].

On peut du même coup s'interroger sur le rôle directeur du CA en matière de gestion de l'établissement. Dans de telles conditions, on peut comprendre que le CA n'a jamais réussi à pleinement s'engager dans la formulation de stratégies claires et cohérentes. Non seulement l'unanimité n'y est guère possible, mais les conditions d'un engagement réel des différents partenaires sur un programme précis ne sont jamais totalement réunies. Le fonctionnement du CA ne favorise pas le développement de réflexes gestionnaires. Le manque d'implication actuel explique qu'il se soit éloigné de sa vraie vocation d'organe de décision et de délibération, et que les débats se résument surtout à la simple énonciation de prises de position diverses, de là cette *fonction tribunicienne* qui explique qu'il vaut toujours mieux "en être" que de rester à la porte. Il est un lieu de cristallisation et d'affirmation des différences.

Finalement, et de manière contre-intuitive, la fausse participation à laquelle a conduit la mise en place d'un organe "représentatif" s'est révélée dommageable pour la gestion du parc. Certes, la démocratie pratiquée a permis que le parc soit accepté, même si c'est avec réserve, ce qui est primordial. Mais elle a aussi conduit à l'immobilisme. Si, comme nous l'avons dit, le CA a du mal à accoucher d'une politique, l'établissement a trouvé aussi la justification de ses propres difficultés dans l'"irresponsabilité" du CA, et dans le fait qu'il est peu épaulé par ceux qui sont censés le diriger; tel est aujourd'hui le cercle vicieux dans lequel se trouve le parc dont la capacité d'action est entravée par le mauvais fonctionnement de son instance dirigeante, mais qui trouve dans cette situation la justification de son propre immobilisme. Une telle logique a conduit en effet à légitimer le manque de dynamisme de l'institution. A courir après une reconnaissance difficile à obtenir, le risque est aussi de se paralyser soi-même, car ne pas vouloir déplaire conduit aussi à ne plaire à personne. C'est là une des raisons qui explique la faiblesse des alliances dont dispose le parc comme l'indétermination de ses missions qui n'est pour une

---

[16] Cf. sur ce point Th. Schelling, *La stratégie du conflit*, Paris, PUF, 1986.

part que la contrepartie de l'absence d'ajustement des intérêts en présence. La nécessité de parvenir à des arrangements négociés conduit à maintenir des objectifs relativement flous et généraux qui ne favorisent guère la consolidation d'une conception instrumentale de l'action. Le maintien d'un minimum de compatibilité entre les membres est donc fonction de la capacité du parc à accommoder des exigences contradictoires; c'est dire que celui-ci ne peut que difficilement en l'état élaborer une stratégie qui nécessite que soit concilier deux objectifs contradictoires: assurer l'intégration de ses membres et agir en organisation efficace. La recherche d'un consensus minimal est paradoxalement liée à la faiblesse des performances de l'organisation! Au fond, la juxtaposition des missions n'est bien que la traduction de l'absence de cohésion des acteurs.

3.4. Une institution en recherche d'identité et de politique

En effet, l'énoncé des missions du parc (protection de la nature, observations scientifiques, accueil du public, développement local) procède plus d'une logique de juxtaposition que d'intégration, et cela a favorisé incontestablement une approche segmentée des problèmes, d'autant que la distinction des missions correspond au découpage des activités organisationnelles, mais aussi de fait des clientèles. Elles ont été progressivement autonomisées, et ressenties du même coup comme contradictoires quand bien même il fallait y voir une possible synergie.

Une telle approche s'est d'autant plus facilement imposée qu'elle s'appuie sur des termes qui peuvent constituer autant d'oppositions possibles: protection de la nature/développement local, observations scientifiques/accueil du public, etc.. Si la protection de la nature peut être antinomique avec toute forme de développement, le travail scientifique ne fait pas nécessairement bon ménage avec la démarche touristique. L'idée de protection est en elle-même une idée d'opposition qui suscite des réflexes négatifs tout comme le zonage conduit à créer des frontières et donc des exclusions. On le voit, l'intitulé des missions, sous sa forme actuelle, n'est pas favorable à l'établissement d'une image cohérente et sans ambiguïté de l'action du parc.

Tout, au fond, a favorisé l'adoption d'une culture d'opposition. Le difficile positionnement du parc a conduit ses agents à trouver leur identité dans l'opposition que leur manifestait un milieu environnant perçu comme hostile plus que dans la réalité d'un métier qu'ils avaient du mal à inventer. Ils ont du même coup contribué à véhiculer une "culture-parc" à l'image de la géographie, fermée comme chacune des vallées qui constitue son univers. Inversement, des collectivités locales faibles ont trouvé dans le parc le support commode à leur opposition à une administration centrale inaccessible, et par là le moyen d'exprimer leur mécontentement. Ainsi la vie du parc est-elle constituée par des jeux d'opposition dans lesquels chaque protagoniste essaie en fait de résoudre son propre problème d'identité résultat d'une même faiblesse à exister pour lui-même, et de se constituer en acteur d'une histoire qu'il ne peut pourtant faire seul. Dans ce contexte, le parc pouvait difficilement devenir l'instrument d'une programmation de la mise en valeur de la zone périphérique par l'ensemble des administrations de l'Etat, que les textes fondateurs appelaient de leurs voeux. Ce souci bienvenu de coordination de l'action publique ne pouvait être porté par une institution dès le départ contestée faute d'avoir été suffisamment opérationnalisée, manquant de moyens comme de légitimité.

L'appartenance au ministère de l'Environnement ne constitue pas de surcroît pour le parc un facteur d'identification compensatoire satisfaisant. Généralement, l'appartenance à une administration ancienne et légitime, comme l'Equipement ou l'Agriculture par exemple, n'est pas sans effet positif sur les perceptions des personnels et des usagers. Dans le cas présent, le ministère ne constitue pas une référence par rapport à laquelle on est susceptible de construire son identité sociale. Non seulement celui-ci est encore jeune et fragile, manquant beaucoup de prestige, mais il n'est pas perçu lui-même avec assez de précision pour offrir une image stable à laquelle se référer. On pourrait même dire que le ministère renforce les attitudes négatives dans la mesure où il est considéré comme très lointain, peu préoccupé du terrain en général, et des parcs en particulier.

La culture d'une institution, c'est autant ses valeurs que ses pratiques. Or les missions, au-delà de leur seule juxtaposition, sont demeurées floues, et n'ont pu de ce fait être traduites qu'imparfaitement en objectifs d'action et en savoir-faire précis. L'incompréhension des autres a fourni au PNPO une justification de ce qu'il est, mais cela ne suffit pas à assurer une légitimité.

A l'évidence, le parc fonctionne, mais il le fait de façon essentiellement routinière et défensive. La conséquence d'une telle situation se lit dans le contenu même de l'action du parc, dont la programmation réelle est pauvre, et sur laquelle il est difficile de communiquer. L'absence d'intégration des tâches et des échelons organisationnels, et la faible articulation des instances administratives aboutissent au fractionnement des activités dont la cumulativité est faible. La preuve la plus évidente en est l'absence d'inventaire rigoureux du patrimoine du parc. Or sans inventaire, il ne paraît guère possible de procéder à une évaluation de la valeur patrimoniale, et par contrecoup de pouvoir arbitrer entre protection, conservation, et exploitation des richesses naturelles. La faiblesse des ressources n'explique pas totalement la faible attractivité du parc, l'absence de stratégie dynamique impulsée par l'institution en est largement la cause. Le parc était, de ce point de vue, davantage géré comme une administration traditionnelle que comme un établissement public qui avait à conquérir sa clientèle et sa légitimité. Une administration telle que la Direction Départementale de l'Agriculture et des Forêts par exemple a ses clients naturels qui la sollicitent et l'obligent éventuellement à s'impliquer activement dans la gestion d'un territoire, mais ce n'est pas directement le cas du parc, qui avait au contraire à se faire reconnaître. Non seulement sa mission, mais aussi la faiblesse de ses ressources n'en ont pas fait un partenaire recherché. Pour parler la langue de l'économiste, la protection de la nature ne constituait pas à ses débuts un marché très porteur, donc elle n'avait pas de clients naturels qui pouvaient être susceptibles de chercher une expertise en la matière. A défaut d'être toujours allé au devant de ses partenaires éventuels, le parc a donc eu une politique de communication figée, peu tournée vers la recherche de partenaires, et a trouvé dans l'opposition de l'environnement la justification d'une telle attitude.

Si le jeu reste ouvert, la difficulté du changement vient du fait que le fonctionnement du parc est aujourd'hui dominé par des logiques de non-communication et d'évitement entre les différents protagonistes. Ces stratégies de non-engagement ont d'autant plus de chances de se maintenir qu'elles sont fonctionnelles pour tout le monde, car personne ne veut cautionner une institution dont l'action n'est, du même coup, pas satisfaisante; c'est là ce qui explique la récurrence de ces stratégies comme la permanence de clivages, souvent plus artificiels qu'on veut bien le dire. On est ainsi dans un cercle vicieux où chacun externalise la responsabilité de la situation présente sur autrui. Cependant l'interdépendance des comportements produit l'immobilisme, et l'incapacité à trouver des solutions lorsqu'un problème surgit, qui oblige les acteurs à se faire face, l'exemple de la protection de l'ours est parfaitement significatif de la faiblesse des processus de négociation.

Actuellement, nous l'avons en partie souligné, le parc ne dispose pas d'alliés puissants qui lui permettent de stabiliser son environnement. A l'évidence, il manque encore de relais, même si l'élection d'un élu à la tête du conseil d'administration peut constituer un premier pas dans cette voie. Les relations avec les collectivités locales sont insuffisamment structurées. L'apprentissage de nouveaux modèles relationnels nécessite la prise de conscience d'enjeux communs à l'ensemble des acteurs. Un enjeu commun ne signifie pas pour autant que les intérêts sont semblables, mais que chacun est impliqué par une même question. La sauvegarde du patrimoine pourrait être de cet ordre, qui pose clairement le problème de l'utilisation, et donc de l'utilité du parc.

4. Reconstruire la negociation

La faiblesse du parc tient donc à un ensemble de raisons qui ont tendance à s'enchaîner et à se renforcer:

- défaut d'alliances fortes;

- manque de perception d'enjeux communs;

- faiblesse des ressources;

- manque de dynamisme propre.

Ce constat est le résultat d'une analyse approfondie qui constitue le préalable à la recherche d'une solution qui ne peut être que collective pour être constitutive par là même d'un ordre réellement négocié. Il faut pouvoir y puiser une connaissance commune qui puisse de ce fait constituer les bases d'une discussion collective qui doit permettre, au moins dans un premier temps, de modifier les représentations dans un sens plus propice à la coopération. Il faut aider en effet à la clarification des enjeux afin de parvenir à une représentation appropriée du territoire. Mais changer les représentations de l'action ne suffit pas toujours à en transformer les conditions, ne serait-ce que parce que, par son caractère public, une institution comme le parc ne peut s'abstraire d'un contexte plus largement politique.

4.1. Vers une conceptualisation conjointe

Le parc est un univers hautement symbolique, et il est important qu'il puisse donner de ses missions une représentation non seulement positive et attrayante, mais également susceptible de pouvoir être traduite dans des stratégies de gestion. Il faut en effet offrir des pistes d'action concrètes susceptibles de permettre de réaliser les apprentissages nécessaires à de nouveaux modèles relationnels. Le problème du parc, c'est de produire de l'intégration. Actuellement, on ne peut penser s'engager sur la voie d'une "négociation intégrative" qui soit susceptible de faire passer l'importance d'une communauté d'intérêts, de valeurs et d'objectifs avant l'affirmation des intérêts particuliers[17]. Comme le note F. Scharpf, le règlement, au sens de *problem-solving*, est un style de décision très fragile, car il reste largement tributaire de l'attachement à des objectifs communs et d'un degré suffisant de confiance mutuelle[18]. Ceci explique qu'il faille s'employer à diffuser des interprétations et des définitions susceptibles d'être admises par tous afin d'augmenter la capacité et le désir des acteurs en présence à s'engager dans une activité de résolution de problème.

4.2. Assurer une meilleure synergie des finalités

Il est possible de passer d'une vision éclatée à une vision homogène, en même temps qu'il est nécessaire de substituer une culture ouverte à une culture fermée. Le choix des mots est toujours important, car il véhicule des images et des représentations comme il conditionne des modes de raisonnement. Pour cette raison, il n'est peut-être pas inutile de chercher le dénominateur commun susceptible d'intégrer l'ensemble des activités du parc afin d'en proposer une vision dynamique et plus unitaire sur laquelle pourraient se retrouver ses personnels comme ses partenaires. Pour l'instant, les participants n'ont aucune capacité à communiquer les uns avec les autres, aucune manière de développer de la confiance, et a for-

---

[17] Cf. sur ce point R. E. Walton, R. B. McKersie, *A Behavioral Theory of Labour Negociations. An Analysis of a Social Interaction System*, New York, McGraw-Hill, 1965.

[18] F. Scharpf, "Echec des politiques et réforme des institutions: pourquoi la forme devrait-elle suivre la fonction?", *Revue Internationale des Sciences Sociales*, UNESCO/ERES, n° 108, 1986.

tiori aucun sentiment d'avoir à partager un avenir commun. Or on sait bien que des acteurs qui n'ont aucun bénéfice à agir en commun ni même un minimum de confiance mutuelle, sans capacité à communiquer et donc à entrer dans des arrangements susceptibles de les lier, ont peu de chances de développer des stratégies communes ou d'alliances. C'est pour cela qu'il est important de modifier les modes de raisonnement et qu'il est important de développer des mécanismes de *conceptualisation conjointe* quant aux interprétations possibles et partagées de ce qui est désiré, recherché. Il faut pouvoir développer des interprétations partagées, en particulier quant au domaine propre d'intervention du PNPO. Le processus de structuration organisationnelle doit correspondre, sous peine de rester vide, à un processus d'institutionnalisation de significations partagées. La formalisation doit représenter une ratification explicite d'une compréhension négociée du domaine d'action. Il n'y a pas actuellement d'attentes partagées. L'absence de points d'équilibre est liée à l'absence de réactions et de références semblables, sinon négativement par la survie du parc, car aucun des protagonistes n'a véritablement intérêt à sa disparition.

L'idée de patrimoine, qui est historiquement au coeur de la réflexion sur la sauvegarde de l'environnement nous paraît être un bon vecteur de ce qui permettrait de trouver un ajustement entre les différentes démarches possibles en matière de gestion d'un parc national, d'autant que la défense du patrimoine est une idée qui peut ici rassembler plus qu'opposer, dans la mesure où c'est un souci qui peut se partager; ce peut être tout autant celui de l'Etat que celui de la région, du département, et de la commune, ou encore des associations qui s'en donnent la vocation.

5. Passer d'une vision eclatee des missions a une vision homogene

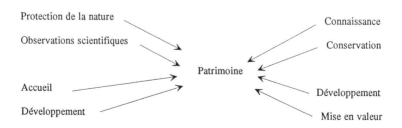

On le voit l'idée de patrimoine permet en fait de retrouver les différentes missions du parc sans qu'il y ait d'oppositions entre les activités qui peuvent découler de la possession d'un patrimoine, car elles sont toutes des composantes d'un seul et même enjeu qui est la gestion du patrimoine naturel. Une certaine forme de hiérarchisation s'impose d'elle-même par sa logique interne, car pour transmettre et améliorer, faut-il déjà avoir su conserver et connaître. Or, à l'heure actuelle, le parc ne dispose d'aucun inventaire sérieux de son patrimoine. De même, on perçoit mieux les possibles combinaisons entre des missions dont la synergie est désormais plus évidente.

L'affirmation claire des missions est essentielle tant au plan externe qu'interne:
- dans le domaine des relations avec l'environnement, elle permet d'assurer la crédibilité des actions mises en oeuvre, de choisir ses interlocuteurs, et de dégager les règles de conduite qui leur sont applicables;

- dans le domaine interne, elle est garante de la cohésion de l'établissement. Particulièrement nécessaire dans les situations de changement ou tout simplement difficiles, elle permet de préserver l'identité des personnels des risques d'éclatement par la référence à un fond commun qui fait la légitimité de l'organisation.

Reste à définir quel en est l'espace de référence, et rompre du même coup avec une interprétation trop générale de l'espace et de son usage, et par là très peu opératoire. A partir d'une interprétation homogène, il est apparu utile, pour des raisons pédagogiques, de s'orienter vers une représentation plus sélective du territoire du parc autour de ses usages, et donc de ses usagers afin de promouvoir une démarche de gestion concertée plus concrète.

5.1. Une gestion de l'espace différenciée pour des publics précis

Là encore en effet, la notion de parc induit une représentation abstraite et indifférenciée de l'espace. L'espace correspond à des usages, dès lors qu'il est lié à l'histoire des hommes. Du même coup, il n'est peut-être pas inutile de différencier l'espace en fonction de l'usage qui peut lui être attribué. Si l'espace doit se gérer, il doit l'être de manière appropriée, c'est-à-dire en fonction d'objectifs spécifiques, suivant des indicateurs adaptés, pour un public précis. Il faut en fait *problématiser le territoire* du parc, autrement dit lier sa gestion à l'identification des problèmes que l'on entend traiter et par là même des acteurs concernés. Il faut partir du concret des situations, et non d'objectifs généraux pour un territoire indéfini, c'est là une condition essentielle au développement d'un engagement réel des partenaires. Il est évident que l'on ne peut gérer un site surfréquenté selon les mêmes principes et les mêmes moyens qu'une zone naturellement abritée et à l'écart des lieux de passage les plus utilisés.

On peut ainsi classer l'espace naturel sur un continuum dont les extrémités symbolisent la fermeture et l'ouverture, et mettre en parallèle les types de public concernés.

PATRIMOINE NATUREL

Fermeture

Quelle nature?	x	**Quel public?**
nature protégée	⟶	scientifiques/parc
nature découverte	⟶	visites guidées et initiés
nature vitrine	⟶	grand public

Ouverture

Il faut bien sûr adjoindre à ce schéma centré surtout sur la zone centrale, une nature "associée" qui correspond en fait à la zone périphérique à la gestion de laquelle le parc doit logiquement participer sans être pour autant dans la même situation de leadership.

Il ne s'agit pas de développer une autre forme de zonage, mais de mettre en place une réelle gestion du territoire en *orientant* les acteurs sur une représentation pratique de l'espace. Une différenciation du territoire en fonction d'enjeux clairs autorise:

- *une gestion spécifique de l'espace*, avec la mise en place d'indicateurs de gestion d'autant plus précis que les finalités sont fixées et connues de tous;

- *une communication appropriée*, dans la mesure où la différenciation spatiale permet d'avoir une approche segmentée du public, et donc de mettre en oeuvre une politique de communication mieux ciblée;

- *un partenariat adapté*, dans la mesure où tout le monde n'est pas nécessairement concerné par le même type d'espace ni le même type de problème. Il est clair que les partenaires pertinents ne sont pas les mêmes suivant la nature des enjeux. Une telle approche offre la possibilité de mieux cibler les interventions nécessaires, et par là même de mieux décider des priorités, et donc des moyens à allouer. En particulier, il est clair que les différents niveaux de gestion de l'espace déterminent des rationalités spécifiques et des possibilités d'alliances variables car ils n'induisent pas les mêmes types de représentation et d'implication. Si les communes ont comme nous l'avons montré, un intérêt généralement à court terme et limité à la portion de territoire qui les concerne, les départements ont par nécessité et vocation une perception plus large et donc plus englobante du parc et de ses impacts qui peut les amener à mieux situer et comprendre les effets structurants à moyen et long terme d'une telle institution et donc à développer avec elle des actions appropriées.

Mais pour s'engager dans une dynamique active de gestion, il faut reconnaître la réalité du parc, à savoir ses effets structurants à long terme en même temps que sa faiblesse institutionnelle qui lui ôte toute valeur en tant que bouc émissaire.

5.2. Prendre la mesure de la réalité

Indiscutablement, le PNPO n'apparaît plus comme une contrainte forte au développement de l'économie locale. Il n'a guère entravé l'aménagement des stations de sports d'hiver, et les difficultés actuelles vécues par les collectivités locales tiennent à des facteurs qui ne lui sont pas imputables. La majorité des élus le reconnaissent, même si le poids de l'histoire veut qu'on se souvienne encore et surtout des promesses non tenues. Cependant, le parc ne doit pas être non plus le bouc émissaire commode d'une opposition à l'Etat, qui ne peut que l'affaiblir et l'empêcher du même coup de participer activement à la promotion de son territoire d'élection. L'ensemble des élus des Hautes-Pyrénées sont aujourd'hui pleinement conscients de la valeur potentielle que représente le parc comme des éléments positifs qu'il a apportés. Il a incontestablement participé à la protection des sites, et il a, par sa seule présence, indirectement protégé les communes de stratégies anarchiques de développement touristique à l'époque où la fièvre de l'"or blanc" pouvait conduire à des aménagements désastreux tant pour les finances locales que pour la qualité de l'environnement. Le parc constitue à l'évidence une image attractive sur laquelle il faut construire. Ainsi une étude sur le tourisme a montré que la fréquentation du département des Hautes-Pyrénées était liée aux multiples possibilités de randonnées, la qualité des paysages et l'aménagement des sites, ce qui légitime largement la présence du parc.

Dans les Pyrénées Atlantiques toutefois, les attitudes demeurent plus hostiles et moins favorables, mais si l'histoire les explique, l'avenir montre leurs limites. Pourtant, là encore, les élus, dès lors qu'ils ne font plus référence au passé, reconnaissent volontiers que le parc ne présente plus d'inconvénients dont on ne puisse raisonnablement débattre; malheureusement leur situation économique délicate et leur isolement les conduisent trop souvent à transposer sur le parc leur mécontentement. La question du développement valléen est complexe et dépend plus de la capacité à mettre en oeuvre une intercommunalité forte pour agir sur les niveaux pertinents de gestion du territoire (Etat, région, département) et un partenariat intelligent avec ces derniers que de la seule pression sur le parc. Jouer sur un acteur faible n'est guère une stratégie gagnante.

Ainsi il ressort que le parc n'est en fait ni une réelle contrainte ni une ressource effective, car il n'est pas perçu comme directement producteur de richesse, et que le développement est un effet induit de sa propre activité de conservation du patrimoine naturel. Mais faire du parc un véritable atout nécessite en particulier un changement de registre temporel, que l'on passe d'une vision à court terme à un raisonnement à moyen et long terme, ce qui implique justement une approche réaliste et informée. Cependant le passage à une rationalité à plus ou moins long terme dépend en particulier de la capacité que l'on a à s'abstraire des contraintes de court terme. Les petites communes ont bien du mal à raisonner sur le long terme qu'implique toute réflexion approfondie sur l'environnement; à l'inverse départements et régions ont assurément plus de distance, ce qui leur permet d'accéder à un raisonnement susceptible d'intégrer dans une même logique d'action contraintes économiques et contraintes d'environnement. La recherche d'alliances suppose que l'on n'oublie pas cela.

En fait, on le voit, les conditions ne sont pas loin d'être réunies aujourd'hui pour assurer une intégration dynamique du parc dans le territoire, mais il est curieusement nécessaire pour cela que l'on reconnaisse dans un premier temps qu'il n'est lui-même qu'un acteur faible, et non le rouleau compresseur d'une action étatique nécessairement technocratique et lointaine, pas plus qu'il n'est complètement asservi à des intérêts locaux nécessairement ignorants des impératifs de protection. Le parc n'est en fait que peu de choses par lui-même, il n'est que ce que les acteurs qui le composent lui permettront d'être. Or, de ce point de vue, le PNPO constitue aussi une arène qui offre une certaine visibilité à l'affrontement des intérêts, et les stratégies des acteurs y sont très largement dépendantes des conditions contextuelles.

5.3. La dramatisation comme solution et le conflit comme mode de communication

Une telle phase de conceptualisation conjointe est à tous égards fondamentale, mais elle ne saurait suffir à l'établissement d'un réel processus de négociation généralisée. Deux exemples de conflit sont là pour l'attester: la protection de l'ours des Pyrénées d'une part, la percée du tunnel du Somport de l'autre. Il convient de ne pas perdre de vue que dans une situation d'interaction, le choix des enjeux comme des coups à jouer sont souvent le résultat d'activités stratégiques, c'est-à-dire en fait de la capacité des acteurs à conduire un processus de mobilisation au mieux de leurs intérêts respectifs. En l'occurrence les jeux d'opposition au sein du parc prennent leur sens dans un contexte qui définit les opportunités d'action plus que dans la personnalité des acteurs. Or le parc est en fait moins un problème qu'une *ressource*, au sens où il offre à certains acteurs le moyen de gérer, à travers lui, des enjeux qui leur sont propres.

Carte du parc National des Pyrénées Occidentales

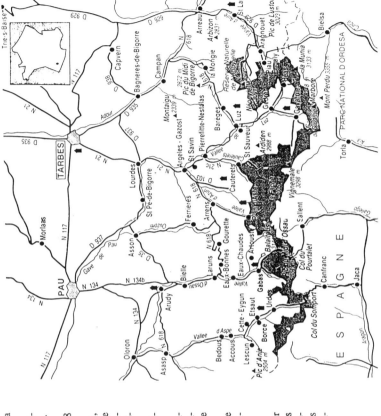

Le Parc National des Pyrénées Occidentales a été créé à la fin de l'année 1967.

Ses 457 km² chevauchent le département des Hautes-Pyrénées (60% de sa surface) et celui des Pyrénées-Atlantiques.

Sa largeur varie entre 1.5 km et 15 km.

De 1.067 m au point le plus bas, il grimpe jusqu'aux 3.298 m du Pic du Vignemale.

Son territoire s'étire de la haute vallée d'Aspe, à l'ouest, jusqu'à la haute vallée d'Aure, à l'est, s'appuyant sur une centaine de kilomètres le long de la frontière; du côté espagnol lui répondent le Parc National d'Ordesa et les réserves nationales de chasse.

L'eau est partout présente, et l'on dénombre 230 lacs d'altitude, sans compter les gaves ou torrents.

Nul n'habite en permanence cette zone de hautes montagnes. Seules activités admises: le pastoralisme - les pâturages représentent 50% de sa surface - et l'activité forestière (12% de son territoire).

Le Parc National des Pyrénées Occidentales se prolonge par les 2.300 hectares de la Réserve Naturelle du Néouvielle, dont la surveillance lui est confiée.

La faune et la flore du Parc son intégralement protégées.

Une zone périphérique de 2.060 km² a été ménagée autour du Parc National. Elle est destinée à préparer l'accès des visiteurs, mais aussi et surtout à encourager le développement local. Car, réparties sur les 6 vallées, 86 communes comptent 30.000 habitants, pour qui l'économie montagnarde est vitale et doit être préservée.

 Zone périphérique

 Parc National

← Maisons du Parc National

Dans le cas présent, l'absence de négociation est liée à la représentation que chacun se fait de ses gains qui conditionne le maintien d'enjeux irréductibles les uns aux autres. Les groupes en présence continue à se percevoir gagnant dans le conflit, car ils n'ont rien à gagner à collaborer, et tant qu'ils le vivront en ces termes, il n'y aura guère de négociation possible. L'épreuve de force est ici vécue comme la stratégie la plus payante, et pour reprendre la formulation d'Adam et Reynaud, elle-même adaptée de Clausewitz: "le conflit est la continuation de la négociation par d'autres moyens"[19]. L'entrée dans le conflit s'explique par la faiblesse des acteurs, renforcée par leur isolement important comme leur absence de ressources négociables; d'un certain point de vue le conflit est aussi pour eux un moyen d'établir une communication.

Ainsi, il n'est pas surprenant que ces deux sujets de conflit se développent dans les Pyrénées Atlantiques. Ce département, comme du reste la Région Aquitaine à laquelle il appartient, ne possède pas, nous l'avons dit, de culture "montagnarde" réellement développée, alors même que la partie montagnarde du département dispose d'une culture très marquée, et le sentiment d'appartenance, très fort, ne fait donc que renforcer une impression d'isolement d'autant plus mal vécue qu'à ces différences culturelles se surajoutent des différences importantes de niveau de développement et de richesses qui se muent rapidement en opposition. La façade atlantique dispose manifestement de plus d'atouts et concentre l'attention des pouvoirs publics. Par ailleurs, cette partie des Pyrénées est elle-même la moins bien dotée sur le plan du tourisme, et manifestement la partie la plus faible sur le plan économique. Le sentiment d'un avenir incertain, voire même d'une absence d'avenir, est très présent. Les vallées comportent un nombre important de toutes petites communes rurales, financièrement exsangues, dont la démographie s'étiole sous l'effet d'un exode rural fort. D'un autre côté, leur capacité d'action collective est faible, les communes sont plus promptes à se réunir sur un objectif de défense que pour la promotion d'actions positives. La mise en place d'une structure intercommunale y est finalement récente, mais il est vrai aussi qu'il n'est pas toujours facile de s'allier quand on a peu de choses à mettre au pot commun.

Nous sommes confrontés ici à une caractéristique essentielle de notre tissu territorial, et aussi son point noir, à savoir l'émiettement communal

---

[19] G. Adam, J. D. Reynaud, *Conflits du travail et changement social*, Paris, PUF, 1978.

Nous sommes confrontés ici à une caractéristique essentielle de notre tissu territorial, et aussi son point noir, à savoir l'émiettement communal et le maintien de structures communales qui n'ont plus lieu d'être sous leur forme actuelle. Elles se trouvent exclues de la prospérité et de la croissance, et la décentralisation n'a guère apporté de réponse à leurs problèmes. Si elles en appellent aujourd'hui encore à Paris, c'est aussi parce qu'elles se trouvent localement marginalisées.

Leurs comportements actuels se doivent donc d'être analysés dans un modèle où la faiblesse des moyens et la non-communication créent et renforcent un sentiment d'exclusion qui trouve dans la protestation non seulement un exutoire à leur mécontentement mais aussi l'expression d'une identité. On comprend aisément pourquoi la dimension morale dont sont assorties les revendications est si prégnante: appels à la dignité, à l'honneur bafoué par les technocrates parisiens ou les urbains en mal de nature. La révolte est la stratégie la plus rationnelle, d'autant que la communication politique n'y est pas plus payante. La représentation politique est faible (quelle que soit la qualité personnelle des élus en présence) par absence de véritable leader, et elle n'est pas de ce fait le lieu le plus pertinent d'expression du mécontentement. C'est bien là du reste ce qui fait problème. L'absence d'expressions instituées selon des procédures légitimes les conduisent à chercher dans des voies plus contestables la résolution de leurs difficultés. La forte connotation morale du discours local est bien liée à un sentiment d'exclusion plus ou moins conscient de laissés-pour-compte. N'ayant rien à échanger dans la négociation, ils jouent sur une des rares ressources disponibles, eux-mêmes, c'est-à-dire l'auto-affirmation de leur valeur.

Un tel contexte permet de comprendre des attitudes qui conduisent à:

- prendre en quelque sorte l'ours en otage, c'est-à-dire en fait que l'ours devient un "médium" de communication et d'échange;

- se réfugier dans la construction de l'équipement miracle.

L'ours est au fond un atout pour chacun des groupes en présence, une ressource que chacun investit de ses propres intérêts. Il est pour les locaux l'occasion de se faire entendre, et d'évoquer leur situation. En l'occurrence, le conflit n'est pas rupture de la négociation, il en est bien là encore la continuation par d'autres moyens. Au fond l'enjeu "sauver l'ours" est un faux enjeu, et paradoxalement, il est même un enjeu mineur, et nous sommes même sûr qu'il existe un relatif consensus sur cette question. L'ours est comme le parc, un intermédiaire.

Malheureusement, prendre en otage n'est jamais une stratégie très honorable aux yeux d'une opinion publique lointaine, et les locaux sont pris au piège d'une "communication" qui leur échappe. Car la généralisation et l'extension du conflit par appel à l'Etat se font bel et bien sur la base de l'ours, non prioritairement sur le développement local. La force de leurs adversaires "protecteurs" se joue bien dans la délocalisation de la scène et la nationalisation du conflit que leur permet leur plus grande capacité d'accès aux médias nationaux, voire son "européanisation" par la saisine des instances communautaires. Dès lors, pour l'opinion publique, la protection de l'ours, avec les côtés proprement symboliques de l'animal liés à l'imagerie enfantine, est une priorité, et vu de Paris, on ne comprend pas ou mal l'entêtement barbare des populations locales. La forte visibilité de l'enjeu, disproportionnée avec la réalité, conditionne du même coup sa nature politique. L'ours est donc aussi une ressource pour ses propres défenseurs qui trouvent là un terrain propice à leurs manoeuvres, comme au ministre de l'environnement lui-même dont l'intervention peut être orchestrée. Souvent en conflit avec des projets gouvernementaux d'équipement, ce dernier peut montrer une grande fermeté sur un enjeu qui laisse pour une fois largement indifférents ses collègues ministres, d'autant qu'il bénéficie sur ce dossier de l'appui du Président de la République.

Tout concourt ainsi à la perception d'un jeu à somme nulle. Les élus craignent que la décentralisation de la négociation et la relocalisation du débat conduisent à enterrer leurs revendications, et à les laisser prisonniers d'un jeu local qu'ils ne maîtrisent pas. Il faut d'ailleurs noter que la classe politique ne leur a pas été en la matière d'un soutien très ardent. Aussi préfèrent-ils interpeller l'Etat comme dépositaire du bien public.

Quant aux "défenseurs" de l'ours, leur faible implantation locale les rend méfiant à des négociations locales où ils pourraient perdre leur assurance, d'autant que la décentralisation de la négociation conduit par nécessité au décloisonnement des problèmes dans la mesure où elle force à raisonner sur une "situation" nécessairement complexe. L'interconnexion des problèmes sociaux montre en effet comment la protection de l'ours ne peut être isolée des questions d'aménagement et de développement. Le maintien de la "pureté" de la revendication et le choix d'un thème étroit rendent en revanche plus pertinente une logique de centralisation de l'action, d'autant plus efficace que la sensibilité écologiste trouve plus facilement à exister nationalement que localement, et que le contexte politique lui est plus favorable.

Autrement dit, la non-communication est payante pour chacune des parties, ce qui explique l'extrême difficulté à parvenir à une solution, et l'existence pour l'instant d'une situation bloquée. Quant au Parc, il a la malchance d'avoir les ours dans la zone périphérique, sur laquelle il n'a pourtant aucune compétence juridique. Mais les protagonistes, en leurs qualités respectives de membres de l'institution sont tentés de lui faire payer leur propre incapacité à se faire face, et à se servir de lui comme d'une arène assurant la visibilité de leurs revendications. Le parc remplit en l'occurrence une *fonction d'amplification,* il est une caisse de résonance.

Le cas du tunnel du Somport est quelque peu différent, car tout d'abord on est en présence d'un enjeu plus clair. Mais là encore c'est le parc par sa présence qui lui donne une dimension symbolique.

La contestation du tunnel par les défenseurs de la nature se fait au nom de la protection des sites, sa défense au nom du développement local. Le tunnel est un enjeu d'aménagement du territoire, car il est un axe important de communication entre Madrid et Bordeaux. C'est bien là une des raisons du soutien plus ferme de la classe politique traditionnelle.

Pour autant il est bien clair que le tunnel est très largement représentatif du mythe de l'équipement lourd. Si sa fonctionnalité est évidente au niveau plus large de la Région, elle est cependant moins évidente au niveau plus local de la vallée d'Aspe. Rien ne dit en effet que les impacts du tunnel seront localement positifs. On est un peu ici dans la situation des communes qui se battent pour obtenir l'arrêt du TGV dans leur gare. Or, l'arrêt ne signifie en aucune manière que des passagers vont descendre, ou même monter, tout dépend, on le sait aujourd'hui, de la capacité des communes à mettre en oeuvre des politiques d'accompagnement. Ce n'est pas le tunnel qui sera par lui-même créateur de richesse.

Mais là encore, on trouve dans cet exemple la marque de la faiblesse des acteurs en présence. En effet les procédures de concertation en amont de la construction d'un équipement lourd sont importantes, et il convient de reconnaître que la France s'est progressivement dotée d'un appareillage appréciable en instrument de concertation. Pourtant leur rendement reste faible. La faiblesse des acteurs, qu'elle soit liée à la faible implantation locale des uns, ou l'absence d'assurance des autres, ne pousse guère à la négociation. Dès lors, la décision de construire l'équipement est prise sans contestation majeure, et c'est une fois que l'on commence les travaux que les oppositions se font jour, car l'existence d'un objet "matérialisable" crée une opportunité d'action. En l'occurrence, le parc prend ici une autre dimension, il n'est pas seulement une tribune, il est l'occasion de poser les questions d'environnement. Par sa seule présence, il impose une autre grille de lecture de la réalité et définit du même coup un *espace de controverse* propice à l'évocation d'une problématique environnementaliste.

6. AU DELA DE L'ILLUSION PEDAGOGIQUE...

Le PNPO est incontestablement une institution fragile, caractérisée par son isolement, et de ce fait en voie de paupérisation relative, s'il ne peut éviter sa marginalisation tant par l'Etat que par les collectivités locales qui constituent son environnement immédiat ou sa réduction à un simple intermédiaire. La question qui se pose aujourd'hui est de savoir si l'on veut en assurer le seul maintien ou le plein développement. Il est probable que, en l'état actuel, il ne puisse faire mieux que ce qu'il fait par défaut de mobilisation et d'organisation, de compétences et de moyens. Si l'on veut éviter d'enfermer le parc dans une conception "jardin public" au détriment d'une conception plus ouverte et plus riche qui vise à faire du PNPO une véritable institution de gestion du patrimoine naturel, il faut le réhabiliter dans ses activités de prestations de services. La vocation du parc a toujours été double, gestionnaire d'un territoire propre, mais aussi partenaire potentiel de nombreux acteurs, communes, départements, régions, associations, universités, etc., auxquels il apporte son concours dans la limite de ses compétences. C'est bien là du reste une mission essentielle de l'Etat qui est d'assurer les collectivités les plus faibles de son aide dès lors qu'elles ne disposent pas des compétences ou des moyens nécessaires à la réalisation de leur volonté. Rappelons d'ailleurs que les services extérieurs de l'Etat ont largement insisté sur cette dimension de leur action dans le contexte même de la décentralisation. L'avenir du parc réside dans la démonstration de ses compétences et dans l'attractivité de ses missions qui ne nécessite pas pour autant le maintien au sein du parc d'une zone périphérique sans signification, et donc qu'il faille en conserver la structure actuelle.

S'il faut selon nous modifier son architecture, c'est bien parce qu'il faut aussi savoir prendre en compte les évolutions susceptibles d'intervenir quant à la nature des problèmes traités. Or l'appréhension de la protection de la nature ne se pose pas aujourd'hui dans les mêmes termes qu'en 1960, et du même coup les modes d'intervention de la puissance publique ont eux-mêmes évolué.

Si les parcs ne peuvent plus s'affirmer comme les seules circonscriptions écologiques, car d'autres existent telles les "massifs" ou les bassins hydrographiques par exemple, on peut faire l'hypothèse que la politique de création des parcs est révolue sous sa forme ancienne, même si l'on ne peut pas totalement exclure la formule qui peut se révéler utile dans des circonstances précises. Non seulement l'environnement constitue une préoccupation générale, qui de ce fait ne peut être l'affaire des seuls spécialistes, mais le problème, dès lors qu'il s'affirme comme l'affaire de tous, exige le partenariat et la contractualisation. Plutôt que de créer des structures lourdes, consommatrices de budgets non négligeables et génératrices de rigidités de fonctionnement, il est probable que l'Etat s'orientera à l'avenir vers des formules plus souples de subventionnement de politiques d'environnement entreprises par les collectivités elles-mêmes, ce qui sera le gage de leur réel engagement et d'une implication active. Les définitions de frontière sont trop délicates et se sont révélées trop coûteuses pour que l'on accepte d'en continuer l'expérience. Non seulement le tracé peu convaincant du PNPO en montre les limites, mais la question actuelle de l'ours en souligne les difficultés. On peut penser que le recours à de telles pratiques se fera plus rare, réservé à des cas exceptionnels et sur des territoires réduits, au profit d'une gestion plus fine et plus souple, plus évolutive du territoire en fonction d'enjeux précis. On le voit très clairement dans le Plan national pour l'environnement, les parcs nationaux ne constituent plus un enjeu fort pour le ministère dont les préoccupations sont ailleurs, et dont le budget demeure bien maigre en dépit d'augmentations substantielles pour entretenir des parcs dont l'existence est toujours plus ou moins contestée. Dès lors le risque pour ceux-ci réside dans l'approfondissement de leur isolement, dans la mesure où, délaissés par l'Etat, ils deviendront d'autant moins attractifs pour les autres collectivités qui se reporteront alors vers des formules moins lourdes de gestion de l'environnement, et seront tentées de ce fait de trouver la présence d'un parc bien pesante autant qu'inutile.

Le parc correspond en effet à une approche de la protection de la nature qui est maintenant ancienne, et qui sera certainement de plus en plus marginale. Elle relève d'une volonté de protection des sites exemplaires contre les dégradations éventuelles que l'homme serait susceptible de lui faire subir. Pour cette raison, la protection est envisagée sous l'angle du zonage et de l'exemplarité. Aujourd'hui, on se situe dans une perspective différente qui est d'intégrer le souci de l'environnement dans les politiques sectorielles. Qui plus est la gestion de l'environnement est de plus en plus reconnue comme affaire d'action collective, et s'incarnera vraisemblablement de moins en moins dans des institutions spécifiques abordant l'environnement de manière trop générale pour un traitement plus différencié de problèmes particuliers tels que la protection des eaux, l'enlèvement des ordures ménagères, etc.. De la même façon, la sauvegarde de l'environnement ne peut relever d'un seul niveau d'action dans le cadre d'une répartition des compétences entre les différents échelons de gouvernement. Les querelles actuelles entre Etat, régions, et départements pour la maîtrise de services de protection de l'environnement attestent de la progression - même si elle peut apparaître encore très insuffisante à beaucoup - d'un souci écologique légitime au sein de collectivités locales très longtemps étrangères à de telles préoccupations.

Il reste au parc à tirer les leçons de l'histoire afin de ne pas être totalement étranger aux évolutions futures. Pour cela, il lui faut se construire une légitimité, autre que purement symbolique, dans l'affirmation de son utilité, qui dépendra de sa capacité à s'organiser et à contracter des relations durables dans le cadre de négociations appropriées.

Aujourd'hui, en particulier du fait de la décentralisation, la réussite du parc dépend beaucoup de l'attitude des élus, qui est liée à une politique plus offensive du parc, mais aussi à leur volonté de s'engager activement auprès de lui. Peut-être conviendrait-il de mieux fixer de les relations avec les collectivités territoriales afin d'éviter leurs fluctuations. Pour ces raisons, il serait utile de recourir à la logique des contrats ou des conventions afin d'établir une coopération stable sur la base d'un échange de service et de la résolution de problèmes concrets. Si l'on veut initier un dialogue entre les différentes parties prenantes à l'environnement qui soit autre chose qu'un "pluralisme mou", il est important de lui donner un fondement réel. Contrairement à une idée, somme toute naïve, qui croyait trouver dans l'organisation une solution à la coopération par l'internalisation des relations partenariales, il faut aujourd'hui *réexternaliser la négociation* afin de la construire sur la réalité des situations plutôt que sur des principes sans signification pour les acteurs. Autrement dit c'est en passant par l'extérieur que l'on parviendra à réaménager la discussion en interne en prenant appui sur la réalité d'engagements concrets, non l'inverse. L'établissement d'une pression externe sur la base d'exigences clairement négociées est un élément clé de redynamisation de l'institution. C'est pour cela que toute stratégie visant à élargir le CA à de nouveaux acteurs ne peut que compliquer encore la tâche du parc. Il ne peut être un lieu d'intégration du territoire, car c'est là la prérogative d'instances politiques et la décentralisation est intervenue entre temps pour disqualifier désormais toute solution qui serait seulement administrative. C'est dans un maillage étroit de relations négociées sur la base d'enjeux précis que le parc peut réaliser l'apprentissage nécessaire à la prise en compte de l'environnement dans la gestion de l'espace. Il lui faut pour cela partir des problèmes plus que se laisser guider par des objectifs sans signification. Pour cette raison, on peut aujourd'hui se poser la question de la pertinence de la notion de zone périphérique. Sa suppression ne marginaliserait pas le parc; tout au contraire, en clarifiant la situation elle obligerait tout à la fois le parc à chercher de manière dynamique des alliances sur la base de projets concrets, et les collectivités intéressées par la démarche du parc à s'impliquer dans une démarche volontariste de partenariat qui romprait avantageusement avec leur participation molle actuelle. D'un autre côté, partir des situations concrètes conduit à avoir une approche décloisonnée des problèmes, et donc à mieux saisir l'imbrication et l'interdépendance des questions de développement local et de protection de l'environnement. Pour cela il faut amener les partenaires du parc à négocier sur la réalité des enjeux locaux afin d'éviter les dérives qui accompagnent toute centralisation des revendications. Plus on s'éloigne du terrain, plus la politisation est forte aboutissant à durcir les positions et à rendre les solutions plus difficiles, car, en changeant de scène, les enjeux de départ acquièrent une dimension symbolique très importante qui les éloigne au lieu de les rapprocher. Il est actuellement essentiel de *fixer* la négociation localement. L'apprentissage de la négociation nécessite en effet que l'on maintienne les relations entre les acteurs à un niveau déconcentré afin d'interdire toute remontée des problèmes et de renouer ainsi avec une logique de face à face qui, sans exclure le conflit, est une condition indispensable à l'établissement d'un dialogue significatif.

Les difficultés de la négociation institutionnalisée montrent à quel point la participation ne suffit pas à créer de la coopération. Toute négociation dépend de l'énoncé et de la définition d'un problème à partir duquel il est possible d'identifier un enjeu susceptible de concerner des acteurs précis. Il ne peut y avoir de négociation sans enjeu commun. La participation et la négociation ne sont pas des solutions en elles-mêmes, elles ne sont que des moyens, faut-il par conséquent les adapter à la structure du problème en jeu comme aux conditions de l'action. Toute interaction ne saurait être assimilée, en fonction d'une quelconque vertu intrinsèque, à de l'apprentissage ou à de la communication.

En un sens, le parc reste une institution qui constitue, en dépit de ses difficultés, une tentative exemplaire d'articulation des grands enjeux des sociétés modernes qui ont à concilier économie, nature, et culture, et il représente de ce simple fait une opportunité d'apprentissage d'une gestion intégrée de ces différents paramètres. Il est ainsi porteur d'enjeux symboliques en terme d'environnement dans une époque où les valeurs d'environnement prennent une importance croissante, et il gère de ce fait des dossiers dont la visibilité peut être forte, et sur lesquels il peut y avoir une réelle plus-value pour le développement du territoire. Faut-il pour cela que l'on passe de la participation octroyée à la négociation volontaire.

REFERENCES

G. Adam J. D. Reynaud, *Conflits du travail et changement social*, Paris, PUF, 1978.

P. Amselek, "L'évolution générale de la technique juridique dans les sociétés occidentales", *Revue de droit public*, mars-avril 1982.

F. Constantin, "Environnement et ressources naturelles, les parcs nationaux", *Jurisclasseur de droit rural*, fascicule B-2, 1984.

M. CROZIER, "Pour une analyse sociologique de la planification française", *Revue française de sociologie*, 6, 1965.

M. Crozier, E. Friedberg, *L'acteur et le système*, Paris, Seuil, 1977.

P. Duran, *Le territoire de l'environnement, le cas du Parc National des Pyrénées Occidentales*, Ministère de l'Environnement/PNPO, 1991.

P. DURAN, "Le savant et la politique, pour une approche raisonnée de l'analyse des politiques publiques", *L'Année sociologique*, 40, 1990.

C. Hood, *Administrative Analysis, An Introduction to Rules, Enforcement and Organizations*, Wheatsheaf books limited, 1986.

P. Gremion, "La théorie de l'apprentissage institutionnel et la régionalisation du cinquième plan", *Revue française de science politique*, XXIII, 2, 1973.

G. Hardin, "The Tragedy of the Commons", *Science 162*, 1968.

P. Mann, *L'action collective, mobilisation et organisation des minorités actives*, Paris, Armand Colin, 1991.

J. G. March, J. P. Olsen, *Ambiguity and Choice in Organizations*, Norway, Universitetsforlaget, 1976.

J. G. March, J. P. Olsen, "The Garbage Can Model of Organizational Choice", *Administrative Science Quarterly*, 17, 1, 1972.

C.-A. Morand, "La contractualisation du droit dans l'Etat providence", in C.-A. Morand (sous la direction de), *L'Etat propulsif*, Publisud, 1990.

E. Ostrom, *Governing the Commons, The Evolution of Institutions for Collective Action*, Cambridge University Press, 1990.

M. Prieur, *Droit de l'environnement*, Paris, Dalloz, 2ème édition, 1991.

S. Ranson, B. Hinings, R. Greenwood, "The Structuring of Organizational Structures", *Administrative Science Quarterly*, 25, 1980.

F. Scharpf, "Echec des politiques et réforme des institutions: pourquoi la forme devrait-elle suivre la fonction?", *Revue Internationale des Sciences Sociales*, UNESCO/ERES, n° 108, 1986.

Th. Schelling, *La stratégie du conflit*, Paris, PUF, 1986.

P. Selznick, *TVA and the Grass Roots*, New York, Harper, 1966.

Vedel, Rapport "Perspectives à long terme de l'agriculture française (1968-1985)", remis le 20 juin 1969 à J. Duhamel, ministre de l'Agriculture.

K. E. Weick, "Educational Organizations as Loosely Coupled Systems", *Administrative Science Quarterly*, 21, 1976.

R. E. Walton, R. B. McKersie, *A Behavioral Theory of Labour Negociations. An Analysis of a Social Interaction System*, New York, McGraw-Hill, 1965.

A. Wolfelsberger, *Les biens collectifs*, Paris, PUF, 1975.

REGULATORY NEGOTIATION IN THE NETHERLANDS: THE CASE OF PACKAGING WASTE

Ida J. Koppen

1. NEGOTIATING WASTE REDUCTION

Packaging waste has been a political issue in the Netherlands since 1973 when Parliament put forward a proposal for legislation[1]. The proposal was not adopted. In 1975, however, when the Draft Waste Act was presented, the Minister for the Environment pointed again to the increasing problem of packaging waste and underlined that waste reduction was an essential element of the new Act[2]. The Act, indeed, authorizes the government to enact Regulations to reduce the flow of waste. One of the four provisions concerns the reduction of packaging waste and the use of deposits to assure the return of packaging materials. Other issues addressed include the separate collection of certain waste types and the prohibition to manufacture products that create problems for an environmentally sound disposal when they are discarded.

Although the Act was passed in 1977, the articles concerning waste reduction were never implemented. Rather than enacting formal Regulations, the Ministry for Housing, Planning and the Environment, often in collaboration with other Ministries, concluded a number of private agreements with sectors of industry about issues regarding waste reduction. A similar trend can be observed in other areas of environmental policy as well[3]. Some of the waste issues for which agreements were

---

[1] Second Chamber 1973-1974, 12 304, no.1 ff.
[2] Articles 27-30. See G.H. Addink (1991) "Biedt het wetsvoorstel afvalstoffen adequate oplossingen voor de belangrijkste knelpunten van het Nederlandse afvalstoffenbeleid?" in R.J.J. van Acht en J.H. Jans, *Afvalstoffenrecht.* Zwolle: W.E.J. Tjeenk Willink.
[3] See C. Lambers (1988) "Beleidsovereenkomsten in het milieubeheer" *Milieu en Recht* 2.

concluded are[4]: the reduction of the use of mercury-oxide batteries (1985); the reduction of waste from PET-bottles (1987); the reduction of phosphates in detergents (1987); the reduction of chloro-fluor compounds in spray-cans (1988); the recycling of plastic crates containing cadmium used by the beer- and soft-drink industry (1988).

The piece-meal *ad hoc* approach to waste reduction changed in 1988 when a comprehensive policy document was presented to the Parliament by the Minister for the Environment, the *Memorandum on Prevention and Recycling of Waste*[5] (hereinafter "the Memorandum"). Besides setting targets for the reduction and recycling of waste, the Memorandum confirms a general ranking of policy objectives that had first been formulated in 1979 by Member of Parliament Lansink. The "motion Lansink", put forward during the Parliamentary debate on the budget[6], is still considered the political basis for Dutch waste policy today. The National Environmental Policy Plan (NEPP) of 1989 refers to the Memorandum for this aspect of Dutch environmental policy[7]. The priority ranking for the objectives of waste policy in the Netherlands is: 1) prevention; 2) product recycling; 3) material recycling; 4) incineration with energy recovery; 5) incineration. Landfill and controlled dumping are last resort options, only to be used for the remainders of waste that are left after the application of some form of treatment.

Each of the objectives offers interesting points of reference for an inquiry into the use of negotiation techniques as they are discussed in this volume. In this chapter we will primarily look at the objectives of prevention and recycling and at the negotiations that take place in the context of their implementation. The Memorandum "institutionalizes" to some degree the informal approach that had developed in practice. It establishes standard negotiation procedures, referred to as *strategic discussions*, as

---

[4] For an overview of the different agreements as well as a detailed analysis of their use and effectiveness, see E.R.C. van Rossum (1988) *Milieuconvenanten*. 's Gravenhage: Staatsuitgeverij; Centrale Raad voor de Milieuhygiëne (1989) *Advies over milieuconvenanten*. 's Gravenhage: CRMH; P-J. Klok (1989) *Convenanten als instrument van milieubeleid*. Enschede: Faculteit der Bestuurskunde; R.J.J. van Acht and L.J.A. Damen (1991) *Effectieve toepassing van milieuconvenanten*. Amsterdam: Centrum voor Milieurecht.

[5] Second Chamber 1988-1989, 20 877, no.2.

[6] Second Chamber 1979-1980, Chapter XVII, no.21.

[7] Second Chamber 1988-1989, *National Environmental Policy Plan. To choose or to lose*, 21 137, nos.1-2, p.147.

the official government procedure to regulate waste reduction. The agreements that are to result from the negotiations are from then on called *covenants*. The strategic discussions and the ensuing covenants epitomize some of the mechanisms under investigation here.

The material presented will focus on the specific use of *policy negotiations*. We will not pay explicit attention to *negotiations that take place to resolve individual, i.e. siting conflicts*. It should be pointed out, however, that most of the mechanisms apply equally to both kinds of decision-making procedures since both, in essence, regard the reconciliation of conflicting interests. The Packaging Covenant that was concluded in June 1991 will be described to demonstrate the underlying principles of the approach as well as the difficulties to put them into practice.

2. CONSULTATION, NEGOTIATION AND CONSENSUS-BUILDING

Before we begin our analysis of Dutch policy negotiations, a few words are needed to explain some of the terms used in this chapter. A distinction must be made between different aspects of the procedures that have so far all conveniently been called "negotiation", namely *consultation, negotiation* and *consensus-building*. Each of these procedures represents a different degree of involvement of societal groups - be they representatives of industry, neighborhood associations, consumer groups or the environmental movement - in public deliberations. We could say that consultation, negotiation and consensus-building "horizontalize" decision-making procedures to different degrees.

Negotiation is used here as a general concept to refer to the interaction between government actors and societal groups in which each participant is in a position to satisfy (part of) the interests of one or more of the other groups. This "something" which each group holds that is of value to one or more of the other groups can be seen as the "bargaining chip" that is

offered in exchange for the attainment of ones own goals or part thereof[8].
Parties will be induced to engage in a negotiation process if a situation of mutual interdependence exists. Although the term negotiation hence implies interdependence and alludes to some form of power-sharing among the different groups involved, it does not give a clear indication of the way decisions are ultimately adopted. For our purpose, the relevant question to ask is to what extent the different societal groups and the government actors involved in a negotiation contribute to the final decision. The term negotiation *per se* does not give any insight in the answer to this question.

The same is true *a fortiori* for *consultation*. The process of consultation is characterized by an unequal distribution of decision-making power among the actors. In the case of public policy, the government asks the opinion of one or more societal groups or individuals affected by proposed policy measures. It might be under an obligation to do so or decide voluntarily to involve the other actors. Some environmental laws require the consultation by the government of interested parties and prescribe that the opinions expressed must be considered explicitly in the final decision. In other instances, the consultation process does not impose similar restrictions. Thus, the amount of influence of the consulted party on the final decision is at least unpredictable and usually limited.

The situation is different when we speak of *consensus-building*. This term is used to refer to a certain type of negotiation in which parties engage if they are determined to find the *optimal joint solution* to a given set of problems. Consensus-building can be seen as a specific type of negotiation characterized by a larger degree of interdependence among the parties or by an increased awareness of the parties of the existing interdependence. Parties recognize that it is in their own interest to make sure that the other parties "interests are satisfied since this is the only guaran-

---

[8] See Gerd Winter (1985) "Bartering rationality in regulation" 19 *Law & Society Review* 219, for the notion of *bargaining chip* in environmental policy negotiations. About the technique of negotiation as a strategy to reconcile conflicting interests, see, among others, Roger Fisher and William L. Ury (1981) *Getting to YES. Negotiating agreement without giving in.* Boston: Houghton Mifflin; Howard Raiffa (1982) *The art and science of negotiation.* Cambridge MA: Harvard University Press; Lawrence Susskind and Jeffrey Z. Rubin (eds.) (1983) "Negotiation: Behavioral perspectives" 27 *American Behavioral Scientist* 135ff (special issue); Roy J. Lewicki and Joseph A. Litterer (1985) *Negotiation.* Homewood IL: IRWIN; (1985) *Negotiation Journal. On the process of dispute settlement.* New York and London: Plenum Press.

tee for a stable, durable solution"[9]. This requires a process of creative problem solving in which *mutual gains* are sought. These can only be found if parties disclose the underlying interests of the objectives which they publicly claim to pursue.

In game theory, the search for a joint solution as opposed to an individual solution is analyzed in terms of cooperative versus competitive behavior in positive-sum games. Gaming exercises like the well-known *Prisoner's Dilemma* based on a simple scoring matrix for two players demonstrate how a cooperative behavior of the players results in an optimal joint solution[10]. If the game is repeated in several rounds, it turns out that cooperation also leads to the best individual results[11]. Exercises like this, in which the scores represent the interests of the groups involved and their relative power, serve to gain insight in the optimal outcome of real-life negotiations. The existence of mutual interests is often only discovered on the basis of the exchange of additional information in the course of a consensus-building process. In game theory language: a perceived zero-sum situation turns out to be a positive-sum situation. The positive return of cooperative behavior in game theory underlines the importance of consensus-building in conflictual public policy situations.

Recent literature on negotiation often tries to show that the best way to negotiate is in a consensus-building process. Since most situations in which negotiations take place are characterized by a high degree of interdependence and by a horizontal power distribution, it is often in the inter-

---

[9] See Lawrence Susskind and Jeffrey Cruikshank (1987) *Breaking the impasse. Consensual approaches to resolving public disputes.* New York: Basic Books, pp.31-33, who list stability as one of the four criteria to evaluate the outcome of a consensus-seeking negotiation, the others being fairness, efficiency and wisdom.

[10] R. Duncan Luce and Howard Raiffa (1957) *Games and decisions.* New York: John Wiley & Sons, pp.94-97; Andrew M. Colman (1982) *Game theory and experimental games.* Oxford: Pergamon Press, pp.101-104.

[11] See Robert Axelrod (1984) *The evolution of cooperation.* New York: Basic Books, pp.7-19. Scharpf proposes a further differentiation of the application of game theory to public policy. In the game called Battle of the Sexes no stable joint solution exists and players alternate between competitive and cooperative behavior. Only in the case that a group identity has developed ("*Wir-Identität*") due to factors external to game-theoretic considerations will cooperation or solidarity prevail and can maximum joint gain be achieved. See Fritz W. Scharpf (1988) "Verhandlungssysteme, Verteilungskonflikte und Pathologien der politischen Steuerung" in Manfred G. Schmidt, *Staatstätigkeit. International und historisch vergleichende Analysen.* Opladen: Westdeutscher Verlag. 19 Politische Vierteljahresschrift Sonderheft 61, pp.72-75; Luce and Raiffa (1957) *op.cit.*, pp.90-94 and pp.97-102; Colman (1982) *op.cit.*, pp.97-98.

est of all parties to find a consensual solution. Negotiation and consensus-building have thus almost become interchangeable concepts. The term negotiation, however, is broader and can also be used to refer to competitive bargaining[12].

If we draw a connecting line between consultation, negotiation and consensus-building, we find an increasing degree of interdependence and horizontal power distribution going from consultation (the lower end) to consensus-building (the higher end). The degree of influence on the final decision increases accordingly. A consensus only exists if each participant has had a say in the final decision and is, moreover, convinced that the package of solutions that has been put together reflects all the individual preferences to the highest degree possible in view of the formulation of a joint solution.

3. THE ORIGIN OF REGULATORY NEGOTIATION

The style of governance that has developed in the Netherlands in the area of waste reduction, can be traced back to two different sets of principles related to different visions of governance and the role of the state as regulator. The first relates to what has been called "the politics of accommodation"[13], the consultative style of governance that is typical for the Dutch political culture in general. The idea of a partnership between government and industry which has recently emerged in environmental policy is really the continuation of a much older and firmly established approach that has dominated issues like labour-, wage- and price negotiations since a long time.

Pieter Winsemius, Minister for the Environment from 1982 to 1986, was the first to formulate the idea of partnership in environmental policy explicitly combined with the notion of "environmental management"[14].

---

[12] See Lewicki and Litterer (1985) *supra* note 8, Chapters 4 and 5 for a description of the different ways to negotiate. The classic example of competitive bargaining is the second-hand car dealer who tries to get the highest price which is obviously not in the interest of the buyer.

[13] See Arend Lijphart (1967) *The politics of accommodation.* Berkeley: University of California Press.

[14] See Pieter Winsemius (1986) *Gast in eigen huis. Beschouwingen over milieumanagement.* Alphen aan den Rijn: Samsom H.D. Tjeenk Willink (especially Chapters 2, 6 and 9).

His motive for introducing these principles in environmental policy was related to the observed shortcomings of the implementation of environmental policy. The effort made to involve the social partners, referred to as *target groups*, early on in the decision-making process must be seen as an attempt to avoid opposition to the proposed measures in a later stage of the policy process[15].

The target group approach and the strategic discussions are coupled with the notion of *verinnerlijking* (internalization), also introduced by Environment Minister Pieter Winsemius. *Verinnerlijking* can be described as the process of sensibilization of the target groups to environmental issues. Communicative instruments, such as information and education are essential elements of this approach[16]. Hajer points out that the notion of *verinnerlijking* reflects the positive-sum game format which Winsemius wanted to confer to environmental policy. "The key to any understanding of *verinnerlijking* is the insight that its success depended on cooperation and consensus"[17].

The next Minister for the Environment, Ed Nijpels, continued the management style introduced by Winsemius. When Nijpels presented the Memorandum on Prevention and Recycling of Waste to the Parliament, he wrote in his accompanying letter: "I regard this Memorandum as the beginning of a process that will cover all aspects of waste policy to discuss with the concerned groups the targets, the measures and the activities needed to achieve a more effective prevention and recycling of waste. It must be obvious that I expect more results from such an approach than from the one-sided use of legislation. Formulating an approach that is not carried by those concerned is at most difficult to uphold and therefore hardly brooking of success."[18]

---

[15] See "The environmental approach. Environmental initiatives among target groups and public authorities", *Milieustrategie*, Journal 91/1, Directorate General Environment, Strategic Planning Unit.

[16] Winsemius (1986) *supra* note 14 pp.61-67, 104-125. See also L.M. van Vliet (1992) *Communicatieve besturing van het milieuhandelen van ondernemingen: mogelijkheden en beperkingen.* Delft: Eburon, Chapter 4.

[17] Maarten Hajer (1994) "Furthering ecological responsibility through "verinnerlijking": the limits to a positive management approach" in G. Teubner, L. Farmer and D. Murphy (eds.) (1994) *Environmental law and ecological responsibility.* London: John Wiley & Sons.

[18] Second Chamber 1988-1989, *Letter of the Minister accompanying Memorandum on the prevention and recycling of waste*, 20 877, no.1, p.1.

The government, in other words, voluntarily renounces its power to impose certain rules unilaterally and places part of the responsibility for solving the problem with the target groups. Besides the strong influence of Pieter Winsemius, this approach was influenced by the early efforts of two or three pioneers at the Directorate General for the Environment to introduce some of the lessons of US environmental policy in the Netherlands. These regarded especially the introduction of consensual, i.e. consensus-seeking[19], decision-making and the use of mediators to assist alternative dispute resolution processes. Both were introduced in the US in reaction to the very confrontational style of regulation that characterized environmental policy in the seventies[20]. The first Dutch project in which scholars and practitioners of the MIT-Harvard Public Disputes Program were involved was called *Risky Decisions* and resulted in a set of policy guidelines for complex decisions involving multiple actors, multiple interests and uncertainty about the scientific data for different alternative trajectories. A follow-up of Risky Decisions started in 1991 with the design of a training program for the personnel of the Ministry for Housing, Planning and Environment (*VROM*), *The Implementation Challenge*. The four-day course is based on the techniques and mechanisms developed in Risky Decisions and is being taught by a group of high-rank officials from within the Ministry who received special training at MIT[21]. All *VROM* officials who carry responsibility for policy decisions are requested to take the course. The other Ministries that are involved in the implementation of environmental policy, such as Agriculture and Fisheries, Transport and Public Works, and Economic Affairs are invited to participate as well. Initiatives to apply US experiences with consensus

---

[19] Lawrence Susskind and Jeffrey Cruikshank (1987) *supra* note 9, p.77.
[20] See, among others, Larry Susskind and Jeffrey Cruikshank (1987) *supra* note 9; Larry Susskind, Lawrence Bacow, Michael Wheeler (eds.)(1983) *Resolving environmental regulatory disputes*. Cambridge MA: Schenkman; Lawrence Bacow and Michael Wheeler (1984) *Environmental dispute resolution*. New York: Plenum Press; Susan Carpenter and W.J.D. Kennedy (1988) *Managing Public Disputes. A practical guide to handling conflict and reaching agreement*. San Francisco/London: Jossey-Bass; Roger Fisher and William Ury (1981) *Getting to yes. Negotiating agreement without giving in*. Boston: Houghton Mifflin.
[21] As the only outside expert participating in this group, the author wishes to thank the other trainers for the constructive collaboration and the Ministry for the trust placed in her.

building were also taken within the Ministry of Transport and Public Works[22].

4. THE LEGALIST CRITIQUE

The first agreements that were concluded in the area of waste reduction were characterized by a high degree of informality. Here we are especially concerned with the legal aspects of the informality and will leave aside for the moment the communicative aspects[23]. The legal informality of the agreements has often been criticised. In essence, the criticism regarded three points. First of all, the ambiguous legal character of the agreements - they were usually referred to as "gentlemen's agreements" - made it unclear if they were legally binding and enforceable. Secondly, third parties were generally unable to influence agreements although the effect of an agreement was often felt outside the circle of its signatories. Thirdly, the democratic control normally exercised over decisions of public authorities by elected bodies was prejudiced by the informality of the interactions[24].

Similar criticism was expressed for the informal agreements between public authorities and regulated firms that characterized the issuance of permits and licenses in other areas of environmental policy[25]. Aalders described how the informal consultations between the licensing authority and the firm that preceded the formal request for a license under the Nuisance Act dominated the ensuing official licensing procedure.

---

[22] See Marianne de Soet (1988) *From competition to collaboration. Environmental decision making tools, used in the USA, beneficial for the Netherlands?* The Hague: Ministry of Transport and Public Works. Also, Raad voor het Milieu- en Natuuronderzoek (1990) *Duurzame ontwikkeling door verbetering van de besluitvorming over milieuproblemen: de (on)mogelijkheden van de consensusbenadering.* Rijswijk: Publikatie RMNO no.50.

[23] The distinction between "communicative informality" and "legal informality" in Dutch environmental policy was developed in Ida Koppen (1994) "Ecological covenants: regulatory informality revisited" in G. Teubner, L. Farmer and D. Murphy (eds.) *supra* note 17.

[24] See the authors cited in note 4.

[25] See for instance Marius Aalders, about the implementation of the Nuisance Act. M.V.C. Aalders (1984) *Industrie, milieu en wetgeving. De Hinderwet tussen symboliek en effectiviteit.* Amsterdam: KOBRA.

In the German literature we find the same phenomenon discussed and criticized by different authors, regarding both policy negotiations and licensing procedures. Bohne, in his seminal work *Der informale Rechtsstaat*, discussed the different dangers that exist if informal interaction replaces the administrative procedures governed by public law and legal principles[26]. Winter described how a *bartering rationality* has replaced the traditional style of unilateral governance[27]. Hucke, similar to Aalders, softened the existing legalist critique by pointing out that the little effectiveness that was achieved in environmental law was often based on informal interactions, in the shadow of law, rather than on formal implementation and enforcement[28].

It was already mentioned that the Memorandum on Prevention and Recycling of Waste institutionalized the informal approach that had existed prior to 1988 by elaborating strategic discussions and waste covenants as part of the official government policy. The question to be answered then is to what extent this institutionalization has accommodated the many points of criticism that had been raised in the literature.

5. STRATEGIC DISCUSSIONS AND COVENANTS AS THE ANSWER?

Strategic discussions were first introduced in the Indicative Multi-year Programs which were formulated in the early eighties for the environmental sectors water, air, soil, waste and noise. The Memorandum elaborated their use as policy instruments with the following description: "The introduction of the Indicative Multi-year Programs on Environment started a process whereby policy and ensuing measures were formulated

---

[26] Eberhard Bohne (1981) *Der informale Rechtsstaat*. Berlin: Duncker & Humblot. By the same author: (1980) "Informales Verwaltungshandeln im Gesetzesvollzug" in *Jahrbuch für Rechtssoziologie und Rechtstheorie*. Opladen: Westdeutscher Verlag; (1982) "Absprachen zwischen Industrie und Regierung in der Umweltpolitik" in *Jahrbuch für Rechtssoziologie und Rechtstheorie*. Opladen: Westdeutscher Verlag; (1984) "Informales Verwaltungs- und Regierungshandeln als Instrument des Umweltschutzes" in 75 *Verwaltungs-Archiv* 343.

[27] Gerd Winter (1985) "Bartering rationality in regulation" in 19 *Law and Society Review* 219.

[28] Jochen Hucke (1978) "Bargaining in regulative policy implementation: the case of air and water pollution control" in 4 *Environmental Policy and Law* 109; Aalders (1984) *supra* note 25 pp.70-74, 97-98 and 193.

together with the concerned target groups. Policies and measures should be carried by the persons they most concern and not wordlessly imposed. Fully appreciative of this line of action, it is my intention to embark upon "strategic discussions" with the persons most involved; to provide a guideline for thorough discussion and to arrive at mutual solutions. In the strategic discussions, policy options will have to be formulated as well as the most suitable means to implement the chosen options."[29]

The procedure that is followed in a strategic discussion contains guarantees with respect to transparency and democratic control. First of all, participation in a strategic discussion is not limited to government and business actors. Other societal groups that have a direct interest in the issues at stake are invited to participate as well. The process is, moreover, structured by outside facilitators that do not have an interest in the outcome of the discussion and assist the participants with the procedure. The position of the facilitator resembles the role played by mediators in the alternative dispute resolution procedures in the US. As "communication experts" they are of particular importance for the constructive exchange of information among the participants as a necessary element of consensus-building. Facilitators can greatly enhance the transparency of the process.

Similar guarantees have been developed for the covenants that might result from a strategic discussion. Covenants are now discussed extensively in Parliament[30] and they contain provisions about the position of third parties. The uncertainty about their legal status seems to have been resolved as well: a covenant is considered a contract under civil law unless some other indication is given[31].

Thus, the conclusion is justified that strategic discussions and covenants do not suffer from the same legal shortcomings as their informal predecessors. This does not mean, however, that the controversy over their use as policy instruments is entirely resolved. Contrary to recent policy practice, the NEPP and its follow-up, the NEPP-Plus, give a limited role to

---

[29] Second Chamber 1988-1989, *supra* note 5, pp.2-3.
[30] See for instance Second Chamber 1990-1991 *Verslag van een mondeling overleg*, 21 137, no.87.
[31] See Van Acht and Damen (1991) *supra* note 4, pp.1-2 and the example of the Packaging Covenant discussed below.

covenants. Covenants are primarily viewed as temporary arrangements, prior to the enactment of formal regulations[32].

6. THE PACKAGING COVENANT: A CONCRETE EXAMPLE

The Packaging Covenant signed on June 6 1991 is often depicted as a successful example of the Dutch target group approach[33]. However, it also demonstrates the difficulties of applying the approach in practice. Only a limited number of groups adhered to the agreement and a real consensus, based on jointly formulated interests, did not emerge.

Packaging waste is one of the twenty-nine waste streams indicated in the Memorandum, for which reduction targets are set. In 1986, 50 percent of packaging waste was dumped, 25 percent incinerated and 25 percent recycled. By the year 2000, these figures will have to change drastically: no more dumping, 40 percent of packaging waste incinerated and 60 percent recycled.

The target groups that were invited to participate in the strategic discussion for packaging waste included three Ministries (Environment, Economic Affairs and Agriculture), representatives of the provinces and the municipalities (organized in national associations), the packaging industry (organized nationally in the Association for Packaging and Environment, *Stichting Verpakking en Milieu, SVM*), consumer and environmental groups (represented by the *Stichting Natuur en Milieu*) and the National Institute for Public Health and the Environment (*Rijks Instituut voor Volksgezondheid en Milieuhygiëne, RIVM*). These groups engaged for two years in a strategic discussion about the proposed targets and the best ways to achieve them.

SVM was set up in the early seventies in reaction to social concern about the rapidly expanding use of one-way packaging. In the seventies, many products in the Netherlands, especially beverages, were still marketed in reusable packaging. The growth of supermarkets was responsible

---

[32] Second Chamber 1988-1989, supra note 7, p.181; Second Chamber 1989-1990, *National Environmental Policy Plan-Plus. Memorandum on policy instruments and sustainable construction*, 21 137, no.22, pp.12-14.

[33] For a description and analysis of another case in which the target-group approach was applied, the so-called *KWS 2000 project* about the reduction of the emission of volatile organic compounds, see L.M. Van Vliet (1992) *supra* note 16, chapters 5, 6 and 7.

for a dramatic shift towards one-way packaging which had three clear advantages for producers and retailers: less storage requirements, easier to handle and more easily adaptable to changing marketing requirements. Moreover, a separate chain of packaging industries had developed with an interest in the increased use of packaging[34].

SVM collected the first data on packaging trends, including the environmental effects of different packaging materials. It supported the early initiatives to recycle glass and paper in the seventies and was well prepared to enter the debate about the waste aspect of packaging. It invested in different ways in developing alternatives to the use of deposits and reusable packaging.

Consumer and environmental groups had organised several successful campaigns against the increased use of one-way packaging. The instrument of consumer boycotts was generally recognised - and feared - as a powerful tool in the negotiations.

Summarising, the context of the strategic discussion on packaging waste was determined by the following factors. A legal framework existed which authorized the Minister to issue Regulations about the reduction of packaging waste. The environmental and consumer movement was well organized and alert to the issue of packaging waste. The branch-organizations in the different sectors of the packaging-chain (production, packaging, distribution, retail) were very competitive and, moreover, some of the dominant firms showed social responsiveness[35]. These factors determined the relative distribution of power among the participants in the strategic discussion and their mutual interdependence.

After two years of negotiations no agreement had been reached. The two main points of conflict had remained the same. First of all, industry had not changed its ideas about the issue of mandatory deposits on containers. It was still strongly opposed to the use of mandatory deposits while environmental groups argued that a deposit-system was the only way to assure a high return rate of containers. Secondly, a disagreement existed over the reduction target itself: environmental groups, supported by several political factions in Parliament, insisted on an absolute reduc-

---

[34] See A.H. Peterse (1992) "Verpakkingsconvenant: element in een alternatieve sturingsstrategie" in N.J.H. Huls and H.D. Stout (eds.) *Reflecties op reflexief recht*. Zwolle: W.E.J. Tjeenk Willink, pp.202-205.
[35] See Peterse (1992) *op.cit.*, pp.207-208.

tion of packaging waste of ten percent by the year 2000[36], whereas *SVM* maintained that the reduction was to be understood as a reduction of the amount excluding the autonomous increase of waste. In the NEPP-plus, the Ministry had explicitly stated that the reduction was a reduction of the total, increased amount. But in the negotiations the point remained unclear and in all its correspondence, *Stichting Natuur en Milieu* insisted on an absolute reduction of ten percent. The Minister himself, in a letter of August 17, 1990 to *SVM* talked about an absolute reduction of ten percent in 2000 relative to the amount produced in the base year 1986. And in a letter of September to *SVM*, the Minister emphasized that this target was valid for waste materials in general while for packaging waste higher targets were feasible. He even mentioned a figure of 50 percent[37].

Later that year, the Ministry for the Environment and *SVM* decided to break off the plenary negotiations and continue bilaterally. This two-way negotiation resulted in the signing of the Packaging Covenant on June 6, 1991. In the covenant, industry has committed itself to a slightly higher objective than the one stated in the Memorandum, but the commitment is not higher than the targets announced in the letters of the Minister. The amount of packaging waste in 2000 shall be *less* than the 1986 level; the quantity recycled shall be *at least* 60 percent. Other commitments are all phrased in the form of intentions: industry shall make an effort to achieve an absolute reduction of 10 percent by 2000 and to recycle at least 50 percent by 1995. A commitment is also made to develop new types of environmentally friendly packaging. Furthermore, the covenant spells out a complex process of monitoring and evaluation. A national Committee is set up, responsible for monitoring compliance with the covenant[38].

The signing of the covenant was reported on the front page of major national newspapers. The Ministry for the Environment and *SVM* described the covenant as a far-reaching environmental measure in the spirit of de-regulation, leaving the packaging industry room to find the most efficient ways to reach the fixed targets. Environmental groups, supported

---

[36] Second Chamber 1990-1991, *Verslag van een modeling overleg*, 21 137, no.87, p.9.
[37] Letters on file with the author. Letter of 17 August 1990, DAM/A no.1970511; letter of 21 September 1990, DAM/A no.1290506. See Ida Koppen (1994) *supra* note 22, for the ambiguity concerning the autonomous growth of the amount of waste.
[38] The Committee has published two annual reports, in September 1992 and September 1993, that scrutinize all implementation measures. Pachaging Committee, P.O.Box 19291, 3501 DG Utrecht.

by a report of the Law Faculty of the University of Amsterdam, criticized the covenant for its lack of binding legal measures and for not introducing mandatory deposit schemes. The fact that the covenant states that it has the legal status of a contract under civil law does not change the criticism since it is not clear that such a contract is acceptable under Dutch public law[39]. During the debate in the Parliamentary Committee for the Environment, the socialist faction insisted that the signing of the covenant should not preclude the adoption of a general Decree on packaging waste[40].

7. CONSULTATION, NEGOTIATION AND CONSENSUS-BUILDING: EVALUATING DUTCH POLICY PRACTICE

In the Memorandum on Prevention and Recycling of Waste, the Dutch Ministry for the Environment has taken a major step to face the challenge of improving the efficiency and effectiveness of waste reduction policy. Rather than adopting and imposing rules about waste reduction unilaterally, the social actors affected by proposed measures are invited to participate in the joint formulation of policy goals and the measures needed to achieve them. The process that is outlined in the Memorandum is characterised by explicit efforts to apply consensus-building techniques (maximize joint gains, disclosure of underlying interests) and by the use of neutral facilitators. Facilitators have the task to organise the meetings from a practical point of view and to make sure that the exchange of information is handled effectively.

---

[39] Under Dutch public law, the government is not free to employ civil law instruments for public policy purposes. In Dutch case law the so-called "*twee wegen leer*", the two-track doctrine, was formulated which grants government actors a large amount of freedom in choosing between public and private law instruments. In subsequent case law, the "*twee wegen leer*" was confined to situations in which the guarantees inherent in public law instruments are equally observed by the private law instruments applied. These concern in particular the publication of documents, the legal position of the citizens directly involved and of third parties and the mechanisms of democratic control by elected political bodies (decisions of the Dutch *Hoge Raad* (Supreme Court) in the *Windmill case*, January 26 1990, reported in *Milieu en Recht* 1991, pp.163-167); *Kunst en Antiekstudio Lelystad*, July 8 1991, reported in *Ars Aequi* 1991, pp. 1133-1142. See also W. Konijnenbelt (1992) *Convenanten met de gemeente: fluiten in het Schemerdnister*. Utrecht: Lemma.

[40] Second Chamber 1990-1991, *supra* note 28, pp.6-8.

The example of the Packaging Covenant demonstrates the difficulties of applying the ideas expressed in the Memorandum and supported by extensive academic research in practice. First of all, policy practice has to account for the legal weaknesses that characterised the early regulatory negotiations. As we have seen, the strategic discussions and policy covenants outlined in the Memorandum have dealt adequately with most of the legal criticism. The second point which must still be evaluated regards the nature of the interaction that takes place in a strategic discussion and the degree to which the government has been able to convey the spirit of consensus-building as a positive-sum game. Have mutual gains been discovered or have parties retained their original ideas as fixed positions without engaging in a constructive exchange of information? A tentative assessment of the *communicative aspects* of strategic discussions shows a less positive appraisal. Here major improvements can still be made.

If we critically look at the interaction that took place during the two-year strategic discussion about packaging waste, we must conclude that although the different parties were consulted, a constructive consensus-building process did not evolve. The environmental and consumer groups were not part of the final outcome. They were consulted and their arguments about the necessity of certain instruments (deposits) were put aside. On this very issue, the two opposing sides, packaging industry and environmental groups, assumed conflictual positions and were not interested to hear the arguments of the other.

In the context of the strategic discussion there were mainly two relevant points to be clarified. First of all, the amount of waste reduction to be expected from deposits as opposed to voluntary recycling schemes and secondly the environmental impact of different packaging materials. Both issues were postponed until after the conclusion of the covenant. In the process of implementing the covenant, life-cycle analyses are carried out for different packaging materials that will show the environmental impact of the different materials. This information is essential for a constructive discussion about the need for reusable packaging. In other words, not enough information was exchanged during the strategic discussion to make consensus-building feasible. Environmental groups were consulted but the points raised were dismissed. The narrow consensus reached between government and industry does not reflect the target group approach as it was presented in the Memorandum, neither is it in line with the lessons to be learned from US environmental policy[41]. Only if the consensus-building process includes the different societal actors that will be affected will the outcome guarantee broad social support for the proposed measures. As long as some groups are left out, opposition may still be expected and the added value of consensus-building as a process of maximizing joint gain is lost. The strategic discussion about packaging waste has failed to resolve some of the major conflicts between the packaging industry and the consumer and environmental groups. Difficult decisions have been postponed until the implementation phase, which is already showing considerable delays. Thus, the main motive behind the new approach - to avoid delays with implementation - is being undermined, and the danger exists that the target group approach turns out to be just a new name for traditional regulation. The only way to dispel this threat is to take the process of consensus-building, with all its implications for creative communication more seriously.

---

[41] Similar Hajer (1994) *supra* note 17, who argues that the "critical potential of environmental NGOs" is not used adequately in strategic discussions that usually end up being bi-partite negotiations.

REFERENCES

M.V.C. Aalders (1984) *Industrie, milieu en wetgeving. De Hinderwet tussen symboliek en effectiviteit.* Amsterdam: KOBRA.

G.H. Addink (1991) "Biedt het wetsvoorstel afvalstoffen adequate oplossingen voor de belangrijkste knelpunten van het Nederlandse afvalstoffenbeleid?" in R.J.J. van Acht en J.H. Jans, *Afvalstoffenrecht.* Zwolle: W.E.J. Tjeenk Willink.

R. Axelrod (1984) *The evolution of cooperation.* New York: Basic Books.

L. Bacow and M. Wheeler (1984) *Environmental dispute resolution.* New York: Plenum Press.

E. Bohne (1980) "Informales Verwaltungshandeln im Gesetzesvollzug" in *Jahrbuch für Rechtssoziologie und Rechtstheorie.* Opladen: Westdeutscher Verlag.

E. Bohne (1981) *Der informale Rechtsstaat.* Berlin: Duncker & Humblot.

E. Bohne (1982) "Absprachen zwischen Industrie und Regierung in der Umweltpolitik" in *Jahrbuch für Rechtssoziologie und Rechtstheorie.* Opladen: Westdeutscher Verlag

E. Bohne (1984) "Informales Verwaltungs- und Regierungshandeln als Instrument des Umweltschutzes" in 75 *Verwaltungs-Archiv* 343.

S. Carpenter and W.J.D. Kennedy (1988) *Managing Public Disputes. A practical guide to handling conflict and reaching agreement.* San Francisco/London: Jossey-Bass.

A. M. Colman (1982) *Game theory and experimental games.* Oxford: Pergamon Press.

R. Fisher and W. L. Ury (1981) *Getting to YES. Negotiating agreement without giving in.* Boston: Houghton Mifflin.

M. Hajer (1994) "Furthering ecological responsibility through "verinnerlijking": the limits to a positive management approach" in G. Teubner, L. Farmer and D. Murphy (eds.) *Environmental law and ecological responsibility.* London: John Wiley & Sons.

J. Hucke (1978) "Bargaining in regulative policy implementation: the case of air and water pollution control" in 4 *Environmental Policy and Law* 109.

P-J. Klok (1989) *Convenanten als instrument van milieubeleid.* Enschede: Faculteit der Bestuurskunde.

W. Konijnenbelt (1992) *Convenanten met de gemeente: fluiten in het Schemerdnister.* Utrecht: Lemma.

I. Koppen (1994) "Ecological covenants: regulatory informality revisited" in G. Teubner, L. Farmer and D. Murphy (eds.).

C. Lambers (1988) "Beleidsovereenkomsten in het milieubeheer" *Milieu en Recht* 2.

R. J. Lewicki and J. A. Litterer (1985) *Negotiation.* Homewood IL: IRWIN; (1985)

R. J. Lewicki and J. A. Litterer (1985) *Negotiation Journal. On the process of dispute settlement.* New York and London: Plenum Press.

A. Lijphart (1967) *The politics of accommodation.* Berkeley: University of California Press.

R. D.Luce and H. Raiffa (1957) *Games and decisions.* New York: John Wiley & Sons.

A.H. Peterse (1992) "Verpakkingsconvenant: element in een alternatieve sturingsstrategie" in N.J.H. Huls and H.D. Stout (eds.) *Reflecties op reflexief recht.* Zwolle: W.E.J. Tjeenk Willink, pp.202-205.

H. Raiffa (1982) *The art and science of negotiation.* Cambridge MA: Harvard University Press.

F. W. Scharpf (1988) "Verhandlungssysteme, Verteilungskonflikte und Pathologien der politischen Steuerung" in Manfred G. Schmidt, *Staatstätigkeit. International und historisch vergleichende Analysen.* Opladen: Westdeutscher Verlag. 19 Politische Vierteljahresschrift Sonderheft 61, pp.72-75.

M. de Soet (1988) *From competition to collaboration. Environmental decision making tools, used in the USA, beneficial for the Netherlands?* The Hague: Ministry of Transport and Public Works.

L. Susskind, L. Bacow, M. Wheeler (eds.) (1983) *Resolving environmental regulatory disputes.* Cambridge MA: Schenkman.

L. Susskind and J. Cruikshank (1987) *Breaking the impasse. Consensual approaches to resolving public disputes.* New York: Basic Books.

L. Susskind and J. Z. Rubin (eds.) (1983) "Negotiation: Behavioral perspectives" 27 *American Behavioral Scientist* 135ff (special issue).

R.J.J. van Acht and L.J.A. Damen (1991) *Effectieve toepassing van milieuconvenanten.* Amsterdam: Centrum voor Milieurecht.

E.R.C. van Rossum (1988) *Milieuconvenanten.* 's Gravenhage: Staatsuitgeverij.

L.M. van Vliet (1992) *Communicatieve besturing van het milieuhandelen van ondernemingen: mogelijkheden en beperkingen.* Delft: Eburon.

P. Winsemius (1986) *Gast in eigen huis. Beschouwingen over milieumanagement.* Alphen aan den Rijn: Samsom H.D. Tjeenk Willink.

G. Winter (1985) "Bartering rationality in regulation" 19 *Law & Society Review* 219.

DER KOOPERATIVE DISKURS: THEORIE UND PRAKTISCHE ERFAHRUNGEN MIT EINEM DEPONIEPROJEKT IM KANTON AARGAU

Ortwin Renn und Thomas Webler

1. EINLEITUNG

Im Sommer 1984 flog eine Delegation von Mitarbeitern der Gulf Coast Waste Disposal Authority des Bundesstaates Texas zusammen mit einer Reihe von Bewohnern des Landkreises Galveston Bay von Houston in Texas nach Denver zum Keystone Zentrum für Konfliktanalyse. Dies war der letzte verzweifelte Versuch der Behörde, nach 15 Jahren Kampf mit lokalen Bürgerinitiativen eine Sondermüllanlage für petrochemische Abfälle im Landkreis Galveston Bay zu errichten. Zwei Anträge der Behörde für eine Genehmigung der Anlage waren durch Einsprüche und Gerichtsurteile bereits gescheitert und so versuchten die Behördenvertreter es mit einem neuen Konzept: Verhandlungen mit den Einwendern. Dafür hatte man das prestigeträchtige Keystone Zentrum gewonnen, das für seine Schlichtungsbemühungen in den ganzen USA hohes Ansehen geniesst. Doch so sehr man sich auch bemühte, so sehr man die Gäste mit Luxussuiten und anderen Annehmlichkeiten verwöhnte, die Bürger von Galveston blieben hart. Sie wollten keine Sondermüllanlage in Galveston. Der Konflikt zog sich noch über fünf weitere Jahre hin. Im Herbst 1989 gab die Behörde entnervt nach. Sie verzichtete auf den Bau der Anlage. Damit noch nicht genug: Bei der Gemeindewahl im Jahre 1989 wurden drei Mitglieder der Bürgerinitiative in den Vorstand der Behörde gewählt. Die Sondermüllanlage war damit endgültig gescheitert. Wie viel der Versuch, die Anlage in Galveston zu errichten, letztendlich gekostet hat, ist nie ermittelt worden. Die Schätzungen gehen über die 10 Millionen Dollar Marke hinaus[1].

Was sich in Galveston abgespielt hat, ist typisch für die Genehmigung und Errichtung von technischen Anlagen mit hohem Risikopotential in nahezu allen Industriegesellschaften des Westens (und zunehmend auch in den Ländern des ehemaligen Ostblocks und in Entwicklungsländern).

---

[1] Heiman 1990a, S. 979 f.

Bürger wehren sich meist erfolgreich gegen die Errichtung von Anlagen in ihrer Nachbarschaft[2]. Diese Haltung, die im amerikanischen Sprachraum gern als NIMBY (not in my back yard) oder im deutschen Sprachraum als St. Florians Mentalität bezeichnet wird, hat sich seit den 70er Jahren weltweit ausgebreitet[3]. Nach einer Umfrage des Umweltausschusses für Abfallbeseitigung von New York wurden von 1980 bis 1987 nur sechs von insgesamt 81 Anträgen zum Bau einer Entsorgungsanlage in den USA genehmigt und eine entsprechende Anlage gebaut[4]. Von diesen sechs erfolgreichen Anträgen betrafen vier reine Übergangs- oder Transportlager; die restlichen zwei fielen auf eine Deponie in Missouri und eine Verbrennungsanlage in Illinois[5]. In Europa sieht die Lage nicht viel besser aus: Müllverbrennungsanlagen stossen überall auf erbitterten Widerstand und können nur in wenigen Einzelfällen politisch durchgesetzt werden[6].

Warum sind gerade Entsorgungsanlagen so in den Strom der öffentlichen Kritik und Akzeptanzverweigerung geraten? Was verbirgt sich hinter der Ablehnung von technischen Anlagen zur Abfallbehandlung und -beseitigung? Ist es Unwissenheit oder Mangel an Gemeinwohldenken? Beide Antworten finden sich häufig in der Literatur zu diesem Thema[7]. Der Begriff der St. Florians Mentalität impliziert, dass der Anwohner die Anlage im Prinzip bejaht, aber er diese nicht in seiner unmittelbaren Nachbarschaft dulden möchte. Doch zunehmend wird bei der empirischen Erforschung solcher Konflikte deutlich, dass die beiden Antworten, nämlich Unwissenheit bez. St. Florians Prinzip zu kurz greifen. Zum einen sind Proteste um so heftiger, je (formal) gebildeter die betroffene Bevölkerung ist. Zudem geht die Ablehnung einer ortsnahen Anlage mit der Skepsis gegenüber der Notwendigkeit einher, solche Anlage überhaupt oder zumindest in dem geplanten Ausmass zu errichten[8]. Wenn also nicht Ignoranz oder Eigennutz die wesentlichen Motive der Ablehnung sind, was ist es dann? Die Literatur zu diesem Thema bietet eine Reihe von zumindest partiellen Erklärungsansätzen:

---

[2] Wiedemann u.a. 1994, S. 215
[3] Frey et al. 1994; Wiedemann u.a. 1991; Rosa 1988; Kraft und Kraut 1988; Crawford 1987; O'Hare 1977.
[4] New York State Legislative Committee 1987.
[5] Heiman 1990b, S. 360.
[6] Fietkau und Weidner 1994, S. 105; Holznagel 1990, S. 23.
[7] vgl. Dettling 1974; Schwarz 1991, S. 7-31f; Heilmann 1985.
[8] Heiman 1990b, S. 360.

- Entsorgungsanlagen werden in der Bevölkerung als wenig attraktiv angesehen. Sie werden mit geringen ökonomischen Vorteilen assoziiert, dagegen oft mit nennenswerten Risiken für Gesundheit und Umgebung verbunden[9].

- Bei grosstechnischen Vorhaben, wie Verbrennungsanlagen oder Deponien, sind Risiken und Nutzen nicht gleich verteilt. In der Regel fällt der Nutzen bei einer Menge meist anonymer Konsumenten oder Produzenten an, während überwiegend die Standortbevölkerung das Risiko trägt. Dies führt zu perzipierten Verletzungen des Fairness-Prinzips[10]. Warum soll eine Gemeinde die Risiken des Konsums anderer Gemeinden tragen? Die Toleranz für technische Einrichtungen ist um so geringer, je weniger Konsens über die Notwendigkeit und Gemeinnützigkeit der Anlage besteht. Ungleiche Risiko-Nutzen-Verteilung kann nur bei allseits geschätzten Einrichtungen (wie etwa Rehabilitationszentren oder Krankenhäuser) mit entsprechender moralischer Überzeugungsarbeit überbrückt werden[11]; ist dagegen der eindeutige Rückgriff auf altruistische Motive nicht möglich, erfolgt in der Regel die Ablehnung.

- Die Risiken von Entsorgungsanlagen sind nicht nur ungleich stark verteilt, sondern bedrohen auch wegen ihres umfassenden Gefährdungspotentials die sozialen Schichten, die ansonsten in der Gesellschaft privilegiert sind. Ulrich Beck hat bei der Analyse der Verteilungswirkungen vor allem auf diesen neuen Egalisierungsgrad der Risiken hingewiesen. Umweltrisiken bedrohen selbst die Reichen und Mächtigen; allerdings können bestimmte Gruppen aus dieser Situation Vorteile ziehen (etwa die Umweltschutzindustrie) oder sich stärker als andere gegen mögliche Gefahren schützen[12].

- Die wahrgenommenen Risiken für Gesundheit und Umgebung sind nicht die einzigen Probleme, die mit Abfallanlagen gedanklich assoziiert werden. Ausser Lärm und Verkehrsbelästigungen befürchtet die Bevölkerung vor allem eine Verringerung der Lebensqualität in-

---

[9] Mitchell 1980; Hadden 1991.
[10] Rayner und Cantor 1987; Consensus 1990.
[11] Jencks 1990, S. 54 f.
[12] Beck 1986, S. 59f f.

nerhalb der Gemeinde, sinkende Grundstückskosten, soziale Veränderungen sowie den 'Imageverlust', der mit der Transformation von einer ländlichen Gemeinde zu einem Industriestandort verbunden ist[13]. Diese Befürchtungen sind oftmals wohlbegründet. So zeigten McClelland u.a.[14], dass die Errichtung von Abfallanlagen die durchschnittlichen Grundstückspreise in den betroffenen Gemeinden negativ beeinflusste.

- Neben die tangiblen Befürchtungen über die negativen Auswirkungen einer Entsorgungsanlage auf Umwelt, Gesundheit und Ökonomie treten symbolische Assoziationen oder Signale. Abfallbehandlung suggeriert negative Bilder von schmutzigen Industrielandschaften, sorglosen Umgang mit natürlichen Ressourcen und Konsum im Überfluss. Gleichgültig ob diese Signale berechtigt sind oder nicht, sie haben häufig handlungsleitenden Charakter und erleichtern die Zuordnung von Objekten zu festgefügten Weltbildern[15] Personen, die Industrie und Marktsystem kritisch gegenüberstehen, sehen in Anlagen zur Beseitigung industrieller oder konsumbezogener Abfälle häufig den Prototypen der von ihnen abgelehnten Wachstumsökonomie. Für sie ist der Kampf gegen Müllverbrennungsanlagen ein Kampf gegen die ihrer Ansicht nach naturzerstörenden Kräfte im Kapitalismus.

- Die Notwendigkeit der Errichtung von Entsorgungsanlagen ist auch unter Fachleuten umstritten - zumindest in dem Ausmass, wie es viele Antragsteller wünschen[16]. Kritiker der bestehenden Abfallwirtschaft weisen darauf hin, dass die Möglichkeiten der Abfallreduzierung sowie der Rezyklierung von gefährlichen Stoffen nicht weit genug ausgeschöpft worden sind[17]. In der öffentlichen Auseinandersetzung um Entsorgungsanlagen lässt sich daher eine ablehnende Haltung immer mit Rekurs auf diesen Disput unter Experten begründen.

---

[13] Rayner 1993, S. 227; Renn et al. 1991, S. 214; Zeiss 1989.
[14] McClelland u.a., 1990.
[15] Jungermann und Slovic 1993, S. 100ff; Buss und Craik 1983.
[16] Wiedemann und Claus 1994, S. 10.
[17] Nader u.a. 1981; Piasecki 1984.

- Der Protest gegen Entsorgungsanlagen nährt sich auch aus der Erfahrung der Bedrohung der eigenen Lebenswelt[18]. Immer mehr Bürger sehen sich in ihrem Alltagshandeln durch professionelle Expertenurteile und institutionelle Eingriffe eingeengt. Was sich in ihrer Gemeinde abspielt, entzieht sich mehr und mehr ihrer Kontrolle und ihrer Einflussnahme. Als Gegenreaktion versuchen sie, alles, was ihnen von aussen aufgezwungen erscheint, abzuwehren und ihre eigene kollektive Identität zu wahren[19].

- Schliesslich ist der Protest gegen eine Entsorgungsanlage häufig auch ein Protest gegen die Art, wie der Beschluss zur Errichtung der Anlage zustande gekommen ist[20]. Der Prozess der Entscheidungsfindung ist mindestens ebenso bedeutend wie die Entscheidung selbst. Mit zunehmendem Bildungsstand und ökonomischem Wohlstand wächst der Wunsch nach Teilhabe an der Entscheidungsfindung, vor allem dann, wenn die persönliche Lebenswelt betroffen ist.

Die Ablehnung gegen Entsorgungsanlagen ist ein vielschichtiges Phänomen. Es ist weder durch die Hypothese des St. Florians-Prinzips, noch durch Ignoranz oder mangelnde Kenntnis der wahren Risikoausmasse bestimmt. Dementsprechend laufen auch alle Vorschläge, die auftretenden Konflikte durch bessere Erziehung, Aufklärung oder Informationskampagnen zu bewältigen, ins Leere[21]. Viele der Befürchtungen von Bürgern sind gar nicht auf der Dimension von Risiko und Nutzen abzubilden; sie beruhen vielmehr auf Aspekten der kommunalen Lebensqualität und der Wahrung der sozialen Identität[22]. Gleichzeitig fordern Bürger, an den Planungen ihrer eigenen Umwelt aktiv beteiligt zu werden. Schliesslich verbergen sich hinter Ablehnung und Zustimmung auch symbolische Zuordnungsmuster, die nur mittelbar mit den instrumentellen Vor- und Nachteilen einer Anlage verbunden sind und sich erst durch die soziale Konstruktion der Zuordnung zu Weltbildern dem Beobachter erschliessen[23].

---

[18] Renn 1987, S. 81 ff.
[19] Rosa et al. 1993.
[20] Zillessen 1993; Kasperson 1986.
[21] vgl. Fritzsche 1991, S. 40 ff.
[22] Otway und von Winterfeldt 1982.
[23] Kemp 1993, S. 118f f.

In diesem Beitrag stellen wir ein Verfahren vor, das wir als kooperativen Diskurs bezeichnet haben. Der kooperative Diskurs zeichnet sich dadurch aus, dass er eine gemeinsame Beschlussfassung der an Entsorgungsfragen beteiligten und davon betroffenen Gruppen vorsieht und nach den Regeln diskursiver Dialogführung strukturiert. Nach der theoretischen Vorstellung unseres Diskursmodell berichten wir über eine Anwendung des Verfahrens bei der Standortfestlegung für eine Deponie im Kanton Aargau.

2. NOTWENDIGKEIT ZUM OFFENEN ZWEISEITIGEN RISIKODIALOG

Das Dilemma im Bereich der Entsorgungspolitik besteht darin, dass zur politischen Bewertung von Abfallstrategien Sachkenntnis über die zu erwartenden Folgen und Risiken verschiedener Lösungsmöglichkeiten vorliegen muss, aber Sachkenntnis alleine nicht ausreicht, um eine demokratisch und ethisch legitimierbare Lösung zu finden. Die Entscheidung den Experten zu überlassen, verletzt die normative Grundlage demokratischer Ordnungen; die Entscheidung dem Markt der politischen Kräfte anheimzugeben, führt in der Regel zur Verkennung physikalisch, chemisch und biologisch gegebener Gesetzmässigkeiten und verfahrenstechnischer Erfordernisse, letztlich damit zu hohen Folgekosten durch inkonsistente Entscheidungen bzw. ineffiziente Lösungen. Gefragt ist also eine Strategie, die kompetente Problemlösung und faire Beschlussfassung miteinander verbindet[24].

Eine solche Strategie setzt zweierlei voraus: eine Risikoabwägung und -legitimation durch Verfahren und einen offenen Dialog mit der Bevölkerung. Im ersteren Fall geht es um einen transparenten und nachvollziehbaren Prozess der Entscheidungsfindung, in dem alle Interessen und Werte berücksichtigt werden[25]; im zweiten Falle um eine angemessene Beteiligung der Menschen, die direkt oder indirekt von den Konsequenzen dieser Entscheidung betroffen sind[26]. Ein offener Dialog muss allerdings nach beiden Seiten hin offen sein, d.h. er darf sich nicht auf die Einbahnstrasse der Information der Betroffenen beschränken, sondern auch

---

[24] Webler in press; Wiedemann et al. 1994, S. 218 ff.
[25] Knoepfel 1994, S. 74 ff.
[26] ebenda S. 78ff und Seiler 1991, S. 17f.

Mitwirkungsrechte der Betroffenen an der Entscheidungsfindung einschliessen. Ohne eine solche Rückkopplung wird jeder Dialog letztendlich im Sande der Frustration verlaufen. Mitwirkung ist also eine notwendige Bedingung für einen erfolgreichen Dialog[27]. Dabei muss zum einen sichergestellt sein, dass eine adäquate Repräsentation der Betroffenen zustandekommt (unter der realistischen Bedingung, dass nicht alle potentiell Betroffenen partizipieren können), zum anderen ist es notwendig darauf zu achten, dass die Beteiligung der Betroffenen die Wirksamkeit des Sachwissens als unabdingbares Element der Entscheidungsfindung nicht einschränkt oder sogar ausschaltet. Gefragt sind also Fairness und Kompetenz[28].

Der Begriff der Fairness ist eng an das Konzept der Beteiligung der betroffenen Bürger an Entscheidungen angebunden. Doch wer repräsentiert die Betroffenen? Selbsternannte Volksvertreter oder Interessengruppen können sicherlich für einen Teil der betroffenen Bürger sprechen, aber beileibe nicht für alle. Ein Beteiligungsverfahren nach dem Freiwilligkeitsprinzip (Jeder ist eingeladen) führt in der Praxis häufig zu Verzerrungen der wahren Bürgermeinungen, weil nur die Aktivisten solchen Einladungen folgen[29]. Bei Verfahren, bei denen Interessengruppen zu einer Verhandlung eingeladen werden, sind meist nicht organisierte Bürger ausgeschlossen. Ein faires Beteiligungsverfahren sollte dagegen jedem potentiell Betroffenen das gleiche Recht einräumen, an der Beschlussfassung teilzunehmen.

Die faire Repräsentanz der Betroffenen kann entweder durch politische Legitimation (etwa Wahlen), durch von den Betroffenen explizit legitimierte Gruppen (etwa Gewerkschaften oder Umweltgruppen) oder durch formale Verfahren der Chancengleichheit (etwa Auswahl nach dem Zufallsverfahren) erzielt werden. In der Regel ist aber schon die Identifizierung der betroffenen Bevölkerung schwierig. Viele Abfallbehandlungsanlagen haben ein breites Nutzenspektrum, aber ein eher lokales Risikospektrum. Wer ist unter diesen Umständen legitimiert, an der Beschlussfassung teilzunehmen? In der Praxis hat es sich häufig bewährt, lokale Interessen durch explizit legitimierte oder durch repräsentativ besetzte Gruppierungen in den Dialog einzubeziehen, während grössere re-

---
[27] Haller 1990, S. 254.
[28] Webler, in press
[29] Reagan und Fedor-Thormon 1987; Cupps 1977.

gionale oder sogar nationale Interessen durch entsprechenden Institutionen bzw. Interessengruppen am besten zu vertreten sind[30].

Gleichzeitig bedeutet eine faire Repräsentation aller Parteien noch lange nicht, dass auch die notwendige Sachkompetenz vorhanden ist, d.h. dass das Wissen um die Konsequenzen von unterschiedlichen Handlungsoptionen auch wirklich adäquat berücksichtigt wird[31]. Der Begriff der Kompetenz wird im Alltag häufig mit Sachwissen in Anlehnung an die Zweck-Mittel-Rationalität gleichgesetzt. Dabei wird Kompetenz danach beurteilt, ob die vorhergesagten Konsequenzen der ausgewählten Optionen sich auch wirklich in der Realität einstellen. Diese Auslegung ist aber wenig hilfreich, da der ex post Zustand noch nicht eingetreten ist, also die Beurteilungsgrundlage fehlt. Gleichzeitig ist die Operationalisierung von Kompetenz als strategisches Wissen für unsere Zwecke zu eng und führt vor allem bei Entscheidungen unter Risiko zu Widersprüchen oder zumindest zu Mehrdeutigkeiten. Aus diesem Grunde ist es notwendig, Kompetenz an der Leistung des Verfahrens zu messen, die im Dialog gemachten Aussagen nach dem Stand des jeweiligen Wissens intersubjektiv nachvollziehbar beurteilen und selektieren zu können. Der Grad der Kompetenz ist also davon abhängig, inwieweit das jeweilige Konfliktlösungsverfahren Möglichkeiten zur Überprüfung von Aussagen bereitstellt und inwieweit bei der Beurteilung dieser Aussagen intersubjektiv gültige Regeln der Überprüfung zur Anwendung kommen[32].

Es ist wichtig darauf hinzuweisen, dass eine solche Selektion selbst im Idealfall keine eindeutige Lösung des Konfliktes verspricht. Auch wenn alle Sachaussagen geklärt sind, die Wahrhaftigkeit von Aussagen überprüft ist und die Angemessenheit von Normen sichergestellt ist, kann es immer noch zu unüberbrückbaren Gegensätzen zwischen den Diskursteilnehmern kommen. Konsens ist nicht die einzige Möglichkeit der Verständigung. Unterschiedliche Strategien in der Behandlung von unsicheren Folgen, unterschiedliche Erfahrungen mit Institutionen in Bezug auf Vertrauenswürdigkeit und unterschiedliche Systeme von Werten und Präferenzen können im Einzelfall sogar Konflikte verstärken und Kompromisse erschweren. Ein Dialog ist kein Garant, nicht einmal eine notwendige Bedingung für eine Konfliktlösung. Oft können Missverständnisse, Doppeldeutigkeiten und strategische Vorgehensweisen Kompromisslösungen eher

---

[30] Carpenter und Kennedy 1991, S. 102 ff.
[31] Moore 1986, S. 100
[32] Webler, in press; Habermas 1989, S. 571 ff.

fördern als die schonungslose Offenlegung von Interessen und Präferenzen[33]. Allerdings bietet nach unserer Überzeugung nur die radikale Offenlegung der eigenen Präferenzen und die Überprüfung aller Aussagen nach konsensualen Regeln intersubjektiver Gültigkeit die Gewähr für eine *faire und kompetente* Problemlösung. Kriterien für erfolgreiche Konfliktschlichtung sind Fairness und Kompetenz, nicht Konfliktlösung um jeden Preis.

3. THEORETISCHE UND METHODISCHE VORGEHENSWEISE

Für eine faire und kompetente Erstellung von Abfallbewirtschaftungplänen bedienen wir uns eines Modells, das auf den Überlegungen von Jürgen Habermas zum rationalen Diskurs und auf dem Planungszellen-Konzept von Peter Dienel aufbaut[34]. An dieser Stelle kann dieses - von uns als kooperativer Diskurs bezeichnete - Modell nicht eingehend erläutert werden[35]. Dennoch erscheint es sinnvoll, die Grundstruktur unseres Ansatzes kurz zu skizzieren.

Das Modell des kooperativen Diskurses beruht auf der Annahme, dass mit Hilfe von Kommunikation gemeinsam erarbeitete und getragene Entscheidungen bez. Handlungsempfehlungen auch bei Interessengegensätzen und Wertkonflikten unterschiedlicher Parteien erzielt werden können, ohne dass eine Partei ausgeschlossen oder ihre Interessen oder Werte unberücksichtigt bleiben. Ein solcher Diskurs ist durch folgende Charakteristika gekennzeichnet[36]:

(1) Die Teilnehmer müssen im Konsens darüber entscheiden, nach welchem Verfahren Einigung über kollektiv bindende Entscheidungen getroffen werden sollen. Die Parteien können Einstimmigkeit, das Mehrheitswahlrecht oder die Einschaltung eines Schlichters vorsehen; wichtig ist aber, dass alle Parteien der vorgesehenen Verfahrensweise zustimmen.

---
[33] von Schomberg 1994, S. 249 ff.
[34] Habermas 1971, S. 101-141; Habermas 1981; Habermas 1989; Habermas 1992; Dienel 1978; Dienel 1989.
[35] siehe dazu Renn et al. 1993; Renn und Webler 1994.
[36] Renn und Webler 1994, S. 40 f.

(2) Die Teilnehmer müssen sich vorab darauf verständigen, dass alle in die Verhandlung eingebrachten Tatsachenbehauptungen nachgewiesen oder durch entsprechende Experten (wobei je nach Wissenstyp nicht nur Wissenschaftler in Frage kommen) bestätigt werden. Lässt sich eine Tatsachenbehauptung, wie häufig zu beobachten, nicht eindeutig nachweisen oder widerlegen, müssen alle legitimen, d.h. innerhalb des jeweiligen Wissenstyp zulässigen Aussagen gleichberechtigt in den Diskurs eingebracht werden.

(3) Die Teilnehmer müssen zur Kenntnis nehmen und einen Konsens darüber erzielen, dass unterschiedliche Interpretationsmuster und Rationalitäten gleichberechtigt sind, sofern sie nicht den Regeln der Logik und anderer formaler Argumentationsregeln widersprechen.

(4) Die Teilnehmer müssen sich gegenseitig verpflichten, alle Aussagen in einem Diskurs zuzulassen, sich aber gleichzeitig damit einverstanden erklären, dass alle Aussagen prinzipiell der gegenseitigen Kritik zugänglich gemacht und gemäss nachvollziehbaren Regeln auf ihre Geltungsansprüche hin untersucht werden.

(5) Die Teilnehmer sollen dazu ermutigt werden, die eigenen Interessen und Werte so weit wie möglich offenzulegen; eine solche Abstinenz vom strategischen Handeln wird sich aber nur dann durchsetzen, wenn Offenheit im Diskurs belohnt und strategisches Lügen wenig Aussicht auf Erfolg hat. Dies mag auf den ersten Blick als "frommer Wunsch" erscheinen. Gemeint ist damit, dass alle Äusserungen von Teilnehmern auf ihre Ernsthaftigkeit und Vertrauenswürdigkeit überprüft werden können und dass sich die Teilnehmer damit einverstanden erklären.

(6) Die Teilnehmer müssen die Bereitschaft mitbringen, eine faire Lösung des Konfliktes anzustreben, bei der alle Interessen und Werte grundsätzlich als legitim und verhandlungswürdig anerkannt werden, ohne damit die Notwendigkeit der Begründung von Interessen oder Werten in Frage zu stellen[37].

---

[37] Bacow und Wheeler 1984, S. 42 ff.

Es gibt keinen Zweifel, dass ein Diskurs, der alle diese Eigenschaften erfüllt, in der Realität nicht stattfindet. Der kooperative Diskurs, wie er hier charakterisiert ist, stellt das Ideal dar, an dem sich Diskurse in der Realität messen lassen müssen. In der Vergangenheit haben wir versucht, praktikable Modelle für Diskurse zu entwickeln und praktisch zu erproben[38]. Die Erfahrungen mit diesen Projekten hat gezeigt, dass die Verwirklichung von kooperativen Diskursen eine Herausforderung darstellt, die theoretisches Wissen, kreatives Denken und praktisches Geschick erfordert. Alle unsere Projekte haben niemals alle Indikatoren eines rationalen Diskurses erfüllen können, mit zunehmender Erfahrung haben wir jedoch mehr und mehr dazugelernt.

Das im folgenden beschriebene Ablaufmodell dient uns dabei als Gerüst, auf dessen Grundlage wir die spezielle Vorgehensweise in jedem konkreten Fall entwickeln. Dieses Grundmodell beruht auf der sequentiellen Verknüpfung von Werten, Wissen und rationaler Abwägung. Die Verknüpfung dieser drei Ebenen geschieht in den folgenden drei Schritten (siehe auch Bild 1):

(1) Im ersten Schritt werden alle in der jeweiligen politischen Arena tätigen Parteien und Organisationen gebeten, ihre Werte und Kriterien für die Beurteilung unterschiedlicher Optionen (etwa Entsorgungsverfahren) offenzulegen. Dies geschieht in Interviews zwischen den Diskurs-Organisatoren und den Repräsentanten der jeweiligen Parteien. Dabei kommt es darauf an, die Gesprächspartner davon zu überzeugen, nicht über die Vor- und Nachteile bestimmter Technologien oder Optionen zu diskutieren, sondern sich auf die Erarbeitung von Zielen und Kriterien einzulassen, die an diese Optionen angelegt werden sollen. Nur wenn es gelingt, allgemeinverbindliche Kriterien festzulegen, die für alle Optionen gelten sollen, kann ein rational begründbares Urteil über die Wünschbarkeit von Optionen gefällt werden. Diese Kriterien gelten dann als Massstäbe, um die bestehenden und noch zu entwickelnden Optionen zu beurteilen. Als methodisches Werkzeug dient dabei die Wertbaum-Analyse, ein in den USA entwickeltes interaktives Verfahren zur Bewusstmachung und Strukturierung von Werten und Attributen[39].

---

[38] Renn et al. 1985, Renn et al. 1989, Renn et al. 1993.
[39] Keeney et al. 1984; von Winterfeldt 1987.

Bild 1: Das Drei-Stufen-Modell der Partizipation: Kriterienerstellung, Folgenabschätzung, Bewertung

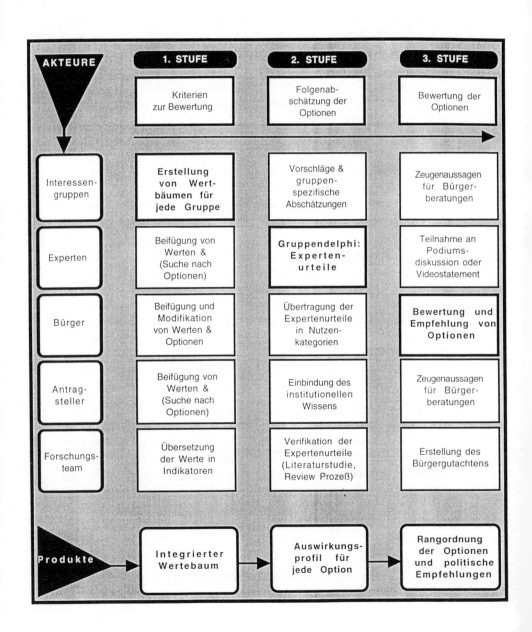

(2) Die Wertdimensionen werden in einem zweiten Schritt durch ein Forschungsteam, das möglichst von allen Parteien als neutral angesehen wird, in Indikatoren überführt. Indikatoren sind Messanweisungen, um die möglichen Folgen einer jeden Handlungsoption zu bestimmen. Als Handlungsoptionen gelten die heute bestehenden Optionen, aber auch die sich schon abzeichnenden technischen oder organisatorischen Neuentwicklungen. Daneben können natürlich auch politische Massnahmen oder Verhaltensänderungen, wie Umweltsteuern oder die Einführung von Abfallsortierung im Haushalt abgeschätzt werden. Da viele der Folgen nicht physisch messbar sind und manche auch wissenschaftlich umstritten sein mögen, ist es nicht möglich, einen einzigen Wert für jeden Indikator anzugeben. Für den Diskurs ist es entscheidend, die Spannweite wissenschaftlich legitimer Abschätzungen so genau wie möglich zu bestimmen. Dazu ist eine Modifikation des klassischen Delphi-Verfahrens sinnvoll, bei dem Gruppen von Experten gemeinsam Abschätzungen vornehmen und Diskrepanzen innerhalb der Gruppen in direkter Konfrontation ausdiskutieren[40].

(3) Hat man die Wertdimensionen bestimmt und die Folgen der jeweiligen Handlungsoptionen abgeschätzt, folgt der schwierige Prozess der Abwägung. Um eine möglichst faire und demokratische Form der Abwägung zu gewährleisten, hat Peter Dienel von der Universität Wuppertal vorgeschlagen, die Bevölkerung als "Schöffen" zu gewinnen und es - ähnlich wie bei einem amerikanischen Gerichtsverfahren - einigen, nach dem Zufallsverfahren ausgesuchten Bürgern zu überlassen, stellvertretend für alle diese Abwägung vorzunehmen[41]. Dieses Verfahren setzt voraus, dass die am Konflikt beteiligten Parteien einer solchen Lösung zustimmen. Alle Parteien erhalten deshalb die Möglichkeit, in einem Koordinationsausschuss mitzuwirken und den Prozess der Information und Diskussion der Bürgergruppen zu beaufsichtigen. Daneben sind sie eingeladen, als Zeugen vor den Bürgern auszusagen und ihre Empfehlungen vorzutragen. Die ausgesuchten Bürger haben mehrere Tage Zeit, die Profile der jeweiligen Handlungsoptionen zu studieren, Experten zu befragen, Zeugen anzuhören, Besichtigungen vorzunehmen und sich eingehend zu bera-

---

[40] Renn und Kotte 1985; Webler u.a. 1991.
[41] Dienel 1978; Dienel und Garbe 1985.

ten. Am Ende stellen sie eine Handlungsempfehlung aus, die sie wie bei einem Gerichtsverfahren in einem Bürgergutachten begründen müssen. Diese Gutachten werden den Konfliktparteien zur Stellungnahme vorgelegt. Aufgrund der Bürgergutachten und der Stellungnahmen kann dann am berühmten "runden" Tisch ein konsistentes und von einer breiten Mehrheit getragenes Paket von Massnahmen oder Entscheidungsvorlagen geschnürt werden.

Das hier beschriebene Verfahren hat den Vorteil, dass es zwischen Werterhebung, Faktenermittlung und Abwägung trennt und dafür verschiedene Verfahrensschritte vorschlägt. Dadurch werden unterschiedliche Prozesse der Trennung von Ideologie und Wissen wirksam, die sich in einem allumfassenden Diskurs oft vermischen. Innerhalb der Bürgerforen lassen sich darüber hinaus die Regeln des kooperativen Diskurses meist besser durchsetzten als in einer Verhandlung zwischen Parteien. Allerdings beruht dieses Verfahren auf der expliziten Zustimmung aller relevanten Parteien, die Empfehlung der Bürger zumindest zu berücksichtigen, wenn nicht sogar für einen selbst als verbindlich anzuerkennen. Gleichzeitig müssen die Profile und faktischen Analysen so aufbereitet sein, dass ein Nichtfachmann mit ihnen umgehen kann. Die Praxis hat jedoch gezeigt, dass Wissenschaftler und Interessengruppen die Urteilskraft des Bürgers meist unterschätzen[42]. Sofern die faktischen Zusammenhänge eingehend erläutert und die Interessen und Werte der beteiligten Parteien transparent gemacht werden, sind Bürger durchaus in der Lage, sachlich richtige und politisch faire Empfehlungen vorzuschlagen. Das Verfahren ist in Bild 1 schematisch veranschaulicht.

4. FALLBEISPIEL: KOOPERATIVER DISKURS FÜR EINE STANDORTFESTLEGUNG "DEPONIE AARGAU OST"

Das folgende Fallbeispiel beschreibt die Anwendung des kooperativen Diskurses für die Bestimmung einer Restabfalldeponie für den östlichen Teil des Kantons Aargau in der Schweiz (siehe Bild 2). Die Abfallbewirtschaftungsleitlinien des Kantons Aargau sehen vor, dass Reststoffe und Bauschutt auf Deponien abgelagert werden. Dabei wird eine faire Lasten-

---

[42] Renn et al. 1985, S. 201.

aufteilung auf die unterschiedlichen Regionen angestrebt. Während der westliche und nördliche Teil des Kantons bereits über eine Deponie verfügen bzw. eine solche in der Planung ist, stand der Bau einer Deponie im Süden des östlichen Kantonsteils noch aus. Aufgrund der zum Teil heftigen Proteste der Bevölkerung gegen die geplante Deponie in Suhr und wegen akuter Umweltprobleme mit zwei Deponie-Altlasten war das Baudepartement der Meinung, man müsse im Fall der Deponieplanung Aargau Ost die Bevölkerung umfassend und frühzeitig in das Planungsverfahren einbeziehen.

Das Evaluationsverfahren für einen Deponiestandort im östlichen Teil des Kantons Aargau wurde vom kantonalen Baudepartement in drei Phasen aufgeteilt. In einem ersten Schritt wurden Gebiete aus dem Verfahren ausgeschieden, die aus juristischen Gründen als Deponiestandorte nicht in Frage kamen (Grundwasserschutzzonen, Gewässerschutzbereich A, rechtsgültige Naturschutzgebiete, Siedlungsgebiete) und auf einem sogenannten Negativzonenplan eingetragen. Da der geologische Untergrund unter dem geplanten Deponiekörper bestimmte Kriterien bezüglich der Durchlässigkeit und Mächtigkeit erfüllen muss wurden alle geologischen Formationen, die diesen Bedingungen voraussichtlich genügten, auf einer geologischen Grundkarte eingetragen. Die Überlagerung des Negativzonenplans mit der geologischen Grundkarte ergab Positivzonen, in denen an topographisch günstigen Lagen insgesamt 32 mögliche Deponiestandorte eingetragen wurden. Die 32 Standortvorschläge wurden von einem Geologiebüro im Auftrag des Baudepartements nach detaillierten Bewertungskriterien überprüft. Nur 13 Standorte erfüllten die Grundbedingungen für einen Deponiestandort und wurden aufgrund einer Nutzwertanalyse in eine Rangfolge gebracht. Im Sommer 1992 ging das Baudepartement an die Öffentlichkeit: Zuerst wurden die 13 betroffenen Standortgemeinden unterrichtet, dann die Presse.

Bild 2: Geographische Informationen über den Kanton Aargau und die Lage der Deponie-Standorte

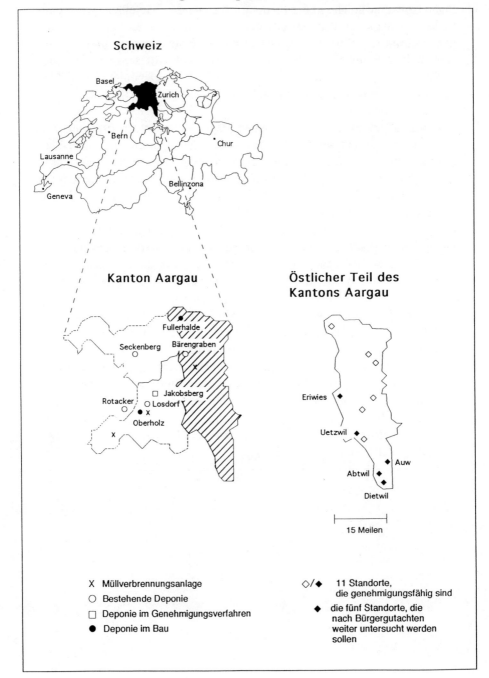

Zu diesem Zeitpunkt erfolgte eine Übereinkunft zwischen dem ETH Polyprojekt "Risiko und Sicherheit technischer Systeme" und dem Baudepartement, für die zweite Phase der Evaluation ein Verfahren des kooperativen Diskurses mit Vertretern der 13 Gemeinden in Gang zu setzen und von den Mitarbeitern des Polyprojektes betreuen zu lassen. Ziel des Diskurses war es, aus den 13 Standorten eine Liste von zwei bis vier ernsthaften Kandidaten zu erstellen, die in der folgenden intensiven Erkundungsphase auf ihre Eignung überprüft werden sollten. Darüber hinaus sollten die Bedingungen für eine Deponie mit den potentiellen Anwohnern ausgehandelt und mögliche politische Ausgleichsstrategien erörtert werden. Parallel zu den Diskursen mit den betroffenen Anwohnern führten verschiedene Geologiebüros Untersuchungen im Bereich der Hydrogeologie und Geotechnik bei allen Standorten der engeren Wahl durch und stellten die Ergebnisse den Teilnehmern des Diskurses vor. Für die Bürgerbeteiligung stellte das Baudepartement rund 150.000 Schweizer Franken zur Verfügung. Aus diesem Fonds wurden die laufenden Unkosten sowie die Sitzungsgelder für die Teilnehmer an den Kommissionen bestritten. Die Arbeit der Moderatoren und die Begleitforschung wurde vollständig von dem Polyprojekt ":Risiko und Sicherheit technischer Systeme" an der ETH Zürich übernommen. Die gesamten Kosten, inklusive Personalkosten, dürften in der Grössenordnung von 400.000 Franken gelegen haben.

In der zur Zeit laufenden dritten Phase werden die in der Auswahl verbliebenen Standorte einer detaillierten geologischen Untersuchung unterzogen. Zudem steht die Zufahrtsplanung sowie die Festlegung des Deponiekonzepts an. Das Baudepartement rechnet damit, in den nächsten Jahren für ein bis zwei Standorte das kantonale Überbauungsplanverfahren einzuleiten.

Tabelle 1:   **Die vier Phasen der Standortwahl**

Evaluations-phase I	Evaluations-phase II	Evaluations-phase III	Überbauungsplan-verfahren / Baubewilligungsverfahren
Grobevaluation aufgrund von rechtlichen und geologischen Kriterien Nutzwertanalyse für 32 potentielle Deponiestandorte: Empfehlung von 13 Standorten	BürgerInnenbeteiligung: - Einbezug von 13 betroffenen Standortgemeinden Geologische Felduntersuchungen Empfehlung von 1-3 Standorten durch die Beteiligtenkommissionen	Detaillierte geologische Untersuchungen Erarbeitung eines detaillierten Deponiekonzepts für die verbleibenden Standorte	Umweltverträglichkeitsprüfung Beschluss des Kantonsparlaments

1991   1992   1993   1994   Zeitachse

5. DER VERFAHRENSABLAUF

Im August 1992 wurden die Gemeinderäte der betroffenen 13 Standortgemeinden über die geplante Beteiligung an der Deponiestandortsuche informiert. Sie wurden eingeladen, einen politischen Vertreter oder eine Vertreterin in ein Begleitgremium, der sogenannten Behördendelegation zu entsenden. Diese Behördendelegation setzte sich aus je einem Vertreter der betroffenen Standortgemeinden und dem Direktor des Baudepartements zusammen. Sie hatte folgende Aufgaben:

- den Ablauf und die Form des Beteiligungsverfahrens zu planen und zu überwachen;
- die Eignungsprüfungen durch die beteiligten Ingenieurbüros zu überwachen und gegebenenfalls zu kommentieren;
- die Öffentlichkeit in den Standortgemeinden über den Auswahlprozesses zu informieren;
- die Empfehlungen der Kommissionen entgegenzunehmen und eine entsprechende Vorlage an die politischen Gremien (wie den Grossen Rat) auszuarbeiten;

- den gesamten Auswahlprozess kritisch zu begleiten.

Die Behördendelegation trat erstmalig im Herbst 1992 zusammen und tagte dann dreimal bis zur Entscheidungsfindung durch die Kommissionen. Es war den Gemeinden freigestellt zu bestimmen, welchen Vertreter sie in die Behördendelegation entsenden wollten. In der Regel wurde ein Mitglied des Gemeinderates ausgewählt, der für die Abfallthematik bzw. Umwelt- und Bauplanung zuständig war.

Die diskursive Verhandlung um die Standortauswahl fand in den Kommissionen statt. Insgesamt wurden vier parallel, aber unabhängig voneinander tagende Kommissionen gebildet. In jeder Kommission waren zwei Vertreter einer jeden potentiellen Standortgemeinde vertreten. Die Kommissionen hatten folgende Aufgaben:

- aus der Sicht der Betroffenen Auswahlkriterien zu formulieren und sie auf die möglichen Standorte anzuwenden;
- die eingehenden technischen Berichte kritisch zu prüfen und entsprechende Rückfragen zu formulieren;
- Vertreter von Interessengruppen und Bürgerinitiativen anzuhören;
- die Rahmenbedingungen für den Betrieb der Anlage weiter auszufeilen; vor allem die Bedingungen für eine mögliche Betreibung der Anlage festzulegen,
- Empfehlungen zur Standortwahl auszusprechen.

Das ETH Team hatte ursprünglich vorgeschlagen, die Kommissionen mit Gemeindemitgliedern, die nach dem Zufallsverfahren repräsentativ bestimmt werden sollten, zusammenzusetzen. Dieser Vorschlag wurde allerdings von dem Baudepartement abgelehnt. Statt dessen wurden die Vertreter der Behördendelegation gebeten, aus jeder Standortgemeinde acht Kandidaten bzw. Kandidatinnen für die Kommissionen zu bestimmen. Dazu erstellte das ETH Team einen Anforderungskatalog. Die Teilnehmer der Kommissionen sollten folgendem Profil entsprechen:

- Repräsentanten der Politik, des sozialen Lebens, der Vereine und der Interessengruppen;
- Mögliche Anwohner oder Eigentümer der ins Auge gefassten Standortgrundstücke;

- (Wenn vorhanden) Vertreter von Naturschutz- oder Umweltschutzgruppen;
- Vertreter der örtlichen Industrien;
- Vertreter der wichtigsten Berufsgruppen (etwa Bauern, Handwerker, etc.);
- Vertreter der Kirchen und kulturellen Gruppen (falls Interesse besteht);
- Interessierte Gemeindemitglieder.

Bis auf eine Gemeinde (Abtwil) nahmen alle vom Baudepartement ausgewählten Standortgemeinden an der Auswahl von Kommissionsmitgliedern teil. Wir hatten vorgegeben, dass die Mitglieder keine spezielle Fachkenntnis im Bereich Deponien oder Abfallwirtschaft besitzen müssten. Die zum Verständnis der geplanten Deponie notwendigen Informationen wurden schriftlich durch eine von der ETH bearbeitete Broschüre und mündlich während der Sitzungen übermittelt. Bei der Auswahl der Mitglieder sollte vor allem auf möglichst breite Erfassung aller Interessen und sozialen Gruppierungen geachtet werden. Aufgrund eines Fragebogens, der an alle Mitglieder der Kommissionen ausgehändigt wurde, ergab sich folgendes Bild der Rekrutierung:

Berufung aufgrund eines Vorschlags des Gemeinderates:	54%
Freiwillige Meldung aufgrund der ausgegeben Information	24%
Vorschlag eines angesprochenen Vereins	10%
Meldung aufgrund einer Annonce im Ortsblatt	3%
andrer Art	9%

Etwas weniger als zwei Drittel der Kommissionsmitglieder war zum ersten Mal in einer Kommission, 16% übten eine offizielle Funktion in der Gemeinde aus, 7% gehörten dem Gemeinderat an. Besonders häufig wurden Vertreter von Naturschutzverbänden, Landwirte, Landeigentümer und Meinungsführer (wie Lehrer oder Ärzte) ausgewählt. Aufgrund dieser Angaben lässt sich eine Streuung über viele Interessengruppen feststellen, insgesamt ist aber eine repräsentative Auswahl aus den Gemeinden sicher nicht zustandegekommen.

Die ersten beiden Sitzungen der Kommissionen wurden mit Ausnahme der zweiten Sitzung der Kommission 4 vom ersten Autor (O. Renn) geleitet. Die Beteiligten wünschten, dass auch die weiteren Sitzungen von dem ETH Team moderiert würden, so dass neben dem Erstautor drei weitere ETH Moderatoren (R. Simoni, U. Dahinden und H. Kastenholz) zum Einsatz kamen. Jeder Diskursbegleiter war für jeweils eine Kommission verantwortlich. Die vier Kommissionen arbeiteten unabhängig voneinander. In rund neun Abendsitzungen bestimmten sie zunächst die weitere Vorgehensweise, legten die Kriterien für die Bewertung der verschiedenen potentiellen Deponiestandorte fest, veranstalteten Anhörungen mit Experten, diskutierten die Resultate der geologischen Gutachten, besichtigten die potentiellen Standorte und führten eine Nutzwertanalyse zu jedem Standort durch[43]. Während der Sitzungen konnten bereits vier Standorte wegen mangelnder geologischer Eignung ausgeschlossen werden. Der gesamte Verlauf des Diskurses ist schematisch in Bild 3 dargestellt.

---

[43] Edwards 1977; Gäfgen 1963.

Bild 3: **Fliessdiagramm der Diskursführung und Entscheidungsfindung im Projekt "Deponie Aargau-Ost"**

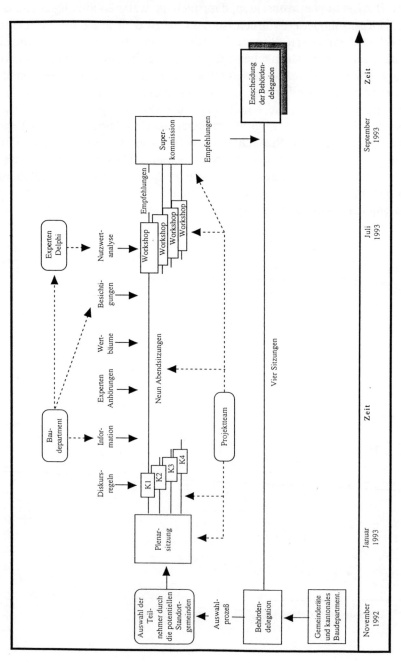

6. ERGEBNISSE DER BÜRGERBETEILIGUNG

Die wesentliche Aufgabe der Kommissionen war es, anhand selbst erstellter Kriterien eine Nutzwertanalyse aller möglichen Standorte vorzunehmen. In Abweichung von dem Drei-Stufen-Modell hielten wir es für sinnvoll, die Wertbäume nicht von organisierten Gruppen, sondern von den Kommissionen selbst erstellen zu lassen. Über mehrere Sitzungen wurden alle Werte und Kriterien gesammelt, in eine hierarchische Ordnung eingebunden und anschliessend nach ihrer relativen Bedeutung gewichtet. Aus diesem Wertebaum wurden dann deduktiv Kriterien und Indikatoren erarbeitet, mit deren Hilfe jeder Standort auf einer Skala von +2 bis -2 beurteilt werden konnte.

Mitte Juni 1993 veranstalteten wir in Kooperation mit dem Baudepartement ein eintägiges Gruppendelphi mit sieben Deponieexperten zur Bewertung der neun verbliebenen Standorte. Als Grundlage dazu dienten die Ergebnisse der Eignungsprüfung durch die technischen Ingenieurbüros. Der Experten-Workshop war, wie im Drei-Stufen-Modell vorgesehen, nach dem Gruppen-Delphi-Verfahren strukturiert[44]. In einem iterativen Erhebungsverfahren wurden Experten mit unterschiedlicher Meinung dazu angehalten, die neun Standorte auf den von den Kommissionen ausgearbeiteten Beurteilungskriterien mit Hilfe eine Skala von 0-10 zu bewerten. Dabei wurde 0 als denkbar schlechter Standort und 10 als denkbar guter Standort definiert. Diese Abschätzungen nahmen die Experten zunächst in drei kleinen Gruppen von zwei bis drei Personen vor. Die Ergebnisse der Gruppenarbeit wurden dann im Plenum allen übrigen Experten vorgestellt. Dabei mussten die Gruppen, deren Ergebnisse am meisten vom Mittelwert aller anderen Gruppen abwichen, ihre Einschätzungen ausführlich begründen. Nach einer Diskussion der Argumente, die zur Rechtfertigung der Gruppenergebnisse vorgebracht wurden, folgte eine weitere Gruppenaufteilung. Die Gruppenzusammensetzung wurde so variiert, dass in jeder neuen Gruppe jeweils ein Vertreter der verschiedenen Standpunkte aus der ersten Runde repräsentiert war. Theoretisch ist es wünschenswert, die Zahl der Runden von Gruppenarbeit und anschliessender Plenumsdiskussion flexibel zu halten und erst dann den iterativen Prozess zu beenden, wenn keine Veränderungen derEinschätzungen mehr auftreten. Am Ende dieses Prozesses steht dann ein Auswirkungsprofil, in

---

44 Webler et al. 1991; Renn et al. 1993.

dem konsensuale Ergebnisse und die Verteilungsfunktion von divergenten Meinungen erfasst sind. Wegen der Kürze der Zeit (der Workshop musste in einem Tag abgewickelt werden) mussten wir uns allerdings mit zwei Runden begnügen. Dadurch konnten nicht alle Fragen abschliessend diskutiert werden: es verblieb ein unausgefüllter Spielraum für mögliche Konsense bez. Konsense über weiterhin bestehende Dissense. Dennoch haben die Ergebnisse des Workshops den Teilnehmern der Kommissionen geholfen, die Profile der verschiedenen Standorte miteinander zu vergleichen. Allerdings fielen den Kommissionsmitgliedern auch manche Inkonsistenzen und Beispiele für strategisches Antwortverhalten bei den Experten auf.

Zur abschliessenden Bewertung der Standorte trafen sich alle vier Kommissionen zu getrennten Workshops, die ein bis zwei Tage dauerten. Ziel des Workshops war es, die Beurteilungen der Standorte und die Gewichtungen der Kriterien zusammenzufassen und in eine Nutzwertanalyse zu integrieren. Als Grundlage für die Beurteilungen dienten einerseits die Abschätzungen aus dem Expertendelphi, andererseits die Resultate der geologischen Untersuchungen. Gleichzeitig spielten die persönlichen Eindrücke aus der Besichtigung der Standorte eine entscheidende Rolle. Die Bewertungen der Standorte nach den Kriterien wurden arbeitsteilig in kleinen Gruppen von fünf Personen innerhalb jeder Kommission vorbereitet und dann im Plenum diskutiert. Nach Verabschiedung der Bewertungen auf einer Skala von +2 bis -2, rechnete der jeweilige Moderator die numerischen Nutzwerte aus und erstellte daraus eine Reihenfolge der Standorte. Die Ergebnisse dieser Nutzwertanalyse sind in den Bildern 4 und 5 dargestellt.

Nach einer intensiven Diskussion der Nutzwertergebnisse wurde über jeden Standort abgestimmt. Neben der Standortbestimmung erarbeiteten die Beteiligten auch Defizitausgleichsstrategien für den Umgang mit nachteiligen Punkten der ansonsten als geeignet empfohlenen Standorte sowie allgemeine Empfehlungen für die Deponieplanung. In allen Punkten, einschliesslich der Festlegung einer Rangfolge der Deponie-Standorte erzielten alle vier Kommissionen einstimmige Ergebnisse. Selbst die von den Standortempfehlungen betroffenen Anwohnern schlossen sich den jeweiligen Gruppenvoten an. Die Ergebnisse der vier Kommissionen waren ähnlich, aber nicht identisch. Auf den ersten Platz landete bei allen Gruppen der Standort Eriwies (in der Nähe von Schinznach). In der weiteren Rangfolge allerdings unterschieden sich die Empfehlungen.

Bild 4: Die Ergebnisse der Kommissionsbewertungen der Standorte (Mensch, Natur, Sozialwesen)

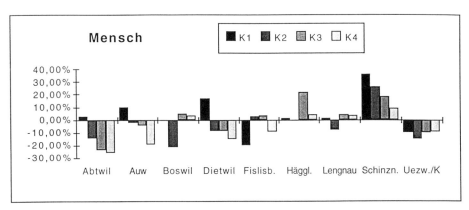

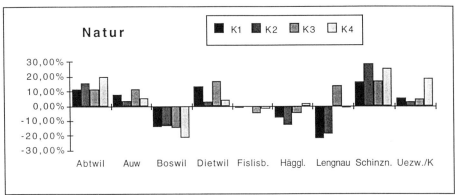

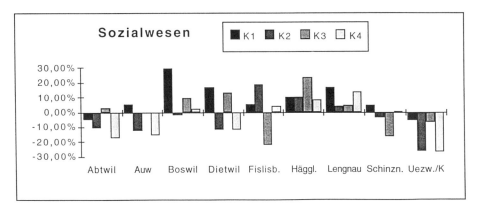

Bild 5: Die Ergebnisse der Kommissionsbewertungen der Standorte (Wirtschaftlichkeit und Gesamt)

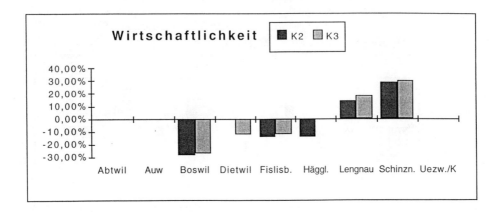
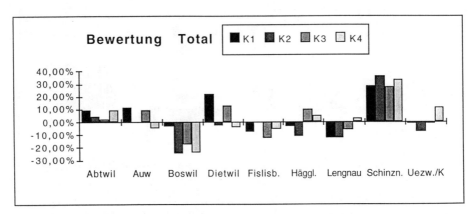
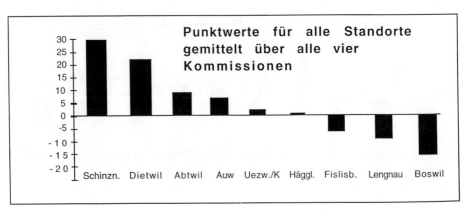

Um diese Unterschiede auszugleichen, wurden aus den vier Kommissionen jeweils fünf Mitglieder ausgewählt, die in einem Kommissionsausschuss (Superkommission) die bestehenden Differenzen ausgleichen sollten. Im Herbst 1993 traf der Kommissionsausschuss zusammen und legte eine Reihenfolge der in Zukunft zu betrachtenden Standorte fest. Neben der von allen Kommissionen bestätigten ersten Priorität für den Standort Eriwies empfahl der Ausschuss an zweiter Stelle die möglichen Standorte Dietwil-Sins und Sins-Auw (gleichrangig) und an dritter Stelle die möglichen Standorte Abtwil und Uezwil. Diese Standorte sollen parallel auf ihre Eignung für eine Deponie weiter untersucht werden, wobei bei ähnlicher geologischer Eignung der jeweils ranghöhere Standort Vorrang haben soll.

Die Behördendelegation schloss sich der Empfehlung des Kommissionsausschusses (dieselben Standorte, jedoch ohne explizite Rangfolge) an und empfahl dem kantonalen Baudepartement, das Ergebnis des Beteiligungsverfahrens politisch umzusetzen. Dies ist inzwischen geschehen und die dritte Phase (nähere Untersuchung der besten Standorte) ist zur Zeit angelaufen. Mit einer Entscheidung für einen oder mehrere Standorte ist im Jahre 1995 zu rechnen.

Das ganze Beteiligungsverfahren war von hohem Engagement der Teilnehmer geprägt, die öfter als vorgesehen und fast immer vollzählig tagten. Kein Kommissionsmitglied kündigte im Verlauf des Verfahrens die Teilnahme auf. Die einzige Gemeinde, die zu Beginn keine Kommissionsmitglieder entsandt hatte, beteiligte sich zum Schluss ebenfalls am Diskurs und akzeptierte die Entscheidungen ebenso wie alle anderen Gemeinden trotz eigener Betroffenheit vom Ergebnis. Es gab keine Opposition gegen die Empfehlungen oder Minderheitsvoten, die abweichende Standpunkte vertraten.

7. BESONDERHEITEN DER SCHWEIZER POLITISCHEN KULTUR

Aufgrund unserer Erfahrungen mit unserem Beteiligungsverfahren im Ausland können wir einige Vergleiche zwischen dem Verhalten der Kommissionsmitglieder im Aargau und dem Verhalten der Bürger in anderen Ländern ziehen[45]. Selbstverständlich sind solche Vergleiche nicht

---

[45] Renn et al. 1985; Renn et al. 1989; Renn et al. 1991; Dienel und Renn, in press.

repräsentativ, sondern beziehen sich nur auf die subjektiven Eindrücke, die wir in diesem Verfahren gewinnen konnten.

Zunächst ist es ein Kennzeichen des Verfahrens in allen Ländern, in denen wir bislang mit Bürgergruppen gearbeitet haben, dass im Gegensatz zu den Unkenrufen vieler Kritiker die Disziplin und das Durchhaltevermögen der beteiligten Bürger erstaunlich hoch sind. Doch die Schweizer Teilnehmer an dem Beteiligungsverfahren verhielten sich in dieser Hinsicht besonders vorbildlich. Keine der teilnehmenden Personen hat ihre Mitarbeit im Laufe der sechsmonatigen Verhandlungsphase aufgekündigt oder von neuen Bedingungen abhängig gemacht. Zu den Sitzungen erschienen stets mehr als 80 Prozent aller Teilnehmer. Die Mitglieder der Kommissionen arbeiteten oft über die vorgesehene Zeit hinaus; sie engagierten sich auch ausserhalb der Sitzungszeiten und setzten sich intensiv mit dem ausgegebenen Material auseinander. Selten haben wir ein solches Engagement erlebt. In den von uns miterlebten Beteiligungsverfahren in den Vereinigten Staaten war die Apathie vieler Mitglieder höher und die Arbeitsmoral weniger stark ausgeprägt. Diese Einsatzbereitschaft der Schweizer Teilnehmer machte uns deutlich, dass die starke Verankerung der Basisdemokratie in der Schweiz mit einem verantwortungsvollen Gebrauch dieser Freiheit durch den Bürger einhergeht[46]. Somit hat uns dieses Erlebnis in unserer Ansicht bestärkt, dass der viel beklagte Vertrauensverlust der offiziellen Politik nur dadurch überwunden werden kann, dass die Politiker auch mehr Vertrauen in die Urteilskraft ihrer Bürger setzen. Das eine bedingt das andere.

Ebenfalls war es für uns interessant zu erfahren, dass die Kommissionsmitglieder in den vier Schweizer Kommissionen sehr viel mehr Vertrauen in die Experten (Deponie-Fachleute) besassen, als wir dies in Deutschland oder den USA erlebt haben. Immer wieder äusserten die Kommissionsmitglieder den Wunsch, mehr Experten zu Wort kommen zu lassen und ihnen die Bewertung der Standorte zu überlassen. Erst nachdem die Teilnehmer Zuversicht in ihre eigenen Urteilskraft entwickelt und gleichzeitig bemerkt hatten, dass die Experten in dem Experten-Workshop zum Teil strategischer antworteten als selbst die von der Entscheidung betroffenen Anwohner (40 Prozent der Kommissionsmitglieder zeigten sich enttäuscht über die Ergebnisse dieses Experten-Workshops), gewannen sie mehr Distanz zu den Fachleuten und fühlten sich auch selbstsicher ge-

---

[46] Tschannen und Seiler 1991; Wehrli-Schindler 1987.

nug, um ihre eigenen Bewertungen vorzunehmen. Dabei ist es wichtig zu betonen, dass sich gemäss unserem Modell die Bewertungen durch die Kommissionsmitglieder an der Sachkenntnis der Experten orientieren müssen, diese Sachkenntnis aber die Bewertung nicht ersetzen kann.

In die gleiche Richtung geht die Beobachtung, dass keine der vier Kommissionen ein Gegengutachten empfohlen oder die Legitimität der eingesetzten Gutachter in Frage gestellt hat. In den USA ist dies fast undenkbar: in den ersten Sitzungen wird meist darum gefeilscht, welche Gutachter eingesetzt werden sollen und welche Finanzmittel den Kommissionen für die Auswahl eigener Gutachter zur Verfügung gestellt werden können[47]. Parteilichkeit der Wissenschaft war dagegen kein Thema der Kommissionen im Aargau. Das hat auf der einen Seite den Konsensfindungsprozess erheblich vereinfacht, führte aber auf der anderen Seite zu einer Hinterfragung der gesamten Beteiligungsmassnahme durch eine Reihe von Mitgliedern. Warum sollen sich sachfremde Laien in eine Entscheidungssituation bringen lassen, die doch viel besser von Fachleuten sachgerecht entschieden werden könnte? Auch in dieser Frage gab es am Ende, so die Ergebnisse unserer Umfrage, einen Umdenkungsprozess. Nur noch wenige Teilnehmer gaben an, dass Experten mehr Kompetenz zur Bewertung der Standorte mitbringen als sie selbst, wiewohl die Sachkompetenz der Experten weitgehend unbestritten blieb.

Der Konflikt um Expertenmeinung versus Laienmeinung setzte sich auf verschiedenen Ebenen fort. Zunächst war es für die meisten Teilnehmer befremdlich, dass die ETH keine Deponiefachleute (die auch im ETH Team vorhanden, allerdings mehr im Hintergrund tätig waren), sondern Prozessexperten, also Moderatoren und Beteiligungsfachleute, geschickt hatte. Es dauerte mehrere Sitzungen, bis die Mitglieder der Kommissionen merkten, dass die von der ETH bestellten Moderatoren wenig Sachkenntnis auf dem Gebiet der Deponieplanung besassen (vielleicht auch zu wenig Kenntnis, wie es im Bericht des Baudepartements von Aargau beklagt wird). Dennoch zeigte sich im Verlauf der Sitzungen, dass die Neutralität der Moderatoren in der Sache und ihre Fähigkeit, Kommunikation zu steuern und anzuregen, wesentliche Bestimmungsfaktoren der Prozessbegleitung waren und auch von den Kommissionsmitgliedern in der Endbefragung als besonders positiv herausgestellt wurden. In der Befragung der Kommissionsmitglieder zu Ende des Beteiligungsverfahrens äusserten

---

[47] Amy 1987, S. 243 ff.

67 Prozent, dass sich ihr Zutrauen in die Kompetenz der Moderatoren gebessert hätte, nur zwei Prozent sprachen von einer Verschlechterung.

Eine weitere Irritation betraf die Vorträge der Gutachter zur Eignungsfähigkeit der verschiedenen Standorte. Eine Reihe von Kommissionsmitgliedern waren fassungslos, dass wir den Gutachtern untersagt hatten, ihre eigene Bewertung der Eignungsfähigkeit der verschiedenen Standorte den Mitgliedern der Kommissionen mitzuteilen. Auch hier stellte sich im Verlauf der Sitzungen ein Lernprozess ein: mehr und mehr erlebten die Teilnehmer die Früchte ihrer eigenen Lernfähigkeit, begriffen die Aufgabenverteilung zwischen Experten und Bewertern und gewannen mehr Zutrauen in ihre eigenen Fähigkeiten.

So sehr zu Anfang das Vertrauen in die objektiv richtige Sachkenntnis der Experten vorherrschend war, so sehr zeigte sich bei einigen Teilnehmern ein ausgeprägtes Misstrauen gegenüber der Behörde. Dabei wurde auch hier nicht mangelnde Sachkenntnis beklagt oder einseitiges Wissen vermutet, die Skepsis galt mehr den Intentionen des Baudepartements in Bezug auf das Verfahren. Vor allem misstrauten viele der Versicherung des Baudepartements und des ETH-Teams, die Empfehlungen der Kommissionen würden auch wirklich ernst genommen und entsprechend bei der politischen Entscheidungsfindung innerhalb der Behördendelegation, des Baudepartements und des grossen Rats in den späteren Phasen des Deponieprojektes berücksichtigt. Mehrere Personen betrachteten das Verfahren als einen psychologischen Trick, um die Bevölkerung ruhig zu stellen und den möglichen Protest der betroffenen Anwohner durch vermeintliche Mitwirkungsrechte aufzufangen. In der ersten Befragung der Teilnehmer wurde dieser Eindruck zum Teil untermauert: Immerhin 30 Prozent stimmten der Aussage voll oder eher zu, dass die Kommissionen nur eine Spielwiese seien, da die Entscheidung längst gefallen sei. Die Hälfte der Kommissionsmitglieder war davon überzeugt, dass die Kommissionen die Bürger beruhigen sollten, damit der Kanton ohne Widerstand eine Deponie errichten könne. Bei den weiteren Sitzungen wurde dieser Eindruck jedoch grossenteils korrigiert. Durch verbale Rückversicherungen, aber auch durch konkrete Handlungen (etwa dass das Baudepartement bestimmte Wünsche von Kommissionsmitgliedern nach Information oder nach Modifikationen des Erkundungsprogramms ausführte) konnte das Baudepartement Vertrauen in seine Integrität vermitteln. Allerdings ging der Prozentsatz derjenigen, die sich am Ende des Beteiligungsverfahrens weiterhin als Statisten auf der Spielwiese des Kantons betrachteten, nur geringfügig zurück.

8. LERNERLEBNIS: BETEILIGUNG

Wie bei fast allen Beteiligungsexperimenten mit Laien, so war auch die Kommissionsarbeit in Aargau ein Paradebeispiel für verantwortungsvolles Lernen[48]. Während Vertreter von Interessengruppen kaum ihre einmal gewonnene Meinung ändern können, ohne vor ihren Mitgliedern das Gesicht zu verlieren, haben Laien den besonderen Vorzug, sich noch nicht und zumindest noch nicht öffentlichkeitswirksam in einer Frage festgelegt zu haben. Sie sind damit nicht nur lernfähig, sondern auch lernbereit[49]. Bei unserer ersten Befragung der Teilnehmer vor der ersten Sitzung der Kommissionen äusserten rund 80 Prozent aller Kommissionsmitglieder, die den Fragebogen beantwortet hatten, dass ihre Wohngemeinde auf gar keinen Fall oder höchstwahrscheinlich ungeeignet für eine Deponie sei. Am Ende der Beteiligung stimmten selbst die Mitglieder der Kommissionen, die aus den ausgewählten Gemeinden stammten, für die von der jeweiligen Kommission ausgearbeiteten Prioritätenliste von Standorten. Offenkundig hat also im Verlauf der Sitzungen ein Umdenkungsprozess stattgefunden. Solche Lernprozesse sind an vielen Stellen deutlich geworden. In persönlichen Interviews mit einem ETH Mitarbeiter äusserten eine Reihe von Kommissionsmitgliedern, dass sie nicht nur mehr über die Sache gelernt hätten, sondern auch über Prozesse der Diskussionsführung und der Konsensbildung[50].

Vor allem war die Beteiligungsmassnahme für die meisten eine Chance, in Zusammenarbeit mit anderen die Möglichkeiten kollektiver Erarbeitung von Normen und Werten zu erleben und in einen Gruppenprozess einzutreten, der eine Transformation des Verhandlungsklimas von anfänglich auf das eigene Interesse fokussierten Individualansprüchen zu einer kollektiven Identifikation mit der Aufgabe mit sich brachte[51]. Diese Verschiebung der Gruppenidentität kam vielfach in der Kommissionsarbeit zum Ausdruck. So erlebten wir bei einer Besichtigung, dass ein Mit-

---

[48] Wynne 1992; Dietz 1988.
[49] Dienel 1978, S. 257.
[50] Bose 1994.
[51] Burns und Überhorst 1988, S. 89ff; Webler et al. 1994.

glied der Kommission von einem Mitbürger an einem Standort aufgefordert wurde, doch die Interessen seines Wohnortes zu wahren und gegen den Standort zu stimmen. Die kühle Antwort des Angesprochenen (sinngemäss): Ich bin in erster Linie meiner Kommission verpflichtet und meiner Aufgabe; da muss ich meine eigenen Interessen hintanstellen.

Die Identifikation mit der Aufgabe und die Entwicklung eines eigenen Gruppenbewusstseins waren Kennzeichen aller vier Kommissionen, sogar bei der abschliessenden Bewertung der möglichen Standorte. Die Gruppensolidarität zerbrach allerdings bei dem Kommissionsausschuss, der sich aus Vertretern der einzelnen Kommissionen zusammensetzte. Zum einen war hier eine künstliche neue Gruppe entstanden, die nur für wenige Stunden zusammenkam, zum anderen waren die Vertreter des Ausschusses von der Behördendelegation vorgeschlagen worden (und nicht wie ursprünglich vorgesehen von den Kommissionen gewählt worden). Diese Delegation durch die Gemeinden brachte eine mehr auf die Lokalinteressen zentrierte Rolle mit sich. So war es kein Wunder, dass strategische Vorgehensweisen die Ausschussarbeit überschatteten. Nichtsdestoweniger waren die Voten der einzelnen Kommissionen so eindeutig und unmissverständlich, dass der Ausschuss eine Einigung herbeiführte, die in Geist und in Intention den Ergebnissen der vier Kommissionen entsprach. Abgeschwächt wurde lediglich der Wunsch der meisten Kommissionen, eine klar gestaffelte Rangordnung der möglichen Standorte herbeizuführen. Dagegen wehrten sich verständlicherweise die Vertreter der Standorte, die auf den obersten vier Ranglisten der Kommissionen standen. Auch die Behördendelegation neigte zu einer Gleichbehandlung der ausgewählten Standorte. Der Kompromiss, alle Standorte gleich zu behandeln, bei ähnlicher Eignung aber den ranghöheren Standort vorzuziehen, schälte sich als bester Kompromiss heraus.

9. GRUPPENDYNAMISCHE BEOBACHTUNGEN

Die Gruppendynamik in der Sitzungen zeigte einen ähnlichen Verlauf, wie wir ihn von den USA und Deutschland kennen[52]. Der Diskurs beginnt meist mit der allgemeinen Skepsis, ob ein solches Verfahren überhaupt etwas bringe. Es folgen Phasen der Frustration (zu viel Lernstoff

---

[52] Garbe und Hoffmann 1988; Renn et al. 1989.

und zu wenig Zeit) und der Rebellion (Auflehnung gegen das Mandat, Opposition gegen bestimmte Tagesordnungspunkte und zunehmendes Unbehagen an der Komplexität der Materie). Erst allmählich wachsen das Gefühl der Gruppenzusammengehörigkeit und damit das Erlebnis von Stärke und Solidarität. Dazu kommen die ersten Erfolgserlebnisse in der Sache. Man kann den Sachverständigen in der Diskussion folgen, man kann Daten vergleichen, man kann sinnvolle Fragen stellen und dann mit den Experten "fast" problemlos kommunizieren. Dieses Erlebnis führt zu einer euphorischen Spannung, manchmal auch zu einer persönlichen Selbstüberschätzung. In der sich daran anschliessenden Arbeitsphase weicht die Euphorie dem produktiven Zweifel an der Richtigkeit des eigenen Vorgehens; dieser Zweifel führt im Idealfall zu einem selbstkritischen, aber auch selbstbewussten Vorgehensweise bei der schwierigen Beurteilung der Eignungsfähigkeit der Standorte. Diese gruppendynamischen Prozesse sind typisch für fast alle Beteiligungsverfahren mit Kleingruppen. Sie verlangen vom Moderator unterschiedliche Strategien der Gruppenführung in den einzelnen Phasen. Während der Phase der Skepsis benötigen die Teilnehmer Rückversicherungen und Gruppenzusammenhalt, während der Phase der Euphorie ist eine konstruktiv kritische Begleitung durch den Moderator gefordert. Dieser phasenspezifische Führungsstil sorgt im Idealfall dafür, dass die positiven Energien in jeder Phase zum Durchbruch kommen und der sachlichen Auseinandersetzung um Argumente zugute kommt. Gruppendynamik ersetzt nicht das Ringen um die richtige Lösung, sie kann aber diese Aufgabe unterstützen oder im negativen Fall behindern.

Während der Sitzungen gab es eine Reihe von kritischen Punkten, die von den Kommissionsmitgliedern thematisiert wurden und oft genug für Sprengstoff sorgten. Darunter fielen:

a) *das Gefühl, nicht alle Informationen zu erhalten.* Dieser Eindruck kam immer dann auf, wenn bestimmte Informationen etwa den Gemeinden oder dem Baudepartement vorlagen, aber den Kommissionen (möglicherweise aus Sparsamkeitsgründen oder aus Kapazitätsmangel) vorenthalten wurden. Da das Baudepartement das Projekt nur durch einen einzigen Betreuer begleitete, war meist Kapazitätsmangel die Ursache für Informationspannen, die zwar selten vorkamen, dann aber von den Mitgliedern der Kommissionen misstrauisch thematisiert wurden. Eine der wichtigen Lehren aus dem Aargau Projekt ist es, dass die ständige Betreuung der Kommissionsteilnehmer sowie die schnelle und gezielte Übermittlung von Informationen und

Literatur ein wesentlicher Bestandteil des Vertrauensbildungsprozesses ist. Logistische Fehler werden vor allem zu Beginn als Zeichen für mangelnde Aufmerksamkeit und mangelnde Achtung gegenüber den Teilnehmern gewertet.

b) *das Gefühl, überfordert zu werden.* Mehrere Teilnehmer äusserten von Anbeginn die Befürchtung, dass sie die geologischen und technischen Details ohnehin nicht verstehen könnten. Dieses Gefühl der Minderwertigkeit wurde z.T. von einigen sachverständigen Mitgliedern innerhalb der Kommission durch bewusste Benutzung von unbekannten Fremdwörtern und einem entsprechenden Habitus verstärkt. Hier half der allgemeine Gruppenprozess der gegenseitigen Verständigung und Solidarisierung weiter. In Phasen starker Beanspruchung aufgrund zunehmender Informationsdichte waren vor allem die Moderatoren gefordert, die langsameren Gruppenmitglieder behutsam zu fördern, ohne die "Schnelldenker" zu verprellen.

c) *das Gefühl, politisch ausgenutzt zu werden.* Mehrfach bestand die Gefahr, dass die Teilnehmer die ganze Aktion als Public-Relation-Instrument zur Durchsetzung des Deponieprojektes betrachteten. Diese Gefahr bestand vor allem zu Beginn der Beteiligungsmassnahme, als den Kommissionsmitgliedern noch nicht ganz klar war, worauf sie sich bei dieser Übung einlassen würden. Häufig versuchten Kommissionen die Bandbreite ihrer Freiheit auszunutzen, nur um herauszufinden, ob die zugesagte Unabhängigkeit auch wirklich eingehalten wurde. So wurden mehrfach Informationen verlangt, die kaum einen Bezug zur Standortplanung hatten. Auch wurde der bei den Sitzungen anwesende Behördenvertreter oftmals mit Bitten überschüttet, wahrscheinlich um seine Bereitschaft zu testen, auf die Anliegen der Teilnehmer einzugehen. Der angesprochene Vertreter reagierte auf diese Herausforderungen mit freundlicher Gelassenheit, entsprach dem Inhalt der gewünschten Bitten, so weit dies zeitlich möglich war, und begegnete gelegentlichen Angriffen und Unterstellungen mit Vertrauensappellen an die übrigen Anwesenden. Besonders positiv hervorzuheben war die Tatsache, dass sich die Vertreter der Baudepartements und alle externen Besucher strikt an die Spielregeln hielten und keine Sonderrechte beanspruchten. Dies ist keineswegs selbstverständlich. Häufig haben wir in anderen Beteiligungsverfahren Experten oder Behördenvertreter ausschliessen müssen, weil sie sich nicht an die Spielregeln hielten oder sich allzu leicht provozieren liessen.

d) *das Gefühl, Versuchskaninchen zu sein*. Die massive Präsenz der ETH und die Notwendigkeit, im Rahmen des Polyprojektes Daten über das Verfahren zu erheben, führte schnell zu dem Eindruck, die Kommissionsarbeit biete eine willkommene Gelegenheit für emsige Sozialforscher, um Bürgerpräferenzen und Willensbildungsprozesse in Kommissionen zu erforschen. Dies widerspricht dem Selbstverständnis der Kommissionen, einen politischen Auftrag zu erfüllen. Die von der ETH gestellten Moderatoren waren deshalb auch angewiesen, ihre Aufgabe im wesentlichen darin zu sehen, den Willensbildungsprozess in den Kommissionen zu erleichtern und eine konstruktive Arbeitsatmosphäre zu schaffen. Mit zunehmenden Vertrauen der Kommissionsmitglieder in die Moderation und in das Verfahren stieg auch die Toleranz (nicht unbedingt das Verständnis) für die Erhebungen.

Insgesamt zeigten sich in der Gruppendynamik sehr ähnliche Verläufe und Probleme, wie wir sie auch in anderen Beteiligungsfällen erlebt haben. Besonders positiv ist allerdings im Fall Aargau hervorzuheben, dass die immer wieder notwendige Schlichtung von Konflikten und das Ausräumen von Missverständnissen oder auch Führungsschwächen von einem kooperativen Geist und dem Wunsch nach fairem Ausgleich getragen waren. Dies erleichterte die Arbeit der Moderatoren und trug massgeblich zum Erfolg der Beteiligungsmassnahme bei.

10. SUBJEKTIVE ZUFRIEDENHEIT DER TEILNEHMER

Wie schon mehrfach angesprochen, haben wir alle Teilnehmern zu Beginn der Kommissionsarbeit, kurz vor der Entscheidung über die Standortwahl und am Ende der Beteiligungsmassnahme mit Hilfe eines formalisierten Fragebogens nach ihren Eindrücken, Erwartungen und Bewertungen befragt[53]. Die Befragung der betroffenen Teilnehmer und Teilnehmerinnen sollte ein Bild des subjektiven Eindrucks der Teilnehmer über das gesamte Verfahrens vermitteln und auch Veränderungen in der

---

[53] Wilhelm und Schild 1994.

Einschätzung der Beteiligten sichtbar machen. Aus diesem Grund wurden insgesamt vier Befragungen durchgeführt, die jeweils vor oder nach wichtigen Phasen der Kommissionsarbeit durchgeführt wurden. Diese Befragungen fanden statt:

1. vor Beginn der eigentlichen Kommissionsarbeit;
2. vor den Standortbewertungen;
3. unmittelbar nach Abschluss der Kommissionsarbeiten;
4. einige Monate nach Abschluss der Kommissionsarbeiten und nach Vorliegen der Entscheidung der Behördenvertreter und des Baudepartements.

Die Abbildungen 6a-c zeigen, dass die Erwartungen an den Diskurs bereits zu Beginn der Verfahrens hoch waren. Die Teilnehmer begannen also ihre Kommissionsarbeiten mit einer positiven Grundeinstellung. Sie erwarteten von diesem Diskurs eine faire Mitbestimmung in einem Entscheidungsprozess, der ihre Interessen betraf. Dass in der dritten Befragung die Erfahrungen mit der gewählten Vorgehensweise mit den hohen Erwartungen übereinstimmten und in der vierten Befragung diese gar noch übertrafen, ist sicherlich als Bestätigung für die gewählte Vorgehensweise zu bewerten.

Bei der subjektiven Beurteilung des Verfahrens wurde einzig die Effizienz der Vorgehensweise in allen drei Befragungen etwas weniger gut bewertet als andere Eigenschaften, die dem Verfahren zugeschrieben wurden. Dies kann als Hinweis gedeutet werden, dass mit 8-10 Abendsitzungen und etlichen Samstagen für Besichtigungen und Workshops die Grenzen des freiwilligen Engagements erreicht sind und nach Möglichkeiten für eine Straffung des Vorgehens gesucht werden müsste. Trotzdem schätzten die Beteiligten den Aufwand als dem Problem angemessen ein.

Während zu Beginn des Diskurses noch 10 Prozent der Befragten das Verfahren für 'eher unfair' (minus 1) bis 'unfair' erachteten, stufte nach Abschluss der Kommissionsarbeiten noch gerade eine Person (von 92) das gewählte Entscheidungsfindungsverfahren als 'eher unfair' ein. In der letzten Befragung schätzte überdies keine einzige Person die Fairness der Vorgehensweise negativ ein. In ähnlicher Weise reagierten die Teilnehmer auf die Frage, ob sie die Vorgehensweise für autoritär oder demokratisch erachten. In beiden Fragen haben offenkundig die gemachten Erfahrungen mit dieser Art der Bürgerbeteiligung zu positiveren Urteilen geführt. Gleichzeitig konnten auch diejenigen, die zu Beginn skeptisch eingestellt waren, von der Fairness und vom demokratischen Gedanken des Verfahrens überzeugt werden.

Sieht man sich den zweiten Fragekomplex (Fragen 2a bis 2f) an, dann fallen zwei Punkte auf: Erstens war die Zustimmung zu den negativ formulierten Aussagen grösser als die Ablehnung der positiv formulierten Aussagen. Dies ist im Prinzip nicht überraschend, weil es einen generellen Trend in der Umfrageforschung widerspiegelt. Gleichzeitig wird aber dadurch die erlebte Ambivalenz der Teilnehmer deutlich. Auf der einen Seite stehen hohe Erwartungen an und später auch positive Erfahrungen mit dem Verfahren (siehe Fragen 2b, 2c und 2f), auf der anderen Seite verbleibt aber das Misstrauen, dass es sich doch um eine "Alibiveranstaltung" handeln könne. Zwar wird dieses Misstrauen im Verlaufe des Verfahrens leicht abgebaut, aber keineswegs überwunden. Mit der Solidarisierung innerhalb der Kommissionen und ihrer Abschottung nach aussen verstärkt sich offenbar der Eindruck, dass sich trotz des breit angelegten Beteiligungsverfahrens die Vermutung eines zunehmenden Widerstands der Bevölkerung gegen die ausgewählten Standorte (2f) im Verlauf des Verfahrens eher verstärkt. Das bedeutet, dass die Teilnehmer trotz des Beteiligungsverfahrens Widerstände gegen den Bau einer Deponie in den ausgewählten Standortgemeinden erwarten. Dies steht im Widerspruch zu den Intentionen des Diskurses, der eine Abkehr von NIMBY-Haltungen zugunsten begründeter Lösungen bezweckt hatte. Interessanterweise beurteilten die Bewohner der nicht ausgewählten Gemeinden diese Frage etwas pessimistischer (61% Zustimmung) als die von der Entscheidung betroffenen Kommissionsmitglieder, von denen laut Fragestellung ja Widerstand zu erwarten wäre (52% Zustimmung). Gleichfalls hat sich bis heute an den ausgewählten Standorten so gut wie kein nennenswerter Protest artikuliert.

Von Anfang an waren die meisten Beteiligten davon überzeugt, dass der Bau einer Deponie im östlichen Kantonsteil notwendig war. Ohne diese grundsätzliche Zustimmung zum Bau einer Deponie wäre die später erzielte Einmütigkeit der Kommissionsempfehlungen nicht möglich gewesen. Gleichzeitig äusserten die meisten Kommissionsmitglieder ihre Skepsis über die mögliche Eignung ihrer Wohngemeinde als Standort. Hier hat sich im Verlauf der Kommissionsarbeit offenkundig eine Wende abgezeichnet. Dabei wurden von Beginn an die negativen Auswirkungen von Deponien wahrgenommen. Diese Einschätzung hat sich im Verlauf der Prozesses auch nicht nennenswert verändert. Die meisten Teilnehmer schätzten auch nach dem Verfahren die geplante Deponie als langfristiges Risiko und als eine Gefährdung für die kommunale Lebensqualität ein. Dennoch hat das Verfahren den Wissensstand und die Meinungen der Teilnehmer nachdrücklich beeinflusst, denn eine grosse Mehrheit gab an, ihre Meinung bezüglich der Abfallproblematik aufgrund der Erfahrungen mit der Diskursarbeit geändert und neue Kenntnisse über Deponietechnik und mögliche Einwirkungen auf Mensch und Umwelt erworben zu haben.

Bild 6: Beurteilung der Vorgehensweise — Vergleich der 1., 3. und 4. Befragung

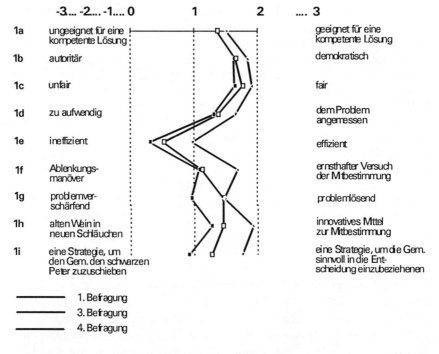

In der Einschätzung ist ein leicht positiver Trend von der ersten zur dritten Befragung zu erkennen. In der vierten Befragung verstärkt sich dieser Trend. Die Frage 1a war in der ersten Befragung noch nicht gestellt worden.

Bild 7: Beurteilung des Verfahrens — Vergleich der 1. und 3. Befragung

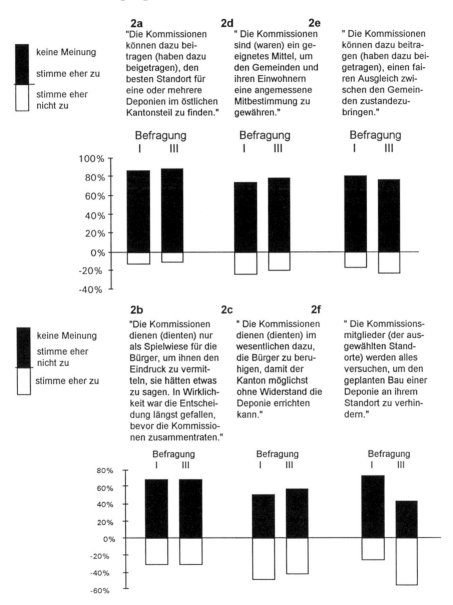

Bild 8: Einschätzung des Deponieprojekts — Vergleich der 1. und 3. Befragung

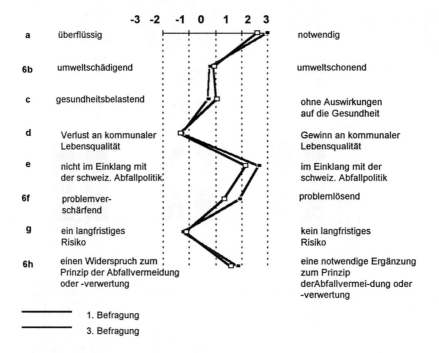

Zwischen den zwei Befragungen sind keine wesentlichen Unterschiede zu erkennen.

Die Analyse der Beurteilungen durch die Gesamtheit der Kommissionsmitglieder zeigt eine weitgehende Zufriedenheit der Betroffenen mit der Art und Weise, wie sie in die Deponiestandortsuche eingebunden wurden. Die Teilnehmer waren der Überzeugung, dass das Verfahren seine primäre Aufgabe, nämlich Kriterien für eine Standortbewertung zu entwickeln und eine begründete Standortauswahl durchzuführen, erfüllt hat. Was in ungenügendem Masse geleistet wurde, waren Empfehlungen über mögliche Ausgleichsstrategien für die von der Auswahl betroffenen Standortgemeinden zu formulieren. Dies wurde aber bewusst an die Gemeinden delegiert, die die vorderen Plätze der Rangordnung einnahmen. Die Beteiligten waren sehr zufrieden mit der Diskursleitung und gaben an, auf verschiedenen Gebieten der Abfallplanung und über das Abfallproblem neue Kenntnisse erworben zu haben. Besonders positiv ist hervorzuheben, dass eine grosse Mehrheit der Beteiligten das praktizierte Diskursverfahren nach eigenen Angaben auch für weitere Entscheidungsfindungen empfehlen wird.

In den Fällen in den USA und in Deutschland, in denen wir ähnliche Befragungen zu Beginn von Beteiligungsmassnahmen haben durchführen lassen, erwiesen sich die Befragten als wesentlich skeptischer und misstrauischer gegenüber dem Verfahren als im Fall Aargau[54]. Das mag damit zusammenhängen, dass wir in der Regel mit einer repräsentativen Stichprobe gearbeitet haben und nicht mit ausgewählten Kommissionsmitgliedern. Sicherlich spielt aber auch die politische Kultur der Schweiz mit der Betonung von freiwilliger Mitarbeit an politischen Entscheidungen (vor allem auf kommunaler Ebene) eine wichtige Rolle[55]. In dieser Hinsicht ist das Schweizer System mit dem an der Ostküste der USA vorherrschenden Kommunalsystem ähnlich. Dort aber waren die Kommissionsmitglieder wesentlich kritischer gegenüber einem externen Verfahrensexperten (wie uns), die ihnen neue Wege aufzeigten, um ihre demokratischen Ansprüche in anderer Form zur Geltung zu bringen. In einem Fall wurden wir sogar von den ausgewählten Kommissionsmitgliedern wieder nach Hause geschickt; sie wollten lieber ohne unsere Hilfe tagen[56]. Dagegen wurde in allen vier Kommissionen im Projekt Aargau die angebotene Hilfestellung der ETH und das Angebot, die Moderation zu übernehmen, ohne grössere Diskussion angenommen. Dass die Moderatoren dennoch zunächst mit Skepsis betrachtet wurden, beweist die Tatsache, dass in der abschliessenden Befragung über ein Drittel der Kommissionsmitglieder die Meinung äusserten, ihre Einschätzung der Moderatoren habe sich im Verlauf der Sitzungen stetig gebessert.

11. SCHLUSSBEMERKUNG

Versucht man eine Gesamtbilanz des Verfahrens zu ziehen, dann scheinen sich die Erwartungen der Teilnehmer, des Baudepartements und der Behördendelegation weitgehend erfüllt zu haben. Sicherlich sind an eini-

---
54 Renn et al. 1989.
55 Linder 1994.
56 Renn et al. 1989.

gen Stellen Schwächen deutlich geworden: manche Informationen kamen zu spät, das Verfahren stand unter einem oft kontraproduktiven Zeitdruck, die technische Betreuung hätte verbessert werden können und die Wahl des Kommissionsausschusses liess zu wünschen übrig. Diese Schwächen konnten jedoch in einem kooperativen und konstruktiven Klima der gegenseitigen Zusammenarbeit weitgehend überwunden werden. In dieser Hinsicht gilt der Grundsatz, dass wohl kein Verfahren der Beteiligung so ideale Bedingungen schafft, dass böser Wille und Mangel an Kooperationsbereitschaft kompensiert werden könnten. Gleichzeitig helfen aber Kooperationsbereitschaft und der Wunsch zur konstruktiven Mitarbeit über manche strukturellen Schwächen der gewählten Vorgehensweise hinweg.

Nach unserer Auffassung ist es die wichtigste Funktion von Diskursen, Konflikte zwischen unterschiedlichen Positionen über die Zumutbarkeit von Risiken zu schlichten und zu einem fairen und kompetenten Kompromiss beizutragen. Dabei begibt sich der Moderator bzw. Diskursorganisator in die Rolle des Katalysators. Er schafft die organisatorischen und strukturellen Voraussetzungen dafür, dass unterschiedliche Parteien sich über Risiken verständigen können und sich aufgrund eines fairen und kompetenten Austauschs von Argumenten auf einen Kompromiss einigen können, ohne dass der Moderator selbst Partei ergreift bzw. den Inhalt des Kompromisses bestimmt. Ein solche Funktion von Risikokommunikation erscheint uns im Rahmen eines kooperativen Diskurses gewährleistet.

Wiewohl die Warnung vor übertriebenen Hoffnungen in Diskurse als Mittel der Umweltplanung und Konfliktlösung berechtigt ist[57], erscheint uns jedoch der Versuch, mit diskursiv strukturierten Verfahren der Bürgerbeteiligung zu arbeiten, nicht nur ein erforderlicher, sondern auch ein gangbarer Weg der Entscheidungsfindung zu sein, und zwar aus folgenden Gründen:

- Das freie Spiel der politischen Kräfte ist dann überfordert, wenn Evidenzen über Folgen umstritten, die moralische Beurteilung der Folgen unsicher und die Verteilungsmöglichkeiten der Folgen auf unterschiedliche Bevölkerungsgruppen variabel sind[58]. Da integrative Mechanismen fehlen, kommt es entweder zur Paralysierung von Entscheidungssystemen, oder aber es kommt zu partiellen Interes-

---

[57] siehe etwa Knoepfel 1994, S. 84 ff.
[58] von Schomberg 1992.

sendurchsetzungen: sei es durch die politische Machtelite oder durch die Gegeneliten, die ein höheres Mobilisierungspotential von politischer Unterstützung bereitstellen können. Beide Folgen sind in der Regel kostenintensiv und suboptimal in Bezug auf das angestrebte Zielsystem.

- Moderne Gesellschaften sind immer weniger gewillt, Entscheidungen nach dem "Trial and error"-Prinzip zu fällen[59]. Sie erwarten von ihren politischen Repräsentanten eine Antizipation möglicher Folgewirkungen und fordern institutionalisierte Formen des Risiko-Managements, um die antizipierten Folgen zu verhindern oder zumindest zu lindern. Dies gilt auch für das Management von Konflikten. Konflikte, die als nicht mehr lösbar erscheinen oder den Einsatz von Gewalt erfordern, werden als Versagen des institutionellen Risiko-Managements bewertet und nicht als alternative Strategie, mit Konflikten umzugehen. Diskursive und antizipative Konfliktaustragung wird also von den jeweiligen politischen Institutionen erwartet, wobei Fairness gegenüber gesellschaftlichen Forderungen und Sachkompetenz eingefordert werden[60].

- Strukturierte Formen diskursiver Entscheidungsfindung stehen nicht im Gegensatz zu pluralistischen Formen der Konfliktaustragung[61]. Im Gegenteil, sie basieren auf dem Grundsatz, dass nur der Diskurs zwischen den pluralen Gruppierungen eine akzeptable und gleichzeitig rationale Lösung des Konfliktes hervorbringen kann. Allerdings ist es nicht ausreichend, alle Teilnehmer um einen Tisch zu versammeln, sondern es gilt, das jeweils relevante Wissen der Teilnehmer funktional in den Prozess der Entscheidungsfindung zu integrieren.

Der kooperative Diskurs, wie er hier charakterisiert ist, ist eine Variante von vielen in der Literatur vorgeschlagenen Konfliktaustragungsverfahren. Wie jedes Modell, ist auch der kooperative Diskurs nur ein theoretisches Gerüst, das immer wieder der Anpassung an die konkreten Bedingungen bedarf. Wir sind aber der Überzeugung, dass dieses Modell als

---

[59] Wildavsky 1982.
[60] Fiorino 1989.
[61] Überhorst und de Man 1990.

Leitlinie für eine Vielzahl von Konflikten im Umweltbereich dienen kann. Eine faire und kompetente Konfliktbewältigung ist mehr denn je notwendig, um das bestmögliche Sachwissen mit den legitimen Werten und Interessen der betroffenen Bevölkerungsgruppen in Einklang zu bringen. Die Forderung nach einem kooperativen Diskurs ist daher nicht nur ein Anliegen zur Verbesserung der politischen Kultur, sondern auch ein Instrument zur Gestaltung einer lebensfähigen und lebenswerten Zukunft.

LITERATURVERZEICHNIS

Amy, D.J., *The Politics of Environmental Mediation* (Cambridge University Press: Cambridge und New York 1987).

Bacow, L.S. und Wheeler, M. *Environmental Dispute Resolution* (Plenum: New York 1984).

Beck, U. *Die Risikogesellschaft. Auf dem Weg in eine andere Moderne* (Suhrkamp: Frankfurt/Main, 1986).

Bose, R., *Standortwahl für eine Deponie im östlichen Aargau. Eine Auswertung von Gesprächen mit sieben TeilnehmerInnen eines Partizipationsverfahrens.* Manuskript (Polyprojekt "Risiko und Sichehreit technischer Systeme. ETH Zürich: Mai 1994).

Burns, T.R. und Überhorst, R. *Creative Democracy: Systematic Conflict Resolution and Policymaking in a World of High Science and Technology* (Praeger: New York 1988).

Buss, D.M. und Craik, K.H., "Contemporary World Views: Personal and Policy Implications," *Applied Social Psychology*, 13 (1983), 258-280.

Carpenter, S.L. und Kennedey, W.J.D., *Managing Public Disputes* (Jossey-Bass Publishers: San Francisco, 1988).

Consensus, "The Facility Siting 'Credo': Guidelines for Public Officials," *Consensus,* 9 (1990), 5.

Crawford, M., "Hazardous Waste: Where to Put It?" *Science,* 235 (1987), 156-157.

Cupps, D. S., "Emerging Problems of Citizen Participation," *Public Administraion Review*, 37 (1977), 478-487.

Dettling, W., *Demokratisierung. Wege und Irrwege* (Deutscher Institutsverlag: Köln 1974).

Dienel, P.C. *Die Planungszelle. Eine Alternative zur Establishment-Demokratie* (Westdeutscher Verlag: Opladen 1978).

Dienel, P.C., "Contributing to Social Decision Methodology: Citizen Reports on Technological Projects," in: C. Vlek and G. Cvetkovich (Hrg.), *Social Decision Methodology for Technological Projects* (Kluwer Academic: Dordrecht 1989), S. 133-151.

Dienel, P.C. und Garbe, D., *Zukünftige Energiepolitik. Ein Bürgergutachten* (HTV Edition "Technik und Sozialer Wandel": München 1985).

Dienel, P.C. und Garbe, D., "Planning Cell: A Gate to Fractal Mediation," in: O. Renn, T. Webler und P.M. Wiedemann (Hrg.), *Fairness and Competence in Citizen Participation. Evaluating Models for Environmental Discourse* (Kluwer: Boston, in press).

Dietz, T., "Social Impact Assessment as Applied Human Ecology: Integrating Theory and Method," in: R. Borden, G. Young, und J. Jacobs (Hrg.) *Human Ecology: Research and Applications* (Society for Human Ecology: College Park, MD, 1988), S. 220-227.

Edwards, W., "How to Use Multiattribute Decision Utility Measurement for Social Decision Making," in: *IEEE Transactions on Systems, Man, and Cybernetics.* SMC-7 (1977), S. 326-340.

Fietkau, H.-J. und Weidner, H.,, "Mediationsverfahren Kreis Neuss," in: F. Claus und P.M. Wiedemann (Hrg.), *Umweltkonflikte: Vermittlungsverfahren zu ihrer Lösung* (Blottner Verlag: Taunusstein 1994), S. 99-118.

Fiorino, D., "Environmental Risk and Democratic Process: A Critical Review," *Columbia Journal of Environmental Law,* 14, Nr. 2 (1989), 501-547.

Fritzsche, A.E., "Die Gefahrenbewältigung in einem gesellschaftlichen Spannungsfeld. Standortbestimmung und Ausblick,: in: J. Schneider (Hrg.), *Risiko und Sicherheit technischer Systeme. Auf der Suche nach neuen Ansätzen* (Birkhäuser: Basel 1991), S. 29-42.

Frey, B.S.; Oberholzer-Gee, F. und Eichenberger, R., *Old Lady Visits Your Backyard: A Tale of Morals and Markets.* Manuscript. Institute for Empirical Economic Research, University of Zürich (Zürich Switzerland, September 27, 1994).

Gaefgen, G., *Theorie der wirtschaftlichen Entscheidung* (Mohr: Tübingen 1963).

Garbe, D. und Hoffmann, M., *Soziale Urteilsbildung und Einstellungsänderungen in Planungszellen.* Werkstattpapier Nr. 25 (Forschungsstelle Bürgerbeteiligung und Planungsverfahren der Universität Wuppertal: Wuppertal 1988).

Habermas, J., "Vorbereitende Bemerkungen zu einer Theorie der kommunikativen Kompetenz," in: J. Habermas und N. Luhmann (Hrg.), *Theorie der Gesellschaft oder Sozialtechnologie. Was leistet die Systemforschung* (Suhrkamp: Frankfurt/Main 1971), S. 101-141.

Habermas, J., *Theorie des kommunikativen Handelns.* Band 1 & 2 (Suhrkamp: Frankfurt/Main 1981)

Habermas, J., "Erläuterungen zum Begriff des kommunikativen Handelns," in: derselbe, *Vorstudien und Ergänzungen zur Theorie des kommunikativen Handelns.* 3. Auflage (Suhrkamp: Frankfurt am Main 1989), S. 571-606.

Habermas, J., *Faktizität und Geltung. Beiträge zur Diskurstheorie des Rechts und des modernen Rechtsstaates* (Suhrkamp: Frankfurt/Main 1992).

Hadden, S., "Public Perception of Hazardous Waste," *Risk Analysis,* 11, Nr. 1 (1991), 47-57.

Haller, M., "Risiko-Management und Risiko-Dialog," in: M. Schüz (Hrg.), *Risiko und Wagnis: Die Herausforderung der industriellen Welt ,* Band 1 (Gerling Akademie, Neske: Pfullingen 1990), S. 229-256.

Heilmann, K. *Technologischer Fortschritt und Risiko: Wege aus der Irrationalität* (Knaur: München, 1985).

Heiman, M., "Using Public Authorities to Site Hazardous Waste Management Facilities: Problems and Prospects," *Policy Studies Journal,* 18, Nr. 4 (Summer 1990a), 974-985.

Heiman, M., "From 'Not in My Backyard' to 'Not in Anybody's Backyard!' Grassroots Challenge to Hazardous Waste Facility Siting," *Journal of American Planning Association*, 56, Nr. 3 (1990b), 359-362

Holznagel, B. *Konfliktlösung durch Verhandlungen* (Nomos: Baden-Baden 1990).

Jencks, C., "Varieties of Altruism," in: J.J. Mansbridge (Hrg.), *Beyond Self-Interest* (University of Chicago Press: Chicago 1990), S. 54-69.

Jungermann, H. und Slovic, P., Charakteristika individueller Risikowahrnehmung." In: Bayerische Rückversicherung (Hrg.), *Risiko ist ein Konstrukt. Wahrnehmungen zur Risikowahrnehmung* (Knesebeck: München 1993), S. 90-107.

Kasperson, R.E., "Six Propositions for Public Participation and Their Relevance for Risk Communication," *Risk Analysis*, 6, Nr. 3 (1986), 275-281.

Keeney, R.L., Renn, O., von Winterfeldt, D. und Kotte, U., *Die Wertbaumanalyse* (HTV Edition "Technik und Sozialer Wandel": München 1984).

Kemp, R., Risikowahrnehmung: Die Bewertung von Risiken durch Experten und Laien - ein zweckmässiger Vergleich?" in: Bayerische Rückversicherung (Hrg.), *Risiko ist ein Konstrukt. Wahrnehmungen zur Risikowahrnehmung* (Knesebeck: München 1993), S. 110-127.

Knoepfel, P., "Chancen und Grenzen des Kooperationsprinzips in der Umweltpolitik," in: Umweltökonomische Studenteniniative OIKOS an der Hochschule St. Gallen (Hrg.), *Kooperationen für die Umwelt. Im Dialog zum Handeln* (Ruegger Verlag: Zürich 1994), S. 65-92.

Kraft M.E. und Kraut, R., "Citizen Participation and Hazardous Waste Policy Implementation," in: C.E. Davis and J.P. Lester (Hrg.), *Dimensions of Hazardous Waste - Politics and Policy* (Greenwood: New York, 1988), S. 63-80.

Kunreuther, H.; Aarts, T.D.und Fitzgerald, K., *Siting Noxious Facilities: A Test of the Facility Siting Credo*. Manuscript of the Wharton School of the University of Pennsylvania (Wharton: Philadelphia, December 1991).

Linder, W., *Swiss Democracy. Possible Solutions to Conflict in Multicultural Societies* (St. Martin's Press: New York 1994).

MacLean, D., "Social Values and the Distribution of Risk," in: D. Maclean (Hrg.), *Values at Risk* (Rowman and Allanheld: Totowa 1986), S. 75-93.

McClelland, G.H., Schulze, W.D., Hurb, B., "The Effect of Risk Beliefs on Property Values: A Case Study of a Hazardous Waste Site," *Risk Analysis,* 10. Nr. 4 (1990), 485-497.

Mernitz, S., *Mediation of Environmental Disputes: A Source-Book* (Praeger: New York 1980).

Mitchell, R.C., *Public Opinion on Environmental Issues: Results of a National Opinion Survey* (Council on Environmental Quality: Washington, D.C. 1980).

Moore, C., *The Mediation Process. Practical Strategies for Resolving Conflict* (Jossey-Bass: San Francisco 1986).

Nader, R.; Brownstein, R. und Richard, J. *Who's Poisoning America: Corporate Polluters and Their Victims in the Chemical Age* (Sierra Club: San Francisco 1981).

New York State Legislative Committee on Toxic Substances and Hazardous Wastes, *Hazardous Waste Facility Siting: A National Survey* (New York Legislative Committee: Albany, June 1987).

O'Hare, M.,"Not on My Block You Don't: Facility Siting and the Strategic Importance of Compensation," *Public Policy,* 25 (Fall 1977).

Otway, H. und von Winterfeldt, D., "Beyond Acceptable Risk: On the Social Acceptability of Technologies," *Policy Sciences,* 14 (1982), 247-256.

Piasecki, B. *Beyond Dumping* (Greenwood Press: Westport 1984).

Rayner, S., "Risikowahrnehmung, Technologieakzeptanz und institutionelle Kultur: Fallstudien für einige neue Definitionen," in: Bayerische Rückversicherung (Hrg.), *Risiko ist ein Konstrukt. Wahrnehmungen zur Risikowahrnehmung* (Knesebeck: München 1993), S. 213-244.

Rayner, S. und Cantor, R., "How Fair Is Safe Enough? The Cultural Approach to Societal Technology Choice," *Risk Analysis* , 7 (1987), 3-10.

Reagan, M., und Fedor-Thurman, V., "Public Participation: Reflections on the California Energy Policy Experience," in: J. DeSario and S. Langton (Hrg.), *Citizen Participation in Public Decision Making* (Greenwood; Westport 1987), S. 89-113.

Renn, O., "Eine kulturhistorische Betrachtung des technischen Fortschritts," in: Hermann Lübbe (Hrg.), *Fortschritt der Technik - gesellschaftliche und ökonomische Auswirkungen* (Decker: Heidelberg 1987), S. 65-100.

Renn, O., Albrecht, G., Kotte, U., Peters, H.P. und Stegelmann, H.U., *Sozialverträgliche Energiepolitik. Ein Gutachten für die Bundesregierung* (HTV Editon "Technik und sozialer Wandel": München, 1985)

Renn, O., Goble, R., Levine, D., Rakel, H. und Webler, T., *Citizen Participation for Sludge Management* . Final Report to the New Jersey Department of Environmental Protection (CENTED, Clark University: Worcester 1989).

Renn, O. und Kotte, U., "Umfassende Bewertung der vier Pfade der Enquete - Kommission auf der Basis eines Indikatorkatalogs", in: G. Albrecht und H. U. Stegelmann (Hrg.): *Energie im Brennpunkt* (HTV Edition "Technik und Sozialer Wandel": München 1984), S. 190-232

Renn, O., Webler T. und Johnson, B.B., "Public Participation in Hazard Management: The Use of Citizen Panels in the U.S.," *Risk: Issues in Health and Safety* , 197 (Sommer 1991), 198-226.

Renn, O.; Webler, T.; Rakel. H.; Dienel, P.C. und Johnson, B., "Public Participation in Decision Making: A Three-Step-Procedure," *Policy Sciences,* 26 (1993), 189-214.

Renn, O. und Webler, T., "Konfliktbewältigung durch Kooperation in der Umweltpolitik - Theoretische Grundlagen und Handlungsvorschläge," in: Umweltökonomische Studenteniniative OIKOS an der Hochschule St. Gallen (Hrg.), *Kooperationen für die Umwelt. Im Dialog zum Handeln* (Ruegger Verlag: Zürich 1994), S. 11-52.

Rosa, E. A., "NAMBY PAMBY and NIMBY PIMBY: Public Issues in the Siting of Hazardous Waste Facilities," *Forum for Applied Research and Public Policy*, 3 (1988), 114-123.

Rosa, E.A., Dunlap, R.E. und Kraft. M.E., "Prospects for Public Acceptance of a High-Level Nuclear Waste Repository in the United States: Summary and Implications," in: R.E. Dunlap, M.E. Kraft und E. A. Rosa (Hrg.), *Public Reactions to Nuclear Waste. Citizens' Views on Repository Siting* (Duke University Press: Durham 1993), S. 291-324.

Schwarz, D., "Ethische und soziale Aspekte in ganzheitlichen Risikobetrachtungen, bezogen auf den Gegenstand Kernenergie," in: S. Chakraborty und G. Yadigaroglu (Hrg.), *Ganzheitliche Risikobetrachtungen. Technische, ethische und soziale Aspekte* (Verlag TÜV Rheinland: Köln 1991), S. 7-1 bis 7-38.

Seiler, H., "Rechtliche und rechtsethische Aspekte der Risikobewertung," in: S. Chakraborty und G. Yadigaroglu (Hrg.), *Ganzheitliche Risikobetrachtungen. Technische, ethische und soziale Aspekte* (Verlag TÜV Rheinland: Köln 1991), S. 5-1 bis 5-26.

Tschannen, P. und Seiler, H., "Halbdirekte Demokratie: Verfassungskonzept und Herausforderungen," *Zeitschrift für Schweizerisches Recht,* N.F. 110. 1. Halbband (1991), S. 117-134.

Überhorst, R. und de Man, R., "Sicherheitsphilosophische Verständigungsaufgaben - Ein Beitrag zur Interpretation der internationalen Risikodiskussion," in: M. Schüz (Hrg.), *Risiko und Wagnis: Die*

Herausforderung der industriellen Welt, Band 1 (Gerling Akademie, Neske: Pfullingen 1990), S. 81-106.

von Schomberg, R., "Argumentation im Kontext wissenschaftlicher Kontroversen," in: K.-O. Apel and M. Kettener (Hrg.), *Zur Anwendung der Diskursethik in Politik, Recht, Wissenschaft* (Suhrkamp: Frankfurt/Main 1992), pp. 260-277.

von Schomberg, R., "Wertsphären, argumentative Vernunft und die gesellschaftliche Bewältigung von wissenschaftlicher und moralisch-ethischer Unsicherheit," in: K.-O. Apel und M. Kettner (Hrg.), *Mythos Wertfreiheit? Neue Beiträge zur Objektivität in den Human- und Kulturwissenschaften* (Campus: Frankfurt am Main 1994), S. 235-255.

von Winterfeldt, D., "Value Tree Analysis: An Introduction and an Application to Offshore Oil Drilling," in: P.R. Kleindorfer und H.C. Kunreuther (Hrg.), *Insuring and Managing Hazardous Risks: From Seveso to Bhopal and Beyond* (Springer: Berlin, 1987), S. 439-377.

Webler, T., "'Right' Discourse in Citizen Participation: An Evaluative Yardstick," in: O. Renn, T. Webler und P.M. Wiedemann (Hrg.), *Fairness and Competence in Citizen Participation. Evaluating Models for Environmental Discourse* (Kluwer: Boston, in press).

Webler, T., Levine, D., Rakel, H., und Renn, O., "The Group Delphi: A Novel Attempt at Reducing Uncertainty," *Technological Forecasting and Social Change,* 39 (1991), 253-263.

Webler, T.; Kastenholz, H. und Renn, O., *Can Public Participation in Impact Assessment Enable Social Learning?* Manuskript eines Vortrags for die Jahrestagung der "Society for Human Ecology" in East Lansing (USA), April 22-24, 1994 (ETH Zürich: April 1994).

Wehrli-Schindler, B. *Demokratische Mitwirkung in der Raumplanung* (SVPW: Bern 1987).

Wiedemann, P.M., "Mediation bei umweltrelevanten Vorhaben: Entwicklungen, Aufgaben und Handlungsfelder", in: F. Claus und

P.M. Wiedemann (Hrg.), *Umweltkonflikte: Vermittlungsverfahren zu ihrer Lösung* (Blottner Verlag: Taunusstein 1994), S. 177-194.

Wiedemann, P.M. und Claus, F., "Überblick und Orientierung," in: F. Claus und P.M. Wiedemann (Hrg.), *Umweltkonflikte: Vermittlungsverfahren zu ihrer Lösung* (Blottner Verlag: Taunusstein 1994), S. 10-24.

Wiedemann, P.; Femers, S. und Nothdurft, W., "Kommunikatives Konfliktmanagement: Trainingsmöglichkeiten," in: F. Claus und P.M. Wiedemann (Hrg.), *Umweltkonflikte. Vermittlungsverfahren zu ihrer Lösung* (Blottner: Taunusstein 1994), S. 215-227.

Wilhelm, U. und Schild, P., *Evaluation des Beteiligungsverfahrens für die Standortbestimmung einer Deponie im Kanton Aargau*. Manuskript (Polyprojekt: Risiko und Sichherheit technischer Systeme der ETH Zürich (Zürich, Juni 1994).

Wynne, B., "Risk and Social Learning: Reification to Engagement," in; S. Krimsky und D. Golding (Hrg.), *Social Theories of Risk* (Praeger: Westport 1992), S. 275-297.

Zillessen, H., "Die Modernisierung der Demokratie im Zeichen der Umweltpolitik," in: H. Zillessen, P. C. Dienel und W. Strubelt (Hrg.), *Die Modernisierung der Demokratie* (Westdeutscher Verlag: Opladen 1993), S. 17-39.

LA GESTION DU PROCESSUS DE CONSULTATION ET DE DECISION: UN NOUVEL ENJEU EN AMENAGEMENT DU TERRITOIRE

Michel Rey

L'auteur a travaillé pendant cinq ans en qualité de chef d'un projet pour le choix de sites en vue de la réalisation d'une installation de stockage pour déchets stabilisés (ISDS) en Suisse romande. La démarche présente la particularité de coupler dès le début des études les aspects techniques et la dimension politique du projet. Cette expérience professionnelle a fait l'objet d'une publication qui est disponible auprès de la C.E.A.T.[1]. Cette démarche a été menée à terme, puisqu'en mars 1993, les trois sites recherchés ont été désignés par les conseillers d'Etat fribourgeois et vaudois en charge de la politique des déchets. Ce choix a été fait avec l'accord de tous les acteurs concernés par l'ISDS. Cet article présente de façon succincte la procédure de consultation suivie dans une démarche qui s'est voulue participative.

1. LE ROLE DE L'ISDS DANS LA POLITIQUE SUISSE DES DECHETS SPECIAUX

Depuis quelques années, la Confédération a élaboré une conception globale de gestion et d'élimination des déchets spéciaux. Cette conception est généralement bien acceptée politiquement, mais sa concrétisation se heurte entre autres à des difficultés dans la recherche de sites aptes à accueillir des installations de traitement ou des décharges: oui à la conception, mais pour autant que ces équipements prennent place sur le territoire des autres communes!

C'est dans ce contexte que s'est inscrite depuis 1986 la réalisation des installations de stockage pour déchets stabilisés (ISDS). La Confédération a décidé de stabiliser au ciment et de stocker en Suisse les résidus des dé-

---

[1] M. Rey: Pour une approche stratégique de la planification et de la réalisation des projets d'aménagement: réflexions et enseignements, à l'exemple de la recherche des sites ISDS pour la Suisse romande, Publication C.E.A.T., Lausanne, mai 1994.

chets spéciaux inorganiques issus de l'épuration des fumées des usines d'incinération des ordures ménagères (9/10) ainsi que les boues inorganiques provenant de l'industrie et de l'artisanat (1/10). Des sites devaient être trouvés pour le stockage de ces résidus, dont trois en Suisse romande, ces derniers devant être exploités l'un après l'autre en fonction des besoins. Un site est prévu pour une quinzaine d'années environ.

2. UNE LEGISLATION LACUNAIRE EN MATIERE DE PROCEDURE D'ETUDE

La Loi fédérale sur la protection de l'environnement du 7 octobre 1983 (RS. 814.01) et l'Ordonnance fédérale sur le traitement des déchets du 10 décembre 1990 (RS. 814.015) contiennent des dispositions précises sur les normes de qualité auxquelles doivent satisfaire les déchets spéciaux après stabilisation; elles énumèrent les exigences applicables à l'emplacement, à l'exploitation et à la sécurité des installations de stockage, qui seront bien évidemment soumises à la procédure des études d'impact.

Les exigences légales sont donc précises sur le "produit", c'est-à-dire l'installation de stockage et les déchets stabilisés, mais elles sont discrètes sur le "processus", sur la manière de conduire les études jusqu'à la réalisation de l'installation de stockage. Rien n'est dit sur les modalités des études: qui doit être associé, comment, dans quel domaine et à quel moment? Et pourtant, en cours d'étude, de nombreux choix sont effectués concernant par exemple les critères de sélection des sites, les options technologiques en matière de stabilisation, les modalités de gestion de l'installation. Or, ces choix ont un caractère politique et conditionnent le "produit" ISDS et le lieu de son implantation.

Selon la loi, il appartient aux cantons de trouver des emplacements adéquats pour l'ISDS. Cependant, la Confédération se réserve le droit de trancher si les cantons ne réussissent pas à trouver une solution. Mais dans la pratique, il n'est pas possible à l'autorité cantonale d'imposer sans information et consultation préalables le choix des sites sur la base des études techniques. De nombreux acteurs politiques, économiques et sociaux ont la capacité de favoriser, freiner ou contrecarrer la réalisation de l'ISDS.

En 1986, l'Office fédéral pour la protection de l'environnement a identifié, à l'aide d'une étude géologique et hydrogéologique réalisée sur base cartographique, une septantaine de secteurs géographiques (zones comprenant entre dix et plusieurs centaines d'hectares), situés sur le Plateau fribourgeois et vaudois, aptes à recevoir un site de 6 ha environ pour une ISDS. Compte tenu de la complexité technique, de la dimension politique potentiellement conflictuelle et de la méfiance de la population, les cantons de Fribourg et de Vaud ont alors confié un mandat conjoint au bureau d'ingénieurs et de géologues CSD au Mont-sur-Lausanne pour les aspects techniques et à la C.E.A.T. à Lausanne pour la définition et la gestion d'un processus d'information et de consultation.

3. DE L'INTERET D'UNE ETUDE PRELIMINAIRE

Compte tenu de ces incertitudes, les deux bureaux ont proposé et réalisé en 1987 une étude préliminaire. Cette étude a permis entre autres de:

o formaliser en termes de variantes le processus de décision qui conduit au choix des sites et de proposer, dès le début des études, une stratégie d'information et de consultation de tous les milieux concernés (qui est associé aux études, comment les acteurs concernés sont-ils associés, dans quels domaines?);

o proposer, également en termes de variantes, les différentes études techniques (géologie, hydrogéologie, relevés écologiques, sondages, etc.) en précisant leurs coûts et leurs implications pour l'information et la consultation;

o rassembler des informations jusqu'alors confidentielles et dispersées sur le marché des déchets spéciaux à stabiliser, informations utiles pour apprécier la clause du besoin de l'ISDS.

Cette étude préliminaire a bien montré que le problème à résoudre ne se posait pas d'abord en termes de choix technique du "bon site", mais surtout en termes de conditions politiques, économiques et sociales à réunir pour réaliser l'ISDS. Il s'agissait de placer cette recherche de sites dans le cadre de la nouvelle politique suisse de gestion et d'élimination des déchets.

La figure suivante schématise les deux variantes d'études proposées: *la démarche administrative* qui propose une sélection rapide des sites par les experts accompagnée d'une campagne d'information, et *la démarche ouverte* qui associe rapidement tous les partenaires concernés. La seconde fut choisie par les conseillers d'Etat. Leur choix a été guidé par le souci de créer un climat de transparence et de confiance permettant non seulement d'éviter les blocages politiques et les oppositions juridiques, mais aussi de prendre en compte tous les intérêts touchés par la réalisation de l'ISDS.

Fig. 1: Les partenaires concernés

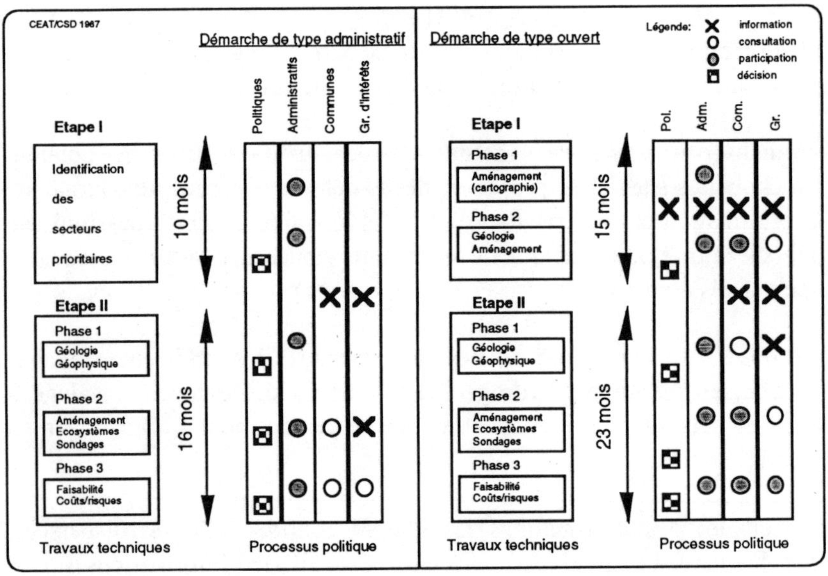

4. UNE DEMARCHE OUVERTE MISE EN OEUVRE PENDANT CINQ ANS

Cette démarche ouverte a été mise en oeuvre depuis le printemps 1988. La première étape des travaux a permis une première sélection de 32 secteurs situés sur le territoire de 51 communes (rendue publique en février 1989), puis une deuxième de 14 secteurs localisés sur 11 communes (rendue publique en juin 1990). Les travaux ont été ensuite affinés pour sélectionner parmi ces 14 secteurs d'abord 5 sites (décembre 1991) puis les 3 sites recherchés (mars 1993). Chacun de ces choix intermédiaires a été décidé par les deux conseillers d'Etat concernés.

Les paragraphes qui suivent présentent l'expérience de consultation qui a accompagné ces sélections successives; ils en font une brève description en faisant ressortir les modalités pratiques et les effets sur le choix successif des sites. Il faut signaler que cette consultation était accompagnée d'une politique d'information (conférences et dossier de presse, articles, conférences publiques dans les communes, argumentaire), politique qui n'est pas évoquée dans cet article, faute de place.

Le tableau suivant résume et synthétise l'ensemble de la démarche générale.

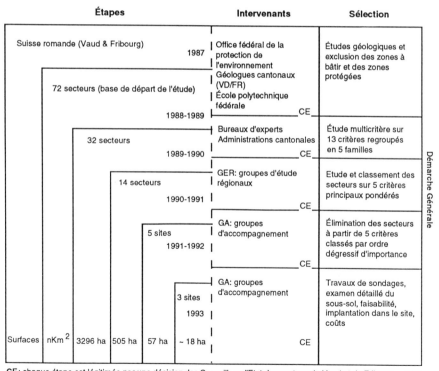

De 72 à 32 secteurs: une sélection par élimination, mais sans consultation.

La première phase de travail a consisté à éliminer une quarantaine de secteurs qui présentaient des caractéristiques les rendant peu aptes à accueillir une ISDS. Cette élimination s'est faite à l'aide de la méthode d'évaluation Electre I sur la base de 13 critères choisis et pondérés par les experts et l'administration cantonale: géologie, hydrogéologie et hydrologie; voies de communication; qualité des terres agricoles, des forêts et des biotopes; paysages et sites, exposition visuelle; proximité des producteurs des déchets et des utilisateurs de marne. Sur cette base, les conseillers d'Etat ont retenu 32 secteurs (plus de 3000 ha) situés sur le territoire de 51 communes et ils ont alors ouvert la procédure de consultation accompagnant les travaux techniques.

S'agissant d'éliminer une partie des secteurs, la consultation est apparue superflue pour cette première sélection par soustraction, d'autant plus qu'elle aurait été lourde puisqu'elle aurait concerné plus d'une centaine de communes. Le coût financier était sans proportion avec l'intérêt qu'on pouvait en escompter. Les modalités et les résultats de cette première sélection ont été communiqués aux 51 communes concernées.

Pourquoi avoir ouvert à ce moment la procédure de consultation? L'appréciation était nettement politique. L'ouverture relativement précoce de la consultation était nécessaire pour créer un climat de confiance et de transparence nécessaire à la prise en compte de tous les intérêts et points de vue; plus tardive, c'est-à-dire après une sélection plus restreinte de secteurs, la consultation n'était plus à même d'influencer les caractéristiques de l'installation et le choix des sites par les conseillers d'Etat, et devenait un exercice alibi.

De 32 à 14 secteurs: le classement des secteurs après consultation des groupes d'études régionaux.

La consultation s'est déroulée dans le cadre de 4 groupes d'études régionaux (GER). Travaillant en parallèle, ils étaient formés d'une quarantaine de personnes provenant pour la plupart des quatre régions potentielles d'implantation (Broye, Nord-Vaudois, Gros-de-Vaud, Cossonay) ainsi que d'experts et de spécialistes. Chaque groupe comprenait 20 à 30 représentants (deux par commune), 6 à 8 représentants des milieux associatifs et de la protection du milieu naturel (WWF, LPN, milieux de la forêt, de l'agriculture) et 6 à 8 représentants de groupes d'intérêts (industriels, UIOM, transporteurs, consommateurs, experts, représentants de l'administration).

Fig. 2: La structure d'un groupe d'étude régional (GER)

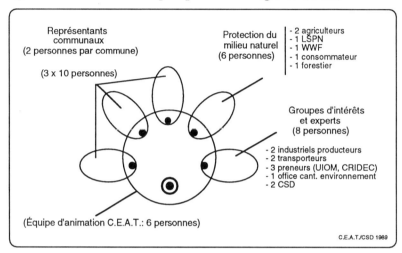

Cette consultation avait trois objectifs qui ont été largement atteints:

o d'abord élaborer et pondérer les critères de sélection (cf. figure 3) à l'intention des conseillers d'Etat en vue de choisir une dizaine de secteurs (14 ayant été finalement retenus);

Fig. 3: Critères de sélection des 32 secteurs avec leur pondération

	Poids
1. proximité du noeud autoroutier	20
2. nombre et qualité des agglomérations traversées	30
3. intégration dans le site	10
4. présence d'une excavation	10
5. qualité moindre des sols (agriculture et forêts)	<u>30</u>
	100
C.E.A.T./CSD	===

o recueillir – ce qui fut le cas – des informations locales plus précises sur les secteurs soumis à évaluation;

o diffuser de l'information sur l'ISDS et sur la politique suisse en matière de déchets.

Les communes, les associations et les groupes d'intérêts ont été invités à désigner leurs représentants par les conseillers d'Etat. Le parti pris a été de privilégier les autorités communales: 51 communes étaient concernées et la population de certaines d'entre elles vivra à proximité de l'installation. Les autres points de vue n'ont pas été négligés, d'autant plus que les choix des GER sont intervenus après discussion et sans recours au vote. La composition de chaque GER a été soumise à l'approbation de ses membres lors de la première séance. Tous les avis, y compris minoritaires ou différents, ont été consignés dans un rapport de synthèse distribué à tous les participants.

De 14 secteurs à 3 sites: le choix après consultation des groupes d'accompagnement (GA).

Depuis l'automne 1990, les travaux de sélection se sont poursuivis en vue du choix définitif des 3 sites. Ils ont été menés dans une procédure de consultation organisée autour de 6 groupes d'accompagnement constitués sur une base communale. Chacun de ces groupes réunissait autour des autorités communales (2 à 4 par commune) 4 à 6 représentants des milieux agricoles, de la forêt et de la protection de l'environnement. Il a été laissé à l'appréciation des communes le soin d'y associer d'autres personnes de leur choix (experts, autres intérêts). Ces GA ont abordé les points suivants:

o discussion et organisation des travaux de reconnaissance sur le terrain; c'est à ce stade seulement que les propriétaires (ils étaient environ 300) ont été sollicités pour la première fois pour une autorisation de pénétration sur les parcelles pour des travaux de terrains; l'appui et les conseils des GA se sont révélés tout à fait pertinents, car seuls quelques propriétaires ont fait opposition et des négociations ont permis de lever ces oppositions;

o prise de connaissance et discussion des résultats des travaux techniques (relevés de terrains, sondages, etc.);

o définition des besoins et des modalités d'information dans les communes;

o avis consultatif sur la sélection des sites;

o discussion des problèmes de chantier, d'exploitation et de surveillance de l'ISDS ainsi que des mesures de compensation.

Jusqu'à cette phase, tous les secteurs avaient été jugés équivalents du point de vue de la qualité de leur sous-sol sur la base des informations cartographiques à disposition. La vérification de cette qualité s'imposait à ce stade des travaux. Cependant, pour éviter d'avoir à effectuer des travaux lourds et coûteux sur l'ensemble des 14 secteurs, un choix intermédiaire de 5 à 6 sites a été prévu, notamment sur la base de travaux de reconnaissance légère sur le terrain.

Pour vérifier les aptitudes de ces 14 secteurs, les travaux suivants ont été entrepris:

o des études indirectes du sous-sol (géologie, géophysique, hydrogéologie et hydrologie);

o des études de surface définissant la qualité écologique, agricole ou forestière des secteurs;

o une étude d'impact sur le bruit induit par le trafic de construction et d'exploitation d'une ISDS.

Elaborés par les responsables des études, les critères et la méthodologie de comparaison des 14 secteurs ont été soumis pour avis aux GA. Les critères retenus et hiérarchisés par les groupes ont alors été repris par les conseillers d'Etat pour qualifier et comparer les secteurs. Il s'est agi d'une pondération qualitative, les critères étant classés par ordre dégressif d'importance:

> 1. la qualité du sous-sol (géologie, géophysique, hydrologie;
> 2. le trafic et la traversée des localités;
> 3. la qualité des terres agricoles et sylvicoles;
> 4. la valeur écologique;
> 5. l'intégration dans le site.
>
> La qualité du sous-sol a été retenue comme un critère discriminant:
>
> - soit le sous-sol n'est pas apte à recevoir une ISDS (auquel cas le site est éliminé);
>
> - soit le sous-sol se révèle favorable avec deux solutions possibles: sans aménagement ou avec des aménagements techniques légers.

Après l'application discriminante du critère de la qualité du sous-sol (3 secteurs ont ainsi été éliminés), l'évaluation et la comparaison des sites se sont opérées sur la base des quatre autres critères. Au terme de ces travaux techniques et de la procédure de consultation au sein des GA, les deux conseillers d'Etat de Fribourg et de Vaud ont retenu 5 sites (3 marnières et 2 sites à excaver).

Des travaux extrêmement fouillés ont alors été entrepris sur ces 5 sites: sondages carottés, implantation dans le site, études des caractéristiques techniques de l'installation dans chaque site (sécurité, étanchéité, infrastructure et bâtiments), coûts d'investissement et d'exploitation.

En ce qui concerne ce dernier aspect, ce n'est qu'à ce stade de la sélection que le critère des coûts a été pris en compte, son estimation étant étroitement liée aux conditions précises d'implantation dans le site et aux travaux d'infrastructure pour sa sécurité.

Les travaux ont été réalisés en collaboration régulière avec les groupes d'accompagnement (GA). L'évaluation et la comparaison des 5 sites ont été effectuées de façon qualitative, en faisant ressortir les avantages et les inconvénients de chaque site, à partir des critères suivants:

> - qualité du sous-sol sur le plan géologique et hydrogéologique, ce critère étant prédominant et discriminant selon les exigences légales;
>
> - la faisabilité technique de l'installation (implantation, accès, coûts, couplage avec l'usine de stabilisation;
>
> - effets environnementaux (nuisances liées au trafic, paysage, qualité des terres et qualité écologique).

L'un des sites a été éliminé, les sondages révélant la qualité déficiente de son sous-sol. Au terme de ces travaux techniques et du processus de consultation, les deux conseillers d'Etat de Fribourg et de Vaud décidaient de retenir:

o Oulens (situé en zone agricole et en forêt) comme site prioritaire à excaver,

o Mathod-Rances-Valeyres (situé en zone agricole ou/et en forêt) comme premier site à excaver de réserve et

o la marnière de Lausanne comme second site de réserve.

Le résultat de cette ultime phase d'étude a fait – comme d'ailleurs les sélections intermédiaires – l'objet d'une dernière conférence de presse à laquelle ont participé tous les acteurs associés à la démarche (autorités cantonales et communales, haut fonctionnaire fédéral, représentants des associations de protection de l'environnement, des associations agricoles, des milieux forestiers ainsi que d'autres groupes d'intérêts).

Le choix n'a fait l'objet d'aucune contestation. Les travaux de détail sont actuellement en cours en vue de la réalisation à Oulens de la première installation de stockage pour déchets stabilisés de la Suisse romande.

5. LES EFFETS CONCRETS DE LA CONSULTATION SUR LA PRISE DE DECISION

Quels sont les effets pratiques et immédiats de la consultation sur la décision en cours d'étude? Dans un sujet complexe et conflictuel comme celui de l'ISDS, les effets de la consultation sont évidents et immédiats sur le processus et le résultat des études. Peut-il en être autrement si la consultation vise à prendre en compte les différents intérêts? Plusieurs exemples le prouvent:

o il y a d'abord le fait que les critères avec leur pondération définis par les GER et les GA ont été repris tels quels par les conseillers d'Etat pour le choix des secteurs, puis des sites; cette reprise était possible parce que ces critères pondérés avaient fait pratiquement l'unanimité des groupes; si tel n'avait pas été le cas, alors les conseillers d'Etat auraient dû procéder à un arbitrage entre les différentes propositions de critères et de pondération;

o préoccupés par la défense des terres agricoles et des forêts de bonne qualité, les représentants des communes et des associations ont exigé la réalisation d'une étude de la qualité des terres agricoles et sylvicoles. Cette étude a conduit à un redécoupage des secteurs et à leur sélection en fonction de cette qualité;

o plusieurs représentants communaux ont demandé, afin d'économiser les terres agricoles, un réexamen des possibilités d'implanter l'installation de stockage dans une zone industrielle, si possible d'une ville; cette demande a conduit les experts à identifier ces possibilités avec leurs avantages et inconvénients. Présentées aux conseillers d'Etat, elles n'ont finalement pas été retenues car cette solution ne résolvait pas le problème de l'économie des terres agricoles, aucune construction n'étant autorisée sur le site de stockage implanté en zone industrielle;

o enfin, on soulignera qu'un seul des trois sites retenus au terme de la sélection finale figurait intégralement parmi les 72 secteurs initiaux soumis à évaluation: celui de Mathod-Rances-Valeyres. Les deux autres sont le "produit" de la consultation. La marnière de Lausanne avait été exclue dans un premier temps par les experts et c'est à la demande des GER qu'elle a été réintroduite dans les sites potentiels après vérification de la perméabilité de son sous-sol; elle a été retenue comme second site de réserve. Le site prioritaire d'Oulens a été proposé à l'ouest de l'autoroute par la Commune d'Oulens qui contestait le site envisagé initialement par les experts à l'est de l'autoroute.

Ces exemples le démontrent: la démarche de consultation a influencé et orienté les choix en cours d'étude. L'ISDS serait certainement localisée dans un autre lieu, si les GER, puis les GA, n'avaient pas été consultés.

Il convient toutefois d'insister sur le fait qu'un processus de consultation n'apporte pas de solutions mais crée plutôt les conditions nécessaires à la reconnaissance du problème à résoudre et à la recherche d'une solution par et avec les acteurs concernés.

6. LES CONDITIONS DU SUCCES D'UNE CONSULTATION

Il faut d'abord que la consultation soit voulue et légitimée par les responsables politiques, à qui il appartient de solliciter l'avis et la collaboration de tous les partenaires; elle ne doit pas apparaître comme un exercice alibi mis en place par un expert, soucieux de faire passer "son" projet.

Mais encore faut-il que les consultés répondent présents. Leur collaboration dépend de leurs valeurs et de leurs intérêts. La politique de gestion des déchets recueille un large consensus dans ses objectifs, même si des divergences existent sur les moyens. L'ISDS n'a pas suscité d'oppositions de principe, mais plutôt des craintes quant aux risques et aux nuisances qu'elle engendre; il n'y a pas eu de refus de l'installation (si cela avait été le cas, la consultation aurait été vaine).

En ce qui concerne la défense des intérêts, les motivations ont été nombreuses pour accepter la consultation: sens des responsabilités face à un problème de société, perspectives de compensations financières, impossibilité de refuser une proposition "crédible" de consultation de la part du canton, souci d'éviter une solution "imposée" par les experts, etc. Ce sont autant de raisons qui ont certainement poussé la quasi totalité des partenaires sollicités à estimer que leurs intérêts seraient mieux défendus en participant à cette consultation plutôt qu'en la refusant. Il convient de remarquer que cette collaboration n'a jamais été acquise définitivement et qu'il a fallu s'en assurer régulièrement en cours d'étude. De même, des partenaires se sont révélés en cours de route et la procédure a permis de les associer à la consultation.

Le refus de participer d'un acteur important est toujours possible, en particulier s'il estime qu'il a les moyens de s'opposer ou de bloquer le projet en restant à l'extérieur de la démarche (par exemple grâce à un droit de recours ou d'opposition). Il appartient alors aux responsables politiques d'apprécier si la consultation conserve sa pertinence ou doit être abandonnée en faveur d'une autre stratégie. Dans un premier temps, certaines communes refusèrent de participer à la consultation. Après discussion et garanties fournies par les Conseillers d'Etat, elles sont revenues sur leur refus et participèrent aux travaux des GER et des GA.

La consultation doit être également menée avec une préoccupation de transparence. Au début de chaque phase, le programme de travail a été présenté et discuté par les conseillers d'Etat avec les groupes de travail. Tous les travaux et décisions des GA et des GER font l'objet de procès-verbaux et de rapports de synthèse distribués à tous les participants.

Une procédure de consultation demande également du temps. Faire circuler de l'information allonge certainement les délais; la faire partager par des partenaires aux connaissances et compétences différentes exige la prise en compte d'un temps d'assimilation; celui d'un maire de commune qui découvre le problème et celui d'un professionnel familier des déchets sont différents, et il faut en tenir compte si l'on veut gagner la participation de certains acteurs moins impliqués dans le projet. Une démarche vise à perdre du temps au début des études pour en gagner à la fin. L'expérience ISDS a prouvé la justesse de cette option, puisque le choix des sites a reçu l'aval de tous les acteurs associés.

Il y a lieu aussi de prévoir une organisation administrative adéquate ainsi que les moyens financiers nécessaires à son bon déroulement pratique. Dans le cas de l'ISDS, les membres des GER et des GA ont été indemnisés pour leurs travaux de séance.

Enfin, il faut rappeler la nécessité de maîtriser les techniques d'animation, de communication et de négociation. Diriger des groupes réunissant plus de 40 personnes exige des compétences en la matière.

Toute consultation renferme des incertitudes quant à ses résultats. Elle tente d'anticiper les blocages en intégrant des avis et intérêts souvent légitimes, et qui sont souvent pertinents pour le projet. Toutefois, elle n'évitera pas toutes les oppositions et recours. Mais si le projet devait être imposé, il le serait alors certainement dans un contexte plus favorable et en meilleure connaissance de cause: participation des communes et des groupes d'intérêts aux études, prise en compte des aspects contestés dans les études, transparence de la démarche, meilleure compréhension de la démarche, existence d'une base plus large de supporters à la politique de gestion et d'élimination des déchets spéciaux. Le choix des sites n'a pas été contesté. En sera-t-il de même lors de la mise à l'enquête de l'installation?

7. EPILOGUE

Les conseillers d'Etat ont opéré le choix des 3 sites en mars 1993. Le site prioritaire d'Oulens a été alors étudié en détail du point de vue technique et financier. Les aspects environnementaux ont été traités dans un rapport d'impact. Situé en zone agricole et forestière, ce site a fait l'objet d'un plan d'affectation cantonal qui a été mis à l'enquête en février 1994. Il n'y a eu aucune opposition au projet qui peut donc entrer dans sa phase de planification pour sa réalisation effective.

Perdre du temps au début de la démarche pour en gagner à la fin, afin d'obtenir l'adhésion des acteurs concernés par l'ISDS: tel était le pari des responsables politiques et techniques des études. Pari gagné!

LÖSUNG VON UMWELTPROBLEMEN DURCH VERHANDLUNG
WAS IST VON VERHANDLUNGSLÖSUNGEN ZU ERWARTEN? STELLUNGNAHME AUS DER SICHT DER PRAXIS DES KANTONS SOLOTHURN

Rolf Maegli

1. EINLEITUNG

An einer Tagung der Vereinigung für Umweltrecht[1] in Solothurn wurde gefordert, dass neue Wege für eine kooperative Bewältigung von Sanierungsproblemen gesucht werden müssen[2]. Insbesondere wurde postuliert, dass der verwaltungsrechtliche Vertrag Einzug in die Praxis finden sollte und dass dem informalen Verwaltungshandeln vermehrt Beachtung geschenkt werden dürfte. Ein Abschnitt beschäftigte sich auch mit dem Einbezug von Drittinteressen. Gefordert wurde, dass die herkömmlichen Legitimationsbeschränkungen fallen gelassen werden, und dass in einem offenen kooperativen Prozess Sanierungsprobleme mit allen Betroffenen zu besprechen seien. Die Einsicht in die Komplexität von Sanierungsvorgängen könne nur durch direkte Teilnahme erreicht werden. Die so erreichte Einsicht in die Problematik sei für eine Lösung der Sanierungsprobleme förderlich. Diese Thesen haben Widerspruch oder doch zumindest kritische Distanz hervorgerufen.

Dass ich damals mit meinen Thesen nicht völlig daneben geraten bin, zeigt der vorgetragene Band, der sich diesem Problem annimmt. Inzwischen ist auch in der Rechtswissenschaft in der Schweiz ein Interesse zu konstatieren[3].

---

[1] Vom 31. Mai 1990.
[2] R. Maegli, *Gesetzmässigkeit im kooperativen Verwaltungshandeln*; in: URP 1990, 265 ff.
[3] Zentralblatt Nr. 9 vom September 1991: Paul Richli: Zu den Gründen, Möglichkeiten und Grenzen für Verhandlungselemente im öffentlichen Recht; 381 ff.

Der vorliegende Beitrag soll aufzeigen, welche Erfahrungen der Kanton Solothurn bis heute[4] mit Verhandlungsmöglichkeiten gemacht hat und welche Perspektiven sich für künftige Fälle aufzeigen.

Ganz kurz sei der Kanton Solothurn vorgestellt: Solothurn mit ca. 230'000 Einwohnerinnen und Einwohnern ist ein ausgesprochener Industriekanton. Die Sektoralstruktur zeigt, dass etwa 50 % der Beschäftigten in der Industrie tätig sind. Solothurn befindet sich im Fadenkreuz der grossen Transportachsen zwischen Nord-Süd und West-Ost. Als einer der wenigen Kantone wird Solothurn auch noch Neubauprojekte von Grossverkehrsanlagen zu bewältigen haben: Autobahn N5, Bahn 2000 Neubaustrecken. Das Gebiet des Jurasüdfusses im Mittelland ist ein Massnahmenplangebiet nach der Luftreinhalteverordnung. Das Bedürfnis nach Rohstoffen führt zu massiven Einschnitten in der Landschaft durch Kiesgruben und Steinbrüche. Weitere Ausbauwünsche führen zu Zielkonflikten.

Ein beträchtliches Konfliktpotential aber auch Möglichkeiten für innovative Problemlösungen im Sinne von Kooperations- und Vermittlungsmodellen sind absehbar.

Erwähnenswert in unserem Zusammenhang sind einige staats- und verwaltungsrechtliche Voraussetzungen. Der Kanton kennt das obligatorische Referendum für Gesetze und hält die Volksrechte ausserordentlich hoch. So müssen beispielsweise Konzessionen für Wassernutzungsanlagen ab einer bestimmten Grösse durch Volksabstimmung erteilt werden. Dass Gesetze dem obligatorischen Referendum unterstehen hat die Wirkung, dass im Rechtssetzungsprozess mögliche Veto-Drohungen - auch von kleineren Interessengruppen - ernst genommen werden.

Das Verhältnis zwischen Bürgerinnen und Bürger zu Staat und Verwaltung beruht zu einem grossen Teil auf dem Grundsatz der Selbstverwaltung. In mehr als 130 Gemeinden sind Kommissionen und Ausschüsse tätig, in denen Bürgerinnen und Bürger im Milizsystem Verwaltungsangelegenheiten erledigen. Gegenüber der Bürokratie und der kantonalen Zentralverwaltung besteht ein hartnäckiges Misstrauen; wenn immer möglich will man Verwaltungssachen auf Gemeindeebene erledigen. Die Gemeinden haben daher eine starke Stellung im Bereich Bau und Planung: In der Regel sind sie zuständig für Baubewilligungen. Bei Abweichungen von der baurechtlichen Grundordnung sind sie die zuständige

---

[4] Abschluss der Redaktion: Oktober 1991 (korrigiert: Juli 1994).

Planungsbehörde für den Erlass von Sondernutzungsplänen (hier Gestaltungspläne genannt). Praktisch alle Projekte mit grösserem Umwelt-Konfliktpotential müssen ein Gestaltungsplanverfahren durchlaufen. Das heisst, dass der Gemeinderat als Exekutive - gebildet aus nebenamtlich tätigen Personen - entscheidet. Der Regierungsrat ist dann noch für die Genehmigung zuständig.

2. VERHANDLUNGSLÖSUNGEN IM KANTON SOLOTHURN - BISHERIGE ERFAHRUNGEN

2.1. Rechtssetzung - Gesetzgebung

2.1.1. Bedeutung der Verhandlungslösungen bei der Rechtssetzung

Es ist wichtig, im Zusammenhang mit der Fragestellung nicht nur einen Blick auf die Verwaltungspraxis - der Gesetzesanwendung also - zu werfen, sondern auch den eigentlichen Gesetzgebungsprozess auf Verhandlungslösungen zu überprüfen. Oben wurde bereits erwähnt, dass der Zwang zur Vorlage eines Gesetzes an das Volk bereits Auswirkungen auf den Einbezug verschiedener Interessen und deren Vermittlung im Rechtssetzungsverfahren hat. Der Gesetzgebungsprozess muss in unserem Zusammenhang auch aus anderen Gründen interessieren:
  Vollzugsprobleme ergeben sich nämlich oft schon daraus, dass beim Erlass eines Gesetzes oder einer Verordnungsbestimmung Konflikte vorprogrammiert werden. Das kann folgende Gründe haben:

- Verschiedene Gesetze stehen zueinander in Zielkonflikten. Interessengegensätze können aber auch innerhalb eines einzigen Gesetzes bestehen. Beispielsweise vertragen sich die Erfordernisse des Lärmschutzes schlecht mit den Anforderungen des Heimatschutzes. Oder die Waldgesetzgebung stellt an den Wald konkurrierende Funktionsansprüche wie Wirtschaftlichkeit, Naturschutz und Erholungsnutzungen.

- Es kann vorkommen, dass in der Gesetzgebung wichtige Standpunkte zu wenig einbezogen oder schlichtweg übergangen werden. Der Gesetzgebungsprozess stellt auf aktuelle politische Stärkeverhältnisse ab, die sich ändern können. Ebenso ist es mit Wertvorstellungen, die im

Verlaufe der Geltungsdauer eines Gesetzes ins Wanken geraten können.

- Gesetze und Verordnungen werden vielfach im Sinne einer Durchsetzungsstrategie erlassen. Wenn sich Interessenkonflikte abzeichnen, neigen Gesetzgeber dazu, einer Lösung auszuweichen um das Gesetz nicht zu gefährden. Anstatt dass dann eine Lösung des Interessenkonfliktes erfolgt, wird dies auf die Realisierungsstufe, den Gesetzesvollzug also übertragen, indem unbestimmte Rechtsbegriffe, Ermessensspielräume und unechte Kompromisse ihren Niederschlag in Gesetzes- und Verordnungsbestimmungen finden[5].

- Machtkonstellationen in den politischen Gremien verhindern, dass berechtigte Anliegen in die Gesetze einfliessen. Es entstehen Regelungslücken, die sich im Vollzug negativ auswirken.

2.1.2. Rechtssetzungsverfahren im herkömmlichen Sinn

Das herkömmliche Gesetzgebungsverfahren ist dadurch gekennzeichnet, dass die Verwaltung Entwürfe erarbeitet, die in ein schriftliches Vernehmlassungsverfahren gehen, dessen Ergebnis mehr oder weniger intensiv ausgewertet wird und zu einer Vorlage an das Parlament mündet. Vollzugsverordnungen werden darauf abgestützt von der Exekutive rein verwaltungsintern erarbeitet und beschlossen.

Gesetzgebungs- und Verordnungsverfahren sind gezeichnet durch rituelle formalisierte Abläufe, die sich stark an der politischen Machbarkeit anhand konkreter Stärkeverhältnissen orientieren. Ergaben sich in Vernehmlassungen entgegengesetzte Meinungen, bleibt es vielfach beim ursprünglichen Vorschlag der Verwaltung oder es wird in unbestimmte Formulierungen ausgewichen.

---

5 Als echten Kompromiss könnten Ergebnisse bezeichnet werden, die auf dem Weg des gegenseitigen Nachgebens zu einer wirklichen Lösung des Problems führen. Vielfach werden die Problemlösungen mit den oben genannten Kompromissen aber aufgeschoben, indem keine Lösung des Konfliktes im Rechtssatz erfolgt sondern dies bewusst oder unbewusst auf die Anwendungsebene delegiert wird.

2.1.3. Kooperative Elemente in der neuen Kantonsverfassung

Die neue Kantonsverfassung von 1986 brachte gewisse Akzentverschiebungen und Innovationen. So wurde insbesondere festgelegt, dass der *Kantonsrat in der Gesetzgebung mitwirken* kann[6]. Vorausgesetzt, dass ein Parlament die Pluralität der Gesellschaft widerspiegelt, wäre darin ein Ansatz zu Konfliktmittlung im Rechtssetzungsverfahren zu erkennen. Leider hat im erst kürzlich geschaffenen Kantonsratsgesetz dieser interessante Gedanke noch keinen genügenden Niederschlag gefunden. Das Gesetz blieb dem herkömmlichen Rollenverständnis eines wechselseitigen Machtkampfes zwischen Regierung und Parlament verhaftet. Es wäre beispielsweise zu prüfen gewesen, inwiefern kantonsrätliche Kommissionen oder FraktionsvertreterInnen bereits im Vorstadium der Gesetzgebung hätten mitwirken können.

Weiter wurde mit der neuen Kantonsverfassung das *Vernehmlassungsverfahren öffentlich* ausgestaltet. Vernehmlassungen werden amtlich publiziert, alle können sich beteiligen und in die Auswertung kann Einsicht genommen werden. Diese Möglichkeiten sollen die Transparenz und die Teilnahme verschiedener Interessengruppen im Gesetzgebungsprozess fördern[7].

Besonders innovativ ist die *Veto-Möglichkeit* des Kantonsrates gegen Verordnungen des Regierungsrates: 20 Kantonsräte können innert 60 Tagen gegen eine vom Regierungsrat beschlossene Verordnungsbestimmung oder Änderung Einspruch erheben. Dann wird das Geschäft traktandiert und der Kantonsrat kann mit Mehrheitsbeschluss die Verordnung zurückweisen[8]. Diese Bestimmung wurde zwar noch selten angerufen,

---

6 Artikel 71 Absatz 1 der Kantonsverfassung vom 8. Juni 1986 lautet:
Der Kantonsrat erlässt alle grundlegenden und wichtigen Bestimmungen in Form des Gesetzes. Er kann an der Vorbereitung der Gesetzgebung mitwirken.
Artikel 79 Absatz 1 der Kantonsverfassung vom 8. Juni 1986 lautet:
Der Regierungsrat leitet das Vorfahren der Verfassungs- und Gesetzgebung. Der Kantonsrat kann in einzelnen Fällen Ausnahmen vorsehen.

7 Artikel 39 der Kantonsverfassung (KV) lautet:
Vernehmlassungen:
1 Vor Erlass von Verfassungs- und Gesetzesbestimmungen und bei anderen Vorhaben von allgemeiner Tragweite kann eine Vernehmlassung durchgeführt werden.
2 Die Vernehmlassungen sind amtlich anzukündigen. Das Recht zur Stellungnahme steht jedem zu.
3 Die Stellungnahmen sind öffentlich zugänglich.

8 Artikel 79 Absatz 2 KV.

hat aber indirekte Wirkung, indem die Verwaltung bemüht ist, bei der Regelung des Vollzuges von Gesetzen auf mögliche Widerstände oder Konflikte Rücksicht zu nehmen, um ein Veto zu vermeiden. Sie hat sich auch so ausgewirkt, dass beispielsweise interessierte Kreise oder die kantonsrätliche Kommission, die ein Gesetz behandelt hat, vor Erlass der Verordnung direkt angehört werden.

Diese Instrumente der neuen Kantonsverfassung können somit in einem kooperativen Sinn und Geist praktiziert werden, sodass unterschiedliche Interessen durch Verhandlung ausgeglichen werden.

2.1.4. Kooperative Rechtssetzung im Kanton Solothurn

Bereits unter der alten Verfassung wurde die Gesetzgebung kooperativ ausgestaltet. Es haben sich verschiedene Modelle herausgebildet: Das Expertenmodell, das Kommissionsmodell oder eine Mischung von beiden.

Beim *Expertenmodell* wird eine aussenstehende Fachperson mit der Erarbeitung eines Entwurfes beauftragt. Diese Person kann in relativer Unabhängigkeit Vorschläge erarbeiten und neues Gedankengut einfliessen lassen. Eine aussenstehende Person kann so unter Umständen stärker Konflikte von Interessengruppen verarbeiten, als dies bei einer rein verwaltungsinternen Gesetzgebung praktiziert würde.

Beim *Kommissionsmodell* wird ein Gesetzesentwurf in einer gemischten Kommission von Verwaltungspersonen und interessierten Kreisen aus Wirtschaft und Bevölkerung beraten. Bei der Zusammensetzung der Kommission wird darauf Bedacht gelegt, dass konkurrierende Interessengruppen unter Berücksichtigung regionaler, sozialer und auch wirtschaftlicher Gesichtspunkte beteiligt werden.

Ideal ist die *Kombination* von Experten- und Kommissionsmodell, indem eine Expertin oder ein Experte in einer gemischten Kommission mitarbeitet oder sogar die Federführung übernimmt. Ansätze zu Mittlerlösungen ergeben sich dann, wenn diese Fachperson als Experte allgemein anerkannt ist und ein gewisses politisch/gesellschaftliches Gewicht verkörpert ("elder statesman"). Konkrete Beispiele aus verschiedenen Gesetzgebungsprojekten sind:

Landwirtschaftsgesetz: Eine Kommission, bestehend aus Bauernverband, Landfrauenverband, Naturschutz, Umweltschutz, Konsumenten und Verwaltungsfachleuten wird begleitet vom Fachexperten, der als ehemaliger Nationalrat, Professor und Oberrichter grosses Ansehen und Akzeptanz geniesst.

Ein *Energiegesetz* ist im zweiten Anlauf endlich zustandegekommen, nachdem ein Verwaltungs-Entwurf in der Vernehmlassung arg zerfetzt wurde und der Regierungsrat anschliessend eine Kommission einsetzte, in der sämtliche Kontrahenten vertreten waren. Diese Kommission hat zuhanden von Regierungsrat und Parlament eine Fassung erarbeitet, die schliesslich vom Volk angenommen wurde. Vertreten waren die Fraktionen des Parlamentes, die Wirtschaftskreise und die Einwohnergemeinden.

Ein kantonales *Abfallkonzept* wurde unter Einbezug der Fachleute der Verwaltung, der politischen Parteien des Kantonsrates, der Wirtschaft, der KonsumentInnen und Umweltverbände erarbeitet. Federführend war ein spezialisiertes Büro in Ökologiefragen, das die materielle Hauptarbeit leistete. Die Kommission wurde von einem Regierungsrat präsidiert. Die Ergebnisse (das Abfallkonzept) mündeten daraufhin in die konkreten Gesetzgebungsarbeiten.

Das *Baugesetz* musste veränderten Verhältnissen, insbesondere auch neuen ökologischen Ansprüchen angepasst werden. Die Kommission setzte sich neben Verwaltungsleuten zusammen aus Vertreterinnen und Vertretern der Einwohnergemeinden, des Schweizerischen Ingenieur- und Architektenverbandes, des Naturschutzes, der Landwirtschaft etc.

Ein neues *Waldgesetz* wurde von einer gemischten Kommission, bestehend aus Verwaltung, Forstwirtschaft, Waldeigentümern, Naturschützern, Raumplanern, Finanzexperten sowie eidgenössischen Parlamentariern erarbeitet.

Die Erfahrungen mit diesen Modellen sind durchwegs positiv. Selbstverständlich können nie alle Ansprüche an ein Gesetz befriedigt werden. Es wird daher immer Gesetze geben, die den einen zu weit, den anderen zu wenig weit gehen. Immerhin führt der kooperative Rechtssetzungsprozess aber zu Ergebnissen, die tragfähig sind. Das politische System beweist damit in gewissen Schranken seine Funktionsfähigkeit hinsichtlich der Vermittlung von Konflikten.

Kooperations- und Mittlermodelle wären im Bereiche der Rechtssetzung noch weiter ausbaufähig. Insbesondere sollte die Zusammenarbeit zwischen Parlament und Verwaltung intensiviert werden. Mittlerlösungen sind durchaus geeignet, aber es wären auch andere Formen der Mitarbeit wie Hearings etc. zu überdenken. Vorausgesetzt wird Dialogfähigkeit, Geduld, Kooperationsfähigkeit, eigentliche Rechtspsychologie und politische Kultur des Miteinanderumgehens. Es muss eine Abkehr vom Blockdenken und Durchsetzungsstrategien stattfinden, hin zu einer Verwaltungstätigkeit, die sich orientiert an einer offenen und pluralistischen Gesellschaft.

2.2. Verwaltungspraxis[9]

Es könnte anhand einer ganze Reihe von Beispielen aufgezeigt werden, wie die herkömmlichen Durchsetzungsstrategien für umstrittene Projekte letztlich naturgemäss gescheitert sind, weil elementare Grundbedingungen zu Vertrauensbildung und Kooperation zu wenig Beachtung fanden. Diese auf Pathologien konzentrierte Betrachtungsweise steht hier aber nicht im Vordergrund; von Interesse sind vielmehr die erfolgreichen und vielversprechenden Ansatzpunkte zu kooperativen und vermittelnden Strategien.

2.2.1. Luftreinhaltung

Die Erfordernisse des Umweltschutzes werden oft den Bedürfnissen der Wirtschaft gegenübergestellt (beispielsweise unter dem Schlagwort Ökologie contra Ökonomie). Die folgenden Beispiele sollen nun aber zeigen, wie die Verwaltung quasi als Anwalt der öffentlichen Interessen funktionieren und kooperativ mit den betroffenen Unternehmen Sanierungsziele erreichen kann.

Es ist vorab zu bemerken, dass die *Sanierungsverfahren* nach Luftreinhalteverordnung keine formellen Publizitätsvorschriften kennen. Demzufolge haben sich in den wenigsten Fällen die Standortgemeinden

---

[9] Für die Darstellung dieser Beispiele danke ich den verantwortlichen Amtsvorstehern für ihre Hinweise: Max Aebi, Arbeitsinspektorat; Franz Adam, Amt für Umweltschutz; Ludwig Looser, Amt für Wasserwirtschaft; Manfred Wyss, Raumplanung.

oder Bürgergruppen eingeschaltet, was aber nicht nachteilig war, weil die Behörde deren Interessen wahrte.

Das Kantonale Arbeitsinspektorat hat bis 1991 über 500 Sanierungsverfügungen gemäss Luftreinhalteverordnung erlassen. Davon wurden gegen fünf Verfügungen Beschwerde beim Departement eingereicht. Dieses bemerkenswerte Ergebnis ist darauf zurückzuführen, dass der Inhalt der Sanierungsverfügungen sorgfältig mit den Adressaten abgesprochen wurde, wobei die gesetzlichen Ziele keinesfalls vernachlässigt wurden. In den meisten Fällen wurde gemäss Stand der Technik und dem Vorsorgeprinzip sogar eine Unterschreitung der notwendigen Grenzwerte und eine Verkürzung der Fristen erreicht. Einige Beispiele von Sanierungen basierend auf Kooperation:

Betrieb	**Schadstoff**	**Stand 1990 (t/a)**	**Reduktion (t/a)**	**Termin**
Kehrichtverbrennungsanlage	NOx	440	340	1995
Zementfabrik	NOx	850	350	1990
Papierfabrik	NOx	270	170	1995
Druckereibetrieb	VOC	250	250	1991
Kunststoffverarbeitung 1	VOC	640	340	1991
Kunststoffverarbeitung 2	VOC	250	180	1991
Summe		2700 (100%)	1630 (60%)	

Die für obgenannte Grossbetriebe verfügte Schadstoffreduktion beträgt 1630 t/a, was 60 % der ursprünglichen Gesamtemissionen entspricht. Eine sensationelle Reduktion um 99,6 % wurde bei einem Druckereibetrieb erzielt.

Sicher stand seitens der Anlageninhaber nicht immer das Ziel der Einhaltung der LRV-Vorschriften im Vordergrund. Die Investitionen sollten auch die Energiebilanz, die Wirtschaftlichkeit und die Modernisierung der Produktionsanlagen fördern. In fast allen Fällen konnte neben der Reduktion der Emissionen gleichzeitig die Produktivität gesteigert werden. Dennoch darf festgestellt werden, dass die Leistungen der Industrie für eine bessere Luft beachtlich und beispielgebend für andere Bereiche wie Privathaushalte und Verkehr sind.

Die Sanierungen in der Industrie konnten mit verschiedenen Kooperationsmodellen erreicht werden.

Ursprünglich arbeiteten die Verfügungsadressaten autonom auf Anweisung der Behörde. Neuerdings ist es dazu gekommen, dass in eine betriebsinterne Projektgruppe neben den Fachleuten der sanierungspflichtigen Firma auch die Beamten des Kantons Einsitz nahmen und somit den Planungs- und Sanierungsprozess von Anfang an begleiteten. Im Falle einer beträchtlichen Sanierung eines grossen Betriebes der Schwerindustrie ist sogar ein gemischtes Projektgremium geschaffen worden, in das neben Vertretern der kantonalen Ämter und der sanierungspflichtigen Firma auch je zwei Vertreter der betroffenen Gemeinden Einsitz nahmen. Es handelt sich um die Standortgemeinde, die am Erhalt der Arbeitsplätze interessiert ist sowie um die Nachbargemeinde, die die Hauptlast der Sanierung zu tragen hat. Es bleibt abzuwarten, welcher Erfolg dieses Vorgehen zeigt. Sicher sind die Voraussetzungen für einen kooperativen Prozess aber gegeben.

2.2.2. Bereich Natur und Landschaft

Für den *Erhalt von artenreichen Wiesen* bestehen Interessenkonflikte zwischen den Bewirtschaftern und dem Naturschutz. Intensive und ertragsreiche Bewirtschaftung hat einen Rückgang der Artenvielfalt zur Folge. Deshalb hat der Kanton bis heute für ca. 700 ha Verträge mit den Bewirtschaftern, den Landwirten abgeschlossen. Nach der kantonalen Baugesetzgebung bestünde zwar die Möglichkeit, diese Flächen durch Schutzverfügungen vor intensiver Bewirtschaftung zu schützen. Aus dem Baugesetz wurde nun auch abgeleitet, dass die Forderungen mit freiwilligen Vereinbarungen erfüllt werden können[10]. Diesen Weg hat der Kanton Solothurn mit beträchtlichem Erfolg begangen; allerdings waren auch die Folgekosten gross. Mit den Bewirtschaftungsverträgen verpflichtet sich der Kanton, den für die Bewirtschaftung notwendigen Mehraufwand und einen Teil des Minderertrages zu entschädigen. Der Landwirt

---

[10] Nach § 128 des Baugesetzes bildet der Kanton aus verschiedenen Einkünften einen Natur- und Heimatschutzfonds. Der Regierungsrat kann diese Mittel unter anderem auch verwenden zur "Förderung freiwilliger Massnahmen" (Absatz 2 litera d).

verpflichtet sich, die Bewirtschaftung im Sinne der Zielsetzung vorzunehmen und auf den Einsatz von Düngemitteln zu verzichten.

Dieses Beispiel zeigt, wie durch Kompensation eine Vermittlung möglich ist. In der Verwaltungspraxis sind dank dieser Kompensationsmöglichkeit die (hoheitlichen) Schutzverfügungen fast bedeutungslos geworden.

In einem andern Fall geht es um den Erhalt eines nationalen, ja sogar übernationalen *Schutzgebietes*, das nicht nur erhalten, sondern wieder in den ursprünglichen Zustand versetzt werden sollte. Die Grenchner Witi ist Feuchtstandort für bestimmte Zugvogelarten und Lebensraum für eine der grössten Hasenpopulation in der Schweiz. Durch den Bau der Nationalstrasse N 5 ist sie stark gefährdet. Dem Bund wurde eine Variante für den Autobahnbau eingegeben, die zum Teil unterirdisch verläuft. Parallel dazu müssen Massnahmen ergriffen werden, um die Landschaft auch künftig zu erhalten, wozu auch Einschränkungen in der bisherigen Landwirtschaft und Freizeit-Nutzung gehören. Das Modell sieht Massnahmen wie Förderung und Abgeltungen, Einschränkungen und Vereinbarungen vor. Heftige Opposition seitens der Standortgemeinde, die um ihre zukünftigen Entwicklungschancen als Industriestandort fürchtet sowie seitens der Landwirtschaft und der vielen Sportvereine müssen am runden Tisch gelöst werden. Der Regierungsrat hat eine Arbeitsgruppe unter dem Vorsitz der Baudirektorin eingesetzt, Vizepräsident der Gruppe ist der Stadtpräsident der betroffenen Gemeinde. Landwirtschaft, Naturschutz, Planer sind mit in der Gruppe vertreten.

2.2.3. Lärmschutz bei Schiessanlagen

Nach der Militärorganisations-Gesetzgebung sind die Gemeinden verpflichtet, Schiessplätze zu unterhalten. Ein von der Verwaltung nach Angaben der Anlageninhaber erstellter Schiesslärmkataster ergab, dass die meisten Anlagen die Lärmschutzvorschriften nicht erfüllen. Zur Beratung der anstehenden Probleme hat der Regierungsrat eine Arbeitsgruppe eingesetzt, die sämtliche Fälle einzeln beraten soll. Vertreten sind die Gemeinden, die Schützenvereine, das Militär und die Verwaltungsabteilungen (Umweltschutz und Raumplanung).

2.2.4. Umweltverträglichkeitsprüfung und Planung

Die Umweltverträglichkeitsprüfung ist wiederholt als Projektverhinderungsinstrument dargestellt worden. Unsere Erfahrungen zeigen, dass in der Einführungsphase der UVP die Bewilligungsverfahren zufolge der Startschwierigkeiten verlängert wurden, dass aber dank der UVP vielfach bessere Lösungen möglich wurden. Eine Besonderheit ist darin festzustellen, dass im Kanton Solothurn die meisten UVPs im Rahmen des Gestaltungsplan (Sondernutzungsplan)-Verfahrens ablaufen. In diesem Verfahren ist die Standortgemeinde zuständige Behörde. Diese führt also die Umweltverträglichkeitsprüfung durch, nachdem die kantonale Umweltschutzfachstelle einen Beurteilungsbericht abgegeben hat. Dieser Verfahrensablauf und die damit vorgeschriebene Publizität zwingt in der Praxis jeden Projektverfasser/Gesuchsteller zur Kooperation. Er muss innerhalb der betroffenen Gemeinde Akzeptanz für sein Vorhaben finden. Das könnte allerdings bei potentiell steuerkräftigen Unternehmungen auch entgegen Umweltinteressen erreicht werden. Immerhin haben aber auch noch die beschwerdeberechtigten Organisationen ein Wort mitzureden, wenn sie sich frühzeitig am Verfahren beteiligen.

Der verfahrensmässige Ablauf der UVP hat konkret folgende Auswirkungen:

Der Gesuchsteller hat, gestützt auf einen Fragenkatalog, den er mit den Umweltschutzfachstellen des Kantons und der Gemeinde abgesprochen hat, ein aussenstehendes Büro mit der Abfassung des Umweltverträglichkeitsberichtes zu beauftragen. Schon damit findet eine gewisse Auslagerung von der Interessensphäre vom Gesuchsteller auf eine Stelle statt, die zwar von ihm beauftragt ist, aber eine gewisse Unabhängigkeit geniesst. Wenn jemand sein Projekt optimierend realisieren will, muss er frühzeitig mit möglichen Opponenten Kontakt aufnehmen.

In einem Fall ging es um die Erneuerung einer Konzession für die Wassernutzung. Die Bestimmung der zukünftigen Höhe der Staumauer eines Flusskraftwerkes führte zu einem Interessenkonflikt: Je höher desto wirtschaftlicher aber auch desto mehr Eingriffe in Landschaft und Flussökologie. Die Verfasser des Umweltverträglichkeitsberichtes haben sich intensiv mit Naturschützern und Fischern auseinandergesetzt und ein Resultat präsentiert, das diesen Interessen gerecht wird und dennoch eine gewisse Wirtschaftlichkeit erlaubt. Die von der Gesuchstellerin beauftragte Ingenieurfirma hat somit als Mittlerin zwischen Wirtschafts- und Umweltinteressen gewirkt.

In einem andern Fall war zu beobachten, dass die Gesuchstellerin für einen Steinbruch mit Informationsveranstaltungen und Strassenständen bei der Bevölkerung um Akzeptanz nachsuchte. Das Vorhaben scheint zu gelingen, indem eine so informierte Bevölkerung einem Projekt aufgeschlossen, mit weniger irrationalen Vorbehalten begegnet.

Spektakulärstes Beispiel einer Umweltverträglichkeitsprüfung, die in Rekordzeit durchgeführt wurde, ist die für den Bau einer neuen Papierfabrik. Die Papierfabrik Biberist eröffnete am 1. Oktober 1991 eine neue Produktionsanlage, die über 500 Mio. Franken kostete und eine Jahresleistung von 120'000 t erlaubt. Der neue Gebäudekomplex weist einen umbauten Raum von 167'000 m3 auf. Es handelte sich um die grösste private Baustelle in der Schweiz. Sämtliche Bewilligungsverfahren konnten planmässig durchgeführt werden. Es ging keine einzige Einsprache ein. Dieses Beispiel zeigt, dass die Umweltverträglichkeitsprüfung nicht - wie vielfach behauptet - ein Projektverhinderungsinstrument ist. Es zeigt aber auch, worauf es besonders ankommt: Auf Vertrauen der Gesuchstellerin bei der betroffenen Bevölkerung und bei den Behörden. Dieses Vertrauensverhältnis ist Basis für eine erfolgreiche Kooperation. Kooperation kann nicht behördlicherseits erzwungen werden, wenn das Vertrauensverhältnis erschüttert ist. Es liegt daher in erster Linie an den Unternehmungen selber, für Akzeptanz und Kooperation besorgt zu sein.

3. SCHLUSSFOLGERUNGEN UND AUSBLICK

Vor dem Hintergrund der amerikanischen Erfahrungen[11], den daraus gezogenen wissenschaftlichen Schlussfolgerungen und der Praxis des Kantons Solothurn kann festgestellt werden:

Im Kanton Solothurn wurden und werden - wie sicher in den meisten anderen Kantonen auch - Vermittlungslösungen mit Erfolg praktiziert. Diese Lösungen haben sich meistens pragmatisch, gestützt auf konkret vorliegende Problemstellungen und ohne dogmatischen Hintergrund erge-

---

11 Wolfgang Hoffmann-Riem/ Eberhard Schmidt-Assmann (Hrsg.), *Konfliktbewältigung durch Verhandlungen*, Baden-Baden, 1990; insbesondere die Beiträge im 2. Abschnitt: Erfahrungen in den USA; sowie Beiträge in diesem Band.

ben. So gesehen ist die Auseinandersetzung um Sinn und Vorteile von Mittlermodellen nicht neu.

Neu wäre es aber, wenn Mittlermodelle systematisch eingesetzt würden. Das heisst, dass verschiedene Mittlermodelle je nach Situation bewusst eingesetzt werden, noch bevor bestimmte Situationen der Verwaltung ein derartiges Vorgehen aufzwingen. Im Gegensatz dazu könnte dies auch dazu führen, dass ganz bewusst keine Vermittlungslösung angestrebt wird, wenn dadurch keine Resultate zu erwarten sind.

Das setzt voraus, dass andernorts gemachte Erfahrungen gezielt ausgewertet und auf ihre Anwendbarkeit überprüft werden müssen. Es wäre zu fragen, wo ausser den genannten Bereichen Mittlermodelle tauglich wären und wie bestehende Praktiken verbessert werden könnten.

Vermutlich wird es für alle Fälle der Vermittlungstätigkeit massgeschneiderte Modelle geben müssen. Wesentlich ist aber in jedem Fall, dass die Modelle gezielt, bewusst und organisiert eingesetzt werden. Hiezu einige Gedanken:

3.1. Rechtsverständnis bei Konfliktvermittlungslösungen

Vermittlungslösungen setzen bei allen Beteiligten Handlungs- und Verhandlungsspielräume voraus. Das gilt auch für die rechtsanwendende Behörde. Hier setzt denn auch die Kritik an den Mittler-Modellen an: Steinberg[12] kritisiert, dass Mittler- und Kooperationsmodelle zu einem Feilschen um und zu einem Verlassen von Rechtspositionen führen können. Er geht davon aus, dass es für jedes Problem eine richtige juristische Lösung gebe, die die Verwaltung möglichst wertfrei durchzusetzen habe. Die Verwaltung sei zur Rechts- und Verfassungsverwirklichung berufen und deshalb müsse die Verwaltung und das Verwaltungsverfahren gestärkt werden.

Unsere Erfahrungen zeigen, dass es für die wirklich konfliktträchtigen Umweltprobleme kaum die einzige richtige juristische Lösung geben kann. Vielfach haben die Behörden in der Rechtsanwendung Ermessensspielräume, die rechtlich schwer fassbar sind. Zudem sind in ver-

---

[12] Rudolf Steinberg, *Kritik von Verhandlungslösungen, insbesondere von mittlerunterstützten Entscheidungen*; in: Konfliktbewältigung durch Verhandlungen, Wolfgang Hoffmann-Riem/ Eberhard Schmidt-Assmann (Hrsg), Baden-Baden, 1990.

schiedenen Gesetzen auf gleicher Stufe Zielkonflikte vorgegeben, die unlösbar sind und deshalb höchstens mit juristisch akrobatischen Subsumtionslösungen zu bewältigen wären, die von der Bevölkerung kaum mehr verstanden würden[13]. Es versteht sich von selbst, dass derartig dogmatische Problemlösungen kaum Akzeptanz und Vertrauen finden. Auch die Komplexität der Sachverhalte führt zu Zweifeln, ob es die einzig richtige Lösung überhaupt geben kann. Es stellt sich deshalb mit Recht die Frage, ob diese Ungewissheit über eine Sach- oder Rechtslage nicht eher durch kooperatives Vorgehen zu lösen wäre. Ziel der Rechtsordnung ist es ja, Rechtssicherheit zu schaffen. Rechtssicherheit wird aber auch durch Akzeptanz begründet. Deshalb sollte es meines Erachtens möglich sein, einen ungewissen Rechtszustand durch eine über Vergleiche erzielte Vereinbarung mittels gegenseitigen Nachgebens in gewissen Rechtspositionen zu regeln. Selbstverständlich kann ein solcher Vergleich nicht contra legem erfolgen.

Erfolgreiches und überzeugendes Praktizieren von Mittlerlösungen setzt somit ein Rechtsverständnis voraus, das der heutigen Komplexität gerecht wird und eindeutig von positivistischen, dogmatischen und formalistischen Rechtsauffassungen abkehrt.

3.2. Transparenz als Voraussetzung von kooperativen Modellen

Voraussetzung für das Funktionieren derartiger Modelle ist eine vollständige Transparenz über Entscheidungsgrundlagen und Entscheidungsabläufe. Die herkömmlichen Bestimmungen zur Beschwerdelegitimation und die damit verbundenen Regelungen über Publizität und Akteneinsicht im Verwaltungsrecht tragen diesen Erfordernissen nicht mehr Rechnung. Es ist eine Schwäche des Verwaltungsverfahrens, wenn auf Einsprachen mit formalistischen Begründungen nicht eingetreten wird, obwohl die aufgeworfenen Fragen einer materiellen Klärung bedürften. Unsere

---

[13] So hat beispielsweise der Regierungsrat des Kantons Solothurn nach 97 Seiten Erwägungen zum Ausführungsprojekt der Nationalstrasse 5 beschlossen:
Die gegen das Ausführungsprojekt der Nationalstrasse N5, Teilstrecke Zuchwil-Nennigkofen, eingereichten Einsprachen werden im Sinne der Erwägungen - insofern ihnen nicht entsprochen wird - abgewiesen, soweit darauf einzutreten ist und sie nicht gegenstandslos geworden sind.
Dieses Dispositiv ist wohl juristisch perfekt aber für Nicht-Juristen kaum mehr zu verstehen.

Erfahrungen zeigen, dass die meisten Einsprachepunkte, auch wenn sie von nicht legitimierten Personen stammen, ohnehin Gegenstand des ex officio Prüfungsverfahrens sind. Die einschränkenden Legitimationsbestimmungen im erstinstanzlichen Verwaltungsverfahren sollten vor diesem Hintergrund kritisch überprüft werden.

Mit zur Transparenz trägt auch die Tatsache bei, dass in die Behördenentscheide und Entscheidungsgrundlagen uneingeschränkt Einsicht genommen werden kann. Gerade im Umweltbereich ist diese Forderung besonders berechtigt, weil letztlich alle in irgendeiner Form von Umweltbelastungen durch Emissionen betroffen sein können. Einzige Schranke bilden nur entgegenstehende Fabrikations- und Geschäftsgeheimnisse, private Interessen also, die durchaus schützenswert sind. Ein konsequenter Schutz dieser berechtigten privaten Interessen gehört aber ebenso klar zu Kooperationsmodellen wie eine Ausweitung und Öffnung. Es wird sich zeigen, oder hat sich bereits gezeigt, dass sich in einer freien demokratischen Auseinandersetzung wirklich berechtigte Anliegen ihren Weg bahnen und das Licht der Öffentlichkeit und eine fundierte Kritik nicht scheuen müssen.

Bei Einsichtsbegehren in Akten kann konkret so verfahren werden, dass den von der Einsichtnahme Betroffenen Gelegenheit zur Stellungnahme gegeben wird. Sind sie mit einer Offenlegung einverstanden, kann diese problemlos erfolgen. Anderenfalls wird mit beschwerdefähiger Verfügung entschieden.

3.3. Aussenstehende Mittler?

In erster Linie sind die Verwaltung und ihre einzelnen Beamtinnen und Beamten aufgerufen, Konflikte durch Kooperation zu lösen. Es gibt aber Fälle, wo diese verwaltungsinterne Lösung versagen könnte. Dies trifft nämlich etwa dort zu, wo eine Verwaltungsabteilung selber Projektträgerin und Anlagbetreiberin ist. Bezeichnenderweise sind die meisten grossen UVP-Fälle derartige Projekte wie Entsorgungsanlagen, Strassenbauten, Eisenbahnbauten etc. In diesen Fällen wäre es sinnvoll, einen Konfliktmittler einzusetzen. Gerade das Beispiel der Autobahn N5 im Kanton Solothurn zeigt auf, wie die bestehenden Strukturen zu leidvollen Konfliktsituationen und Interessenkollisionen führen können: Hier ist eine Abteilung des federführenden Bau-Departementes mit der Ausarbeitung des Projektes beauftragt. Diese hat natürlich ein Interesse an der Durchsetzung. Eine verwaltungsinterne Umweltschutzkommission hat die Beurteilung des vom Bau-Departement verfassten Umweltverträglichkeitsberichtes durchzuführen. Schlussendlich entscheidet der Regierungsrat auf Antrag des Bau-Departementes über das Projekt und über die Einsprachen. Die Ausarbeitung des Projektgenehmigungsentscheides und die eigentliche Umweltverträglichkeitsprüfung erfolgt somit durch das gleiche Departement, das die Planung für das zu prüfende Projekt durchführt. Derartige Konstellationen sind sehr fragwürdig und nicht mehr länger haltbar. Die Glaubwürdigkeit derart zustandegekommener Entscheide ist mehr als fraglich. Der Einsatz eines aussenstehenden Mittlers, der zwischen Projektträger, Einsprecher und Genehmigungsbehörde funktionierte, könnte Vertrauen schaffen.

Andere Perspektiven eröffnen sich beispielsweise bei Sanierungen, wenn ein von Behörde und Anlageninhaber gemeinsam beauftragtes Ingenieurbüro Expertenvorschläge ausarbeitet. Analog der UVP-Fälle, wo die Verfasser des UV-Berichtes vermitteln, könnten die Experten bei Sanierungen funktionieren. Die Experten müssten wie eine Verwaltungsabteilung der Gesetzmässigkeit verpflichtet sein. Somit könnte auch ein Teil des Verwaltungsaufwandes "privatisiert" werden.

3.4. Wo liegen die Grenzen der Kooperationsstrategien?

In der amerikanischen Literatur wurde bereits erwähnt, dass Kooperationslösungen voraussetzen, dass allseitig Verhandlungsspielraum vorhanden ist[14]. Wenn es aber um Schwarz-Weiss-, Ja-oder-Nein-Fragestellungen geht, wo es nur Verlierer und Sieger geben kann, ist kein Verhandlungsspielraum gegeben.

Optimal dürften deshalb Kooperationsmodelle bei Variantenentscheidungen und Standortevaluationen anwendbar sein. Dies setzt voraus, dass ein Projekt grundsätzlich nicht bestritten ist.

Eine Grenze der Kooperationsstrategien sehe ich auch im Führungsgebot. Exekutive und Verwaltung müssen in gewissen Situationen Füh-

---

[14] Dazu die Beiträgein in diesem Band und jene im 2. Abschnitt (Erfahrungen in den USA) in: Konfliktbewältigung durch Verhandlungen, Wolfgang Hoffmann-Riem/ Eberhard Schmidt-Assmann (Hrsg), Baden-Baden, 1990.

rungsstärke zeigen und müssen Verantwortung für Entscheidungen übernehmen. Eine Gefahr der Kooperationsmodelle könnte darin bestehen, dass diese Führungsverantwortung abgeschoben wird. Führungsverantwortung ist nicht gleichzusetzen mit den hier kritisierten Durchsetzungsstrategien. Führen heisst entscheiden, wenn die Diskussion unter den Kontrahenten nicht zu Ende kommt oder wenn sich einzelne Parteien in offensichtlichen Fällen nicht flexibel zeigen.

3.5. Neue Verfahrensregelungen - Vertragliche Lösungen

Rein schriftliche Verfahren haben keine Zukunft mehr. Die Verwaltung kommt nicht umhin, sich mit den Gesetzmässigkeiten menschlicher Kommunikation intensiver auseinanderzusetzen. Dabei wird eingesehen werden müssen, dass unsere Prozessgesetzgebungen nichts anderes als ritualisierte Kommunikation sind. Sie sind im Grunde genommen eine Abstraktion von Gesprächen und Konfliktlösungen auf allerdings nicht mehr ganz zeitgemässer Ebene. Ein Grossteil von Konflikten - sei es nun im zwischenmenschlichen Bereich oder im Verhältnis unter Geschäftspartnern oder zwischen Bürgern und Staat - beruhen auf Kommunikationsproblemen. Wenn es gelingt, diese Kommunikationspannen und Missverständnisse in den Griff zu bekommen, ist bereits ein grosses Ziel erreicht. Zu den Kommunikationsproblemen gehören auch ungleiche Kenntnis- und Informationslagen von Beteiligten. Hier müssen kooperative Prozesse ansetzen: Alle beteiligten Parteien müssen bei Null beginnen und sich gleichzeitig und gleichmässig im Informations- und Kenntnisstand hinaufarbeiten. Wichtig ist dabei, dass die Parteien von Anfang an und in sämtlichen Verfahrensstadien mit von der Partie sind. Das Vertrauen kann nur da gewahrt werden, wo keine geheimen Absprachen erfolgen. Diese Spielregeln müssen zu Beginn eines Kooperationsprozesses festgelegt und bewusst gemacht werden.

Der Einsatz von Konfliktmittlern hat also durchaus Zukunft. Warnen möchte ich aber davor, dass dieses neuartige Modell sofort in Verfahrensgesetzgebungen und ritualisierte Abläufe gepresst wird. Mittlermodelle müssen kreativ und innovativ eingesetzt werden können. Sicher sind sogar bestehende Verfahrensgesetzgebungen dahingehend interpretierbar. Allerdings sollte eine wichtige Lücke geschlossen werden: Der verwaltungsrechtliche Vertrag muss für die gesamte Verwaltungstätigkeit

allgemein anwendbar werden und schliesslich sollte auch noch die
Möglichkeit von Vergleichsverträgen gegeben sein. Es lohnt sich an dieser Stelle einmal mehr, das deutsche Verwaltungsverfahrensgesetz zu zitieren[15].

3.6. Privatisierung von Verhandlungslösungen in parastaatlichen Organisationen

Ein weiterer Gedanke betrifft die Privatisierung von Konflikten in parastaatlichen Gremien. Der gegenwärtige Zustand der öffentlichen Finanzhaushalte zwingt zu einer drastischen Infragestellung bisheriger Verwaltungstätigkeiten. Das Schlagwort der Privatisierung kann unter dem Eindruck von Konfliktvermittlungsstrategien neu überdacht werden. Beispielsweise sieht das Energiegesetz des Kantons Solothurn vor, dass der Staat Beiträge für bestimmte energiepolitisch wünschbare Massnahmen gewähren kann. Darunter verbirgt sich natürlich auch ein Konfliktpotential zwischen den einzelnen Anhängern verschiedener Energieträger oder Methoden. Es wird naheliegend sein, das Problem dieser Förderung an eine noch zu schaffende Körperschaft zu delegieren, in der sämtliche Kontrahenten und Interessenten zusammengefasst sind: Energiewirtschaft, Einwohnergemeinden, Bauwirtschaft, Konsumenten, Umweltverbände etc. Der Kanton könnte diesem Gremium - verbunden mit einem Leistungsauftrag - Kompetenzen zum einvernehmlichen Vollzug und zur Mittelverteilung übergeben. Ähnliche Modelle wären im Bereich der Landwirtschaft oder des Naturschutzes denkbar. Diese Beispiele umfassen selbstverständlich die leistende Verwaltung. Eine Delegation von

---

[15] § 54 des deutschen Verwaltungsverfahrensgesetz vom 25. Mai 1976 lautet wie folgt:
"Ein Rechtsverhältnis auf dem Gebiet des öffentlichen Rechts kann durch Vertrag begründet, geändert oder aufgehoben werden (öffentlich-rechtlicher Vertrag), soweit Rechtsvorschriften nicht entgegenstehen. Insbesondere kann die Behörde, anstatt einen Verwaltungsakt zu erlassen, einen öffentlich-rechtlichen Vertrag mit demjenigen schliessen, an den sie sonst den Verwaltungsakt richten würde."
und § 55 (Vergleichsvertrag):
"In öffentlich-rechtlicher Vertrag im Sinne des § 54 Satz 2, durch den eine bei verständiger Würdigung des Sachverhalts oder der Rechtslage bestehende Ungewissheit durch gegenseitiges Nachgeben beseitigt wird (Vergleich), kann geschlossen werden, wenn die Behörde den Abschluss des Vergleichs zur Beseitigung der Ungewissheit nach pflichtgemässem Ermessen für zweckmässig hält."

hoheitlichen Befugnissen wäre verfassungsrechtlich bedenklich. Hingegen könnten hoheitlichen Entscheidungen Konsensfindungen vorangehen, die in solchen parastaatlichen Gremien erzielt würden.

3.7. Konfliktvermittlung als Aufgabe der Verursacher?

Das Postulat nach Konfliktmittlung könnte dazu führen, dass die eigentlichen Verursacher von Konflikten, die Projektträger und Anlageninhaber sich zurücklehnen, sich auf ihren Parteistandpunkt versteifen und die Ausmittlung (getrost) der Verwaltung oder den Mittlern überlassen. Hier ist zu fragen, ob es nicht in erster Linie Aufgabe der Problem- und Konfliktverursacher ist, die Akzeptanz ihrer Position zu erkämpfen. So finden sich etwa in einem Unternehmensleitbild einer bedeutenden solothurnischen Firma folgende Ausführungen:

> *"Wir sehen uns in eine ökologisch-marktwirtschaftliche Verantwortung eingebunden. Wir wollen mit unserem Tun und unserer Technik einen Beitrag für eine bessere Umwelt leisten und unsere Produkte und Dienstleistungen zum Wohle der Menschen einsetzen. Dazu gehört auch eine möglichste umweltschonende Produktion."*[16]

Aus diesem Leitbild darf ein beträchtliches Engagement auch für Konfliktvermittlung und Konfliktlösung abgeleitet werden.

Man darf von einer Unternehmung für die Belange des Umweltschutzes die gleiche Sorgfalt und das gleiche Engagement verlangen wie für das Marketing. Aufwendige Marktstudien, Produktanpassungen, riesige Absatzorganisationen etc. sollen den Umsatz steigern. Genau gleich wie der Absatz der Produkte geplant und durchgesetzt wird, sollte die Akzeptanz des Produktionsprozesses verfolgt werden. In diesem Sinne ist zu hoffen, dass der zitierte Grundsatz praktiziert wird und Nachahmung findet, womit eine Art Privatisierung der Vermittlung auf der Basis der Selbstverantwortung erfolgen könnte.

---

[16] Leitbild "Technik für den Menschen und seine Umwelt" der von Roll AG, Gerlafingen.

3.8. Vermittlung durch die Verwaltung - Projektmanagement

Ständig neue Gesetze und damit neue Verwaltungsabteilungen, Zuständigkeiten, Verfahren und Verfügungen führten in der Verwaltung zu einem Sektoraldenken. Verschiedene mit der gleichen Sache befasste Personen und Ämter betrachten diese aus dem beschränkten Gesichtswinkel ihrer Zuständigkeit und Kompetenz. Damit ist eine integrale Gesamtschau, die auch die Vermittlung von Konflikten einschliesst, nicht mehr gegeben. Das Bundesgericht hat deshalb die Kantone verpflichtet, für eine materielle und teilweise auch formelle Koordination der Verfahren zu sorgen[17].

Bei der Umsetzung dieses Auftrages wird man sich Gedanken machen müssen über neue Formen der Verwaltungsarbeit. Anstatt dass viele Beamte in ihrem Sektor tätig sind und sich niemand federführend verantwortlich fühlt, sollte für ein Geschäft von grösserer Tragweite ein Projektmanager eingesetzt werden, der die Gesamtverantwortung übernimmt für eine koordinierte Behandlung (formell-materiell), für eine integrale Betrachtung und für den Einbezug von Drittinteressen und für die Vermittlung von Konflikten. Der Projektmanager ist Anlauf- und Vermittlungsstelle für alle Beteiligte (Amtsstellen, Gesuchsteller, Drittinteressenten, Gemeinden etc.).

Dieses Modell setzt voraus, dass bestehende Schranken, die im Hierarchie- und Zuständigkeitsdenken begründet sind, überwunden werden.

Die Verwaltung muss sich von der Vollzugsbürokratie hin zum eigentlichen Projektmanagement entwickeln. Das heisst u. a., dass verwaltungsseitig für wichtige Dossiers eindeutige federführende Zuständigkeiten geschaffen werden. Dabei soll sie auch die Kommunikation stärken, eine Kommunikationskultur pflegen und sich bewusst sein, dass Projektverwirklichung heute heisst, miteinander umgehen zu können - auch mit unterschiedlichsten Standpunkten.

---

[17] BGE 116 Ib 50ff ("Chrüzlen").

LITERATURVERZEICHNIS

R. Maegli, *Gesetzmässigkeit im kooperativen Verwaltungshandeln*; in: URP 1990, 265 ff.

Wolfgang Hoffmann-Riem/ Eberhard Schmidt-Assmann (Hrsg.), *Konfliktbewältigung durch Verhandlungen*, Baden-Baden, 1990.

Rudolf Steinberg, *Kritik von Verhandlungslösungen, insbesondere von mittlerunterstützten Entscheidungen*; in: Konfliktbewältigung durch Verhandlungen, Wolfgang Hoffmann-Riem/ Eberhard Schmidt-Assmann (Hrsg), Baden-Baden, 1990

VON DER KONSTITUTIONELLEN KONKORDANZ ÜBER ADMINISTRATIVE KONSENSLÖSUNGEN ZUM DEMOKRATISCHEN DEZISIONISMUS
- ZUR VIELFALT VON VERHANDLUNGSARRANGEMENTS IN KONFLIKTLÖSUNGSVERFAHREN DER SCHWEIZ[1]

Peter Knoepfel

1. EINLEITUNG

Wer im politisch-administrativen Alltag Helvetiens nach Mediationslösungen für konflikthafte Konstellationen sucht, wird nur dann fündig, wenn er den Begriff der Mediation relativ weit fasst. Das schweizerische politisch-administrative System ist nämlich traditionsgemäss auf allen Ebenen gewissermassen durchtränkt von einer Vielzahl von institutionellen Mustern für Kompromisse aller Art. Solche Muster finden sich bereits im klassischen Zivilprozess, für dessen Einleitung in vielen Kantonen auch heute noch ein Leitschein seitens des "Vermittlers"[2] notwendig ist, in dem attestiert wird, dass eine aussergerichtliche Streitbeilegung nicht gelingen will. Auch im streitigen Verwaltungsverfahren sehen die Prozessordnungen vieler Kantone explizite Stationen vor, an denen mit den streitenden Parteien über mögliche Kompromissformeln verhandelt wird, bevor sich die Richter zur definitiven Rechtsfindung zurückziehen. Das Parlamentsrecht der Kantone und des Bundes sowie langlebige politische Usanzen sichern auf der Ebene der Kantone und des Bundes schliesslich auch in der hohen Politik Kompromissformeln ab, die den jeweils unterlegenen Minderheiten ein faire Beteiligung ermöglichen sollen.

---

[1] Dieser Beitrag ist in leicht überarbeiteter Version auch erschienen in: A. Dally, H. Weidner, H.-J. Fietkau (Hrsg.): *Mediation als politischer und sozialer Prozess, Loccumer Protokolle 73/93*, Evangelische Akademie Loccum, (31545 Rehberg-Loccum), 1994, S. 145-182.
[2] = Friedensrichter.

In einem solchen Kontext fällt es schwer, Mediationslösungen im engeren Sinne zu identifizieren und diese von den übrigen Konsensbeschaffungsinstrumenten fein säuberlich zu isolieren. Als Mediationsprozesse im engeren Sinne seien hier (mit der Berliner Equipe[3] oder mit den Juristen um W. Hoffmann-Riem[4]) Verhandlungsprozesse verstanden, "mit deren Hilfe Interessenkonflikte zwischen zwei oder mehr Parteien unter Hinzuziehung einer neutralen, vermittelnden Person (Mediator) beigelegt werden sollen"[5]. Solche Verfahren bezwecken die Suche von Problemlösungen, "die möglichst für alle am Konflikt Beteiligten akzeptabel sind (...) Im Zentrum steht ein wechselseitiges Ausloten von Handlungsspielräumen und (...) die Suche nach neuen Lösungen in einem fairen Dialog sowie (...) der Einbezug von Personen oder Gruppen, die in förmlichen Verfahren keine oder nur schwache Beteiligungsrechte hätten (...)"[6]. Solche Verfahren setzen mithin nicht nur die in der Schweiz durch zahlreiche institutionelle Vorkehren sichergestellte Suche nach Kompromisslösungen unter den beteiligten Partnern, sondern auch die Intervention eines Konfliktmittlers (Mediator) voraus. Wie zu zeigen sein wird, ist eine solche Person in Konfliktlösungsprozessen, in denen es unter den Parteien zu wichtigen Verhandlungen kommt, nur selten zu finden. Denn die Parteien kommen meist von sich aus überein, den Spielraum möglicher Kompromissformeln sorgfältig auszuloten, um etwa den Scherbenhaufen eines - im voraus nicht kalkulierbaren - negativen Volksverdikts oder eines autoritativen Gerichtsspruchs aus dem fernen Lausanne zu vermeiden. In diesem Sinne stellen wir im folgenden, nach einem kurzen (und eher impressionistischen) Rückblick auf drei wichtige historische Konfliktlö-

---

[3] Dargestellt etwa bei H. J. Fietkau, H. Weidner, *Mediationsverfahren in der Umweltpolitik, Erfahrungen in der Bundesrepublik Deutschland,* in: Aus Politik und Zeitgeschichte, B 39-40/1992 (Beilage zur Wochenzeitung "Das Parlament"), S. 24 ff.
[4] Vgl. dazu etwa W. Hoffmann-Riem, E. Schmidt-Assmann (Hrsg.), *Konfliktbewältigungen durch Verhandlungen,* Band I (Informelle und mittlerunterstützte Verhandlungen in Verwaltungsverfahren), Baden-Baden (Nomos), 1990 und Band II (Konfliktmittlung in Verwaltungsverfahren), Baden-Baden (Nomos), 1990.
[5] H. Weidner, *Der verhandelnde Staat. Minderung von Vollzugskonflikten durch Mediationsverfahren,* in: Schweizerisches Jahrbuch für Politische Wissenschaft, 33/1993: Vollzugsprobleme, Bern (Haupt), 1993, S. 232.
[6] H. Weidner, ibid., S. 232.

sungen (Kap. 2), einige typische Konfliktkonstellationen der helvetischen Grosswetterlage dar, um vor diesem Hintergrund auf Mediationsverfahren im engeren Sinne einzugehen (Kap. 3). In Kap. 4 wird schliesslich gezeigt, dass die schweizerische politisch-administrative Kultur eine Vielzahl anderer Konfliktaushandlungsmechanismen kennt, die den Stellenwert von "Mediationsverfahren" deutlich relativieren (Kap. 5).

2. (IMPRESSIONISTISCHE) GESCHICHTLICHE REMINISZENZEN: DIE SCHWEIZ UND IHRE MEDIATION

Der auch heute noch in praktisch allen Volksabstimmungen über neue Kompetenzen des Bundes[7] aufschimmernde Zwist zwischen "Zentralisten" und "Föderalisten" hat in der Schweiz eine lange Tradition. Stellvertretend dafür seien hier zwei markante historische Ereignisse erwähnt:

- *Das "Stanser Verkommnis" vom 22. Dezember 1481:* Dieses "Verkommnis" kann als erster historischer Kompromiss zwischen den auf Stärkung (und Expansion) der Position der Zentralgewalt[8] drängenden Stadtorten und den die föderalistische Eigenständigkeit betonenden Landkantonen angesehen werden. Dazu schreibt der Chronist:

"Ob dem Begehren von Freiburg und Solothurn, in den Bund aufgenommen zu werden, brach die Entzweiung vollends hervor: Die Länder wünschten keine weiteren Städte mehr. Die Dinge waren bereits arg verfuhrwerkt, als man sich nach ergebnislosen Verhandlungen noch einmal (...) zu einer Tagsatzung in Stans traf. Die Einigkeit zu gewinnen schien aussichtslos. Da (...) betrat,

---

[7] Solche Kompetenzübertragungen bedürfen nach schweizerischem Bundesstaatsrecht immer einer Verfassungsänderung, die ihrerseits sowohl von der Mehrheit des Volkes (Volksmehr) als auch von der Mehrheit der Kantone (Ständemehr), in einer Volksabstimmung genehmigt werden muss.

[8] Die in einem - sehr lockeren - Staatenbund zusammengefassten Alten Orte verfügten bereits damals über einige wenige gemeinsame (zentralstaatliche) Organe und gesetzgeberische Erlasse.

mitten in der kühlen Aufbruchstimmung, der Pfarrer von Stans, Heinrich Imgrund, den Tagungssaal, um im Namen des Einsiedlers Niklaus von der Flüe und als Überbringer von dessen dringenden Worten die Einigkeit unter den Eidgenossen zu fordern. Das Unmögliche gelang diesem Boten des Bruder Klaus. Niemand reiste ab, die Verhandlungen begannen von neuem und mündeten in ein friedliches Sichverstehen ein. Am 22. Dezember wurden Freiburg und Solothurn in den Bund der acht Orte aufgenommen und das sogenannte Stanser Verkommnis wurde unterschrieben."[9]

Bruder Klaus soll damals den berühmten Satz gesprochen haben: *"Stecket den Zun nid zu wit"*. Der besorgte Historiker kommentiert: *"Städte und Länder, im Begriff sich endgültig zu entzweien, fanden (...) den Weg zueinander zurück"*[10].

- Die "helvetische Mediationsakte" vom 19. Februar 1803: In diesem Falle kam der Schlichter nicht aus dem eigenen Land, sondern aus dem fernen Paris: Es war seine Exzellenz, der erste Konsul der Französischen Republik Napoleon Bonaparte höchstpersönlich, der die fast hoffnungslos zerstrittenen Parteien der Zentralisten (Vertreter des helvetischen Einheitsstaates) und der Föderalisten (restaurative, oft antidemokratische Kantone) zu einem Kompromiss in Gestalt einer neuen Verfassung zwang, die explizit als "Mediationsakte" bezeichnet wurde. Darin machte der spätere Kaiser und Verfechter jakobinischer Einheitsideale den seit dem Untergang der alten Eidgenossenschaft in der Opposition stehenden Föderalisten einige wichtige Zugeständnisse, für die sich nach längeren Verhandlungen auch die Zentralisten erwärmen konnten. Der Preis für die feldherrliche Schlichtungstätigkeit bestand allerdings im Abschluss einer Militärkapitulation der Schweiz mit Frankreich, in der Bonaparte das Recht eingeräumt wurde, für seine Welteroberung in der Schweiz 16'000 Soldaten anzuwerben. Helvetien wurde im gleichen Dokument verboten, Militärallianzen einzugehen[11].

---

[9] P. Dürrenmatt, *Schweizer Geschichte*, Zürich (Schweizer Druck- und Verlagshaus AG), 1963, S. 133
[10] Ibid., S. 134.
[11] Vgl. dazu Schweizer Lexikon, Zürich (Schweizer Lexikon), Band 4, 1992, S. 500.

Nicht selten wurden die Konflikte zwischen Zentralisten und Föderalisten auch durch teilweise parallel verlaufende religiöse Spannungen verschärft, deren Wurzeln - wie im übrigen Europa - in den kriegerischen Auseinandersetzungen der Reformation der ersten Hälfte des 16. Jahrhunderts liegen. Auch heute noch stimmen in gewissen, besonders werteträchtigen Sachfragen katholische Kantone anders als protestantische. Entlang dieser Konfliktlinie haben sich ebenfalls zahlreiche Kompromissmechanismen herausgebildet, deren historische Ursprünge weit in die Vergangenheit zurückgehen. Dazu seien folgende zwei Vorkommnisse in Erinnerung gerufen:

- *Die "Kappeler Milchsuppe" vom Oktober 1531:* Anlässlich dieser historischen Mahlzeit, die Freund und Feind in den Religionswirren zwischen Zürich und den Innerschweizer Orten nach getanem Kriegswerk vorübergehend vereinigte, soll der katholische Chorherr Hans Schönbrunner über den eben gefallenen und "ketzerischen" Reformatoren Huldrych Zwingli gesagt haben: *"Wie du auch glaubenshalb gewesen, so weiss ich, dass du ein redlicher Eidgenosse gewesen bist. Gott vergebe dir deine Sünden".* Bis zum heutigen Tag wirken solche konfessionellen Gräben nach; etwa im Appenzeller Land, wo es 1597 zur religionsbedingten Landteilung kam: Noch heute güllt mancher katholische Innerrhoder mit besonderer Freude am Karfreitag, wenn die protestantischen Ausserrhoder mit einem feierlichen Kirchgang des Kreuztodes "ihres" Heilandes gedenken. Dennoch sind diesseits und jenseits der Grenze zwischen den beiden Halbkantonen gleichermassen "treue liebe Mitlandleute und Bundesgenossen"[12] anzutreffen.

- Die radikalen protestantischen Stände und die konservativen katholischen Kantone lieferten sich in der zweiten Hälfte der vierziger Jahre des letzten Jahrhunderts einen erbitterten *"Sonderbundskrieg".* Dieser konnte weder durch einen Bruder Klaus verhindert werden, noch wurde er durch eine feierlich ausgelöffelte Milchsuppe unterbrochen: Nach gescheiterten Vermittlungsversu-

---

[12] Diese Formel verwenden die Landammänner der beiden Kantone jeweils zur Anrede der Mitglieder der traditionellen Landsgemeinden am letzten Aprilsonntag.

chen verliessen die Abgeordneten der Sonderbundskantone die Tagsatzung, worauf die Gesandten der radikalen Stände am 4. November 1874 schlicht eine militärische Intervention beschlossen. Der Sieg der Radikalen machte den Weg frei für die Gründung des schweizerischen Bundesstaates durch die Verabschiedung der Bundesverfassung vom 12. September 1848, die in ihren Grundzügen[13] auch heute noch gilt. Bis zum Auftreten der sozialistischen Bewegung anfangs des 20. Jahrhunderts bildete der Gegensatz radikal/protestantisch und konservativ/katholisch die Grundstruktur der eidgenössischen Politik. Weil die beiden Lager auf der Ebene der jeweiligen Kantone je deutliche Mehrheiten hinter sich scharen konnten, mussten sie auf der Ebene des Bundes Kompromisse schliessen, waren (und sind) doch die zuständigen Behörden für den Vollzug der Bundespolitik die diesbezüglich weitgehend souveränen Kantone. Nur kompromissfähige Bundespolitik hatte eine Chance, im ganzen Land sowohl von radikalen wie von konservativen Behörden vollzogen zu werden.

Mit dem Aufkommen der Sozialisten öffnete sich - insbesondere in den städtischen Kantonen, aber auch in einigen ländlichen Textilkantonen der Ostschweiz - ein weiterer Graben zwischen zwei Lagern, der helvetische Politik und Administration von den Gemeinden bis zum Bund auch heute (noch?) deutlich prägt. Es ist dies der Gegensatz zwischen "Bürgerlichen" und "Sozialdemokraten", der seine vermutlich letzten Zuspitzungen in den fünfziger Jahren der Hochzeiten des Kalten Krieges erfahren sollte. Die Art und Weise, wie dieser Konflikt "abgearbeitet" wurde, kommt in folgenden zwei Kurzreminiszenzen zum Ausdruck:

- *Die Niederschlagung des "Generalstreiks" vom 11. November 1918:* Ausgehungert von den Folgen des eben erst zu Ende gegangenen Ersten Weltkriegs und heimgesucht von einer epidemischen Grippe beschloss die schweizerische Arbeiterbewegung im Herbst 1918 zum ersten (und zum letzten) Mal die Ausrufung eines landesweiten Generalstreiks. Die Historiker sind sich heute einig,

---

[13] Die Totalrevision vom 29. Mai 1874 brachte insbesondere eine Ausweitung der Volksrechte.

dass gedrückte Löhne, mangelnde Verhandlungsbereitschaft der Arbeitgeber und das fast vollständige Fehlen von Sozialversicherungen die Gewerkschaften und die politische Linke damals zu diesem Schritt zwangen. Es fehlte an all jenen auf Konsens angelegten Verhandlungsmechanismen, die später zur Aushandlung von Gesamtarbeitsverträgen und zur Sicherung des relativen Arbeitsfriedens führen sollten. Die bürgerliche Parlamentsmehrheit und die ausschliesslich aus Bürgerlichen zusammengesetzte Landesregierung entschlossen sich daraufhin, die Generalstreikbewegung unter Einsatz der schweizerischen Armee zu liquidieren. Jene betrüblichen Novemberereignisse führten in der Generation unserer Grossväter hüben und drüben zu Lernprozessen. Diese hatten insbesondere im unternehmerischen Lager, bereits in den späten zwanziger Jahren eine Anhebung der Verhandlungsbereitschaft zur Folge. Spätestens seit dem Abschluss des ersten Friedensabkommens in der Maschinen- und Metallindustrie in der 2. Hälfte der dreissiger Jahre[14] herrscht in der Schweiz hinsichtlich der Arbeitswelt eine geradezu beispiellose Verhandlungsmentalität, die dafür verantwortlich ist, dass bis heute - selbst in konjunkturell schwierigen Zeiten - immer wieder gesamtarbeitsvertragliche Lösungen zustande gekommen sind.

- Auf der politischen Ebene des Bundes sollte es indessen erst eine Generation später zu jener berühmten Konkordanz kommen, die eine definitive Beteiligung der Sozialdemokraten an der Regierungsverantwortung in Gestalt der sog. *"Zauberformel"* ermöglichte. Dazu kam es im Dezember 1959[15]. Seither wird auch auf Bundesebene bei allen referendumsgefährdeten Vorlagen das "wechselseitige Ausloten von Handlungsspielräumen"[16] zum zentralen Fluchtpunkt eidgenössischer Politik.

---

[14] 1. Friedensabkommen zwischen dem Arbeitgeberverband Schweiz. Maschinen- und Metall-Industrieller und dem Schweiz. Metall- und Uhrenarbeiter-Verband vom 19.7.1937.
[15] In den Jahren 1943-53 verfügten die Sozialdemokraten über eine Einervertretung im Bundesrat.
[16] Nach der Formel von H. Weidner, op. cit., Anm. 5., S. 232.

Demgegenüber konnten - allen gegenteiligen Beteuerungen zum Trotz - bis zum heutigen Tag demgegenüber im Konflikt zwischen den Geschlechtern keine validen Verhandlungslösungen gefunden werden. Bekanntlich konnte sich der schweizerische Souverän erst 1968 (!) zur Anerkennung des Frauenstimmrechts auf eidgenössischer Ebene durchringen, und es bedurfte 1990 gar einer Entscheidung des Bundesgerichts, um auch den letzten Kanton (Appenzell Innerrhoden) diesbezüglich zur grundrechtlichen Räson zu bringen. Der am 14. Juni 1981 von Volk und Ständen genehmigte Gleichberechtigungsartikel der Bundesverfassung blieb bis Mitte der neunziger Jahre politisch, wirtschaftlich und gesellschaftlich weitgehend uneingelöst. Erst in der Märzsession des Jahres 1994 kam es in den eidgenössischen Räten zur Debatte über ein eigentliches Gleichberechtigungsgesetz. Wie stark der latente Geschlechterkonflikt die berufliche, politische und gesellschaftliche Realität weiterhin durchdringt, zeigten die heftigen Reaktionen wirtschaftsnaher Parlamentarier auf einzelne Bestimmungen dieser Gesetzesvorlage, die trotz der darin enthaltenen Selbstverständlichkeiten auf harsche Ablehnung stiessen[17].

3. TYPISCHE HELVETISCHE KONFLIKTKONSTELLATIONEN DER GEGENWART

Neben diesen historisch gewachsenen und auch heute noch latent vorhandenen strukturellen Konfliktpotentialen lassen sich in der schweizerischen Gegenwart - aus einer eher analytischen Perspektive - folgende vier typischen Konfliktkonstellationen identifizieren:

- *Kompromissen nur schwer zugängliche "Nullsummenkonflikte"*: Diese Konflikte waren auch in den Zeiten der Hochkonjunktur und der überbordenden öffentlichen Budgets nicht durch Kompensationsleistungen überwindbar. Darunter zählen zum einen eigentliche Wertkonflikte, die sich (gegenwärtig) nicht oder nur

---

[17] Etwa die - abgelehnte - Forderung der Beweislastumkehr im Falle geschlechtsspezifischer Diskriminierungen bei Beförderungen, Gratifikationen und dergleichen.

schwer auf (auflösbare) Interessenkonflikte reduzieren lassen[18]. Diese betreffen in der Schweiz vermutlich bis heute die nukleare Entsorgungsfrage, die Abtreibungsproblematik oder - neuerdings - die Frage der kontrollierten Abgabe von harten Drogen an Drogenabhängige durch den Staat. Bei diesen Fragen zögert nach allgemeiner Praxis auch eine durchaus vorhandene Mehrheit der Bundesversammlung, der Minderheit Lösungen aufzuzwingen. Die guteidgenössische Lösung solcher Konflikte besteht jeweils eher in der Kantonalisierung (z. B. in der Abtreibungsfrage), in der Zuflucht zu Leerformeln (etwa in der nuklearen Entsorgungsfrage) oder im Lamentieren über eine angeblich entscheidungsunfähige Landesregierung, die man mit der Konfliktlösung geflissentlich allein lässt (Beispiel: Drogenproblematik).

- Ähnliche, substantiellen Kompromissen nur schwer zugängliche Konflikte bestehen (meist innerhalb der Kantone) entlang der Achse *Kernstädte - periurbane Umliegergemeinden - ländlicher Raum*[19], zwischen der *Suisse romande und der deutschen Schweiz* sowie in - etwas abgeschwächter Form - entlang den Demarkationslinien *zwischen den Konfessionen* (katholisch/protestantisch). Während sich die Konfliktlinien Stadt/Land und Deutschschweiz/Westschweiz vor allem in ökologie- und verkehrsbezogenen Themen sowie bezüglich der Europafrage manifestieren[20], führt die unterschiedliche Zugehörigkeit zu den beiden Landes-

---

[18] Vgl. zu dieser für Mediationsverfahren zentralen Unterscheidung etwa H. Weidner, op. cit., Anm. 5., S. 239 oder S. Wälti, *Neue Problemlösungstrategien in der nuklearen Entsorgung*, in: Schweizerisches Jahrbuch für Politische Wissenschaft, Nr. 33/1993, Vollzugsprobleme, Bern (Haupt), 1993, S. 212.

[19] Vgl. dazu U. Klöti, Th. Haldemann, W. Schenkel, *Agglomerationsprobleme und vertikale Zusammenarbeit, Umweltschutz und öffentlicher Verkehr in den Grossagglomerationen Lausanne und Zürich*, Bericht 49 des NFP "Stadt und Verkehr", Zürich, 1993 oder Peter Knoepfel, Rita Imhof, Willi Zimmerman: *Massnahmenpläne zur Luftreinhaltung. Wie sich Behörden beim Umweltschutz arrangieren*. Bericht 57 des NFP "Stadt und Verkehr", Fonds national suisse de la recherche scientifique, Zürich.

[20] Insbesondere im Bezug auf Umwelt- und Verkehrsthemen. Vgl. dazu die UNIVOX - Umfrage zum Thema Umwelt 1993, GfS - Forschungsinstitut Adliswil und IDHEAP, Chavannes-près-Renens.

kirchen in der Regel eher zu den oben umschriebenen Wertekonflikten[21].

- *"Sonderopfer" für Politikbelastungsräume:* Es gibt in der Schweiz - wie in anderen europäischen Ländern - Räume, die überdurchschnittlich an nachteiligen Folgen von verräumlichten[22] zentralstaatlichen Politiken zu leiden haben[23]. Das sind etwa die Regionen entlang der Nord-Süd-Transitachse (insbesondere das Urnerland und der nördliche Tessin) oder der Kanton Aargau, wo praktisch die gesamte nukleare Energieproduktion der Schweiz konzentriert ist. Ähnliche Politikbelastungseffekte lassen sich auf kantonaler Ebene auch auf dem Territorium der Kantonshauptorte oder anderer grösserer Städte feststellen (Pendlerexpositionen). Daraus können Konflikte zwischen der Hauptstadt und der Kantons- bzw. zwischen der Kantons- und der Bundesregierung entstehen. Solche flackern vielfach im Zusammenhang mit zusätzlichen oder kapazitätsmässig auszubauenden Infrastrukturwerken des Bundes[24] oder der Kantone[25] auf. Mit der zunehmenden Verräumlichung zentralstaatlicher Politiken nehmen diese vertikalen Spannungen zwischen dem Zentralstaat und der lokalen Ebene auch in der Schweiz zu[26].

- *"Fremde Richter":* Den Eidgenossen sind Volksrechte und die eigene Souveränität heilig. Mit Schrecken denkt man in den früheren "Untertanenkantonen" an die Fremdherrschaft durch die eidgenössischen Vögte, die in gewissen Kantonen (z.B. Waadt) bis ins Revolutionsjahr 1798 herrschten. Für die Jurassier dauerte die

---

[21] Beispiel: Abtreibungsfrage.
[22] Vgl. zum Begriff Peter Knoepfel, Ingrid Kissling-Näf, *Transformation öffentlicher Politiken durch Verräumlichung - Betrachtungen zum gewandelten Verhältnis zwischen Raum und Politik*, in: A. Héritier (éd.), Policy-Analyse, Kritik und Neuorientierung, PVS-Sonderheft 24/1993, Opladen (Westdeutscher Verlag), S. 267-288, insbesondere S. 274 ff.
[23] Natürlich gibt es umgekehrt auch Räume, die von solchen Bundespolitiken überdurchschnittlich profitieren (z.B. die Stadt Bern, die praktisch die gesamte unmittelbare Bundesverwaltung beheimatet).
[24] Insbesondere Nationalstrassen oder neue Bahnlinien.
[25] Etwa Müllverbrennungsanlagen oder Sondermülldeponien.
[26] Vgl. dazu im einzelnen P. Knoepfel, I. Kissling-Näf, op. cit., Anm. 22, S. 277 ff.

bernische Fremdherrschaft sogar bis in die jüngste Vergangenheit (1979); eigene Richter haben ihnen die Berner und die Schweizer Bevölkerung erst anlässlich der Kantonsgründung im Jahre 1982 zugestanden. Umgekehrt beisst auf Granit, wer in der Schweiz die Kantonsgrenzen antasten oder die Gemeindeautonomie in Frage stellen möchte. So ist etwa die Schaffung angemessener regionaler Körperschaften mit hoheitlichen Zuständigkeiten in der Agglomeration auf der regionalen Ebene zwischen den Gemeinden und den Kantonen bisher nirgends zustande gekommen, obwohl dazu sowohl aus der Sicht der Raumplanung als auch (neuerdings) aus der Sicht einer angemessenen Ausgestaltung des Verkehrswesens und einer entsprechenden Reduktion der Luftbelastung durchaus Anlässe bestünden. Hier dreht sich der Konflikt nicht einmal um "fremde", sondern um neue "eigene" Richter. Dass man auch mit Zugeständnissen an die angeblich "technokratischen" Richter in Brüssel nicht gerade freigiebig ist, zeigt das negative Ergebnis der Volksabstimmung vom 6. Dezember 1992 über den Beitritt zum Europäischen Wirtschaftsraum (EWR) deutlich.

4. ACHT MEDIATIONS- ODER MEDIATIONSÄHNLICHE VERFAHREN AUS DER JÜNGSTEN VERGANGENHEIT UND DER GEGENWART

Die hier vorgestellten Konfliktlösungsverfahren stammen allesamt aus dem engeren oder weiteren Umfeld der Umweltpolitik. Betroffen sind die Bereiche Abfall, Energie, Naturschutz und Verkehr. Die Darstellung basiert auf laufenden oder abgeschlossenen Fallstudien, auf Zeitungsberichten, Kursmaterialien des IDHEAP und auf anderer Literatur[27].

---

[27] Insbesondere: Das Schweizerische Jahrbuch für Politische Wissenschaft, 1993, das dem Thema "Vollzugsprobleme" gewidmet ist.

4.1. Abfall

Von den zahlreichen konflikthaft verlaufenen und (noch) verlaufenden Verfahren zur Festlegung von Standorten für Anlagen der schweizerischen Abfallwirtschaft stellen wir im folgenden drei exemplarische Fälle vor. Alle drei betreffen Sondermüllanlagen, wie sie nach der neuesten Abfallgesetzgebung in der Schweiz inskünftig errichtet werden müssen, weil der Export von Sondermüll untersagt werden soll[28]. Solche Anlagen sind nicht nur auf der Ebene der Technologieauswahl umstritten[29]; auch die Standorte für technologisch nicht bestrittene Anlagen sind vielfach wegen der durch solche Anlagen induzierten Nebenbelastungen (Verkehr, Eingriffe in die Landschaft etc.) kontrovers. Dass dabei lokale Minderheiten für gemeinnützige Leistungen gegenüber der Mehrheit regelmässig übermässig belastet werden, braucht nicht besonders betont zu werden. "Die betroffene Minderheit ist (...) nicht ohne weiteres bereit, dieses "Opfer" zu erbringen (...) Warum gerade bei uns? Im Zusammenhang mit Standortentscheiden ist im Volksmund oft vom Weitergeben des Schwarzen Peters (...) die Rede. Auf den gleichen Sachverhalt bezieht sich auch das Sankt-Florians-Prinzip (...) "[30].

- *Das Genehmigungsverfahren für eine Sondermüllverbrennungsanlage der Firma CIBA-GEIGY in Basel-Stadt*[31]
  In diesem Verfahren, das im Sommer 1985 eröffnet und am 2. Mai 1991 erfolgreich abgeschlossen wurde, standen sich die Firma CIBA-GEIGY, zusammen mit den Firmen Sandoz und Hoffmann-La Roche, mit einer aus elf Gruppen bestehenden Opposition konfrontiert. Die Gruppierungen stammen aus der unmittelbaren Standortumgebung[32], aus dem benachbarten Deutsch-

---

[28] Art. 30, Abs. 4 des Entwurfs für die Revision des BG über den Umweltschutz, veröffentlicht in der Botschaft des Bundesrates vom 7. Juni 1993, S. 45 f. (Kommentar) 121 (Text).
[29] Die Verbrennung von Sondermüll an sich ist in der Schweiz weniger umstritten als in Deutschland (Dioxinverdacht).
[30] S. Wälti, op. cit., Anm. 17, S. 211.
[31] Dargestellt bei P. Knoepfel, U. Zuppinger, *Etude de cas d'une usine d'incinération de déchets spéciaux à Bâle, Suisse*, (vorläufig interner Bericht zuhanden des Schweizerischen Nationalfonds), Lausanne, 1994.
[32] Aktion Selbstschutz und Gruppe Sondermüllofen-Gegner - SMOG.

land[33] sowie aus dem Kanton Basel-Stadt [34] und aus der gesamten Schweiz[35]. Seitens der Behörden waren in das Verfahren nicht nur die für die Erteilung der Genehmigung zuständige Koordinationsstelle für Umweltschutz des Kantons Basel-Stadt, sondern auch der Vorsteher des baselstädtischen Baudepartements und das baselstädtische Verwaltungsgericht beteiligt. Als Befürworter der Anlage traten die Schweizerische Kommission für Abfallwirtschaft, das Bundesamt für Umwelt, Wald und Landschaft (BUWAL) und der Nachbarkanton Basel-Landschaft auf, der sein Interesse an der Verbrennung seiner Sonderabfälle anmeldete. Naturgemäss beteiligten sich an diesem Verfahren auch verschiedene mehr oder weniger neutrale Ökobüros. Eines dieser Büros zauberte das für solche Situationen geradezu "obligatorische" Alternativ-Verfahren aus der Tasche.

Nach heftigen und offenen Auseinandersetzungen zwischen der Firma CIBA-GEIGY und den Opponenten, unter denen vor allem die aus Deutschland stammenden Gruppen immer wieder die Dioxinfrage ansprachen, konnte bez. dieser heissumstrittenen Problematik eine Einigung erzielt werden. Dies gelang wohl letztlich auch deshalb, weil die Firma CIBA-GEIGY nach den ersten Verhandlungen mit den Opponenten im atmosphärisch schwierigen Kontext des etwa gleichzeitigen Sandoz-Brandes (vom 1. November 1986) höchste technologische Anforderungen an die Anlage stellte und das Projekt nicht mehr als bloss firmeneigenes, sondern als regionales Vorhaben und damit als Dienstleistung gegenüber der Öffentlichkeit zu konzipieren begann. Die Opponenten zogen schliesslich ihre verwaltungsgerichtliche Beschwerde zurück, nachdem zwischen ihnen und dem Projektträger eine schriftliche Vereinbarung unterzeichnet worden war. Darin verpflichtete sich die CIBA-GEIGY zur Einhaltung strengerer Grenzwerte für Staub-, NO_x- und Dioxin-Emissionen als in der eidgenössischen und kantonalen Gesetzgebung vorgesehen. In der gleichen Übereinkunft wurde eine permanente Überwachung der Luftschadstoffemissionen durch eine Kommission vereinbart, in

---

[33] Interessengemeinschaft Morgenluft (Weil am Rhein), Landratsamt Lörrach, Stadt Weil am Rhein, Regierungspräsidium Freiburg i.B., SPD Baden-Württemberg.
[34] WWF Sektion Basel, Sozialdemokratische Partei des Kantons Basel-Stadt.
[35] WWF Schweiz, Demokratische Juristen.

der auch die Umweltschutzorganisationen vertreten sein sollten. Ein eigentlicher Mediator ist in diesem Verfahren nicht aufgetreten. Einen wesentlichen Anteil am Zustandekommen der Vereinbarung hatte der Leiter der Koordinationsstelle für Umweltschutz des Kantons Basel-Stadt, der mit den verschiedenen Konfliktparteien einzeln und am runden Tisch intensive Gespräche führte, und die Beteiligten schliesslich zum Einlenken brachte.

- *Standortfestlegung für eine Sondermülldeponie in der Suisse romande*[36]
In diesem Verfahren, das fünf Jahre in Anspruch nahm (1989-1993), gelang es, für den Bau einer Sondermülldeponie für die Reststoffe aus fünf westschweizerischen Kantonen[37] drei Standorte mit einer Fläche von insgesamt 18 ha rechtsverbindlich und ohne eine einzige Einsprache auszuweisen. Das im Beitrag von M. Rey beschriebene Verfahren verlief von Anfang an im Rahmen einer eigentlichen Projektmanagement-Struktur und damit, bis kurz vor dessen Abschluss ausserhalb der Bahnen des üblichen Verwaltungsverfahrens[38]. Zunächst wurden aus 72 hydrogeologisch geeigneten Standorten unter Anwendung von 13 Kriterien durch ein spezialisiertes technisches Beratungsbüro 32 Orte ausgewählt. Der Schritt von diesen 32 zu den später verbleibenden 14 Standorten wurde unter Einsatz von fünf gewichteten Kriterien vorgenommen, die durch Repräsentanten der betroffenen Standortgemeinden, der Umweltschutzorganisationen und weiterer interessierter Kreise im Rahmen sog. Regionalgruppen erarbeitet wurden. Diese Kriterien waren (mit abnehmender Gewichtung)

---

[36] Vgl. dazu M. Rey in diesem Band.
[37] Freiburg, Waadt, Neuenburg, Jura, Wallis.
[38] Solche Projektmanagement-Strukturen werden mittlerweilen in zahlreichen anderen Kantonen für die Durchführung von Planungsverfahren für Grossanlagen verwendet (Beispiele finden sich etwa in den Kantonen St. Gallen, Aargau, Thurgau und Wallis - vgl. dazu insbesondere die einschlägigen Regierungsratsbeschlüsse des Kantons Thurgau vom 9.7.1985 (RRB 1244) sowie die Richtlinien des Walliser Regierungsrates vom 8.7.1993 betreffend Verfahrensbeschleunigungen. Generell dazu: I. Kissling-Näf, *Staatliche Steuerung über Verfahren und Netzwerkbildung, die Umweltverträglichkeitsprüfung als zeitgemässe Antwort auf komplexe gesellschaftliche Probleme im Umweltbereich*, Chavannes (IDHEAP), 1995 (Diss., in Ausarbeitung).

eine möglichst geringe Forst- und landwirtschaftliche Qualität der betroffenen Böden, eine vertretbare Zahl und Dichte der in den betroffenen Ortschaften zu erwartenden Verkehrsbewegungen, das Vorhandensein eines nahen Autobahnanschlusses, die möglichst harmonische Integration der Anlage in die Landschaft und das Vorhandensein einer geeigneten Grube (etwa: Steinbruch, Kiesgrube etc.).

Diese im Konsensverfahren mit repräsentativen Vertretern der potentiellen Standortgemeinden erarbeiteten Kriterien wurden von einer ähnlich zusammengesetzten Begleitgruppe auch in der nächsten Stufe angewandt; aus diesem Prozess resultierten Ende 1992 schliesslich fünf mögliche Standorte. Von der Verwaltung in Auftrag gegebene Detailstudien führten im Verlaufe des Jahres 1993 zur Verabschiedung rechtsverbindlicher Zonenpläne für drei dieser fünf Standorte. In dieser letzten Phase wurde die Projektmanagement-Struktur sukzessive wieder in die ordentliche Raumplanungsverwaltung des betroffenen Kantons (Waadt) integriert, so dass schliesslich die zur Ausweisung der Standorte notwendigen kantonalen Nutzungspläne im ordentlichen Planungsverfahren erfolgen konnte. Dieses Verfahren sieht bekanntlich die öffentliche Planauflage mit Einsprachemöglichkeiten seitens der betroffenen Grundeigentümer, Drittinteressierter und der Gemeinden vor. Die Einsprachefrist lief ab, ohne dass auch nur eine einzige Einsprache erhoben worden wäre.

Die Besonderheit der gewählten Projektmanagement-Struktur liegt darin, dass ihr operatives Zentrum bewusst ausserhalb der Verwaltung angesiedelt wurde: Es war dies die Communauté d'études pour l'aménagement du territoire (C.E.A.T.), eine von den westschweizerischen Kantonen getragene Stiftung, die administrativ der Eidgenössischen Technischen Hochschule in Lausanne untersteht. Ihr Zweck liegt in der Durchführung von Studien und Aufträgen zu raumrelevanten Vorhaben aller Art. Für die technischen Fragen, die sich im Planungsprozess stellten, war ein (ebenfalls nicht staatliches) Planungsbüro zuständig. Die Instanzen der beiden betroffenen kantonalen Verwaltungen (Freiburg und Waadt) waren lediglich im Lenkungsausschuss vertreten, der die wichtigsten strategischen Entscheidungen zu treffen hatte. Diese Struktur kennt prinzipiell keinen Mediatoren. Sie ist nicht primär auf Konfliktlösung, sondern auf die Durchsetzung einer - angemessenen - Problemlösung angelegt. Die Konfliktbewältigung ist damit lediglich Mittel zum prinzipiellen Zweck der Management-Struktur. Sie wurde indessen von Beginn an als zentrales Projektinstrument angesehen, ging man doch davon aus, dass eine Standortausweisung gegen den Willen der betroffenen Gemeinde politisch kaum durchsetzbar wäre. Der C.E.A.T. als operativem Zentrum dieser aus der Staatsadministration ausgelagerten Projektorganisation fiel darin auch die Aufgabe einer Mediation zu, obwohl weder sie selbst noch irgendein Dritter als eigentliche Mediatoren auftraten. Ihre Mitarbeiter[39] waren keine "neutralen" Personen, sondern eher - glaubwürdige, weil inhaltlich und prozedural von der nicht unbedingt geliebten Staatsverwaltung unabhängige - Makler für eine gemeinnützige Sache. Ihr Auftrag bestand in der - professionellen - Konsensbeschaffung. Man kann mit Fug von einer sozialtechnologischen Dienstleistung für die Verwaltung sprechen.

- *Standortsuche für eine "Reststoffdeponie" im Kanton Aargau*[40]
  Dieses im Beitrag von O. Renn und Th. Webler in diesem Buch beschriebene Verfahren verlief teilweise bis in die Details gleich wie jenes in der Suisse romande, obwohl es erheblich später einsetzte (Ende 1992), praktisch nur ein Jahr dauerte (bis Ende 1993) und die ausserhalb der Verwaltung angesiedelte Projektgruppe "Vorbeugendes Konfliktmanagement" der ETH Zürich (erstaunlicherweise) keine Kenntnis vom westschweizerischen Ex-

---

[39] Und namentlich ihr Generalsekretär, Michel Rey, der das Projekt persönlich leitete.
[40] Vgl. dazu den Beitrag von Ortwin Renn und Thomas Webler in diesem Band; ferner: O. Renn, *Risikodialog statt Sankt-Florians-Prinzip. Erfahrungen aus einem Modellversuch im Kanton Aargau*, in: NZZ vom 27./28. November 1993, Nr. 277, S. 23 f.

periment hatte[41]. In zwei Schritten wurden von ursprünglich 32 in Frage kommenden Standorten bis Ende 1993 27 eliminiert. Bis zur Jahrtausendwende beabsichtigt der Kanton Aargau im Ostaargau die planungsrechtlichen Voraussetzungen (Nutzungsplan) für maximal drei Deponiestandorte zu schaffen. Für den zweiten Schritt wurde unter den damals noch in Frage kommenden Standortgemeinden ein sog. "demokratisches Mitwirkungsverfahren" institutionalisiert, das von einem Expertenteam der ETH Zürich durchgeführt und wissenschaftlich begleitet wurde. Im Laufe eines halben Jahres bewerteten über 80 Bewohner aus den betroffen Standortgemeinden in vier Kommissionen während eines halben Jahres die möglichen 11 Standorte und gaben eine Empfehlung zur Weiterbearbeitung der projektierten Standorte an eine aus Vertretern der Staatsverwaltung unter der Leitung des Baudirektors zusammengesetzte "Behördendelegation"[42].

Das explizit auf dem Konzept des sog. Bürgergutachtens von P. Dienel[43] aufbauende Verfahren kennt ebenfalls keinen Mediator im engeren Sinne. Der Projektleiter[44] betreute das Projekt fachlich von der Seite des Kantons und die ETH-Projektgruppe führte den Konsensbildungsprozess durch. Sie stellte den Rahmen für Konfliktmittlungen zur Verfügung, ohne selbst eine etwa dem Mediator im Neusser Verfahren in der Bundesrepublik Deutschland[45] vergleichbare Position des neutralen Mittlers einzunehmen. Ähnlich wie beim Experiment in der Suisse romande, kann bei dieser Form alternativer Streitbeilegung von einem durch ein

---

[41] Erstaunlich ist dies deshalb, weil über das Westschweizer Verfahren in einer Publikation zum Thema "Konfliktbewältigung durch Verhandlungen" bereits 1990 berichtet wurde. Der Bericht: P.Knoepfel, M. Rey, *Konfliktminderung durch Verhandlung: Das Beispiel des Verfahrens zur Suche eines Standorts für eine Sondermülldeponie in der Suisse romande*, in: W. Hoffmann-Riem, E. Schmidt-Assmann (Hrsg.) Konfliktbewältigung durch Verhandlungen, Konfliktmittlung in Verwaltungsverfahren, Band II, Baden-Baden (Nomos), S. 257-286.
[42] Vgl. NZZ vom 20./21. November 1993, Nr. 271, S. 22.
[43] P.C. Dienel, *Die Planungszelle. Der Bürger plant seine Umwelt, eine Alternative zur Establishment-Demokratie*, Opladen (Westdeutscher Verlag), 1991.
[44] Werner Baumann.
[45] Prof. Füllgraff, vgl. dazu den Beitrag von Helmut Weidner in diesem Band.

Projektmanagement unterstützten Politikdialog gesprochen werden[46].

4.2. Bereich Energie

Die drei im folgenden aus dem Bereich Energie vorgetragenen Verfahren wurden entweder erst kürzlich abgeschlossen oder sind gegenwärtig (März 1994) noch hängig. Zwei Verfahren gelten der für die schweizerische Elektrizitätsproduktion an erster Stelle stehenden Wasserkraftnutzung; ein Konflikt bezieht sich auf die Endlagerung radioaktiver Abfälle, die aus den vier schweizerischen Kernkraftwerken stammen, die ihrerseits rund 40% der helvetischen Stromproduktion decken.

- *Leistungserweiterung des Grosswasserkraftwerkes "Cleuson / Dixence" im Kanton Wallis*[47]
  In diesem Verfahren, das auf Planungen im Herbst 1988 zurückgeht, sah sich der vom Kanton Wallis unterstützte Projektträger, die Aktiengesellschaft "Ouest-Suisse SA et Grande Dixence SA" einer harten und recht aussichtsreichen Opposition des WWF Schweiz sowie des WWF Wallis ausgesetzt. Am 4. November 1992 unterzeichneten die Umweltschutzorganisationen mit dem Kanton Wallis und dem Projektträger vor Abschluss eines bundesgerichtlichen Rechtsmittelverfahrens eine aussergerichtliche Vereinbarung. Darin verzichteten die Umweltschutzorganisationen auf ihren Rekurs gegen die geplante Leistungssteigerung um 1,100 MW (Projektsumme: 1,1 Milliarden Franken) zum Zweck der Erzeugung von Strom für Spitzenzeiten. Der Projektträger und der Kanton Wallis verpflichteten sich im Gegenzug auf folgende vier Leistungen zugunsten der Allgemeinheit:

---

[46] Im Sinne der von H. Weidner in diesem Band vorgeschlagenen Terminologie.
[47] Vgl. dazu P. Knoepfel, A. Eberle, G. Gerhäuser, N. Girard, *Energie und Umwelt im politischen Alltag. Energie et environnement dans la vie quotidienne. Drei Fallstudien für den Unterricht*, Bern (EDMZ), 1995, S. 19-181.

- Sicherung von Restwassermengen durch Verzicht des Einbezugs verschiedener Bäche in das Wasserregime des Kraftwerks (mit regelmässigen Kontrollen);

- Schaffung einer ökologischen Ausgleichsfläche im Talboden (Kiesgrube "Des épines") und deren Unterstellung unter eine Naturschutzzone unter Mitwirkung einer paritätischen Kommission;

- Studium der Auswirkungen der Bauarbeiten und des Betriebs auf das Wasserregime der Rhône;

- Schaffung von Biotopzonen in den Gemeinden Nendaz, La Praya und Hérémence.

Die Gesamtinvestitionen der Firma Ouest-Suisse SA et Grande Dixence SA für diese Kompensationsleistungen belaufen sich auf ca. 5 Millionen Franken.

In diesem Verfahren stand der Verhandlungslösung wiederum ein institutioneller Zwang in Gestalt eines unmittelbar bevorstehenden und inhaltlich für keine Seite vollumfänglich vorhersehbaren Bundesgerichtsentscheides zu Pate. Auch hier bedurfte es keines eigentlichen Mediatoren, der die Parteien an den Verhandlungstisch gebeten hätte. Die Einsicht, dass beiden Parteien durch eine vermittelnde Lösung mehr geholfen wäre als durch einen Volltreffer der einen oder anderen Seite via Gerichtsbeschluss, reichte als mediationsstiftendes Agens aus. Sicherlich half im Hintergrund die integrierende Persönlichkeit des Wallisers und ehemaligen Präsidenten der Eidgenössischen Bankenkommission (Bodenmann) mit, der sich hüben und drüben für eine solche Lösung einsetzte. Auch die formelle Einladung des Bundesgerichts an die Parteien, sich in seinen Gebäulichkeiten zum Gespräch zu treffen und die moderierende Diskussionsleitung durch den instruierenden Bundesrichter dürften einiges zur Konsensbildung beigetragen haben. Aktive Mediation liegt gleichwohl in diesem Verfahren nicht vor.

- *Konfliktlösungsgruppe "Wasserkraft" beim Eidgenössischen Verkehrs- und Energiewirtschaftsdepartement ("KOWA")*
Am 23. September 1990 stimmten Volk und Stände dem neuen Verfassungszusatz zu, der "für die Dauer von 10 Jahren ... keine Rahmen-, Bau-, Inbetriebsnahme- oder Betriebsbewilligungen gemäss Bundesrecht für neue Einrichtungen zur Erzeugung von Atomenergie (Atomkraftwerke oder Atomreaktoren zu Heizzwecken)" mehr zulässt[48]. Dieses verfassungsrechtliche Moratorium für Kernkraftwerke veranlasste den Bundesrat damals, das Ziel eines "Energiefriedens" zu proklamieren. Unter dieser Devise sollten Mittel und Wege gesucht werden, das sog. Programm "Energie 2000" zu realisieren, das u. a. für das Jahr 2000 einerseits eine Stabilisierung des Energieverbrauchs auf der Basis von 1990 anstrebt, und andererseits bei der Energiegewinnung eine Anhebung des Wasserkraftanteils um 5% vorsieht. Das Eidg. Verkehrs- und Energiewirtschaftsdepartement berief in der Folge vier Konfliktlösungsgruppen ein, die themenweise sämtliche interessierten Gruppierungen zu Konfliktlösungen um den runden Tisch zusammenbringen sollten. Die Gruppe, die wahrscheinlich am schnellsten am Ziel sein wird, ist die "Konfliktlösungsgruppe Wasserkraft (KOWA)". Sie steht, wie die drei anderen Gruppen, unter der Leitung einer neutralen Person, die von allen angesprochenen Gruppen gleichermassen als Mittler anerkannt wird. Im Falle der KOWA ist dies der ehemalige NZZ-Inlandredaktor Walter Schiesser. Die Gruppe umfasst Vertreter der Umweltschutzorganisationen, der Elektrizitätswirtschaft, der Bundesverwaltung[49] und der Kantone. Sie zählt 24 Mitglieder.

Seit ungefähr zwei Jahren versucht der Mediator, die Konfliktparteien zu einer - vermutlich im Sommer 1995 verabschiedungsreifen - Vereinbarung zu bewegen. Darin soll sich jede Partei zu spezifischen Massnahmen verpflichten, die sie im Hinblick auf die Zielsetzung einer leicht angehobenen Energiegewinnung aus der Wasserkraft einzugehen bereit ist.

---

48 Art. 19 der Übergangsbestimmungen zur Schweizerischen Bundesverfassung vom 29. Mai 1874, angenommen in der Volksabstimmung vom 23. September 1990 (Initiative "Stopp dem Atomkraftwerkbau").
49 Vertreten sind die 3 Bundesämter für Wasserwirtschaft, für Energiewirtschaft und für Umwelt, Wald und Landschaft.

- *Standortsuche für ein Endlager für radioaktive Abfälle*[50]
1972 gründeten die Elektrizitätsgesellschaften, die Atomkraftwerkbetreiber und der Bund die Nationale Genossenschaft für die Lagerung radioaktiver Abfälle (NAGRA). Diese veröffentlichte Ende März 1982 eine Liste von 20 möglichen Standorten für ein Endlager für schwach- und mittelradioaktive Abfälle. Ende 1983 beantragte die NAGRA bei den zuständigen Instanzen der Kantone und des Bundes den Bau von Sondierstollen an drei Standorten (Oberstock/UR, Ollon/VD und Piz Pian Grand/GR). Aufgrund des Vernehmlassungsverfahrens erteilte der Bund zwar die Bewilligung für die Sondierbohrungen, beauftragte die NAGRA indessen mit der Abklärung eines zusätzlichen Standorts. Nach langem Suchen fand man schliesslich den Standort am Wellenberg (NW). Die Untersuchungen an allen vier Standorten sollten 1993 abgeschlossen werden. Der Entscheid des Bundesrates zur Rahmenbewilligung soll dem eidgenössischen Parlament vorgelegt werden. Bei einem nächsten Schritt sollen dann auf kantonaler und kommunaler Ebene weitere Genehmigungsverfahren folgen. Das Verfahren ist hoch konfliktträchtig: "Mit Einsprachen, Initiativen, Demonstrationen und direkten Aktionen auf kantonaler und kommunaler Ebene bewirkten die Kritiker der Entsorgungspolitik immer wieder Verzögerungen. Die Opposition konnte zwar in den meisten Fällen die Arbeiten nicht verhindern; sie ist jedoch im Stande, die NAGRA und die Behörden in ihren Bestrebungen zu behindern und insbesondere die anstehende Standortwahl wesentlich zu verzögern. Im Bestreben, die Akzeptanz gegenüber der Entsorgungspolitik in der Schweiz zu verbessern und dem Standortentscheid den Weg zu ebnen, fand 1991 auf Bundesebene eine erste Aussprache zwischen Behörden, Ausführenden (NAGRA, Energiewirtschaft) und Umweltschutzorganisationen statt."[51] Diese "Entsorgungskonferenz" platzte indessen kurz darauf, weil die Umweltschutzorganisationen ihre Teilnahme aufkündigten, nachdem der Bundesrat eine Leistungserhöhung des Atomkraftwerks Mühleberg genehmigt hatte.

---

[50] Vgl. dazu den Aufsatz von S. Wälti, op. cit., Anm. 18, 1993, S. 205 ff. sowie das Bulletin d'information du Forum Vera (parution trimestrielle), Zürich, Nr. 1/1994.
[51] S. Wälti, ibid., S. 208.

Die Entsorgungspolitik stösst aber auch bei den betroffenen Gemeinden und bei den potentiellen Standortkantonen auf erbitterten Widerstand. So widersetzte sich die Bevölkerung der potentiellen Standortgemeinden den Plänen der NAGRA teilweise recht heftig. Dabei schwappte die Opposition recht rasch von der Standortfrage auf die generelle Ebene der Abfallproblematik und der Energiepolitik über; ausserdem transformierte sich der Streit mitunter auch in eine institutionelle Auseinandersetzung über die Gemeindeautonomie[52]. Die Kantone, denen dank der kantonalen nichtnuklearen Bewilligungsverfahren laut Raumplanungs- oder Umweltrecht "eigentliche Vetofunktionen"[53] zukommen, haben sich insbesondere in der Innerschweiz, in die Reihen der Opposition eingegliedert. Hochinteressant ist der Fall des Kantons Nidwalden, wo der Kanton - mit Zustimmung des Bundesgerichts (Entscheid vom 30. August 1993) - auf sein Bergregal pocht und die Verfügungsgewalt über dieses Regal nach einem Landsgemeindebeschluss 1994 der Landsgemeinde übertrug[54]. Es steht zu erwarten, dass die Nidwalder Bevölkerung "mit einer deutlichen Mehrheit gegen das Endlagerprojekt"[55] stimmen wird.

In ihrem Kommentar zu diesem Prozess stellt S. Wälti zunächst fest, dass das traditionelle Verfahren auch in diesem Falle in einer Krise steht. Zwar habe die NAGRA als parastaatliche Institution nach mehrmaliger Korrektur des Zeithorizontes in relativ kurzer Zeit ein umfangreiches und detailliertes Entsorgungsprogramm vorgelegt. Aber sie habe damit einen wachsenden partizipatorischen Druck ausgelöst. Deshalb träten Verzögerungen der nuklearen Entsorgung in erster Linie in der Standortsuche auf. Der Versuch, mit einer Änderung des Atomgesetzes die Verfahrensregeln selbst zu ändern und das Prozedere zu zentralisieren, dürfte jedenfalls auf erheblichen Widerstand stossen[56].

Vorläufig sei auch der Versuch gescheitert, anstelle von Konfrontation Kooperation zu praktizieren. Der Einbezug eines neutralen Dritten, der von den Bundesbehörden gewählt wurde,

---

[52] Vgl. S. Wälti, ibid., S. 212.
[53] S. Wälti, ibid., S. 213.
[54] Vgl.dazu Luzerner Neueste Nachrichten vom 28. Januar 1994.
[55] S. Wälti, ibid., S. 214.
[56] Vgl. dazu auch P. Knoepfel, I. Kissling-Näf, op. cit., Anm 21, S. 277 f.

"sollte sicherstellen, dass alle Beteiligten (Umweltschutzorganisationen, Ausführende, Behörden) als in den Entscheid involvierte und an dessen Ausgang interessierte Gruppen"[57] berücksichtigt wurden. Indessen verliessen die Umweltschutzorganisationen diese Gesprächsrunde relativ rasch. Zwar wurde die Notwendigkeit einer sicheren Entsorgung der radioaktiven Abfälle von niemandem bestritten. "Die Entsorgung wird jedoch von einem Teil der Umweltschutzorganisationen untrennbar an die hoffnungslos polarisierte Energiepolitik geknüpft: Keine Endlager ohne Ausstieg aus der Atomkraft (...). Der Ende 1992 vom Bundesrat getroffene Entscheid zur Leistungserhöhung des AKW Mühleberg hat dabei das labile Vertrauensverhältnis ... aus den Fugen gehoben. Alles deutet darauf hin, dass im Zeitpunkt der Mediationsbemühungen die Situation schon derart verfahren war, dass der (Ver-) Handlungsspielraum Konzessionen und Kompromisse kaum zuliess."[58].

4.3. Naturschutz

Als Gegenvorschlag zur kurz darauf zur Abstimmung gelangenden Rothenturm-Initiative[59] verabschiedeten die eidgenössischen Räte am 19. Juni 1987 eine Revision des Bundesgesetzes über den Natur- und Heimatschutz (NHG)[60]. Darin wurde die gesetzliche Grundlage für den Biotopenschutz gelegt, welcher über die Verabschiedung von entsprechenden Inventaren sicherzustellen ist (Art. 18a). In Erfüllung dieses Gesetzesauftrags verabschiedete der Bundesrat am 21. Januar 1991 die Verordnung zum Schutz der Hoch- und Übergangsmoore von nationaler Bedeutung[61], die eine Liste von 518 Hochmoorgebieten mit einer Oberfläche von 15 km² inventarisiert. Hinzu traten im Rahmen einer weiteren Verordnung Bestimmungen

---

57 S. Wälti, ibid., S. 218.
58 S. Wälti, ibid., S. 219.
59 Angenommen in der Volksabstimmung vom 6. Dezember 1987 - Bundesverfassung der Schweizerischen Eidgenossenschaft vom 29. Mai 1874, Art. 24sexies, Abs. 5.
60 Vom 1. Juli 1966, SR. 451.
61 SR. 451.32.

über den Schutz von Flachmooren von nationaler Bedeutung[62], die 1084 Biotope mit einer Fläche von 185 km² inventarisierten (vornehmlich in den Kantonen Bern, Luzern und Schwyz). In Erfüllung des neuen Verfassungsauftrags und der Art. 18a und 5 des NHG will der Bundesrat schliesslich eine dritte Verordnung zum Schutze von Moorlandschaften von besonderer Schönheit und nationaler Bedeutung (Moorlandschaftsverordnung) erlassen[63]. Ihr zufolge sollen 91 Standorte mit einer Oberfläche von insgesamt 926 km² durch besondere Massnahmen der Kantone geschützt werden. Zweck der Verordnung ist der (durch Bundessubventionen mitfinanzierte) Unterhalt der Biotope von nationaler Bedeutung.

Diese geballte Ladung[64] bundesrechtlicher, räumlich festgelegter Schutzanordnungen führte bei den betroffenen Kantonen zu einer eigentlichen Fronde. Diese kam 1992 und 1993 in fünf Standesinitiativen der Kantone Obwalden, Schwyz, Graubünden, Nidwalden und Zug zum Ausdruck, welche die zuständige nationalrätliche Kommission zu einer Motion veranlasste, in der Abschwächungen des absoluten Moorschutzes im Sinne einer nochmaligen Revision des entsprechenden Verfassungsartikels gefordert wurden[65]. Die Beratungen über die auch in anderer Hinsicht denkwürdige Revision des NHG[66] sind gegenwärtig (Frühjahr 1995) noch nicht abgeschlossen. Es will scheinen, dass sich die zunehmend kritischere Stimmung in der Bevölkerung gegenüber dem Umweltschutz nun anhand der Naturschutzpolitik zum ersten Mal Luft gemacht hat.

---

[62] Verordnung über den Schutz von Flachmooren von nationaler Bedeutung vom 7. September 1994 (SR. 451.33); (Inkrafttreten: 1. Oktober 1994).
[63] Moorlandschaftsverordnung; geplantes Inkrafttreten: 1. Juli 1995.
[64] Neben diesen drei Schutzinventaren bestehen weitere Inventare. Zu erwähnen sind insbesondere das Bundesinventar der Landschaften von nationaler Bedeutung vom 21.11.1977 (121 Standorte), SR. 451.11, das (in Bearbeitung befindliche) Inventar der historischen Verkehrswege der Schweiz von nationaler Bedeutung, das Bundesinventar der Auengebiete von nationaler Bedeutung vom 28.10.1992, SR. 451.31 und das Inventar der schützenswerten Ortsbilder der Schweiz aufgrund der entsprechenden Verordnung vom 9.9.1981, SR. 451.12 sowie das kantonal erhobene Inventar der Trockenstandorte der Schweiz.
[65] Année politique suisse - Schweizerische Politik, 1992, S. 195.
[66] Zur Debatte steht das Beschwerderecht der Umweltschutzorganisationen (Beschluss des Nationalrates vom Dezember 1993: Abschaffung dieses Beschwerderechts mit 101:86 Stimmen).

Aber nicht nur auf der Ebene der Gesetzesrevision, sondern auch bei der Umsetzung bereits verabschiedeter Gesetze und Verordnungen zum Naturschutz äussert sich die beschriebene Opposition der betroffenen Kantone gegen die Inventarisierungspolitik des Bundes. Die Kantone wehrten sich insbesondere gegen die aus ihrer Sicht zu weit gezogenen Perimeter der Schutzgebiete und gegen die angeblich zu strengen Nutzungsbeschränkungen für diese Gebiete. In Anbetracht dessen setzte das Bundesamt für Umwelt, Wald und Landschaft (BUWAL), zusammen mit dem schweizerischen Tourismusverband, eine Arbeitsgruppe ein. Diese sollte "die verschiedenen Interessen zwischen Landschafts- resp. Moorschutz, Fremdenverkehr und Landwirtschaft unter einen Hut"[67] bringen[68]. Im Zusammenhang mit der Pflege und Erhaltung von Moorlandschaften und den daraus resultierenden Ertragsausfällen für die Landwirtschaft zeigte eine Studie des BUWAL und des Bauernverbandes jährliche Kosten zwischen 27-29 Millionen Franken (Basis 1991) auf. Im Rahmen der laufenden Revision des NHG soll eine gesetzliche Grundlage für die Entschädigung der Landwirtschaft in der Höhe von 90% der Ausfälle vorgesehen werden[69].

Neben diesen allgemeinen Abklärungen hatte das BUWAL an einer Vielzahl von Sitzungen mit den betroffenen Kantonsregierungen Verhandlungen über die definitive Festlegung der Schutzparameter und der Nutzungsvorschriften zu führen. Ähnlich wie im Falle der vom Bund "via Dekret" an die Kantone verteilten landwirtschaftlichen Fruchtfolgeflächen[70] empfanden die Kantone die einseitige und durch Wissenschaftler vorgenommene Definition des Schutzperimeters durch Beamte aus Bern als einen eigentlichen

---

[67] Année politique suisse - Schweizerische Politik, 1993, S. 195.
[68] Hauptstreitpunkt war insbesondere die Frage, ob in den inventarisierten Moorgebieten von nationaler Bedeutung weiterhin touristische Einrichtungen betrieben, erneuert oder erstellt werden dürften.
[69] Année politique suisse - Schweizerische Politik, 1993, S. 195 f.
[70] Gemäss Art. 16 ff. der Verordnung vom 2. Oktober 1989 über die Raumplanung (SR. 700.1) - vgl. zu jenen harten Auseinandersetzungen zwischen dem Bund, den Kantonen und den Gemeinden die Fallstudie *Fruchtfolgeflächen Kanton Bern (Rüfenacht/Spiez): Schulterschluss zwischen Raumplanung, Landwirtschaft und Ökologie?*, in: W. Zimmermann, P. Knoepfel, *Umwelt und Landwirtschaft im politischen Alltag. Drei Fälle für die Schule*, im Auftrag des Bundesamtes für Forstwesen, des Bundesamtes für Umweltschutz, des Bundesamtes für Raumplanung und des Bundesamtes für Landwirtschaft, Bern (EDMZ), 1987, S. 252-355.

Affront. Sie waren nicht bereit, die immer dichter werdenden Schutzanforderungen der sich vielfach überlappenden Bundesinventare auf ihrem Gebiet hinzunehmen. So hatten denn im Laufe des Jahres 1993 die behördlichen Vertreter des eidgenössischen Natur- und Landschaftsschutzes etliche Schlichtungssitzungen zu bestreiten, an denen sie sich teilweise mit recht "wüsten" Vorwürfen seitens der kantonalen Raumplanungs-, Volkswirtschafts-, aber auch seitens der Naturschutzbehörden selbst konfrontiert sahen. Ungefähr 90 Schutzobjekte wurden anlässlich dieser Sitzungen im Detail durchbesprochen und in den meisten Fällen zugunsten der Kantone arrondiert bzw. bezüglich Nutzungsauflagen etwas gelockert.

Dieses Vorgehen zur Schlichtung von Konflikten zwischen Bund und Kantonen ist ein recht übliches Verfahren. Auch hier treten keine formellen Mediatoren auf. Das Verfahren ist auch nicht anderwertig formalisiert. Auslöser ist die meist von Kantonsregierungen artikulierte Opposition gegen eine bestimmte Politikumsetzungsmassnahme eidgenössischer Behörden, die in einem Schreiben der Kantonsregierung an den Bundesrat, in formellen Beschlüssen kantonaler Parlamente für Vorstösse bei den Bundesbehörden[71] oder gar in der informellen Unterstützung von Volksinitiativen zur Abänderung der Bundesverfassung durch eine Kantonsregierung[72] Gestalt annimmt.

Die Bundesbehörden sind - wie etwa im erwähnten Fall der Moorschutzverordnung - formell nicht verpflichtet, auf die Proteste der Kantone einzugehen, sofern sie vor Erlass der entsprechenden Anordnungen die Kantone gebührend angehört hatten. Genau über diesen Punkt bestand im vorliegenden Verfahren ein Dissens: Während die zuständige Bundesbehörde (BUWAL) der Meinung war, mit den Kantonen im Rahmen des Vernehmlassungsverfahrens über die einschlägigen Verordnungen ausreichend über die zu inventarisierenden Objekte diskutiert zu haben, sahen sich die Kantone ihrerseits von den Inventaren schlichtweg "überrumpelt". Dass dem - in Anbetracht der zunehmenden Flut von Vernehmlassungsverfahren über

---

[71] Im Extremfall: Standesinitiative für die Behandlung eines Geschäfts gemäss Art. 93, Abs. 2 der Bundesverfassung.
[72] So geschehen bei der am 20. Februar 1994 - unerwartet - angenommenen Alpeninitiative, die insbesondere vom Landammann des Kantons Uri öffentlich unterstützt wurde.

wichtige und unwichtige Gegenstände bei den Kantonen - durchaus so sein kann, ist nicht von der Hand zu weisen. Denkbar ist indessen auch, dass sich die zuständigen Kantonsbehörden erst im Nachhinein und auf Druck interessierter Kreise der politischen Tragweite der Inventare bewusst geworden sind und "Nachverhandlungen" verlangten. Umgekehrt dürfte man sich in Bern auf eine solche Reaktion insofern vorbereitet haben, als man sich bei den Entwürfen für die Schutzgebietsperimeter einige Rückzugspositionen offenhielt. Insofern war auch hier eine spätere Konfliktlösung durch Verhandlung durchaus Bestandteil der Strategie zur Umsetzung bundespolitischer Zielvorgaben vor Ort.

4.4. Verkehr

Noch in den späten sechziger Jahren lief jeder kantonale Baudirektor oder jeder Ständerat Gefahr, abgewählt zu werden, wenn es ihm nicht gelang, für seinen Kanton in Bern ein "Stück Nationalstrasse" zu ergattern. Seit den späten siebziger Jahren ist eher das Gegenteil der Fall: Jedenfalls die unmittelbar betroffene Bevölkerung lässt sich kaum mehr auf das "Geschenk" neuer oder erweiterter Nationalstrassenstücke ein. Vermutlich markiert diesen Wendepunkt die unter dem Druck einer Volksinitiative durch die eidgenössischen Räte am 22. Juni 1977 erfolgte Einsetzung einer Kommission zur Revision des Nationalstrassennetzes ("Kommission Biel"). Die Kommission brauchte fast 10 Jahre, um das mit einfachem Bundesbeschluss[73] am 21. Juni 1960 verabschiedete Nationalstrassennetz zu überprüfen[74]. Auf der Liste der sechs von der Kommission Biel zu überprüfenden Teilstrecken figurierte die Nationalstrasse N9 im mittleren und oberen Teil des Kantons Wallis nicht. Trotzdem akzeptierten die Räte 1979 eine aufgrund einer Petition von Umweltschützern aus dem Kanton Wallis zustande gekommene Motion, in der eine Revision

---

73 D.h. ohne Referendumsmöglichkeit.
74 Das Ergebnis der Überprüfung führte bekanntlich zur Elimination der N6 (Verbindung zwischen den Kantonen Bern und Wallis durch den Bau des sog. Rawyltunnels).

bzw. eine Rückdimensionierung der als solche in jenem Gebiet nicht in Frage gestellten Nationalstrasse gefordert wurde[75].

Das Bundesamt für Strassenbau beauftragte daraufhin Professor Philippe Bovy von der Eidgenössischen Technischen Hochschule Lausanne (EPFL) mit der Überprüfung der Linienführung. Das Mandat sollte die generelle Linienführung und die Kapazität, die Zahl der Autobahnzubringer und das Verhältnis der neuen Strasse zum kantonalen Strassennetz überprüfen. Zu eruieren waren ausserdem die Möglichkeiten einer etappenweisen Realisierung der Strasse. Dabei sollten die gegenwärtigen und künftigen Verkehrsbedürfnisse sowie die Auswirkungen des Werkes auf die Umwelt, die Landschaft, die Landwirtschaft, den Tourismus, die Strassensicherheit und die kantonale Volkswirtschaft genauer analysiert werden.

Der Experte führte daraufhin in den Jahren 1980-1982 ein für die damalige Zeit in mancherlei Hinsicht bemerkenswertes technisch-politisches Sozialexperiment durch. Er unterteilte die Strecke von Riddes (Mittelwallis) bis Brig (Oberwallis) in acht Teilstücke, die er in einem iterativen Verfahren nacheinander reevaluierte. Fast zehn Jahre vor dem Einsetzen einer eigentlichen "Mediationswelle" in der französischen und deutschen Literatur und vor der praktischen Verwendung von Mediations- oder mediationsähnlichen Verfahren in der Verwaltung führte der Ingenieurwissenschafter Bovy im Wallis gewissermassen im Alleingang und ohne Kenntnisse der (früheren) einschlägigen sozialwissenschaftlichen Literatur[76] ein solches Verfahren durch. Er bildete für jede Teilstrecke regionale Bürgergruppen, in denen die interessierten Kreise (Landwirte, Umweltschutzorganisationen, Dienststellen der kantonalen Verwaltung) und die Gemeinden vertreten waren. In diesen Gruppen wurden zunächst zahlreiche Varianten entwickelt, die einer technischen Machbarkeitsstudie unterworfen wurden. Diese Varianten wurden in einem

---

[75] Vgl. zum folgenden die Fallstudie *Martigny-Brigue: Enthousiasme - contestation - réexamen. Comment protéger la forêt de Finges contre les nuisances de la N9 en Valais?* (présentée par P. Knoepfel et W. Zimmermann, Dossier de cours, Lausanne (IDHEAP), 1987).

[76] Für die schweizerischen Verhältnisse aufgearbeitet bei P. Knoepfel, *Demokratisierung der Raumplanung. Grundsätzliche Aspekte und Modell für die Organisation der kommunalen Nutzungsplanung unter besonderer Berücksichtigung der schweizerischen Verhältnisse*, Berlin. (Duncker & Humblot, Schriften zum Öffentlichen Recht, Band 323), 1977.

nächsten Schritt von den Regionalgruppen anhand von Kriterien zu den Bereichen "technische Merkmale", "Umwelt und Natur", "gebaute Umwelt" sowie "Verkehrseignung" bewertet. Die in diesen Bewertungen bestplazierten drei Varianten wurden vor Ort durch Mitarbeiter der Equipe Bovy in Planzeichnungen umgesetzt und von den Regionalgruppen erneut evaluiert[77]. Auf diese Weise konnte eine wesentliche Verbesserung der Linienführung erzielt werden[78], die mit einer einzigen Ausnahme (Strecke Sierre-Leuk durch den Pfynwald) auch vom harten Kern der Opposition akzeptiert wurde. 1984 wurde der Grossteil der von Bovy erarbeiteten Vorschläge im ordentlichen Plangenehmigungsverfahren ohne Schwierigkeiten genehmigt[79].

Wahrscheinlich kommt das von Bovy gewählte Verfahren, das seit 1982 unter Raumplanern und Politikwissenschaftern der Westschweiz gewissermassen als Geheimtyp gehandelt und an zahlreichen Lehrveranstaltungen präsentiert wurde, unter den bisher in der Schweiz durchgeführten Prozeduren zur Lösung von Konflikten durch Verhandlung am nächsten an die eingangs vorgetragene Definition von Mediationsverfahren heran. Denn "Mediator" Bovy hatte niemals die Gewissheit, dass ein Konsens erzielbar und eine erzielte Konsenslösung für die im ordentlichen Verfahren zuständigen Behörden auch akzeptierbar wäre. Falls das Verfahren scheitern sollte, hätte man immer noch auf die bereits im ordentlichen Verfahren verabschiede-

---

[77] Dargestellt im einzelnen bei Ph. Bovy, *Rapport final de synthèse du réexamen de la N9*, Lausanne (EPFL), 1982.

[78] Bessere Integration der Strasse in die Landschaft, markante Reduktion der sichtbaren Strassenabschnitte (von 32,3 km auf 8,2 km), Lärmentlastung (Reduktion der lärmausgesetzten Siedlungsflächen um 62%), geringerer Flächenverbrauch (Reduktion um 23%), geringerer Materialverbrauch (Reduktion um ca. 50%), Verbesserungen im Bezug auf den Naturschutz (Reduktion der betroffenen Objekte von 12 auf 3). All diese Verbesserungen hatten lediglich eine Kostensteigerung von 10% zur Folge.

[79] Für das erwähnte Stück zwischen Sierre und Leuk, das nicht befriedigend gelöst werden konnte, arbeitete das kantonale Amt für Nationalstrassenbau zwischen 1984 und 1993 unter hohem Kostenaufwand zahlreiche Varianten aus. Mit der am 20. Februar 1994 angenommenen Alpeninitiative und der unmittelbar danach vom Eidgenössischen Verkehrs- und Energiewirtschaftsdepartement verfügten Planungssperre kam es zwar zu einigen Verzögerungen. Weil die N9 von den eidgenössischen Räten nicht als Transitstrasse im Alpenraum klassiert wurde, dürfte die Planung dieses Strassenabschnitts in naher Zukunft (Mitte 1995) abgeschlossen sein.

te, umstrittene Ursprungsvariante zurückgreifen können. Damit war der Experte bei seinem Ausloten eines Konsenses erheblich freier als etwa die beiden Konsens-Manager Michel Rey oder Ortwin Renn, deren Auftrag eindeutig darin bestand, mit einer - umsetzbaren - Standortentscheidung aus dem Feld zurückzukehren.

4.5. Résumé und Diskussion

Ohne Zweifel wird man im helvetischen Alltag auf der Ebene der Kantone oder der Gemeinden noch manche andere Fälle solcher mediationsähnlicher Verhandlungen finden, in denen parallel zu oder anstatt der förmlichen Verwaltungsprozeduren (teil)öffentlichen Foren zur Konfliktbewältigung eingesetzt wurden. Die hier getroffene Auswahl aus Umweltkonflikten der jüngsten Zeit dürfte jedoch einigermassen repräsentativ für die schweizerischen Verhältnisse sein. Als Schutzobjekte stehen heute jedenfalls weit mehr der Natur- und Landschaftsschutz im Vordergrund als etwa der Lärmschutz, der bisher noch wenig politisierte Bodenschutz, die behördlich privilegierte Luftreinhaltung[80], der (qualitative) Gewässerschutz oder der Schutz vor Störfällen bzw. vor umweltgefährdenden Stoffen.

Zu mediationsähnlichen Verhandlungsprozessen kommt es in den erwähnten Bereichen immer dann, wenn eine gesetzgeberische Lösung durch Parlament und/oder Volk (aus welchen Gründen auch immer) ausgeschlossen ist und die Realisierung von - verräumlichten - Bundes- oder Kantonspolitiken auf zähe örtliche Widerstände stösst. Diese Aushandlungsprozesse sind als Konsensbildungsverfahren anzusehen, die der "Einkontextierung" zentralstaatlicher Politiken in örtliche bzw. regionale "Politikteppiche" dienen. Solche Politikteppiche schränken den Zugriff der übergeordneten Ebene stark ein. "Die Einflechtung einer neuen zentralstaatlichen Politik ist ohne die Zustimmung der Akteure der bestehenden Arenen nur schwer mög-

---

[80] Im Rahmen der kantonalen Massnahmenpläne für lufthygienische Belastungsgebiete; vgl. dazu R. Imhof, *Luftreinhaltung und Verkehr in 11 Kantonen - Situation, Akteure und Massnahmenplan*, Cahiers de l'IDHEAP no 125, Chavannes-près-Renens (IDHEAP), 1994

313

lich."⁸¹ Auch wo legislatorische Entscheidungen getroffen wurden, braucht derjenige, der die Ressource "Lebensraum" in Anspruch nehmen will, "heute nicht nur eines repräsentativ-demokratischen Mandates durch ein nationales Parlament, sondern er benötigt (...) ausserdem den stillschweigenden Konsens der betroffenen Bevölkerung zur Einfügung seines Werkes in örtliche oder überörtliche Politikteppiche (...). Konsens ist eine wertvolle, knappe und daher durch Sinnstiftung permanent zu alimentierende Ressource. Die Verhandlungsposition des Zentralstaats zwingt die Behörden dazu, täglich neu Sinn zu stiften, bzw. den Nutzen der Raumbeanspruchung und -verwendung zu rechtfertigen. Der verhandelnde Staat ist jener Staat, der nicht nur abstrakt, sondern konkret und vor Ort Sinn stiftet, Verständnis für seine Belange sucht und sich durch ausgehandelte Leistungen und Gegenleistungen legitimiert"⁸².

Bezeichnenderweise geht es in den meisten dieser Verhandlungsprozessen um Mehrebenenkonflikte. Der Sondermüllverbrennungsofen der CIBA-GEIGY führte zu Verhandlungen zwischen örtlichen Opponenten und kantonalen Behörden. In den Standortsuchverfahren in der Waadt und im Kanton Aargau wurde ebenfalls zwischen einer Vielzahl kommunaler, regionaler und kantonaler Akteure verhandelt, und am Konflikt über die Erweiterung der Grande Dixence waren Vertreter der betroffenen Standortgemeinden, des Kantons Wallis, der in der ganzen Suisse romande aktiven Elektrizitätsgesellschaft "Ouest-Suisse SA" und des WWF Schweiz beteiligt. Die dornenvolle Suche nach einem Endlager radioaktiver Abfälle ist schliesslich von Verhandlungen zwischen Bundesämtern, Kantonsregierungen, Gemeindevertretern mit örtlichen und nationalen Umweltschutzorganisationen und der (gesamtschweizerischen) Genossenschaft NAGRA begleitet. Selbst bei der Revision der Linienführung der N9 im Kanton Wallis waren und sind der Bund und die Gemeinden gleichermassen wie der Kanton Verhandlungspartner.

Verhandlungen, die über das normale Ausmass des helvetischen Alltags hinausgehen und daher auch besondere Strukturen benötigen, werden offenbar immer dann geführt, wenn ein Projektstreit

---

81 P. Knoepfel, I. Kissling-Näf, 1993: *Transformation öffentlicher Politiken durch Verräumlichung - Betrachtungen zum gewandelten Verhältnis zwischen Raum und Politik*, Cahiers de l'IDHEAP no 109, Lausanne (IDHEAP), S. 13.
82 Ibid., S. 17.

gleichzeitig das zunehmend fragilere Gleichgewicht zwischen dem Bund, den Kantonen und den Gemeinden nachhaltig beeinträchtigen könnte. In diesen Fällen steht nicht nur das umstrittene Projekt als solches, sondern gleichzeitig auch das eine Vielzahl geronnener historischer Konflikte repräsentierende Glasperlenspiel eines vollumfänglich kaum erklärbaren helvetischen Kompromisses als staatspolitische Errungenschaft auf dem Spiel.

5. ANDERE (WENIGER AUF VERHANDLUNG BASIERENDE) KONFLIKTLÖSUNGSMECHANISMEN

Solche eher langwierige, auf intensivem wechselseitigem Ausloten von Handlungsspielräumen basierende Verhandlungslösungen sind auch in der Schweiz nicht die einzigen Mittel zur Streitbeilegung. Selbst ohne statistischen Belege[83] ist festzustellen, dass derartige Konfliktlösungsmechanismen auch für den schweizerischen Alltag eindeutige Ausnahmefälle darstellen. In der Regel werden hier ebenfalls "kürzere" Konfliktlösungsprozesse vorgezogen, aus denen nicht um jeden Preis ein vollständiger Konsens unter sämtlichen Betroffenen resultiert. Allerdings dürfte ein internationaler Vergleich zeigen, dass auch bei diesen nicht auf einer vollumfänglichen Aushandlung basierenden Konfliktlösungsmechanismen bei den opponierenden Parteien gleichwohl eine relativ hohe Akzeptanz der erzielten Ergebnisse zu verzeichnen ist. Die auf Kompromiss angelegte Grundstruktur der politisch-administrativen Kultur unseres Landes führt selbst in diesen Verfahren in der Regel zu relativ breit abgestützten und daher "akzeptierbaren" Lösungen, in denen die Belange der Unterlegenen ebenfalls Berücksichtigung finden.

Im Sinne eines Überblicks fügen wir im folgenden die u. E. wichtigsten fünf nicht auf vollumfänglichen Verhandlungen basierenden Konfliktlösungsmechanismen des schweizerischen politisch-administrativen Systems an. Es sind dies:

---

[83] Etwa die von H. P. Kriesi vorgenommene Dokumentation der politischen Konflikte in der Schweiz (vgl. dazu H. P. Kriesi (Hrsg.), *Bewegung in Schweizer Politik. Fallstudien zu politischen Mobilisierungsprozessen in der Schweiz*, Frankfurt (Campus).

- *Die Lösung von Konflikten durch Parlaments- oder Volksentscheid*
Wo auch nach längerem Verhandeln keine Einigkeit erzielt werden kann, wird abgestimmt. Das gute alte Mehrheitsprinzip der parlamentarischen und/oder der direkten Demokratie hat gerade in der Schweiz, schon viele Streitigkeiten beigelegt. Dazu finden sich auch in der Umweltpolitik zahlreiche Beispiele. So mussten es die Tessiner Behörden aufgrund einer Volksinitiative dem Volk überlassen, über die "umweltfreundlichste" Verbrennungstechnologie zu entscheiden, womit ein langwieriger Expertenstreit über ein kurzes Wochenende (am 6. Juni 1993) zugunsten des berühmt-berüchtigten "Thermoselect-Verfahrens" entschieden wurde. Ähnlich erging es den Winterthurer Stadtbehörden, denen nach harzigen Verhandlungen schliesslich gegen ihren Willen durch Kantonsratsbeschluss ein Standort für eine Sondermüllverbrennungsanlage in der östlichen Industriezone "gesichert" wurde[84]. Der Expertenstreit über die Tragbarkeit von Atomkraftwerken wurde am Wochenende des 23. Septembers 1990, jener über die Tragbarkeit des Wasserkraftwerks in der Rheinlandschaft in Rheinau schon am Wochenende des 23. Februar 1953 kurzerhand vom Volk entschieden. In gleicher Weise fanden die langwierigen Verhandlungen über die ökologische Tragbarkeit von Waffenplätzen[85], von drei Autobahnteilstücken[86] oder von Moorlandschaftseingriffen[87] bzw. über die Tragbarkeit des Transitsverkehrs auf den Alpenstrassen[88] ihr Ende. In all diesen (und in zahlreichen weiteren) Fällen werden durch mehr oder weniger intensive Aushandlungsprozesse eingeleitete Verfahren schliesslich jäh abgebrochen und dezisionistisch entschieden. Das Mittel des Gegenvorschlages gegen Volksinitiativen bzw. die in Parlamentsdebatten übliche Berücksichtigung von Referendumsdrohungen ermöglicht es, der jeweiligen Minderheit ein Stück weit entgegenzukommen.

---

[84] Richtplanentscheid des Zürcher Kantonsrats vom 14. Februar 1992. Dagegen erhob die Stadt Winterthur eine staatsrechtliche und eine verwaltungsgerichtliche Beschwerde, die das Bundesgericht am 17. Juni abgewiesen hat (AZ: 1A 226/1992; 1 P 634/1992).
[85] Abstimmung vom 6. Juni 1993 (abgelehnte Initiative).
[86] Volksabstimmung vom 2. Juli 1987 (abgelehnte "Kleeblatt-Initiative").
[87] Angenommene Volksinitiative vom 6. Dezember 1987.
[88] Angenommene Volksinitiative vom 20. Februar 1994.

- *Entscheidung durch den Richter*
Das in Umweltkonflikten etwa in der Bundesrepublik Deutschland, übliche Verwaltungsgerichtsverfahren wird in der Schweiz zur Streitbeilegung deutlich weniger in Anspruch genommen. Dies liegt zum einen daran, dass das schweizerische Rechtsschutzsystem[89] - im Gegensatz etwa zum Grundgesetz der Bundesrepublik Deutschland[90] - keine Generalklausel zugunsten des verwaltungsgerichtlichen Rechtsschutzes kennt. Gemäss den Art. 97 ff. dieses Gesetzes sind gewisse gerade für das Umweltrecht bedeutsame Entscheidungen verwaltungsgerichtlichen Verfahren nicht zugänglich. In diesen Fällen müssen Rechtsstreitigkeiten vom Bundesrat entschieden werden[91]. Hinzu kommt vermutlich auch der sich in dieser Grundordnung widerspiegelnde Faktor, dass man in der Schweiz politische Konflikte nur ungern einem Richter vorlegt[92].

- *Kooperationslösungen*[93]
Die Umsetzung des schweizerischen Umweltschutzgesetzes vom 7. Oktober 1983[94] und der zahlreichen darauf abgestützten Verordnungen durch die Kantone hat namentlich im Bereich der Sa-

---

[89] Bundesgesetz vom 16. Dezember 1983 über die Organisation der Bundesrechtspflege, SR. 173.110.
[90] Art. 19., Abs. 4.
[91] Dies war etwa der Fall beim konfliktreichen Rekursverfahren gegen die Genehmigung einer zweiten Hochspannungsleitung über den Gemmi-Pass, das schliesslich vom Eidgenössischen Justiz- und Polizeidepartement in erster Instanz (im Sinne der Ablehnung der Hochspannungs-Leitung) entschieden wurde. Vgl. zu diesem Verfahren: P. Knoepfel, W. Zimmermann, *Le cas de la ligne électrique de la Gemmi: un retournement furtif de situation, en cinq actes*, Cahiers de l'IDHEAP no 52, Lausanne, 1989, 72 p. Gleiches gilt auch für Rekurse gegen Plangenehmigungen, gegen die Erteilung von Konzessionen oder von Subventionen aller Art (Art. 99 des Organisationsgesetzes).
[92] Der Bund kennt denn auch keine Verfassungsgerichtsbarkeit, in der etwa Bundesgesetze vom Bundesgericht auf ihre Verfassungsmässigkeit hin überprüft werden könnten. Dieser Grundsatz ist bereits in der Bundesverfassung vom 29. Mai 1874 (SR. 101.) verankert (Art. 113, Abs. 3).
[93] Vgl. allgemein dazu die Beispiele bei P. Knoepfel, *Chancen und Grenzen des Kooperationsprinzips in der Umweltpolitik*, in: Oikos, Umweltökonomische Studieninitiative an der HSG (Hrsg.): Kooperation für die Umwelt. Im Dialog zum Handeln, Chur/Zürich (Rüegger), 1994, S. 73 ff.
[94] SR. 814.01.

nierung von Altanlagen zu einer kaum vorhersehbaren Entwicklung des informellen Verwaltungshandelns geführt. In den meisten Kantonen kam es bisher kaum je zu einer förmlichen Sanierungsverfügung, wie sie in diesem Gesetz (Art. 16) vorgesehen ist. Verfügt wird im Sanierungsverfahren lediglich, dass die betroffenen Industrie- und Gewerbebetriebe den kantonalen Ämtern bis zu einem festgesetzten Zeitpunkt Sanierungsvorschläge einzureichen haben. Diese Vorschläge konnten in aller Regel zur Befriedigung der Ämter und der Anlagebetreiber auf dem Verhandlungswege bereinigt werden. Zu definitiven Anordnungen individueller und spezieller Sanierungsmassnahmen, denen sich der Betreiber widersetzt hätte, kam es gesamtschweizerisch gesehen nur in ganz wenigen Fällen. Davon berichtet auch der Beitrag von R. Maegli in diesem Band.

- *Professionalisierung und Standardisierung*
Manche Umweltkonflikte, um die noch vor einigen Jahren fallweise zäh verhandelt worden wäre, können heute erheblich leichter abgearbeitet werden, weil sich mittlerweile hüben und drüben eine gemeinsame Konfliktsprache entwickelt hat. Diese erlaubt es, ehemals immer wieder aufgetretene Missverständnisse zu beseitigen. Dies ist zum einen auf die eingetretene Standardisierung vieler früher umstrittener Belastungsgrenzwerte, zum andern aber auch auf eine ökologische Professionalisierung des beteiligten Personals der staatlichen Umweltschutzfachstellen, der Umweltschutzorganisationen und der Industrie- und Gewerbevertreter zurückzuführen. Diese letztere verdanken wir einer eigentlichen Ausbildungsoffensive der schweizerischen Hochschulen und der höheren technischen Lehranstalten in den letzten zehn Jahren. Ein professionalisiertes Angebot ist heute aber auch in bezug auf Streitkultur und Konfliktregelungstechnologien im Entstehen[95]. Ein Beweis dafür sind insbesondere die oben angeführten Fälle mediationsähnlicher Konfliktbeilegungsverfahren.

---

[95] Etwa rund um das ETH Polyprojekt "Risiko und Sicherheit technischer Systeme", das im Aargauer Fall eingeschaltet wurde (vgl. O. Renn, Th. Webler in diesem Band). Vgl. allgemein dazu H. Weidner, *Der verhandelnde Staat. Minderung von Vollzugskonflikten durch Mediationsverfahren*, in: Schweizerisches Jahrbuch für Politische Wissenschaft, Nr. 33/1993, S. 240 ("Öko-sozialer Komplex").

- *Konfliktvermeidung*
 Würden in Helvetien alle Konflikte durch Verhandlung, Abstimmung, Rechtsmittelverfahren, Kooperation oder Professionalisierung gelöst, gäbe es die Schweiz nicht. Im Gegenteil: Unser Land hat vielleicht sogar deshalb bis heute recht gut mit all seinen Konflikten gelebt, weil alle schweizerischen Behörden von den Gemeinden bis zum Bund, eine recht reichhaltige Palette von Strategien zur Nichtentscheidung von Konflikten entwickelt haben. Das Leben mit - jedermann bekannten - Vollzugsdefiziten an der Front von jedermann bekannten Kantonen, mit mehr oder weniger bekannten "Übersetzungsfehlern" in deutschen, italienischen und französischen Gesetzestexten oder mit offenen oder verdeckten Bundesrechtswidrigkeiten in der Verwaltungspraxis des einen oder anderen Kantons ist einfacher und wohl auch erspriesslicher als die Lösung eines jeden Konflikts à tout prix. Augenzwinkern, angebliches "Übersehen" oder die geradezu geniale Handhabung eines "beschränkten Gesichtswinkels der Willkür" durch Bundesbehörden und die Bundesjustiz[96] können allesamt als - m. E. recht weise - Instrumente einer solchen Konfliktvermeidungsstrategie angesehen werden. Diese Instrumente, die dem helvetischen Glasperlenspiel sein besonderes Gepräge verleihen, wurden unter den Bedingungen der ausgezirkelten Autonomiebereiche der verschiedenen ethnischen, kulturellen und sprachlichen Gemeinschaften sukzessive entwickelt und stetig verfeinert.

6. SCHLUSSFOLGERUNGEN: DIE SCHWEIZ HAT UND BRAUCHT KEINE MEDIATOREN

Mit den obigen Ausführungen meinen wir hinlänglich belegt zu haben, dass die Schweiz deshalb kaum eigentliche Mediatoren braucht, weil ihre gesamte politisch-administrative Kultur und ihre Institutio-

---

[96] Der "beschränkte Gesichtswinkel der Willkür", den das Bundesgericht bei verfassungsgerichtlichen Beschwerden wegen Verletzung von Art. 4 der Bundesverfassung anwendet, ist für diese "staatspolitische Weisheit" m. E. immer noch eine einmalige Leistung helvetischer Konflikttechnologie. Auch heute wird wohl kein Jurist in der Lage sein, die wundersame Welt dieser "Willkür-Überprüfung" exakt abzumessen.

nen mit einer Vielzahl von Verhandlungselementen durchsetzt sind, deren Produkt der vielzitierte "helvetische Kompromiss" ist. Heute und morgen wird der Stellenwert von Mediationsverfahren äusserst gering bleiben, weil beim Bund und bei den Kantonen trotz zahlreicher und im Vergleich zum Ausland wohl auch fundamentalerer Konfliktpotentiale vielfältige andere Konfliktlösungsmechanismen bestehen, die Verhandlungen in mehr oder weniger ausgeprägtem Ausmasse zulassen. Ein Mediator als "neutrale, vermittelnde Person"[97] ist für die meisten Verfahren zur Lösung von Umweltkonflikten daher nicht erforderlich; vielerorts würde eine solche Institution vermutlich sogar auf Ablehnung stossen, weil sie als Eingeständnis einer Unfähigkeit der (traditionellen und neuen) Institutionen, aber auch der "mündigen" Konfliktparteien zur selbständigen Streitbeilegung angesehen würde.

Demgegenüber konnte der Aufsatz anhand der Frage nach dem potentiellen Stellenwert von Mediation in der Schweiz den bedeutenden Stellenwert von Verhandlungslösungen in diesem Land näher umschreiben. Ausserdem konnten wir darlegen, dass für die beachtliche Konfliktverarbeitungskapazität unserer Institutionen eine ausgesprochene Fähigkeit der schweizerischen Interessengruppen aller Art zur Konfliktlösung durch Verhandlung verantwortlich ist. Diese Fähigkeit bedarf der Weiterentwicklung und der Pflege im Rahmen der Konfliktschulung[98], von Forschung und Entwicklung im Bereich "social engineering" bzw. "Risikodiskurs"[99] oder im Zusammenhang mit neuen Organisationsentwicklungen in der öffentlichen Verwaltung[100]. Es könnte durchaus eintreffen, dass auch andere Länder dereinst auf die reichhaltige Verhandlungskultur Helvetiens zurückgreifen werden.

---

[97] Im Sinne der eingangs zitierten Definition von H. Weidner.
[98] Wie dies etwa am IDHEAP für Kommunalpolitiker angeboten wird (Kurs: *La gestion des conflits au niveau communal,* durchgeführt von K. Horber-Papazian im Sommersemester 1994).
[99] Durchgeführt z. B. von der Projektgruppe des ETH Polyprojektes "Risiko und Sicherheit technischer Systeme".
[100] Etwa zum Projektmanagement oder zur kundenfreundlicheren Verwaltung.

LITERATURVERZEICHNIS

Ph. Bovy, *Rapport final de synthèse du réexamen de la N9*, Lausanne (EPFL), 1982

P. C. Dienel, *Die Planungszelle. Der Bürger plant seine Umwelt, eine Alternative zur Establishment-Demokratie,* Opladen (Westdeutscher Verlag), 1991

P. Dürrenmatt, *Schweizer Geschichte*, Zürich (Schweizer Druck- und Verlagshaus AG), 1963

H. J. Fietkau, H. Weidner, *Mediationsverfahren in der Umweltpolitik, Erfahrungen in der Bundesrepublik Deutschland,* in: Aus Politik und Zeitgeschichte, B 39-40/1992 (Beilage zur Wochenzeitung "Das Parlament"), S. 24 ff.

W. Hoffmann-Riem, E. Schmidt-Assmann (Hrsg.), *Konfliktbewältigungen durch Verhandlungen*, Band I (Informelle und mittlerunterstützte Verhandlungen in Verwaltungsverfahren), Baden-Baden (Nomos), 1990 und Band II (Konfliktmittlung in Verwaltungsverfahren), Baden-Baden (Nomos), 1990.

R. Imhof, *Luftreinhaltung und Verkehr in 11 Kantonen - Situation, Akteure und Massnahmenplan,* Cahiers de l'IDHEAP no 125, Chavannes-près-Renens (IDHEAP), 1994

I. Kissling-Näf, *Staatliche Steuerung über Verfahren und Netzwerkbildung, die Umweltverträglichkeitsprüfung als zeitgemässe Antwort auf komplexe gesellschaftliche Probleme im Umweltbereich,* Chavannes (IDHEAP), 1995 (Diss., in Ausarbeitung)

U. Klöti, Th. Haldemann, W. Schenkel, *Agglomerationsprobleme und vertikale Zusammenarbeit, Umweltschutz und öffentlicher Verkehr in den Grossagglomerationen Lausanne und Zürich,* Bericht 49 des NFP "Stadt und Verkehr", Zürich, 1993

P. Knoepfel, *Chancen und Grenzen des Kooperationsprinzips in der Umweltpolitik,* in: Oikos, Umweltökonomische Studieninitiative an der HSG (Hrsg.): Kooperation für die Umwelt. Im Dialog zum Handeln, Chur/Zürich (Rüegger), 1994, S. 65-92

P. Knoepfel: Kommentar zur UNIVOX - Umfrage zum Thema *Umwelt 1993*, GfS - Forschungsinstitut Adliswil und IDHEAP, Chavannes-près-Renens

P. Knoepfel, *Demokratisierung der Raumplanung. Grundsätzliche Aspekte und Modell für die Organisation der kommunalen Nutzungsplanung unter besonderer Berücksichtigung der schweizerischen Verhältnisse*, Berlin. (Duncker & Humblot; Schriften zum Öffentlichen Recht, Band 323), 1977

P. Knoepfel, A. Eberle, G. Gerhäuser, N. Girard, *Energie und Umwelt im politischen Alltag. Energie et environnement dans la vie quotidienne. Drei Fallstudien für den Unterricht*, Bern (EDMZ), 1995.

P. Knoepfel, R. Imhof, W. Zimmerman: *Massnahmenpläne zur Luftreinhaltung. Wie sich Behörden beim Umweltschutz arrangieren*. Bericht 57 des NFP "Stadt und Verkehr", Fonds national suisse de la recherche scientifique, Zürich, 1994

P. Knoepfel, I. Kissling-Näf, *Transformation öffentlicher Politiken durch Verräumlichung - Betrachtungen zum gewandelten Verhältnis zwischen Raum und Politik*, in: A. Héritier (éd.), Policy-Analyse, Kritik und Neuorientierung, PVS-Sonderheft 24/1993, Opladen (Westdeutscher Verlag), S. 267-288

P. Knoepfel, M. Rey, *Konfliktminderung durch Verhandlung: Das Beispiel des Verfahrens zur Suche eines Standorts für eine Sondermülldeponie in der Suisse romande*, in: W. Hoffmann-Riem, E. Schmidt-Assmann (Hrsg). Konfliktbewältigung durch Verhandlungen, Konfliktmittlung in Verwaltungsverfahren, Band II, Baden-Baden Nomos), S. 257-286

P. Knoepfel, W. Zimmermann, *Le cas de la ligne électrique de la Gemmi: un retournement furtif de situation, en cinq actes*, Cahiers de l'IDHEAP no 52, Lausanne, 1989

P. Knoepfel, W. Zimmermann, *Fruchtfolgeflächen Kanton Bern (Rüfenacht/Spietz): Schulterschluss zwischen Raumplanung, Landwirtschaft und Ökologie?*, in: W. Zimmermann, P. Knoepfel, Umwelt und Landwirtschaft im politischen Alltag. *Drei Fälle für die Schule*, im Auftrag des Bundesamtes für Forstwesen, des Bundesamtes für Umweltschutz, des Bundesamtes für Raumplanung und des Bundesamtes für Landwirtschaft, Bern (EDMZ); 1987

P. Knoepfel, W. Zimmermann, *Martigny-Brigue: Enthousiasme - contestation - réexamen. Comment protéger la forêt de Finges contre les nuisances de la N9 en Valais?* dossier de cours, Lausanne (IDHEAP), 1987

P. Knoepfel, U. Zuppinger, *Etude de cas concernant une usine d'incinération de déchets spéciaux à Bâle, Suisse*, (vorläufig interner Bericht z. Hd. des Schweizerischen Nationalfonds), Lausanne, 1994

H. P. Kriesi (Hrsg.), *Bewegung in Schweizer Politik. Fallstudien zu politischen Mobilisierungsprozessen in der Schweiz,* Frankfurt (Campus), 1985

O. Renn, *Risikodialog statt Sankt-Florians-Prinzip. Erfahrungen aus einem Modellversuch im Kanton Aargau*, in: NZZ Nr. 277 vom 27./28. November 1993

Schweizer Lexikon, Zürich (Schweizer Lexikon), Band 4, 1992

S. Wälti, *Neue Problemlösungsstrategien in der nuklearen Entsorgung*, in: Schweizerisches Jahrbuch für Politische Wissenschaft, Nr. 33/1993, Vollzugsprobleme, Bern (Haupt), 1993, S. 205-224

H. Weidner, *Der verhandelnde Staat. Minderung von Vollzugskonflikten durch Mediationsverfahren*, in: Schweizerisches Jahrbuch für Politische Wissenschaft, Nr. 33/1993, S. 225-244

Autorenverzeichnis

Thomas W. Church, JR., Professor and Chair of the Department of Political Science, Rockefeller College, State University of New York, 135 Western Avenue, Albany, NY 12222, United States
☎: 1 518-442-5285 - fax: 1 518 442-5298 or 3398

Phillip J. Cooper, Professor of Public Administration, Dept. of Public Administration, University of Kansas, Lawrence, Kansas, United States

Patrice Duran, Professeur en sociologie de droit, Groupe d'Analyse des politiques publiques, Université de Paris I, Département de science politique, 13, rue du Four, F-75006 Paris, France
☎: 33 1 43 54 11 09 - fax: 33 1 43 29 72 90

Arturo Gàndara, Professor at the School of Law, University of California at Davis, Davis, California 95616, United States
☎: 1 916 752-0243 (752-2892), Fax: 1 916 752 4704

Wolfgang Hoffmann-Riem, Professor für Öffentliches Recht und Verwaltungswissenschaft, Direktor des Hans Bredow Instituts für Rundfunk und Fernsehen, Universität Hamburg, Edmund-Siemers-Allee 1 Pv. Ost, D-20146 Hamburg, Deutschland
☎: 49 40 4123-5416/5625

Peter Knoepfel, Professor und Direktor des Institut de hautes études en administration publique (IDHEAP), Route de la Maladière 22, CH-1022 Chavannes-près-Renens, Schweiz
☎: 41 21 691 96 79/80 - Fax: 41 21 691 08 88 - e-mail: PETER.KNOEPFEL@idheap.unil.ch

Ida J. Koppen, JD, Environmental Research and Consultancy, Loc. S. Chiara, 5, I-53019 Castelnuovo B.ga (Siena), Italia
☎: 39 577 359 125 - Fax: 39 577 359 125

Irene Lamb, Dr. jur., Verwaltungsrichterin, Rellingerstrasse 1, D-20257 Hamburg, Deutschland
☎: 49 40 24 86 41 23

Rolf Maegli, lic. jur., Chef des Rechtsdienstes / Departementssekretär, Volkswirtschafts-Departement des Kantons Solothurn, Rathaus, CH-4500 Solothurn, Schweiz,
☎: 41 65 21 24 36, Fax: 41 65 21 29 81

Daniel A. Mazmanian, Luther Lee Professor and Director of the Center for Politics and Economics. The Claremont Graduate School, Claremont, California 91711-6163, USA
☎: 1 909 621-8284 - Fax: 1 909 621-8390 -
e-mail: (INTERNET) Mazmanid@CGSVAX.Claremont.edu

Robert Nakamura, Professor of Politcal Science, Rockefeller College, State University of New York, 135 Western Avenue, Albany, NY 12222, United States
☎: 1 518-442-5285 - fax: 1 518 442-5298 or 3398 - e-mail: ROBERT.NAKAMURA@CNSIBM.Albany.edu

Ortwin Renn, Professor für Technik- und Umweltsoziologie (Universität Stuttgart) und Mitglied des Vorstandes der Akademie für Technikfolgenabschätzung, Industriestrasse 5, D-70565 Stuttgart, Deutschland
☎: 49 711 9063 160 - Fax: 49 711 9063 299

Michel Rey, Economiste, secrétaire général de la Communauté d'études pour l'aménagement du territoire (C.E.A.T.), CP 555, (14, ave de l'Eglise anglaise), CH-1001 Lausanne
☎: 41 21 693 41 65 - Fax: 41 21 693 41 54

Michael Stanley-Jones, Graduate Student, Program in Politics and Policy, The Claremont Graduate School, Claremont, California 91711-6163, USA

Thomas Webler, Doktor, 132 Farley Road, Wendell, MA 01379, USA
☎: 1 508 544 7201

Helmut Weidner, Dr. phil., wissenschaftlicher Mitarbeiter am Wissenschaftszentrum Berlin für Sozialforschung (WZB), Reichpietschufer 50, D-107 85 BERLIN. Deutschland
☎: 49 30 25 49 12 69 - Fax: 49 30 25 49 12 54

Ökologie & Gesellschaft / Ecologie & Société

Herausgegeben von PETER KNOEPFEL und HELMUT WEIDNER
Publié par PETER KNOEPFEL et HELMUT WEIDNER

Band 1 STEFAN SCHWAGER/PETER KNOEPFEL/HELMUT WEIDNER: Umweltrecht Schweiz – EG. Das schweizerische Umweltrecht im Lichte der Umweltschutzbestimmungen der Europäischen Gemeinschaften – ein Rechtsvergleich. 1988.

Band 2 STEFAN SCHWAGER/PETER KNOEPFEL/HELMUT WEIDNER: Droit de l'environnement Suisse – CE. Le droit suisse de l'environnement à la lumière des Actes officiels de la Communauté européenne dans le domaine de la protection de l'environnement. Etude comparative des régimes juridiques. 1989.

Band 3 PETER KNOEPFEL (Hrsg.): Risiko und Risikomanagement. 1988.

Band 4 PETER KNOEPFEL (Hrsg.): Landwirtschaftliche ökologische Beratung – ein Modell für die allgemeine Umweltberatung? 1990.

Band 5 DANIELA BARONI/VERENA BRUNNER/PETER KNOEPFEL/PIERRE MOOR: Strassenverkehrsrecht im Lichte des Umweltrechts/Le droit de la circulation routière face à la législation de l'environnement. 1991.

Band 6 SIBYLLE GRUNDLEHNER/PETER KNOEPFEL(Hrsg.): Défis des déchets. Réalités politiques et administratives de la Suisse romande. 1992.

Band 7 PETER KNOEPFEL/WILLI ZIMMERMANN: Gewässerschutz in der Landwirtschaft. Evaluation und Analyse des föderalen Vollzugs. 1993.

Band 8 ANDREAS BALTHASAR/CARLO KNÖPFEL: Umweltpolitik und technische Entwicklung. Eine politikwissenschaftliche Evaluation am Beispiel der Heizungen. 1994.

Band 9 PETER KNOEPFEL/RITA IMHOF/WILLI ZIMMERMANN (Hrsg.): Luftreinhaltepolitik im Labor der Städte. Der Massnahmenplan – Wirkungen eines neuen Instruments der Bundespolitik im Verkehr. 1995.